THE DEATH OF
Marco Pantani

Also by Matt Rendell

A SIGNIFICANT OTHER
Riding the Centenary Tour de France
with Lance Armstrong

KINGS OF THE MOUNTAINS
How Colombia's Cycling Heroes Changed
Their Nation's History

Edited by Matt Rendell

The Official Tour de France Centennial 1903–2003

Athens to Athens: The Olympic Games 1896–2004

THE DEATH OF
Marco Pantani

A Biography

MATT RENDELL

Weidenfeld & Nicolson
LONDON

First published in Great Britain in 2006
by Weidenfeld & Nicolson

10 9 8 7 6 5 4 3

A CIP catalogue record for this book
is available from the British Library.

ISBN 13: 978 0 297 85096 0
ISBN 10: 0 297 85096 2

Typeset by Input Data Services Ltd, Frome
Printed in Great Britain by Butler and Tanner Ltd, Frome and London

The Orion Publishing Group's policy is to use papers that
are natural, renewable and recyclable products and made
from wood grown in sustainable forests. The logging and
manufacturing processes are expected to conform to the
environmental regulations of the country of origin.

Weidenfeld & Nicolson

The Orion Publishing Group Ltd
Orion House
5 Upper Saint Martin's Lane
London, WC2H 9EA

www.orionbooks.co.uk

CONTENTS

FIGURES

ABBREVIATIONS AND DEFINITIONS

INSTITUTIONAL ABBREVIATIONS

IOC   International Olympic Committee

CAS   Court of Arbitration for Sport, an independent institution, based in Lausanne, which facilitates the settlement of sports-related disputes through arbitration or mediation

UCI   Union Cycliste Internationale, cycling's world governing body

CONI Italian Olympic Committee

CSAD Scientific/Anti-doping Committee of the Italian Olympic Committee

FCI   Italian Cycling Federation

CDFN Federal Disciplinary Committee of the Italian Cycling Federation (court of first instance)

CAF   Federal Appeal Committee of the Italian Cycling Federation (court of second instance)

NAS   *Nucleo antisofisticazione*, the branch of the Carabinieri dealing with health and hygiene matters – including doping in sport – responsible to the Health Ministry

Ser.T. *Servizio tossicodipendenza*, the substance-abuse service in the Italian health service

DSM-IV *Diagnostic and Statistical Manual of Mental Disorders*, fourth edition, published by the American Psychiatric Association

Turin CTO Centro Traumatologico Ortopedico e di Malattie Sociali e del Lavoro, the Orthopaedic Traumatology Centre of the Maria Adelaide Hospital in Turin

PCI   Partito Comunista Italiano, the Communist Party of Italy

CYCLING ABBREVIATIONS

DS   *Directeur sportif* (see below)
GC   General classification – in stage races, table giving total time taken by each rider to complete every stage
GP   (In race names) *Gran Premio*, 'Grand Prix'

CYCLING TERMS USED IN THIS BOOK

bidon Plastic drinks bottle with hands-free stopper
directeur sportif Team boss who recruits riders, dictates race programmes, provides training routines and directs race strategy from team car
domestique Rider employed to work to further team-leader's prospects of victory
dossard The race number worn on the rider's back
peloton A large compact group of cyclists
rouleur A cyclist capable of riding in the lead position on flat or rolling stages for long periods
soigneur Paramedical assistant who gives massage, etc.

A NOTE ON CURRENCY CONVERSION

For the period post-1990, old Italian lire have been converted into the more universal euro at the rate of 2,000 lire per euro.

LIST OF ILLUSTRATIONS

Marco and Sotero (*Tonina and Paolo Pantani*)
Marco's first racing licence (*Vanni Caroni*)
Racing with Fausto Coppi (*G C Fausto Coppi, Cesenatico*)
    before
    winning
    warming-down
    going home
Marco, Poli and Andreani (*Bruno Ronchetti*)
Marco, Induráin and Ugrumov
Marco and Amaducci
Marco and Roncucci (*Giuseppe Roncucci*)
Marco and Pregnolato
Conconi, Marco and Pregnolato (*Roberto Pregnolato*)
Marco the rebel leader
Marco in the mountains
Marco leading (*Fotoreporter Sirotti*)
Marco's paintings (*Tonina and Paolo Pantani*)
Marco with the Pope
Car crash (*La voce di Cesena*)
With carabinieri
Marco alone

Every effort has been made to trace copyright; we will be happy to rectify any omissions in subsequent editions.

To SD, RF and EO

Io amo la montagna, ma nel momento della fatica ho dentro un grande odio. Così cerco di abbreviare la mia agonia.

'I love the mountains, but in the moment of exertion, I'm filled with deep hatred. So I try to shorten the suffering.'

Marco Pantani

I tried to speak to him in Italian: '*E allora, com'è la forma?*' He just laughed: '*Sììì, la forma. La forma di formaggio . . .*'

Lance Armstrong

Prologue

A block from the seafront, Viale Regina Elena stretches south, one-way, from central Rimini. Midsummer, the town's population swells sevenfold and the Viale teems. Out of season, the arcades and ice-cream parlours close, the boutiques offer discounts and, with little else to do, the Viale resets its cobbles, points its façades and waits for spring.

The figure who booked into 46, Viale Regina Elena, Hotel Residence Le Rose, at 2 p.m. on Monday 9 February 2004, his only luggage a miniature backpack and a small bag of medicine, was in a poor state of repair. From room 5D he made two telephone calls, then left the hotel for twenty minutes. It was the last time he stepped outside. Back in his room, he closed the windows, drew the curtains and turned up the heating. Not half a decade before, Marco Pantani had been one of sport's most distinctive, most inspiring figures. Now he was withdrawing from the world.

Shortly before 9 p.m. he phoned out twice from his room. At 10.10 he took an incoming call. Instants later, a visit: two minutes, no more. At twenty to midnight there was another phone conversation: his last. For the next four days, at each sign of life on the landing he would open the door and start an incoherent conversation. Lorissa, the Ukrainian cleaner, worked around him. Pantani, quiet, courteous, asked her where she was from, and Lorissa replied. But her Italian mostly consisted of concrete nouns and infinitives, so when, on the morning of Friday 13 February, he posed a less straightforward question – 'How do I look?' – she could only garble, 'I don't know. I don't know you,' and he sent her away.

At eight that evening he called reception for an omelette, prosciutto, cheese and fruit juice. Oliver Laghi, the owner of the restaurant and pizzeria Rimini Key, two blocks from Le Rose, brought the order to reception. Pantani's name was mentioned, and Laghi, once a competitive amateur rider, asked to deliver it himself. He collected three small bottles of pear juice from the bar and took the lift to the fifth floor. There, a foul-smelling, emaciated figure in filthy clothes greeted him with a terrible vacancy: 'He opened the door with a smile. He seemed tired, like someone in crisis, very depressed. He was thin and drawn, and spoke quietly. His breath was bad. I made conversation with him anyway and told him dinner was on me. He thanked me and patted me on the back. I said, "I'll see you tomorrow, and we'll celebrate."' But Marco never ate another meal.

The following morning Pantani repeatedly telephoned reception to complain about noise, although the only noise was his. Perhaps seeking the source of the rattle and scrape inside his head, he was dismantling the room. He asked the receptionist to call the Carabinieri. When Lorissa came to clean, Pantani swore through the door at her. Soon afterwards, he opened the door on a couple crossing the landing, gave them a look of suspicion and said something like, 'I know who you are.' At 3.30 p.m., a Sicilian student named Pietro Buccellato started his shift on reception. He rang up repeatedly, but the line was always engaged. At the door he could hear no movement. From street level he could see no lights. He tried the numbers Pantani had dialled on Monday, but no one answered. He tried again.

'Hello?'

'Hello? This is the Residence Le Rose. Reception. We have Pantani here and he seems to be in crisis. Our records show he called you, so I wanted to let you know . . .'

'If you're talking about Pantani the cyclist, you've got it wrong. I don't know him, so he can't have dialled my number.'

The hotel owner had taken the weekend off. Mid-afternoon, he called to make sure all was well. Buccellato told him nothing had been seen or heard of Pantani.

'Make an excuse and go and see what's going on.'

He turned the master key in the door. The light was on, but the door was blocked. Not knowing what to do, he went back downstairs. The owner called again and, this time, insisted. At 8.40 p.m., Buccellato took up two towels. He turned the key and forced back the furniture piled behind the door.

The room was in disarray. The fitted microwave ha
and stacked in the barricade. Shards of mirror glisten
floor. Medicine boxes, some empty, were strewn ar
A bed sheet and a tube extracted from the air-con
had been tied to the banister of the stairwell leading up to th
bedroom. Climbing the steps to the bed, Buccellato's eyes met Pan
The former champion was lying on one side beside the bed, face down,
as if he'd fallen out. His famously bald head was swollen and badly
bruised. He had been dead for hours. More medicine boxes lay on the
bedside table, over a dusting of fine white powder. Marco Pantani was
certified dead at 9.20 p.m. The time of death was estimated at 5 p.m. At
10.42 p.m. Italian time his death was published by the Italian news
agency ANSA. By 2 a.m. on Sunday 15 February the body was being
removed from the hotel. The cause of death, determined by the autopsy
report with unqualified confidence, was published on 18 March: acute
cocaine poisoning.

Marco Pantani had emerged in the first half of the 1990s when the
superlative Miguel Induráin, the winner of five consecutive Tours de
France, two Giros d'Italia, as well as World and Olympic titles,
dominated cycling through a combination of prodigious strength and
tactical conservatism. Induráin won by losing nothing on the flat
stages, little in the mountains, and making colossal gains in the individual time trials. His essential talent was not the jolting acceleration,
the sudden, perceptible transition from one state to another, but something altogether harder to discern: sustained, unchanging speed. The
pleasure in observing Induráin at work was the blissful contemplation
of changelessness. Nothing astonished but the calm enigma of his
strength.
    Then Marco had appeared, a ball of inspired chaos, full of subversive
trickery – full of *style*, and capable – who knew how? – of Promethean
accelerations whenever the road turned skywards. Where Induráin
defied the invisible resistance of the air, Marco challenged those most
evident of hurdles, the mountains. Strange rivals: Induráin, the master
of a mystical form of tedium, with flotation-tank lungs and the sleepy
manner of the plankton-feeder; Marco, minuscule and flamboyant,
prone to dart, fish-like, out of the pack and disappear into the blue. In
this often unfathomable sport, Marco's only method was to quicken

the altitude until, looking down from a great height, his rivals
emed a distant distraction, lost somewhere far below. One terse acceleration after another against the dizzying massif until his rivals dropped
back, battered, in his wake.

At the 1994 Giro d'Italia, Marco's second appearance in a great
professional stage race, he had won two epic mountain stages and
finished second overall, ahead of Induráin. A month later, he went to
the Tour de France, and finished third. It wasn't just his results that
attracted the fans. With his bent nose, protrusive ears and thinning
hair, he was recognisable the way few movie stars ever are, and not just
in Italy or to followers of cycling.

To step up from those podium places to outright wins, Marco faced
not only an austere physical trial but formidable mental barriers. The
advent of wind-tunnel testing, aerodynamic time-trial bikes, teardrop
helmets and low-friction bodysuits had given powerful physiques like
Induráin's the decisive edge in stage racing. On long, flat time-trial
stages, they could gain five minutes or more on any diminutive climber –
yet, in the mountains, they could keep the climbers in sight and their
losses to a minimum. Induráin's became the model package of skills for
the modern stage-race champion. His apparent successors, the Russian
Evgeni Berzin and the German Jan Ullrich, conformed to the model.
Marco, it seemed, could only ever hope for stage wins.

And there was more. Marco, an Italian rider with Italian sponsors,
couldn't miss the Giro to concentrate his efforts on the Tour; if he was
ever to win in France, he would have to complete the Giro–Tour double,
achieved only by legends like Coppi, Merckx and Induráin himself.
However, since Induráin's failed attempt in 1994, again the belief had
spread that the demands of modern cycling had made the double
unattainable.

Marco, however, specialised in the impossible. He'd train for eight hours,
then, on the final climbs, the final fifty, sixty kilometres, he'd take
himself to the limit, push himself to the edge of the abyss, gauging just
how far he could lurch, just how much his body could take. And that
was how he won, free-diving within himself to greater depths and
darknesses than others dared, surfacing barely alive, tasting blood,
from the great apnoea. There was self-mutilation in these performances,
a shedding of everything worldly, before that indestructible heart

brought him back, as it did every time, no matter the altitude or depth, to the applause of millions. That was on the climbs. On the descents, he'd bury the saddle in the hollow of his abdomen and lower his weight over the back wheel, his crotch millimetres over the tyre, arms outstretched to grasp the handlebars. It made you wince to watch: the lightest contact between buttock and tyre, the smallest stone beneath the front wheel might not actually have emasculated him, but it would surely have destroyed his delicate balancing act, catapulting the bike front into the air, leaving no reaction time. He'd have fallen the way a dead body falls. But he accepted the risks: in this death-inviting tuck, his flyweight frame could stay ahead of a pack of heavier riders.

The cruelty of his attacks was belied by the naïve warmth of Marco's smile. There was an innocent appeal, a childlike vulnerability about him; a lack of sophistication that rather contrasted with what sport had become, and was becoming even more. An innocent élan, authentic, immediately winning: this was the meaning of Marco. When, despite the mental and historical barriers, he won the 1998 Giro d'Italia, and followed it with the Tour de France, cycling braced itself for a new period of dominance. Not for Marco, Induráin's impregnable citadel. He would suffer catastrophic failures in the valleys, then compensate with sublime solo victories in the quiet of the mountains.

Indeed, at the 1998 Tour de France, only Marco's epic performances in the mountains had sustained the sporting interest of an event mired in scandal following the arrest, shortly before the Tour had started, of a 53-year-old *soigneur* named Willy Voet at the wheel of a car in the colours of the Festina team. A rapid search had revealed the presence of hundreds of doping products. Untouched by the scandal, Marco was branded the saviour of his sport.

His expected period of dominance started at the 1999 Giro d'Italia, where he won four remarkable mountain stages. It ended there, too. On the morning of 5 June 1999, at the mountain town of Madonna di Campiglio, he was stopped. After a mandatory health test, Marco was suspended on suspicion of doping, and the Giro he had dominated was snatched from his grasp. He could have returned to competition two weeks later and ridden the Tour de France; instead, invoking a plot to destroy him, he took refuge in cocaine. There were half-hearted comebacks, amid fresh doping allegations, forensic investigations and a long suspension. Then, nothing.

*

In the sudden orange tower that rises gantry-like over the A14 motor-way at Imola, Romano Cenni, whose supermarket chain Mercatone Uno sponsored Marco from 1996 to 2003, is telling me: 'If they hadn't stopped him, we'd be standing here today saying, "We won the Giro and Tour in 1999, 2000, 2001, 2002, 2003."' He might have added that, with the support of a *team* instead of that disparate pool of freelancers, Marco might have won the 1994 Giro d'Italia and improved on his third place in the Tour de France. Or that only a wretched series of accidents had deprived him of likely podium places – wins, why not? – in 1995 and 1996. 'In 1997', he resumes, 'he fell at the Giro d'Italia, couldn't train because of his injuries, then went to the Tour de France and finished third.' Yet that recurring conditional – 'If they hadn't stopped him . . .' – circumscribes Cenni's reminiscences: 'He told me in many ways that he was clean, very clean, but they wanted to destroy the man and the athlete. We destroyed a man, and we destroyed an athlete. Perhaps we also destroyed a sport.'

Cenni places Marco's extinction in a dismal perspective: if he was clean, as he protested to the end, he was certainly robbed of wins rightly his throughout his career. If not, he had been living a lie – and with mind-boggling conviction.

Cenni, I was told, has aged since Marco's death. He seems indes-tructible to me, slow and barrel-chested, with the priestly tone of a survivor remembering others less robust. There was his late friend and business partner Luciano Pezzi, a former cyclist – a team-mate of the legendary Fausto Coppi – and one of Marco's mentors. 'They understood each other. If Luciano hadn't died, things would have turned out dif-ferently.' There was a beloved nephew, an artist-suicide whose sculp-tures and paintings adorn Cenni's office and the Mercatone Uno building foyer. And there was Marco, 'a man, an athlete, whose equal has perhaps never existed'. Are those tears welling in his eyes? 'Of *that* dimension of greatness. Who sent people in the street – old women, housewives – hurrying home when they knew the Giro was on, to see it on television. Perhaps this will never happen again, because no one will be capable of such epic exploits. Or perhaps I'm wrong. Perhaps I'm in love with him and when you're in love, perhaps you make technical errors, or errors of evaluation. Still, what Marco gave Italy, what he gave my company, is something I'll always be grateful for.' There is integrity in this tribute, and pertinence too. For, although Cenni isn't saying and solid figures are hard to come by, Mercatone Uno is said to have doubled its turnover and tripled its outlets during the Pantani years.

There, encoded in Cenni's grief, are the horizons Marco's biography must confront: the intimate, personal truth of a man driven to such extreme peaks and depths; the social and political reality of a society in which sport, sponsorship and television form an inseparable ternary system, in which athletes – whether a few or most we can only ever know in retrospect – poison themselves in order to perform; the psychology of a civilisation in which we bind ourselves together with illusions, necessary and unnecessary, at every point. At every moment, abstract, impersonal issues cleave to private pain and grieving. And, at the centre of it all, the sinister subject of that conditional proposition: 'If *they* hadn't stopped him . . .', and the edifice of ambiguity slowly rising around his memory.

Already, we are in the gravitational pull of two very Italian principles: *dietrologia*, the sometimes madcap search for hidden dimensions to surface reality, and *omertà*, the silence of those in the know. Common to both is the idea of menace, a hint of which sometimes accompanied this odyssey through Marco's existence. To some, no doubt, the danger must have seemed to emanate from me. Marco lived in many worlds and compartmentalised his existence. He shared his transgressions with friends, although not every friend would wish to be associated with every transgression. A foreigner, with foreign standards of discretion, looking into episodes that could have destroyed reputations and wrecked marriages must have seemed dangerous. Yet there were also moments during my research when I too felt, or imagined I felt, threatened, perhaps even physically, by interviewees who argued that Marco's private life must remain off-limits – although other supporters of this view nonetheless showed me great kindness. If any such threat existed, it was misplaced: there was never any choice but to write about the man. Elite sport makes absolute demands of its initiates. The soul is its raw material, no less than the body. 'Nothing goes to waste,' as Marco's adversary Lance Armstrong put it. 'You put it all to use; the old wounds and long-ago slights become the stuff of competitive energy.' In these circumstances, we can hardly hope to understand the athlete without understanding the man, or, more interestingly, the relationship between the two.

But let's be clear: writing Marco's story means confronting two types of substance abuse. One is, supposedly, private, personal and recreational. The other is professional, vocational and centred on a milieu – that of global sport – that brings together sometimes vast corporate interests and potentially uncontainable public passions. Both depend on organised crime and involve vast sums of money. Trespass on those interests, and the threat is unlikely to be purely imaginary.

Yet, to go back, it would seem possible to write a book about Marco's sporting career without touching on his life at all. Or on the final weeks of his life without connecting it to his sporting career. Or again, on his downfall at Madonna di Campiglio or his relationship with his manager without connecting *them* to the mechanisms that made Marco a sporting icon, and asking what that icon meant (and means). All of these books have been written. What no one has so far attempted is to examine the entirety of Marco's existence in a sympathetic manner and to place the vital questions at its heart: what did Marco mean to Italy and the outside world, and what did his meaning to others ultimately mean to him? Did he, or did he not, abuse doping products? Was his suspension at Madonna di Campiglio, as he claimed, the result of a plot? How and why, given that cocaine, too, is a banned substance, did he continue to compete? Was his death a private, individual tragedy, or one in which sport played the decisive role? The answers suggest another question to which this biography, taken as a whole, tries to respond: what made Marco Pantani, for all his extravagant panoply of faults, so extraordinary?

Early in my research, during the first, preliminary interviews, two fundamental questions arose: could a biography of Marco Pantani be morally justified? and was it even possible to write? They came up not as abstract, philosophical issues, but as urgent practical problems. The ethical question stemmed from the pain such a book might cause his loved ones. The manner of his death is still deeply felt in the several small communities he belonged to in life. The first of these was his home town of Cesenatico, with its population of 23,000, almost too small not to be overwhelmed by the passion that came to surround Marco. Another was the world of professional cycling, many, perhaps most, of whose members have been traumatised by the deaths and maimings of team-mates and friends on the road, and some of whom have seen doping as, more than an occupational hazard, a secretive subculture. A third was the wider sporting community, including the journalists and writers who cover professional cycling. All three are no doubt worlds where comradeship is accompanied by jealousy and rumour abounds – which is, perhaps, to say no more than that Marco was one human being living among others.

The practical question was raised by the unwillingness of many who knew him to talk. Marco's own attitudes to media interest added to the quandary for, in life, Marco was an introvert as well as an icon. He valued his privacy above all else and media attention put him on edge. If there was affection in the coverage – if the media even sought to protect him – he didn't notice, or care. All he knew was, his face sold newspapers. True, he cashed in on the emotions he stirred in the public – his image rights made him a multimillionaire – but what choice did he have? A poorer Pantani would have been guaranteed no less serious invasions of his privacy than the rich one suffered.

However, I soon found that in-fighting between many of those who knew him made it possible to compile an enormous quantity of information, even if not all was reliable. There seem to be legions of spokespeople, all well intentioned, no doubt, and deeply hurt, each in conflict with the others, ever ready to tell 'the truth about Marco Pantani'. Several, like tyrannical mother-figures, had literally drawn up lists of Marco's 'real' and 'false' friends, without perhaps recognising that Marco chose his own friends, using his own criteria. As well as the books, there were monuments, a play, the first streets named after him, and an imminent television drama. There have been celebratory DVDs and some dreadful TV documentaries, one of which set a benchmark for bad taste even in contemporary television by showing images of his corpse. A charitable foundation was competing with any number of fan clubs to 'manage' that vague entity, Marco's 'image' – a word already suggesting something two-dimensional, half-true. At the time of his death, much was unknown about his existence, even to those close to him. He had organised his affairs to ensure that no one had more than a partial view of his existence. This and the fanatical possessiveness Marco inspired among his confidants led to a bitter struggle over his memory. Few of those closest to him, then, seemed to want to let Marco rest in peace. On the other hand, there seemed to be no sceptical, investigative work going on to piece together Marco's many manifestations and incorporate the mass of forensic, medical and psychological documentation into a complex portrait. In other words, there seemed to be a great deal of 'image management' and very little interest in historical truth; of the two, it occurred to me, history is altogether more difficult to fix, resistant to 'management' and harder to turn to a profit. This ended my dilemma over whether this book could be morally justified. In the real, fluid world of memory and human interactions, it can be hard to put our finger on the truth about any of us. At best, we can try to grasp the horizons within which Marco grew, how he exercised his free will and why, and then evaluate his actions by the standards of what alternatives lay before him at the time. If, in the process, we find the dead, at times, coming to life before us, the purposes of biography will have been served.

1

The Miracle

(1970–84)

At 11.45 in the morning of 13 January 1970 Marco Pantani entered the world in Cesena, a small administrative centre in the Italian region of Romagna. His first journey, to nearby Cesenatico, took him fifteen kilometres and a world away. For, although Cesenatico owes its name and existence to Cesena, whose medieval merchants opened it as their gateway to the Mediterranean in 1303, Cesena directs its imagination northwards across the agricultural plain that extends as far as Treviso, and westwards to Bologna, whose university has faculties in the town. Cesenatico, by contrast, dreams of the sea, from which it has been inadvertently claiming land since the fourteenth century, thanks to the Port Canal, which affects the currents carrying sand and silt down the Adriatic coast. In the sixteenth century Leonardo was commissioned to renovate the port: among the da Vinci manuscripts at the Institut de France, Codex L, folios 66, 67 and 68, dated 6 September 1502, show the designs of the waterways that remain the heart of the town. Not so the brightly coloured barges that came and went with goods and people for half a millennium. A few now float listlessly in the canal, but most were museum pieces as long ago as the nineteenth century, when Turner depicted one with a smear of colour against a haze of sea and sky. Today, occasionally rigged for the tourists, the barges travel only on picture postcards, although Cesenatico was said to be closer to Venice, Trieste, even Dalmatia, than to Cesena, as recently as the 1930s. The fishing fleet is still intact, though, and thriving. One lunchtime, six vessels chugged into port before me, brimming with mullet they'd pulled out in less than half an hour. Today the town's main sources of wealth are its generous beaches. Even hundreds of yards inland, a fine layer of sand covers every horizontal surface.

Yet Marco would turn his back on the sea and head out into the hinterland, where the land crumples not into mountains but into a succession of abrupt knolls. Their scale can be deceptive; the highest promontory, the Maiolo, gestures rather than towers into the sky – the pass summits at Pugliano, 787 metres above sea level, and the gradient, at its steepest, grazes 9 per cent. The Barbotto, by contrast, peaks at barely 500 metres, but the pitch gathers with the climb and the final kilometre tops one-in-eight. The rain pours off it into a river, the Rubicon, that starts on its slopes. In 49 BC Caesar crossed the river, which marked the boundary between Italy and Cisalpine Gaul, to conquer or perish against Pompey. In a paradox that must have delighted him, Marco used these squat hills to become a great climber of high mountains, crossing the Rubicon almost every day from adolescence to the end of his short life as he pursued the gruelling métier of the professional road-racer.

At the top of the Pieve di Rivoschio – four kilometres of climbing, four more of gentle descent and then a sudden, steep ramp for the final stretch – lies the village where, as the tumult of the Second World War receded, on a smallholding large enough for the family home, four sheep and a clutch of chickens, Marco's grandmother Delia Gemelli, who called herself Alfea, lived with her husband, Marco's grandfather Sotero, known as Bacón. The family had deep regional roots: Sotero had grown up twenty-five kilometres away at Sársina, where he had inherited his trade from *his* father, Ciro, whom everyone called Ferdinando. Marco's forebears, then, were itinerant shoe-repairers, travelling from village to village, patching and sewing the tough hide boots of the *contadini*. Alfea, meanwhile, bore Sotero four children: Dino, Luciana, Ferdinando – Marco's father – and Ersilia.

Italy, at the time, was still a peasant nation. There were oases of technological progress, but most fortunate enough to be wage-earners worked in labour-intensive firms, the glut of small shops, the countless trades and, above all, the fields. Then, between 1950 and 1970, as Marco's father and his siblings grew up, backward Italy became an advanced industrial nation. Three million migrants from the impoverished South kept wages low in the North and made Italy a massive exporter of cars, typewriters and domestic appliances, with European market leaders in Zanussi, Ignis, Indesit, Olivetti, Fiat and Pirelli. Industrial production expanded from the established 'industrial triangle' between Turin, Milan and Genoa, reaching the Adriatic coast at Ravenna, thirty kilometres – not twenty miles – north of Cesenatico.

The years of the 'economic miracle' were years of change in other ways, too. At the end of the war, American troops in Ray-Bans had handed out chocolate and chewing gum. Rock and roll from jukeboxes competed with the rattle of pin-ball machines, washed down with Coca-Cola. American icons like Marilyn Monroe and James Dean entered the Italian imagination, and American money – Marshal Aid, but also covert US sponsorship of the Christian Democrats as a bulwark against the Communists – entered the national coffers. Meanwhile, the tourist industry of the Adriatic Riviera emerged from the ravages of war. The charming villas that had housed the pre-war gentlefolk now became bed-and-breakfasts, and the first high-rise buildings appeared. In 1947 Cesenatico received the boost of a visit by the Giro d'Italia, that monument of national sporting events, which brought two national heroes to town in the cyclists Gino Bartali and Fausto Coppi.

This was the new world in which Sotero and his family made their way. In 1951 they moved to Villalta, 2.8 kilometres from Cesenatico. The move, perhaps fifty kilometres, was a modest one by Italian standards: between the end of the war and 1970 hundreds of thousands of Italians left for the Americas and Australia; similar numbers crossed to France, Switzerland and Belgium, while perhaps ten million internal migrants changed region. Nonetheless, their day's journey took the Pantanis from the back-breaking toil of agricultural labour to the tourist-fuelled boom of the Adriatic coast.

Marco's father – Alfea's third son – had been born Ferdinando, but the name was too long-winded for Alfea, so she called him Paolo. When he was ten or eleven, the family was on the move again, this time into the heart of Cesenatico, to a home in Via Giusti. Sotero found work with the local authority, cleaning the streets. In the afternoons, despite the resolute atheism of his Communist convictions, he played cards and gossiped with the parish priest. Like Sotero, Cesenatico had radicalism in the blood. Several sons of the town had fought for Garibaldi and, in August 1849, the General himself had found temporary safety there. He and two hundred of his troops had regrouped, grabbed some sleep, then boarded twelve barges bound for Venice to help break the Austrian siege. A plaque above what are now numbers 57 and 58, Corso Garibaldi – a charming cobbled street on the south bank of the canal –

announces: 'In this house, on 2 August 1849, Anita and Giuseppe Garibaldi, chased by four armies, found refuge after the events of Rome.' This historic building was also Marco Pantani's first home.

In 1966, soon after Ferdinando, now called Paolo, had completed his military service, he met Tonina Belletti at a dance along the coast at Bellaria. Tonina – the -*ina*, an affix of endearment, is part of her birth name – had been born in Rimini, the daughter of a sailor, Bruno, known to all as Baiò, and Maria, known as Poppona. Paolo was twenty-two, Tonina sixteen and a half. By the time they were married, in 1968, Tonina was pregnant with a daughter, Laura, who would be known as Manola. After their first year of marriage Paolo and Tonina moved into the Garibaldi building. Tonina, disarmingly open, dizzying with energy, tells the story quickly, with an anxious enthusiasm that confuses the chronology: 'We came to Cesenatico and spent a year in Via Cremona, where I was already expecting Marco. When we were married, I was already five months pregnant with Manola. When Manola was born, immediately afterwards, after five months, I fell pregnant with Marco. Because I couldn't have children. I said, "I won't get married if I can't have children." I saw several doctors, and they said, "No, you can't have children." Yet I had Manola and straight afterwards I had Marco.'

Yet the two miracle births in quick succession triggered a family drama Marco was too young to experience directly, but which would shape much of his life. Soon after the arrival of the children she had longed for, Tonina fell into a devastating emotional crisis and took a razor to her veins. There were economic difficulties too: Paolo had trained as a plumber and worked for himself for a spell, but there were problems and, when a number of clients refused to pay, Paolo's business failed and he was forced to find a boss.

The indomitable Tonina decided to look for work. She continues: 'My husband didn't want me to because, here in Romagna, a man feels inferior if his woman works. I started in hotels: the Hotel Esplanade, then the Hotel Conti. I used to take Marco with me to the Hotel Conti – he wasn't three – and he got up to everything you can think of. Once, I was making the beds with the owner's wife, high in the building; I turned around and saw Marco climbing from one balcony to the other! Another time, he was shouting and shouting, and I told him, "Don't cry or they'll send us home." But he was rubbing his eyes, poor thing, because they were full of plaster, the sort you put on walls. He was full of life. Yes. His life was all hurry. I remember that when he went to school, everything was at the last moment. Shoes, everything: "Come here quickly, because you've forgotten your cap" ...', and her reminiscence fragments into a mass of frenzied detail.

The Adriatic Riviera in which Marco was growing up was a world of change. The picture postcards of old fishermen mending fishing nets contain a truth: the force of habit has inexplicably failed to blind the locals to the beauty of the surroundings. They carry with them a sense of belonging, even if experienced individually (and it's hard for a community of hoteliers and restaurateurs so exposed to the mutability of the market – a community where everyone wants so much from the tourists, and from life itself – to maintain that old-time sense of aggregation). An intimate relationship, then, and an evolving one, for, as recently as the 1950s and 1960s, the local variant of Romagnolo dialect was still very much the common tongue. A survey conducted no further back than 1955 showed that, taken as a whole, 66 per cent of Italians couldn't speak Italian. Think of the migrant workers from the South, who can only have spoken dialects incomprehensible in the northern cities: they must have faced a difficult integration. Marco's uncle, Dino, freely admits he expresses himself more readily in Romagnolo than in Italian. The national language gained ground thanks partly to formal schooling but mostly to the informal education of the television: in the course of four years in the late 1960s the number of television sets in Italian homes doubled to seven million and, by the time Marco was growing up in the 1970s and 1980s, dialects throughout the peninsula began to fall out of use, a trend as sudden and unprecedented as the economic upturn. Kids of Marco's generation still slipped into dialect to deliver a *battuta* – a 'one-liner'. Someone who knew Marco for most of his life, Giuseppe 'Pino' Roncucci, his *directeur sportif* when he was an amateur, told me: 'When there was a *battuta*, he could say it in dialect. *"Andemm, Pieno, andemm"* – "Let's go, Pino, let's go." If you made a *battuta* in dialect, he'd reply in dialect, but I heard him speak very little in dialect. He spoke a lot of Italian.' Again, after he'd won the Giro and the Tour in 1998, he walked round in a T-shirt with the dialect line: *'U gne n'è par nisèun'*– 'There's nothing left over for anyone else.' But the T-shirt was designed by someone else.

And so, the old tongues lost their nuance, and the languages of the current generation's parents and grandparents began to run out of speakers. Henceforth, dialect would be nothing more than a rhetorical device inserted into the conversation the way we insert a metaphor or an expletive. A tragedy, in its way, although more obvious tragedies accompanied Marco's first ten years. Less than a month before he was born, a terrorist bomb exploded in a Milan bank, killing sixteen. The blame was attached to left-wing anarchists, although it soon proved to have been the work of the far right, aided by the secret services and protected by the police. It opened a decade of terrorist incidents, some horrific in scale, which culminated, in 1978, in the kidnap and execution by the leftist Red Brigades of perhaps Italy's most distinguished states-man, Aldo Moro and, in 1980, in an explosion in a crowded waiting room at Bologna railway station which left eighty-five dead. Between these atrocities, dozens of journalists, police, magistrates, industrialists and academics were maimed and killed by terror attacks.

Amid shadowy State involvement in lethal plots and the framing of the innocent, the expression *dietrologia* – the conviction that hidden dimensions underlie surface reality – became current; so too did the phrase *'tutto in nero'* – 'everything under the counter' – for these were also years of systematic tax evasion that would have brought another country to its knees. Shop-owners and artisans often declared incomes equal to or smaller than those of their employees. Self-employed pro-fessionals, small entrepreneurs and shopkeepers survived and prospered by defrauding the State, once by tax evasion, and twice by investing the proceeds in the high-interest bonds which financed Italy's public debt. Italy carried on regardless and, on the Adriatic Riviera, the holiday industry, its hotels full and margins wide from 1 March to 20 September, year in, year out, saw the boom continue for another decade even as the rest of the country went through a complex and painful economic and social transition. In the course of a generation, a peasant culture was supplanted by a culture of consumption which took over the High Street and, to an even greater extent, the consumer's imagination, in the form of daydreaming and longing.

Marco had little personal experience of this world of shining objects. Tonina told me there had been no money for toys. 'He bought his first toy when he began to earn money with his bicycle, aged twelve or thirteen. He bought a missile-launcher, Robobox, and I've still got pieces of it about the house. But Marco loved fishing and hunting. As a child he could name every fish in the Adriatic, and he'd go miles to fish for freshwater trout.' He would return to these pastimes of withdrawal into nature, of stealth and wordless concentration, all his life, although it was not his father but Sotero who would load Marco on to his bicycle to take him fishing. And it was Sotero who collected him from school. Paolo told me: 'I had commitments. I was often away for two to three weeks because I didn't always work here in town. So he spent most of his time with his grandfather Sotero, who was like a second father, maybe more.' Looking at a photograph of Sotero and his grandson, Tonina remembers, 'They had a marvellous relationship. Sotero was my father-in-law, not my father, but I was very fond of him. He wasn't beautiful on the outside, but he was on the inside!'

The move to Corso Garibaldi on the Port Canal conditioned much of Marco's future life by giving him a neighbour named Guerrino Ciani, who belonged to Sotero's generation. Tonina told me, tenderly: 'From infancy, Marco always had this love for old people and for children. He was very attached to Guerrino.' Guerrino was also a keen cyclist and a founder member, in the 1960s, of the Fausto Coppi Sports Club, known in Cesenatico as 'the Fausto Coppi'. In 1971 the Fausto Coppi had held the first Nove Colli, or Nine Hills, an all-day amateur ride skirting San Marino and searching out the hardest climbs in the Cesenatico hinterland. The annual Nove Colli quickly ballooned, and the Fausto Coppi with it. Marco would have seen the bikes in the courtyard, and Guerrino set off with the Fausto Coppi riders. Then, in 1979 or 1980, Guerrino was one of the founders of the Fausto Coppi's youth section, intended to introduce children to racing cycling. This was where Marco would start to compete. Guerrino's influence was decisive in Marco's decision to take up cycling.

Yet Marco's choice of sport was surprising. Cesenatico had produced footballers: the international goalkeeper Giorgio Ghezzi, nicknamed 'Kamikaze', had won league titles with Inter in 1953 and 1954, was then sold to Genoa – a decision Inter fans found incomprehensible – before ending his career with Inter's bitter city rivals, AC Milan; and Alberto Zaccheroni, who had an undistinguished career as a full-back before becoming one of Italy's leading managers, winning the league title with Milan in 1999. Both had connections with the holiday industry: Ghezzi

17

retired to Cesenatico, where he owned the Hotel Internazionale, named after the team with which he is still associated; Zaccheroni was the son of a Cesenatico restaurateur.

As Tonina describes it, 'Marco, ever since he was small, wanted to be seen. At the nursery school in Viale Trento, he protected the other children. When he was a bit bigger, he played football, but they never let him play because he was small and skinny. He spent a lot of time on the bench, so he gave up.'

Mario Pugliese, the Cesenatico correspondent for the newspaper *La Voce di Cesena* – 'The Cesena Voice' – was Marco's classmate at school. He told me, 'If you wanted to practise sport in Cesenatico, you either played football or you joined the cycling team. Marco wasn't a good footballer. He played for Cesenatico, but he was really very ordinary. He was absolutely individualist, and therefore unsuited to a team game. We were always yelling, "Get rid of it! Here! Here!" But he never passed.'

Yet cycling came to Marco thanks as much to his shyness as to his inability to pass the ball. His inhibitions were of such crippling intensity that he could come across as retarded. Guerrino Ciani's son-in-law, Nicola Amaducci, noticed as much. Tonina recalls: 'In the courtyard of the house where we lived the boys used to meet to go out training with Amaducci. Amaducci began to say, "Come on, Tonina; let him come out with us." I said, "We'll see what his father says, but we don't have much money." We'd married with nothing; we'd bought an apartment; we had two children. He said, "We'll provide the bicycle." It's the bicycle that's now hanging in the bar.'

After Tonina's animated turmoil, the contrast of Amaducci's gentle melancholy. We met in Amaducci's Bar del Corso, yards from the Garibaldi building, and there was immediately a tenderness about him and a sense of apprehension that subsided only a little as the conversation became more natural, although even then he nervously curled a piece of card around a finger, or into a slim tube. His beard is no longer the proud jet-black you see in the photographs, where Marco, his thirteen-, maybe fourteen-year-old scalp still covered by dense locks, always seems to have his arms locked around Amaducci's neck. Grey hairs now outnumber the dark, and Nicola Amaducci looks across the room with warm, sad eyes and speaks with a voice put on edge by the presence of

18

a microphone, then softened by his deep courtesy and the slightest of lisps. Christened Nicola in memory of his great-grandfather by parents who didn't like the name so called him Roberto, he has worked with schoolchildren all his life – call it a vocation – albeit as an administrator, not a teacher, overseeing school canteens and transport, and the relations between the education services, pupils and their families. A career spent caring for local kids. And when, in 1972, his own son was born, Nicola, called Roberto, called him Roberto too, as if to correct the earlier oversight. Amaducci knew Marco almost from the moment he was born: then, in 1977, the Pantanis and the Amaduccis were two of eighteen families who formed a cooperative and built a three-storey apartment block at 136, Via dei Mille: the First of May Condominium. The Amaduccis moved into an apartment on the third floor of stairwell C; the Pantanis took a flat on the first floor of stairwell A. Where Tonina portrays a gregarious, outgoing child, Amaducci paints a quite different picture: 'He was always strong-headed, impetuous, introverted, rather solitary. He had difficulty making friends. Marco had a small vegetable garden alone, below the flat, which he cultivated on his own, and he often went fishing alone. Roberto and Marco were only two years apart, so they sometimes played together in the garden, although it often ended in an argument. It was Marco's personality, you see? He was a solitary child, quiet, but always full of energy. My wife, who was a primary-school teacher, worked with him one summer at a camp for children with working parents, and he was always up a tree or on a roof, full of life, but rather alone. And when a ten- or eleven-year-old child is isolated, it's not nice, so to try and help him make friends with other children, I invited him to take up cycling with us. I thought his personality would suit him to cycling. I wasn't thinking of results, I was just thinking that group sports, going out to train with friends, would help calm him down a little. Because life can be difficult for young people . . .'

Amaducci first got involved in the Fausto Coppi Sports Club when his son Roberto started to ride in 1982. 'I joined too, first accompanying the kids, then as vice-president of the club. Very soon we were taking out more than fifty children to ride every Sunday. I didn't think of myself as a *directeur sportif*: I experienced sport as something to enjoy, as something in which to progress, to reach a certain level of proficiency, but above all as fun. Everything that came after that was extra. I was always with those boys. I worked in the office during the day and at Fausto Coppi in the afternoons for training and in the evenings when there were races. It was almost a form of social work, although I was directly involved because of my son, and later my daughter, who began to ride. My wife was always there too, and my father-in-law was involved. We had a lot of fun: it was a commitment that brought responsibility with it, but enjoyment always came first. They were the most beautiful years of my life.'

Despite, or perhaps because of, this nurturing philosophy, the youth section of the Fausto Coppi quickly produced a group of talented and highly competitive riders: 'Of the children of Marco's age, four others progressed to become Category One amateurs: Andrea Agostini, Anthony Battistini, Renato Baldassari and Francesco Buratti. All got to within a step of the professional ranks. All four were good riders, but Baldassari and Battistini especially so. Except that, for various reasons, they never took that final step: Battistini, because his mother died at a critical moment of his development; Baldassari, because of his character, although nowadays he's always on his bike, competing as an amateur and regularly winning. Andrea Agostini, too; when the amateur circuit races end in a sprint, he's always the favourite to win.'

But the jewel was Marco: 'He enjoyed riding his bike, and we saw in a matter of a year or two that he had something the other children didn't. In 1983, when he started racing, the races for the juniors still included climbs, and he was always ahead on them, despite the fact that his way of riding was always to ride at the back, never at the front. But even in those days he went well – very well. But you never think one of your children will do what Marco did. You think they'll ride well, finish high up in the field, but not become what Marco became. He was different from the others as a child, and he achieved what he did because he was different.'

The affection that bonded Marco and the man who introduced him to cycling is suggested, in twenty-year-old photographs, by Marco's embrace. But Amaducci's words seem to refer not just to those childhood years but to the end of Marco's life: 'What he needed was affection. He needed someone to be near him. With me, he was always himself. With me, he never changed.'

Perhaps it was the idea of shared experience; perhaps cycling allowed him the silence he enjoyed when he was hunting, or fishing, or taking watches apart and playing with the parts for hours and hours. This blissful absorption, losing himself in time as he dissected some mechanical device, perhaps mimicked his adored grandfather, bent over a shoe, forcing a needle through leather with strong, accurate fingers. Perhaps he simply forgot his shyness in the heat of competition. Either way, Nicola Amaducci was right: cycling allowed Marco to break through his chronic inhibitions and enjoy friendship, showing the extroversion he could otherwise only achieve with his mother. It gave him an outward persona, a mask he could use to face the world. It also gave him deep bonds with other boys – bonds which would survive him. But if, in one direction, cycling set Marco free, in another, it added to Tonina's burden of anxiety, which lives on in her memories, liberated by the years from chronological order: 'For me, the anguish was continuous, every time he went out. If I met him at the crossroads, I'd turn the other way in fear, because he was a bit reckless. Every time he went out, I was afraid. Because, many things had not yet happened, but . . . after the first accident, the second, the third, the fourth, that is – and I remember one day I went to work, and he was going out with two or three other boys; I was on my bike going to work, and I said, "Helmets for those boys!" and my husband said, "Go away!" When I got home to the condominium, the other boys asked me, "How's Marco?" I said, "Why, where is he?" He was in hospital because he'd been hit by a car. He had been descending; the car was coming up the other way.'

In 1983 Sotero had part-funded Marco's first racing bike, which would supplant the model loaned by the Fausto Coppi. To do so, grandfather, father and son visited the Vicini factory in the outskirts of Cesena, founded by the 1939 champion of Italy, Mario Vicini, known locally as Ghaibera Vicini. Paolo told me: 'We wanted to buy a bike we'd already seen. But Marco saw this "Tour de France" bicycle, twenty or thirty thousand lire more than the other. It was dark red, bull's blood, metallic.' At a distance of two decades the cost is still imprinted in Paolo's memory. 'The other bicycle was 260,000 lire. We paid 290,000 lire' – €145. 'Two or three years later, when Marco had to ride a team bike, we sold it to a mechanic.'

Marco learned to dismantle and reassemble his bike with great expertise; and, later on, as Tonina recalled, 'He always went training with an Allen key in his pocket, because he analysed his position. A bit higher, a bit lower, a bit here, a bit there. He almost always went training alone. He often told me he heard voices. He never told me whose voices they were. They were his affair. Even when he dropped Tonkov at Montecampione, he threw away his glasses and everything, and he heard voices. Perhaps it was his grandfather.'

Initially, it was not Marco's father but his uncle Dino who accompanied him to races. Dino also lived on Viale dei Mille, in the Condominio Gabbiano – the 'Seagull Condominium' – a hundred metres away. A timber-yard hand during the week, Dino was passionate about cycling. In the newspaper, he always lingered over the cycling pages, and rode himself, although not competitively. Even today Dino cycles two or three mornings a week. For the past twenty years he has taken part in recreational events all over Italy and France. We met in a bar near the railway station where Dino plays cards each afternoon, like his father before him. 'We were the ones who put him on a bike. Sotero gave him his first bike, but we were the ones who went with him every Sunday. Paolo didn't want to follow. He used to play football, until we put him on a bike. People were always saying, "Where did you get a son like that from?" I was always replying, "I'm not his father, I'm his uncle." Because I was bald, they thought I was his father – until Paolo started shaving his head.' But that was not for a decade yet.

Given the circumstances, for young people on the Riviera, German or English were more use than Romagnolo. Like the other holiday resorts of the Adriatic Riviera, from upmarket Riccione and swaggering Rimini further south, to the nightclubs of Milano Marittima halfway to Ravenna, Cesenatico was thriving on tourism, especially West German tourism, as early as the 1960s. The Deutsche Mark bought comfortable accommodation, good food, brilliant sunshine, golden beaches, at a favourable exchange rate. A cheap family holiday for the Germans, then, and for the locals, initially at least, an eye-opening tide of temporary revellers from a more emancipated world. And some German girls, of course, had (and still have) a fantasy about Italian men which made them easy pickings for smooth-talking beach boys. For a local boy with a little charm, the odds have always been favourable: in summer the seafront is crowded with beautiful girls in bikinis, some of whom have certainly come in the hope of meeting a Latin lover. The massive and continuing internal migration of the early 1960s, the liberalisation of sexual habits, the diffusion of contraceptive devices, the divorce and abortion laws, all created a decisive break between the generations.

The tourist industry here did little to combat the idea of the Riviera as a place of sensual, if not downright sexual pleasure: even today, in perhaps more conservative times, the postcards depict young temptresses baring breasts, and sometimes more, and gazing alluringly out at you. The models are mostly blonde, not at all Italian-looking: they depict local identity loss – or, perhaps, though the idea feels forced, identity gain.

Mario Pugliese looks back with affection at the adolescence he and Marco shared: 'We went to school together from when we were eleven to when we were fourteen or fifteen. We were close friends, together every day. Actually, there were three of us; they called us the "MPs": Mario Pugliese, Matteo Panzavolta and Marco Pantani. We were hyperactive, and we were always being called into the headmaster's office after getting caught doing something wrong. Marco had an innate intelligence that allowed him to get by in school without ever doing any work. He'd arrive half an hour before school and copy our homework, but he was the quickest copier. He had the art of getting by – something typically Italian. But we were thirteen-year-olds, full of hormones, and we sometimes went a bit too far with respect to the girls in our class. Don't get me wrong: they liked it, but we weren't very elegant. If there was a girl in a miniskirt, we'd pick on her and make sure it got lifted up. Nothing disproportionate, nothing that wasn't essentially healthy.

'Marco was attractive enough as a twelve- or thirteen-year-old; but by the time he was fifteen, he was already losing his hair. It was a big problem for an adolescent, especially in those days. Today, baldness is fashionable to some extent, in part, thanks to Marco himself. But in those days, losing your hair was a problem; it meant trying all sorts of treatments. It was anti-aesthetic. Adolescence can be difficult enough for everyone, especially for a boy of extraordinary sensitivity like Marco. With a balding head, ears that suddenly stuck out ... We're moving from facts into opinions, here, but a person who is extremely shy, extremely introverted, closed within themself, will develop a greater sensitivity. He'll learn to listen to himself much more, and refine his sensitivity – quite different from someone who has absolutely normal social interactions; and he was extremely sensitive.'

Marco's incipient hair loss took place in a nation in which a deep-rooted passion about appearance, style and fashion had assumed the traits of the consumer culture of the 1980s and 1990s: a 1992 survey showed no less than 37 per cent of Italians claimed to wear designer labels. As in other southern European countries, spending on pharmaceuticals was unusually high. Sales of aftershave lotions and anti-wrinkle creams were rocketing. Italian youth was obsessed with the word *bello* – 'beautiful'. To be a *bel ragazzo* or a *bella ragazza* – the adjective before the noun signifying beauty that is surface deep – meant peer-group acceptance and popularity; hair loss was not part of the type. Marco spent a great deal on scalp treatments and hair-restorers – to no avail.

Isolated from the common experience of Cesenatico's youth, he went out into the nearby hills alone to ride hundreds of kilometres. It was a simple defensive strategy. Pugliese continues: 'In adolescence, when others were having their first relationships with girls, for him it wasn't so easy. This no doubt increased his introversion.

'As an eleven-, twelve-, thirteen-year-old, he was expressive. Then things changed. He was a little taciturn, although obviously it depended on the company. But I think here is where a gap opened between Pantani the athlete who sits in the saddle and acquires charisma, security, and can impose his will very persuasively, and Pantani in plain clothes, not on the bike, who finds it harder to impose his charisma, and finds it harder to be secure.'

This teenaged insecurity built on a fragile possessiveness Marco had shown as a young child. Tonina recalls: 'He attached himself to [Guerrino], like another grandfather. He was so attached that when Guerrino's real grandson visited, Marco would hit him, because he didn't want him there. The other boy's grandfather belonged to Marco.' A school friend recalls that, as a teenager – his temperament already showing a terrible sense of hurt – Marco would not take part in playful wrestling like other boys: 'He would hit you in the face. He wasn't big, but it wasn't normal for a thirteen-year-old, and the other boys were slightly wary of him.' Only with the prop of cycling could he achieve togetherness.

Many years later, his manager Manuela Ronchi would find, 'On the few occasions I embraced him, he became rigid, and blushed. He wasn't used to receiving displays of affection.' In this most tactile of cultures, it was a noticeable eccentricity: great warmth with an inner circle of same-sex intimates, and a wary coldness with others. Nonetheless, success would camouflage this and, perhaps, other conspicuous character traits. In later years, Ronchi continues, 'Because he was very reserved, and had a forbidding charisma, people who wanted to show him affection perhaps held back.'

The quality of the group that included Marco led the club to look for expert help, so in 1984 the Fausto Coppi called Vittorio Savini, a former technical director of the amateur Giro d'Italia and the brother of a journeyman professional, Claudio Savini. Savini had been to school with Marco's father Paolo at Villalta when they were both ten, although they'd had no contact since. Savini told me: 'They said, "We've a group of youngsters who show promise, and you're the only one here who knows anything about cycling." I didn't really have time to get involved, but I told them I'd go along and take a look, and from the day I did, a Sunday I'll never forget, I fell in love with them all; not just Marco, but the whole group – kids who were trying so hard.'

Busy, intense, slightly bullying, Savini reminisces in the office of the Renault dealership he manages in Cesenatico: 'Marco wasn't the strongest of them. At that moment there were two or three boys who were as strong and, in the sprint, perhaps stronger: Anthony Battistini, Andrea Agostini and Francesco Buratti, a powerful *rouleur* who won a lot as an amateur. He could do sixty kilometres an hour on the flat, but he was a very poor climber. All in all, it was an exceptional group of boys, and wherever we went to compete, our group scared the hell out of the other riders.'

Marco rather resembled his father, but his peculiar character was all his own. It lodges in Savini's memory as it does in everyone's who knew him in childhood: 'Marco didn't have an easy personality, even as a child. He could be a very good, sweet boy, but there was anger in him: you only had to say a word against him and he could fly off the handle. When he was racing, even as a child, he was wilful. He didn't listen, and he lost a lot of races because of it. But even as a fifteen-year-old you could see he climbed well. There were no great mountain passes in the age-group race profiles, only small climbs; but each time we went over a road bridge, Marco would start right at the back, and by the brow of the climb he'd be in front. I used to say to him, "But why do you always ride at the back of the group?'' And you know what he said? He enjoyed looking into the faces of the other boys as they suffered. This was the pleasure he drew from it.

'When he was climbing, he was something else. Mother Nature had given him a gift. He hardly breathed; he didn't break into a sweat. People forget that. Marco had a capacity for riding we'll have to wait another fifty years to see the likes of again. When you told him to attack, he attacked, and no one could stay on his wheel.'

Savini became one of Marco's confidants. 'He used to come here and sit where you're sitting, and in the evening, at closing time, we'd talk again, and he'd let off steam, and sometimes we even argued, because we saw things differently. I'd known him as a child, and to me I suppose he was still one of my boys, when in reality he was thirty years old. It's not that I didn't understand him: it's just that I felt he was still a child, clean, pure, not a thirty-year-old with commitments, involvements, who reasoned differently.'

2

The Meaning of Success
(1980–88)

There are other beginnings here. In 1980 the Cesena authorities created a new economic zone south-east of town, alongside the Via Emilia, the old, straight Roman road projecting north-west out of Rimini. A triangle of land with planning rights was divided into plots and sold off to small entrepreneurs. The resulting community, Case Castagnoli, is cut off from the town; the Vicini bicycle factory, already outlying, must be two kilometres behind you by the time the taxi swings right and into the industrial zone where, at length, you find the lock-up where Giorgio Fagioli, 64, supplies professional tools – heavy-duty pumps, drills – to the building trade.

'I knew Marco's father. He was a plumber, and a customer of mine. He came here because I sell pumps. But he stopped coming. I don't know what happened to him: there's good money in plumbing, but only for those who know how to do it. If you don't keep up to date, you soon lose out. He wasn't' – Giorgio looks for the word – 'a *sophisticated* type.' These days, Fagioli's clients are mostly Senegalese and Albanian. 'They do the menial jobs Italians won't perform any more. Some take the next step, and set up small businesses.' Perhaps aware of my foreignness, and of Italy's sometimes virulent racism, he adds, 'Good people.'

With a smile as warm as Marco's, and a wag of the tail, Giorgio's dog Rocky follows us next door, into the hall of the Nuova Case Castagnoli Sport, a sports and social club Giorgio helped set up in 1982, 'to bring a bit of life to the area. I'd been a rider myself – amateur, nothing special. So, among other things, we organised a bike race.' Which, on 22 April 1984, became the first race Marco ever won, even if the details now escape Giorgio: 'I can't remember whether it was on the flat, or if

27

it was the year it had a climb. It seems to me now that he was second the year it was on the climb, and first the year it was on the flat. What I remember is that when he finished second, he cried. He won it in a sprint. He wasn't anyone at the time. There are things I don't remember any more. When he started winning, in 1994, I asked if it was the same Pantani, or another one.'

By then, of course, Marco's early race record was being organised into a semi-official canon. However, despite the temptation there must be to play up those early sightings, to graft the certainty of the written record onto the fading memories, Giorgio can't quite bring it to mind. The truth is, of course, you know at the time you're looking at *something*, an outline looming in the fog. Only years later can you know what it was — and this Giorgio has the equanimity to accept.

Soon after Marco's victory, Giorgio's club launched an annual ten-day Festival of Sport, with tournaments, dinners and guests. 'Thanks to the factory, some great champions came to visit us. Bartali came. He liked his wine, so we took him to a local producer of Sangiovese, and by the time we left he couldn't drive and his son had to take the wheel. Francesco Moser came too: we presented him with a gold medal. Marco came twice. I heard he charged others, but he came to us for free. He should have come here last year, too . . .' Giorgio had founded a Marco Pantani fan club in 1994. No doubt they wanted to celebrate its tenth anniversary with Marco. But Giorgio's voice has dwindled to silence. I hold a hand out to the dog, still grinning and wagging his tail, but he won't come any nearer. Giorgio throws him a glance — 'You know, he won't come within a metre of anyone' — then resumes: 'Many of my friends went up to Madonna di Campiglio to see the stage. When they heard Marco had been suspended, they left in their camper vans. They didn't even wait for the race to pass.'

Marco's parents remember Marco's first win vividly. Paolo told me: 'They always finished in a sprint, and Marco, for a sprint, was very light — there were boys his age who were twice his size . . . Before the race, I wrote a note and hid it in his pocket. He was reading it when he rode past Amaducci's wife. It said, "Marco, don't be afraid. To win, you have to attack them. Where there's a ramp, a climb, or something, they're big, and if there's a sprint, they'll beat you, but if you have the courage to attack first and get away, you'll beat them. Come on." I wrote something like that; and that's what he did.' Tonina smiled: 'He finished alone, we saw him just before the final curve – I was with Ciani – and we hugged with joy.' On 13 May Marco won again at Serravalle di San Marino. This time the win was a means of mourning. Guerrino Ciani, with whom Tonina had celebrated Marco's first win, had since died. Marco dedicated his second victory to his memory. It was his first experience of mourning someone close; Tonina recalls, 'Marco was still small, but he was very sorry.' So soon in his cycling career, success mingled with loss.

His third and fourth wins came in quick succession: on 29 July, at Pieve Quinta, Forlì, he crossed the finish line three and a half minutes ahead of his nearest rival. A week later, on 5 August, at Val di Noce, also Forlì, he took victory number four in a race remembered vividly by a future regional chairman of the Italian Cycling Federation, Celestino Salami: 'I already knew Marco, but we met properly on 5 August 1984. The Forlì–Val di Noce was a thirty-three-kilometre race and finished with a three-kilometre climb at a gradient of 17 to 18 per cent: it wasn't really suitable for thirteen-to-fourteen-year-olds, and after that year it was removed from the calendar. We arrived at the foot of the climb together, and I attacked. Then Marco came past, like a truck. He was amazing, a phenomenon, even aged fourteen.'

One of Marco's Cesenatico friends would later recall that Marco, incapable of sharing his feelings after his victories, would return home and shut himself in his room for two days. From Giorgio Fagioli we know that finishing second could reduce Marco to tears. Winning bicycle races quickly became a fundamental prop for his sense of self and, in this sense, 1984 marked a watershed in his emotional development.

Between this and his next win, Marco moved to agricultural college, stepped up into the 'schoolboy' category, and suffered two accidents. A collision with a truck left him with a broken nose and cuts to the lip that would leave a permanent scar over his mouth. A fall in a race left Marco nursing a blow to the head and collarbone fractures that required the insertion of a wire to hold the bone fragments in place. Tonina recalls the accident as part of a family drama: 'In 1985 many things happened. Marco fell from his bike and broke his collarbone. My daughter was operated on urgently and was saved by a miracle. My father died, and I had to open the kiosk. My father would have liked to see it, but he didn't even have time to see it. It was a very bad year.' However, Tonina's initiative was rewarded. The kiosk in Viale Torino selling a traditional snack, the *piadina*, was a success. It must have made the family visible in this small community: but visibility is not always a blessing, as Marco and his family would discover.

Marco, meanwhile, missed weeks of college. He never caught up, failed his exams and then, instead of retaking them, moved to a technical college, where he studied radio repair for three years. He must have shown ability: silent absorption was one of his characteristic moods. It was the mental state of cycling, too, monitoring the exertion, but also the movements of the rider in front. A marathon runner can from time to time allow himself to be hypnotised by the rhythm. Not a cyclist, for whom the slightest tyre contact means a lost race and probable injuries to the collarbone and face. He rides, eyes turned monkishly downwards, in absolute concentration. All his life Marco would tinker with radios, retune mopeds and, later, motorbikes to increase the power. He maintained his hunting rifles serviced and oiled. He became an expert bike mechanic. Out fishing and hunting, too, he must have found the same stillness and self-emptying. And on the starting line before his races, as other riders exchanged greetings and chattered idly, Marco would stand apart in silence. He wasn't there to socialise.

We can only imagine the impact of the first kill, out with Sotero in the hills: cycling must have mimicked it, each victory a kill rekindled, a precious moment with his beloved grandfather relived. Cycling helped him make his way in the world, but it also represented proud moments with his grandfather and uncle. It returned him home to his doting mother, perhaps allowing him to become what he imagined she wanted him to be: the successful man in her life. Marco's accidents, then, caused him physical distress, of course; worse, by keeping him out of the saddle, they might even have caused him emotional deprivation.

Two days short of a year separated his last win of 1984 and his first of 1985, at Montefiorino, Modena on 4 August. On 15 September Marco took his first victory outside Emilia-Romagna. It was in Tuscany: the Ilario Vignali Trophy, at Donnini di Regello, near Florence. Vanni Caroni, whose son Alberto rode for the Fausto Coppi, was there. His account gives something of the flavour of those years: 'We left Cesenatico at 5.30 to 6 a.m. Normally, we fathers went with our sons: they wanted us there. In Marco's case, it was his uncle, Dino, who used to accompany him. We had to sign in as soon as we arrived, and collect lunch vouchers for the riders and staff. Then we went to eat: I can't remember what – probably local specialities in a restaurant. I remember, in the race, Battistini was in a breakaway, two minutes thirty seconds ahead of the peloton. We drove past them in the car, then pulled over to watch the pass. And Dino said, "Marco isn't in good shape today." But Marco always rode defensively on the flat, while Battistini launched furious attacks, often wasting a lot of energy. The race finished with a climb, and there, Marco suddenly attacked. His attack effectively neutralised Battistini's breakaway, which didn't go unnoticed. There were recriminations later. But Marco rode straight past the breakaway, and Battistini won the sprint for second place. One-two for the Fausto Coppi.'

There were three wins in 1986, and two placings worth mentioning: second in the regional championship, and a finish somewhere in the top ten – the exact result is lost – in the national championships. Then, into the 'junior' category, for seventeen- and eighteen-year-olds, where Marco began the transition from being just another teenager to becoming a noted athlete. The mechanisms that would achieve it began to be assembled around him: journalistic comment, broadcast images, the first nervous interviews.

And, suddenly, there he is, in moving pictures, for perhaps the first time – seventeen and on edge, his hair fastidiously brushed and, from a distance, still dense. Luciano Draghi believes the highlights of the junior-category Forlì–Montecoronaro hill climb, on 7 July 1987, are the first televised images of a Pantani victory. If so, they represent a decisive step in the process that made Marco a public figure. Draghi created *Ultimo Kilometro*, a weekly television review of amateur cycling in Romagna – 'Although we also covered national-level events like the Coppa Placci and the Coppi and Bartali, and some events outside the region' – in 1986. Now in his seventies, Draghi announces proudly, 'We recorded the thousandth *Ultimo Kilometro* last week [at the end of May 2005]. It goes out at 9 p.m. We don't have figures for the programme, but we do for the station: we have an average of about eighty thousand viewers. We cover every category up to élite, starting with the very young. Marco began riding in 1982–3. When he began to ride well, we started to cover him.'

The coverage has none of the paraphernalia of specialised sports coverage, none of the authoritative aura afforded by technology and celebrity: no expert analyses, onscreen graphics or slow-motion replays. By today's standards, it's home video standard, or lower. And similar footage that would now be considered precious has long since been dumped, or recorded over. It seems incredible, until you think: how many local stars make the grade? How many miss their chance through a poorly timed off day or injury? How many more invent one to explain away failure, when the truth is simply that their physique reached peak performance at sixteen, or nineteen, or twenty-two, and developed no more?

Montecoronaro, 865 metres above sea level, squats on the shoulder of Monte Fumaiolo – the 1,407 metre peak on whose southern slopes the Tiber is born. The pass, once a key artery between northern and central Italy, has been superseded by tunnels that channel the traffic down towards Umbria. Only the cyclists celebrate its tortuous turns and upward journey. The race precedes the annual wild-boar feast by a week. Claudio Della Vedova of the Canduccio Club from Udine, up in Friuli, is dominating the category, and is thought of as unbeatable in hill climbs. The gradient and Della Vedova have kept the field small: just forty-seven have paid their race subscription, and only forty-one have actually turned up to ride. Draghi's commentary berates the cowards who stayed at home: 'You have to have the courage to take part in races that are supposedly a foregone conclusion.' That's certainly how Della Vedova rides it, forcing the pace from the front as if no one else is in the race – as if he is racing against himself, not the other riders. Early in the race, his team-mate, Luca Facchin – also an excellent climber – joins a decoy breakaway. Marco's Fausto Coppi team-mates cover the attack, before they reach the spa town of Bagno di Romagna, and the pass rises through open countryside for eight kilometres, to the village of Verghereto. There the gradient relaxes for one and a half kilometres, before the final two-kilometre climb up to the Válico.

On the long climb up from Bagno di Romagna, Della Vedova accelerates, dispatching all but his team-mate Facchin and Marco. Facchin stays with them for some kilometres, then falls away. Now, curved grimly over the frame, low over the tops of the bars, Della Vedova's only body movement is a slight pendulum movement in the shoulders. He never sits up or stands on the pedals; it is an exercise in physical confinement. He looks like a time-triallist reducing the wind resistance, although wind resistance is the least of his worries on this sustained climb. The images show mostly the back of his shirt: 'Canduccio' is printed in black letters on white. Three wide hoops – blue, red and yellow – circle the midriff. His race number is 27.

Right behind him, Marco is more slender, perhaps taller than his more muscular rival. *Dossard* number 7 is pinned to his light-blue GS F. Coppi–Gelati Menni–Conad shirt. He is full of nervous energy, often out of the saddle, moving his hands from the centre of the bars to the horns of the brake levers, or to the flat lower ends. His torso is straighter; he can very probably breathe more easily than Della Vedova, taking more air into the lungs, absorbing more oxygen. He throws occasional glances to either side and down the hill, checking where the other riders are, eyeing the camera-bike. He turns the pedals eighty times a minute; eighty-five when the gradient eases. Della Vedova manages a funereal seventy-two, maximum seventy-five turns per minute. He sets the pace, Marco matches it, and they creep up the hillside with their centres of gravity locked into a binary system, despite every moving part being out of sync. Della Vedova's team-mate, Facchin, is now over a minute behind. If the pace had been allowed to relax, perhaps the two Can-duccio riders could have launched coordinated attacks and worn Marco down. Instead, Della Vedova depends on Marco cracking.

The monotonous grind is broken only as they approach the sign marking the final kilometre – not the traditional triangular red flag but a white canvas placard stretched like a hammock between a tree and a road sign. Della Vedova is still forcing the pace as Marco reaches down to tighten first his right shoe, then his left. They have a minute and a half more of racing. Della Vedova increases the tempo. Marco grips the handlebars on the lower part of the curve, then stands on the pedals – an unusual position that will become his signature. Then he raises his hands on to the upper part of the bars, still standing. Della Vedova's pendulum movement becomes more pronounced; to the sideways motion his torso adds a vertical pitch.

There is an elastic vitality about Marco. He rides, back in the saddle now, towards the final corner, then rises, perhaps impatient, perhaps just stretching before the sprint. Local knowledge. He sits and takes the bend close on his rival's wheel. They coast through ninety degrees. Then, the 'Arrivo' banner appears, straight ahead, draped over the finish line, white on red, disappearing into the rooftops. Before you can rise out of the saddle, you have to reach that phase in your pedal action where your pedal stroke is at its apogee; Marco reaches it a fraction of a second before Della Vedova. It is still uphill. The lateral movement of his bike is controlled, the front wheel aimed directly at the line, the power directed tight into the pedals which accelerate to a hundred and ten breathless strokes per minute, a fast spin. Della Vedova's loose style dissipates energy: the pendulum motion has spread down through his body and into the bike; the wobble to his steering adds inches to the distance he covers from here to the finish line. Pushing a larger gear than Marco, he cannot reach a hundred pedal strokes per minute. Marco takes the left-hand side of the road, steering into the narrowing gap between Della Vedova and the wall. The Friulan threatens to force him into the wall, then, sportingly, eases out to allow Marco a clean sprint. Marco's final pedal strokes must touch a hundred and twenty per minute. For several tantalising lengths they are shoulder to shoulder like kids holding their breath under water, looking into each other's eyes. Physical attributes come into it – lung capacity, oxygen absorption, lactic acid clearance – but so does willpower, and it is Marco who prevails. He gains an inch, then two, and Della Vedova knows he has lost. Victory is clear, although the margin is less than a length.

The two riders have covered the 105 kilometre course at an average speed of 37.951 k.p.h. Two hours, forty-six minutes of racing, much of it spent locked together in combat. Yet there is no handshake, no nod of the head in acknowledgement of experience shared. Anywhere but here you'd wonder where they lay on the spectrum of autism. A minute and fifty seconds pass before Facchin crosses the line in third place. Eighteen riders will finish inside the stipulated time limit. Six will finish outside it, and seventeen will abandon, or probably have done already.

After recorded highlights of the Forlì–Montecoronaro, Marco, his Fausto Coppi team-mate Anthony Battistini and their *directeur sportif* Vittorio Savini were interviewed in the studio. Marco was nervous. Tightly focused questions would have allowed him to structure his thoughts and, perhaps, overcome his anxiety. Instead, he was fed open-ended statements and left to talk into silence. Worse, he was asked to summarise the almost eventless race. The best raconteur would have struggled, and Marco wasn't the best of raconteurs: tongue-tied, self-correcting, repetitive, peppered with meaningless spacers, his was a lifeless description:

> Della Vedova showed you know from the first kilometres that he was strong, indeed, he showed he was very strong climbing, he climbed at a high tempo, very str– he climbed very strongly and at a high tempo, he always, nearly, rode at the front always, I was always, let's say I rode defensively, and at the end of the race, you know, let's say Della Vedova paid a little for his presumption, saying – let's say –

At which point Draghi mercifully interrupted with, 'But he's a generous rider, Della Vedova, eh? A rider who throws everything he's got into the mix without tactical abstruseness . . .' and terminated Marco's humourless, above all anxious performance.

Draghi then turned to Savini, who told him: 'We have trained with blessed calm, we have perhaps suffered humiliation from other teams based in Romagna, but we've always carried on with our head held high.'

Savini was celebrating victories by Marco and Battistini in the same weekend, yet his moment of triumph evoked not the glow of contentment but memories of former humiliations. Like Marco, he endured the interrogation unsmilingly. The interview suggested the beginning of an antipathy between Marco (and his entourage) and the medium of television. With the years this aversion would mature into a hostility to journalism, and journalists, across the board.

Aged eighteen, Marco decided he had outgrown the Fausto Coppi. He took several team-mates and joined a team based at the village of Gambettola, near Forlì. The move proved fruitless: Marco waited until August for his single race win, down at Pescara, on the Abruzzo coast. He lost the rest of the season by driving his first car, a Fiat Ritmo, into a wall, and breaking bones in his foot that had to be set in plaster. After forty interminable days, he came back at the 1988 Forlì–Montecoronaro, and finished fifth, despite his lack of training.

By now, Marco was living the life of an athlete. Mario Pugliese told me: 'We lost sight of each other for a while. I remember I met him one Saturday evening. I said, "You still riding?" and he said, "Yes, this year, I'm going to try to do well at the amateur Giro d'Italia. If it goes well,

I'll continue. Otherwise, I'll go and sell *piadine*." Six or seven months later, he finished third in the amateur Giro d'Italia, and his great ascent started there.' Pugliese began working as a journalist aged seventeen. When Marco attained his first major results, Pugliese did some of the first interviews. 'So we saw each other again after a long time, in the Port Canal, and I said: "Just think how it is: you're a cyclist, I'm a journalist, and I'm writing about you, and tomorrow you'll buy the newspaper," and so on. I covered him for some time, until he stepped up a level, and it became difficult to get near him.'

3
Red Riders
(1989–JUNE 1992)

In 1989, aged 19, Marco moved up into the 'amateur' category, in which he would compete against twenty-six- and twenty-seven-year-olds who'd narrowly missed professional contracts or failed to renew them, or against East Europeans capable of holding their own against the professionals but whose regimes either barred them from trying or lacked the resources to make it possible. The under-23 restriction had yet to be introduced.

Marco was especially close to his Communist grandfather, and his home, the First of May Condominium, was the creation of a leftist cooperative. Now, Italian Communism influenced his life in a surprising new way. His new team, Rinascita, was one of two cycling clubs in the industrial town of Ravenna, thirty kilometres to Cesenatico's north. It had been founded in 1947 by fifteen former combatants in the twenty-eighth Garibaldi Brigade, the partisan group that had fought Ravenna's battle of liberation from the Nazi army. Medardo Bartolotti, the Rinascita president from 1981 to 1988, told me: 'After the war it was clear Ravenna would assume a left-wing configuration because 90 per cent of the partisans had been Communists. Pedale Ravennate, the first of the cycling clubs, had been founded by a group of thirty Republicans; the Republican Party in Ravenna was among the strongest in Italy. They had a lot of votes in Ravenna, although nationally they only polled 1 or 2 per cent. At Rinascita, 40 per cent of us were members of the PCI' – the Italian Communist Party – 'I've been a member for forty years. But the clubs weren't Party organisations as such; they were run by men who were inspired by their political ideals to contribute their experience to the clubs.'

Italian history had made these Party connections, which seem so odd to the outsider, inevitable. After the Second World War and the birth of the Italian Republic, the opposing ideological forces of the Catholic Church and the Communist Party had created organisations to involve the masses through social and cultural activities. In majority Communist regions like Emilia-Romagna, Party influence could extend into the most apolitical corners, one of which was cycling, a sport that requires a vast organisational apparatus diffused from village to village to secure local sponsorship, coordinate local administrations, close the roads, marshall the traffic and direct the riders. Hosting an event invariably highlighted the dynamism of local politicians, and race organisation became closely tied to political activism. Elsewhere in the peninsula, other institutions made amateur cycling possible. Across Italy's so-called 'Red Belt', from Emilia-Romagna and the Marches in the east, across Umbria to Tuscany in the west, Italian Communism, not as a doctrine but as a dry-eyed system of alliances, coloured by principles one step short of strategic – a strenuous, insistent, often rather conservative moralism – smoothed the way before the peloton.

Marco's amateur career was mostly restricted to the Red Belt and as a first-year amateur his results were promising. In June, second in the Riccione–Misano Adriatico to another first-year amateur, Marco Fincato, later a Mercatone Uno team-mate; fourth in the Memorial Pancotti at Ostra Vetere, in the hills inland from Ancona; fourth again in the Pistoia–Sammomé, a race created by the great Loretto Petrucci, twice winner of the Milan–Sanremo in the 1950s; and third, to a future pro three years his senior, Massimo Donati, in another Tuscan race, the Socchi Trophy, ending in Volterra. In July, on a rare visit to the northern Lombard Alps, he finished second in the Sondrio–Livigno hill climb, dropping future Giro winner Ivan Gotti.

But if Marco's stint at Rinascita was memorable at all, it was for his first experience of stage-racing. Nine days after the Sondrio–Livigno he was in Calabria at Italy's other extreme, for the Six Days of the Sun. Marco took two stage wins, and finished fourth overall. The winner, Daniel Efraín Castro, was an Argentine four years his senior. It whetted Marco's appetite for stage-racing. He made up his mind to win the amateur Giro d'Italia.

The predominant amateur stage races of the day were the Tour de l'Avenir, unofficially known as the amateur Tour de France, and the Peace Race, based on the axis Warsaw–Berlin–Prague, but they were of no interest to Marco. Italy had many prestigious amateur stage races, the Giro della Valle d'Aosta, the Giro delle Regioni among them; but the only one that mattered to Marco was the amateur Giro d'Italia. Each year, six to eight national teams were invited from countries as far apart as Colombia and the Soviet Union; Soviets had won nine of the previous ten amateur Giros d'Italia: the 1984 winner, Piotr Ugrumov, would later be one of Marco's greatest rivals. The 1998 winner, Dmitri Konychev, would later be one of his most accomplished team-mates. Strangely, the amateur Giro d'Italia allowed Marco to showcase his skills to the wider world, while remaining in the regional reality of his childhood, for the race had been created by Rinascita on the basis of its Communist roots.

In 1966, during the preamble to the Prague Spring, the Czechoslovak Cycling Federation had encouraged its affiliates to establish relations with counterparts in Western Europe. A Slovak club, ZVL of Zilina, wrote to Rinascita asking to enter a twinning relationship. There were exchanges between delegations, Rinascita riders took part in the Okolo Slovenska, the Slovakian 'national' Tour, and ZVL riders took part in Italian races wearing Rinascita colours. In 1968 the president of Rinascita had the idea of organising a Friendship Race crossing the Iron Curtain, starting at Zilina and stopping at Bratislava, Vienna, Graz, Maribor, Lubiana, Udine, Venice and Ravenna. After positive first contacts the project became mired in bureaucracy, and the idea was quietly abandoned as a beautiful but unrealisable dream.

Bartolotti told me: 'With the help of the Republican Party and the Socialists, we had organised a Giro delle Antiche Romagne in 1963. In 1969, when the idea of an amateur Giro d'Italia occurred to Adriano Rodoni' – the President of the Italian Cycling Federation (FCI) – 'our experience organising the Giro delle Antiche Romagne, and the ambition shown by our Friendship Race project, persuaded the FCI to offer the project to us.'

Between the first edition of Il Piccolissimo Giro d'Italia Dilettanti, in 1970, and Marco's participations in the early 1990s, the event had been hijacked by profit-making organisers in Rome, gone bankrupt, been suspended, been taken over by the *Gazzetta dello Sport*, failed again, before reverting, at last, to Rinascita. Marco's first amateur Giro, the 1990 edition, was the last organised by the *Gazzetta dello Sport*. But by then, he was no longer a Rinascita rider.

It had become clear to him that, to win the amateur Giro, he would need a stronger team, one with proper commercial sponsorship and more professional structures. Vittorio Savini put him in touch with one of Italy's leading amateur teams, Giacobazzi, sponsored by a wine-producer based at Nonantola, ten kilometres north of Modena, and directed by Giuseppe Roncucci, universally known as Pino. Now in his seventies, too old to worry too deeply, Roncucci is tall, slim, with great hands and a manner that is both warm and authoritative. The bookcases that line his study are packed with trim files containing the archives of three and a half decades at the forefront of Italian amateur cycling. He was once an amateur rider himself, but his career ended after four post-war seasons with a pharynx injury suffered in a fall. So he took up Graeco-Roman wrestling and was national champion four years later. But cycling remained his passion and in 1968 he took one of Italy's first training courses for *directeurs sportifs* at the Servadei Velodrome in Forlì. Roncucci impressed, and in 1969 he was invited to direct the youth team based at the velodrome, Servadei–Alessandri. In 1977 Giacobazzi joined Alessandri as a co-sponsor of the junior team. He told me, 'Giacobazzi had a major team, one of the strongest in Italy, and they hadn't been able to win anything. So I was given their junior team. I felt I could try a month with these boys they had. I asked them for carte blanche for a month, we had a training camp in Romagna, and by the end of the year we'd won twenty-four races. They gave me a contract for life! Giacobazzi was a gentleman, passionate about his sport, one of those sponsors who never wanted to break the mould. He said, "I'll give you two hundred or three hundred million lire (€100–150,000). Now put together a team." We were better organised than many professional teams. One year, we had a professional team on the track, directed by Luciano Pezzi. But Giacobazzi didn't like profession-alism: he said, "I like to bring through boys, who then become champions."'

Roncucci had first seen Marco at the 1984 Forlì–Val di Noce, the race Celestino Salami had told me about – meaning Marco had been known to the country's top amateur *directeur sportif* for three years. Roncucci had seen him again at the 1987 Forlì–Montecoronaro, where Marco had beaten Della Vedova, and told me, 'We went to see Della Vedova to sign him for Giacobazzi, but he pulled and pulled and pulled, and Pantani followed and followed and followed. And then, in the final three hundred metres, Pantani – toh! – and won. He had that sudden acceleration on the climbs that he could repeat. As an amateur he was already winning the way he would as a professional.'

At the end of 1989 Roncucci received a call from Savini. 'He said, "Pino, are you interested in taking Pantani?" Now, we were a team of strong riders, and we still had Della Vedova. But we wanted to win this blessed Giro d'Italia, the one title Giacobazzi had never won. So I went to the *piadina* kiosk to meet him. I asked him why he wanted to come to Giacobazzi, seeing that when he'd become an amateur he'd joined Rinascita. He said, "I want to come to Giacobazzi because you have a strong team, and I want to win the Giro d'Italia." It was as simple as that!'

If the organisational structures that allowed Marco to emerge came from Italian Communism, the finance came from what has been called 'molecular capitalism', that extensive network of small and medium-sized entrepreneurs, producing anything from components and partly finished goods to sophisticated products for niche world markets, each with the autonomy to spend the firm's money, and often with a passion for, and sometimes a past in, cycling. The collective work that is the organisation of a stage race – it makes little difference whether amateur or professional – is helped enormously by the pre-existing ties binding together another peculiarly Italian construct, the industrial district.

The industrial district has nothing to do with the industrial park or free-trade zone: the term refers to an area (often a small town, including the surrounding countryside) in which local economic pressures have produced an array of small firms specialising in one sector, often contributing collectively to the final product. The industrial districts in the towns of Prato and Carpi, for example, specialise in textiles, Poggibonsi and Arquate in furniture, Lumezzane in cutlery, Sassuolo in ceramics, Vigevano in shoes. A considerable minority produces complex machinery, or precision instruments: Belluno is a centre for eye-glasses and frames, Mirandola for artificial kidneys, Emilia-Romagna for agricultural equipment, Verona and Cremona for bicycle components. By 1991 there were at least 238 industrial districts, employing 1,700,000 workers. The industrial district has become the very paragon of Italy's entrepreneurial vitality, its deep-rooted artisanal skills and its flair for design and export. The ceramics firms of Emilia-Romagna alone include any number of cycling sponsors, including Jolly, Ariostea, Panaria, Refin and Ceramica d'Imola.

In early May 1990 these networks combined to create the four-day Giro dell'Emilia-Romagna for amateurs, organised by the Nonantola cycling club, politically and culturally Communist, like Rinascita. The organisers brought together no fewer than eight local authorities and five regional businesses to finance and coordinate the event, while the twenty-one participating teams of six brought a panoply of riders with a future in professional cycling, some local, like Stefano Cembali from Lugo, others from further afield, including Eros Poli and Andrea Ferrigato from Verona, and Stefano Zanini from Varese. Marco, aged twenty, reinforced his status as a stage-race specialist by securing second place in two stages, and finishing second overall, in the same time as the winner. Yet, in the official photographs, Marco, his hair visibly thinning, stands alone, stage right. When the gregarious and astonishingly tall Poli lifted his sprinter's prize in one hand and the tiny winner, Cristiano Andreani, in the other, there was general laughter. Marco laughed too, but there was no eye contact. One second place could be too much for him to bear – and he'd suffered three.

Then, on 27 May, the 1990 Giro d'Italia for amateur riders began with an individual time trial at Pietrasanta, just north of Viareggio on the Tuscan coast. Since 1982 only Russians had won the amateur Giro. Roncucci told me, 'In those days the stages of the amateur Giro set off two hours before those of the professional Giro, on the same roads, but slightly closer to the stage finish, and then we did the same route as the professionals. It was the year Bugno won among the professionals, and we were often in the same hotel as Bugno. We had Dr Sturla as our team doctor, who was Bugno's doctor. The riders were incorporated into regional teams and directed by the *directeur sportif* of the riders who were in a majority. Giacobazzi had five riders in the team, which made me the DS. The prologue took place in a downpour, and Marco hit a patch of oil and fell badly. He dislocated his shoulder and he was badly cut. I called his father and told him to come and collect him, but Marco raised hell and convinced us to let him carry on. He'd lost five minutes – four minutes and something . . . The Giro doctor, Semensini, said: "Let's try to put him on his bike, then I'll dress the wounds; we'll put something on the handlebars so he'll be able to ride in that position, although it'll only be in that position . . ."'

Marco rode the following seven stages as a seated statue. Incredibly, on stage four, through the mountains of the Trentino to Baselga di Piné, he was fourth. On stage seven, through the Dolomites to the Passo Pordoi, fifty kilometres west of Cortina d'Ampezzo, he managed third, and climbed from ninth to fifth in the general classification – despite another fall when a rock detached itself from the mountainside and rolled into his rear wheel when he was descending.

That evening Roncucci asked a rival team to allow its masseur to treat Marco's thigh muscle, which appeared to be badly torn. The masseur, Roberto Pregnolato, set the injury, and at Aprica the following day Marco took second place on the stage. These performances helped him finish the Giro in third place overall, one minute, one second behind the winner, Wladimir Belli. Roncucci told me, 'Without the fall he'd have won it comfortably.' The same would be said of Marco many times in future.

Pregnolato had met Marco before. Earlier that year, Davide Boifava, the *directeur sportif* of the professional team Carrera, had introduced them. At the time, Marco wore his hair long, and Pregnolato, seeing him first from behind, commented: 'How can a cyclist have so much hair?' At the 1990 amateur Giro, Marco dubbed Pregnolato 'Robespierre' for his theatrical good looks. Pregnolato shortened Pantani into 'Panta'. The reassuring pleasure of Robespierre's hands and the sweet aromas of his liniment and oils brought them together. It was the greatest friendship of both their lives, and would last, despite one or two interruptions, until Marco's death.

Difficult not to like, with the calm presence you would want after a 280 kilometre training ride through frozen rain, Pregnolato, today the proprietor of a beauty centre in central Modena, is professionally surrounded by pretty girls and the occasional transvestite. Sparkling and full of innuendo, he has gifted hands. By the time he met Marco he had already worked at the highest level in many sports, including a spell with the football team Fiorentina and the great Brazilian Zico. But his name will always be indelibly linked with that of Marco Pantani, whose face looks down on him from the photographs, the newspaper and magazine articles that decorate the walls of his massage room, as though, in death, Marco has become his guardian angel. In life, their roles were reversed. With Pregnolato, Marco was relaxed, generous, fun – everything he couldn't be with others. But Marco was already showing a different part of himself to everyone who knew him; little wonder his various associates would later argue over which of Marco's identities was the real one.

In a 1995 interview Pregnolato described the physique his hands knew so well. 'You see how skinny he is? How can someone like that have a great muscle mass? Marco is wiry; he's different, all muscle. At times it's laughable to call my manipulations of his legs "massage". Bear in mind I've massaged a lot of famous sportsmen, but I've never come across a musculature as powerful as his.'

Marco came out of the amateur Giro with excellent form, and won a two-man sprint in Le Marche on 10 July and a mountain time trial at Parma towards the end of the month. At the end of August he became amateur champion of Emilia-Romagna. That winter, no doubt funded by their race winnings, Marco and his childhood friend and team-mate Andrea Agostini went to Thailand. Marco sent Roncucci a postcard that read: 'I came to train, but it's easier to go to the beach.' Pino showed me the postcard, in one of his meticulous files, alongside an envelope bearing Marco's signature. 'I said, "What are you doing?" "Training to write autographs."' Marco's discomfort in television interviews was clearly not an outright aversion to celebrity. And there is something peculiar about the autograph Marco sought to perfect. The 'Marco' was an italic, but the 'Pantani' leaned backwards, a reverse italic; since Marco always signed his name 'Pantani Marco', his two names seemed to be trying to escape each other. Marco was the only member of his family with neither a nickname nor even an affix of endearment like Tonina. His autograph suggests that Marco, so uncomfortable in his skin, was uneasy with his own name.

Early in 1991 Marco was selected for the Italian national 'B' team for the Settimana Bergamasca, a ten-day stage race pitting amateurs against professionals, with teams representing sixteen countries. The profile didn't suit Marco: there weren't enough long, steep climbs; and, despite the prestige of his first national call-up, he no doubt had his sights fixed on the amateur Giro. Nonetheless, he finished tenth overall, and fourth in the 'young riders' classification. The race was won by a nineteen-year-old American named Lance Armstrong.

More high placings followed: second place in the Trofeo Matteotti at Marcialla, in the hills of Chianti; second overall in the Giro del

Friuli-Venezia Giulia, won by Gilberto Simoni; third in the Trofeo Minardi at Lido di Classe, north of Cesenatico, behind Davide Rebellin and Wladimir Belli. Simoni, Rebellin and Belli would all become highly accomplished professional riders. Each missed opportunity for victory was undoubtedly endured for a greater cause: the amateur Giro. It started on 19 June 1991 with a semi-stage – one of two stages in the same day – that decided the race prematurely. Roncucci recalls it like this: 'I said, "Marco, watch out, because these short semi-stages are dangerous. A little wind, a breakaway gets away and doesn't get caught ..."' And that's how it happened: the Tuscan Francesco Casagrande finished the first part of day one with a two-minute, thirty-four-second lead over Marco, who had preferred to mark the favourites Belli, Piccoli, Rebellin and Bartoli. Casagrande spent the rest of the week on Marco's wheel. It won him the race. Marco won stage nine, and took second place the following day, but he couldn't shake off Casagrande. 'He lost the race through naïvety,' Roncucci concludes.

In late August 1991 a new phase of the season began with a series of important races. Roncucci arranged a training camp. Ten days before it started, Marco asked him for time off to go to the beach with his friends. 'I told him, "Marco, you go to the beach, but when you come home, we'll go to a training camp in the mountains to prepare for the final races of the season." At the training camp he destroyed anyone who tried to stay on his wheel. Because when he was training, *u gne n'è par nisèun.* He was a boy who loved the bicycle, but he wasn't a monk. His ten days were his ten days, and you had to leave him alone. I remember, we spent seven days in the mountains, and when we came down, he won a race here at Meldola' – fifteen kilometres south of Forlì – 'with a hard climb repeated five times. He broke the frame, changed bikes, and still won by minutes.'

There were also two mountain time trials: the first at Fonte San Moderanno, on the border where Tuscany meets Emilia; the second, the Gàstone Nencini Memorial, northwards from Barberino di Mugello, in the Tuscan hills, to the Passo della Futa. Earlier in the year Marco had finished second on the same road, the eleventh century Strata Florencie between the Tuscan capital and Bologna, but in the opposite direction, speeding south from Bologna to the Passo della Raticosa. The Raticosa and the Futa were classic climbs, whose sporting heritage encompassed motorsport as well as cycling: the old Mille Miglia had threaded Nuvolari, Moss et al. through these hills.

On 1 September 1991, Marco, a third-year amateur, burst up the Futa at speeds even Gianni Bugno, the recently crowned world professional road-racing champion, had difficulty matching. Before twenty thousand fans who lined the climb's fourteen writhing kilometres, Marco won the amateur race in a time of twenty-nine minutes thirty-seven seconds, with an average speed of 28.359 k.p.h. Later, Bugno won the professional race convincingly. The only tension was in whether he would beat the time set in the amateur race: enveloped in the moving stream of air created by a convoy of camera-bikes and motorbike-bound photographers, Bugno beat Marco's time by 10.3 seconds. The *Gazzetta di Modena* eulogised, 'A wonderful feat for Pantani at the start of what could be the decisive week for his move into professional cycling.' On 21 September Marco won the Giro dell'Emilia, with an uphill finish. Roncucci then told him to rest: 'I said, "You've raced enough this year. In 1992 you're turning professional, and we've got to win this blessed Giro. Now go and rest."'

On 20 November Luciano Draghi of Telerimini awarded Marco the 'Ultimo Kilometro' prize. At the ceremony, Marco wore his thinning hair brushed back into a mad professor's mullet. He looked strikingly like Vittorio Savini.

From his papers Roncucci produces a cutting, the newspaper title and date cropped out, but summarising Giacobazzi's 1991 season. It picks out Marco, and records: 'His results have earned a professional contract with the Carrera team after the Barcelona Olympics.' The timing of Marco's agreement with Carrera is unclear. In an interview immediately after the amateur Giro d'Italia, Marco had said: 'If I'm left out of the Olympic team, I think I'll make the big jump into the professionals. If I'm included in the Olympic team, we'll talk about it at the end of 1993. As far as Carrera is concerned, nothing has yet been decided. There have been contacts with Carrera and others. I'll weigh up the offers in the coming days, and then decide. All offers being equal, I'll choose Carrera because I already know them: I spent a couple of weeks of the winter holidays with the riders.'

Roncucci knows nothing of any pre-contract, but there is evidence, as we shall see later on, that Marco's agreement with Carrera had already started in 1991.

*

On 22 March 1992 Marco rode the Memorial Giuseppe Gemelli, starting and finishing in the small town of Bagnacavallo, twenty kilometres west of Ravenna. The sheer profusion of prizes and competitions for amateur riders in Romagna emerges from the race description: the sixth Memorial Giuseppe Gemelli was also the fifth Memorial Antonio Arniani; it counted towards the third Banca Popolare Pesarese–Ravennate Trophy, the fourth Due Galli Trophy and the fifth Tuttauto Trophy. The cream of Italian amateur cycling took part: the national champion Roberto Giucolsi; Francesco Casagrande and Wladimir Belli, victors in the two most recent amateur Giros d'Italia. Luca Colombo, a member of Italy's world-champion 100 kilometre team time trial quartet; Fabio Casartelli – the previous year's champion – and other leading amateurs, including Daniele Nardello and Marco. Before the race, a group of Giacobazzi riders chatted on the starting line. Marco was not among them. Even as a professional, Marco became remote before races; he was never chatty on the starting line. Roncucci told me: 'No, he wasn't a chatterbox. At races he concentrated. He was there to race. He wanted to know what he needed to know, with no distractions. He always said to me, "Pino, if I turn professional, I'll do two years. If I get results, OK. If not, I'll stop." He always had this sense of not wanting to waste time.'

The severe route suited him. The peloton, tightly bunched, circled Bagnacavallo, then sped south and over a semblance of a hill in the Faenza railway bridge, thinning and stretching on the climb, broadening and contracting on the other side. There were no attacks: awaiting them was the short, steep, rhythm-destroying Montecarla after fifty-three kilometres, starting at the village of Marzeno, on the river of the same name; then, after the village of Brisighella, the race's major problem, Monte Cottignola; and then, after second ascents of the Montecarla and Monte Cottignola, and a final climb of Montecarla, thirty-five flat kilometres northwards to the Bagnacavallo finish line.

The peloton was intact at Marzeno, fifty-three kilometres into the race. Low on the Montecarla, without quickening, Marco and Vincenzo Galati tested the elasticity of the group. It narrowed and elongated, and the first breaches, twenty, thirty metres long, opened in the line. On the descent, the peloton tightened back into shape, its suppleness damaged, but unbroken.

Then, on Monte Cottignola, another elongation – and the first fissure.

Eleven riders became detached at the front and gelled into a stable state. Four were team-mates riding for Domus 87: Casartelli, Galati, Pellegrini and Lusignoli. Two represented De Lorenzi: Davide Taroni and Massimo Bazocchi. Then there were Michele Poser of Trevigiana, Leonardo Piepoli of Casano and Francesco Casagrande – the commentary calls him Stefano Casagrande – of Vellutex. Marco was there too, with his Giacobazzi team-mate Riccardo Ragni. Unable to maintain the pace of the climbers, Casartelli lost contact, then rode back up to the group at his own pace. Higher up the hill, the group subdivided; five of the eleven formed a new pact: Marco was there, with Galati, Casagrande, Poser and Piepoli. Piepoli fell away first, followed by Poser. Marco set the pace. His pedal stroke had a weightlessness it had lacked in earlier years.

On the descent eight riders, including three of Casagrande's Vellutex team-mates, bridged the gap to the trio. But the group lasted only as far as the second climb of the Montecarla: perhaps a hundred spectators watched as Marco crossed the col alone, with Galati, Pellegrini and Casagrande strung out in his wake.

By the second climb of Monte Cottignola, there were three leaders. Marco rode at his speed; Galati and Casagrande followed. All gripped the top of the handlebars, but elsewhere, their styles diverged: Marco led, turning the pedals seventy-five times each minute, his torso prone to a faint lateral sway, his head motionless. He gave the impression that he was pushing down as little weight as Galati, whose faster cadence sent his shoulders into an eccentric alternation. Behind them, Casagrande churned the cranks laboriously, sixty-five circles a minute. His body movement was even more pronounced: he rocked sideways and up and down, nodding his head rhythmically.

In sight of the brow, Casagrande and Galati eased past Marco. He feigned disinterest in the mountain prize. But, as the reshuffle settled temporarily, Marco reached down to the gear levers, shifted the chain onto a smaller sprocket, and stood on the pedals to sprint past the '100m to go' sign. By the time Galati was level with Casagrande, Marco had passed them both, his leg speed reaching a hundred and twenty turns per minute. Before they reached the white line marking the mountains prize, Marco was taking an unhurried look over his right shoulder and into his opponents' eyes. After the tortuous drop from the col, the three had just two minutes on the chasing group. They worked together on the plain before the final climb of Montecarla.

Marco led Casagrande and Galati around the tight corner and into the climb.

Speed is important here: they cannot hope to hold a slender lead on the long pursuit to Bagnacavallo, especially into a headwind. Low on the climb, Marco allows Galati and Casagrande to lead, and changes gear. His acceleration is impulsive and unanswerable. We cannot see Galati's face, but the sense of asphyxiation must be unendurable. He lets Marco go, knowing that to do so will mean certain capture by the chase. Casagrande watches Marco dart away, then manages the gap. He closes in; Marco flits away again. Casagrande watches, inert. The col is approaching. Marco will have the mountain prize, but Casagrande will catch him on the descent.

On the flat road leading back to Bagnacavallo, Galati is caught. The chasers take turns riding into the wind. Marco and Casagrande, meanwhile, enter the final phase of the race. Their lead is three minutes fifteen seconds. There is time for an extended endgame. Casagrande is the more powerful sprinter: Marco's hope can only be that his repeated accelerations have worn Casagrande down. But, with less than five hundred metres to go, he is already positioned badly, leading his rival, unable to see him, gifting him the slight vacuum in his slipstream. At speed, Casagrande's muscle mass gives him the advantage, so Marco slows, perhaps hoping to catapult his slighter frame out of a nearly standing start faster than his larger rival. At little more than walking pace, the two twenty-two-year-olds pause: Marco's position is hopeless. He eyes the camera and smiles ambiguously. He looks over his right shoulder (the first look is always over his right shoulder), then stands in the pedals, half-turns the pedals and, coasting, looks over his left shoulder. Four more half-turns, and another coasting glance. Three half-turns, and a half-look. Three more half-turns, and another half-look. One half-turn, and a glance. One more, and a lingering glance. Still standing, Marco begins to pedal continuously. Casagrande does nothing. There are less than two hundred and fifty metres to the finish line. After eleven seconds, Marco sits — and Casagrande drives down into the pedals, flinging himself across the road to keep his slipstream from Marco's reach. By the time Marco reacts, Casagrande leads by three lengths. Marco closes in, but his trajectory meets that of Casagrande beyond the finish line. He loses by a length, and rides past as Casagrande celebrates. There is no eye contact or handshake. On the podium,

Casagrande smiles. Marco stands to his right, chewing, swaggering – the arrogance of the acutely shy. His eyes dart about the crowd, more in contempt than curiosity, then look down. There is none of the small child in his face.

Post-race, Casagrande is asked what happened to Galati: 'Pantani's repeated accelerations must have finished him off.' Marco never looks at his interviewer, and listens to his questions, at times, with a smirk. His answers are self-important: 'The onus was on me to lead. I almost always pulled on the climbs: they didn't relay me . . . Casagrande came after me . . . He immediately gave me two lengths, and I couldn't – despite gaining on him – I couldn't catch him.'

A week later, on Sunday 29 March 1992, Marco rode the GP Città di Nonantola. The camera pans across the riders on the start line. Marco is not among the Giacobazzi riders. The race profile is absolutely flat. The race commentary's sole mention of Marco is to report a fall one and a half kilometres from the finish. In an interview after the race, Marco plays down the incident: 'It doesn't seem to be serious. I have a few scrapes, but nothing important. The good thing is that we've managed to win. I have some regrets because of the pain of the fall, but I think it's repaid by the victory for the team. It was about time.' Prosaic words, but the interview is remarkable for Marco's eyes, which roll in their sockets without coming to rest on anything. The demands of the post-race interview seem to leave him flummoxed.

The GP Città di Nonantola is commemorated in a book with the dialect title La 'Cursa ed Nunántla' e altri sport, compiled by Bruno Ronchetti, for many years the official speaker of the professional Giro d'Italia, and his colleague Claudio Vaccari. Their precious volume gives a brief description of every GP Città di Nonantola from the first edition on 12 March 1975 to the 1999 race. It also gives, where possible, details of the riders who stood on the podium during those years – their town of origin and future profession – and lists the guests of honour at each race. This database offers a rare sociological panorama of amateur cycling in Italy, and of the milieu in which Marco spent the years 1989 to 1992.

In the twenty-five GP Città di Nonantola covered by the volume, sixty-eight different riders stood on the podium. Twenty-six became professional cyclists; one died in a road accident while training. Both statistics seem high. Of the forty-two who did not become professional cyclists, Ronchetti and Vaccari give the post-cycling professions of twenty-six. The professions of only two, an IT expert and an engineer, suggest a possible university education.

The vast majority of the sixty-one riders for whom a province of origin is given are natives of Emilia-Romagna (twenty-three). Then follow Lombards (eleven), Venetians (ten), Tuscans (five), and then, in almost negligible numbers, Piedmontese (three), Sicilians (two), Friulians (two), and one from each of Liguria and Le Marche. The numbers suggest the degree to which, for instance, amateur cycling in Lombardy and the Veneto merged with amateur cycling in Emilia-Romagna, while amateur riding in other regions had a quite separate existence. As many Poles (two) rode the GP Nonantola as Ligurians and Marchigiani. Above all, perhaps, the figures suggest how important home victories were to riders and their sponsors. The special guests – mostly former or active professional riders, often former competitors in the GP Nonantola, occasionally cycling officials, champions in other sports and the odd regional politician – served, symbolically, to cast an ancestral shadow over the amateur competitors, cementing them firmly in a tradition.

Between Nonantola and the amateur Giro, Marco achieved another series of high placings: third in the Coppa Apollo 17 at Colbuccaro di Corridonia (near Macerata); second in the Nereto Grand Prix near Teramo; second – to Gilberto Simoni – in the hardest mountain stage of the Tour of Friuli–Venezia Giulia, and fifth overall; second to Fabio Casartelli in the Trofeo Minardi, at Sant'Ermete, between San Marino and Rimini. His one victory was a mountain time trial in Tuscany, from the port of Livorno inland to Valle Benedetta. Once again he no doubt shouldered the burden of losing only in view of the greater goal of victory in the amateur Giro d'Italia.

Before it started, Marco signed the contract with Carrera, one of the leading professional teams, to start riding professionally at the start of August 1992. He presented himself in Davide Boifava's office with his father and DS Pino Roncucci. Roncucci told me: 'Marco said, "The contract is fine, but what about if I win the Giro d'Italia? What about if I win the Tour?" Boifava, I remember, took another blank sheet of paper, and wrote, "If you win the Giro, if you win the Tour, if you win a stage, if you win this, or that ..." At that point, we relaxed, and

Boifava said, "Now, you must be happy. You've got a good deal." And Marco said, in reply, "You're the ones who've got the good deal." And it was a great deal.' The contract, he said – the comment is recorded in a local newspaper – left him free to prepare for his goals in tranquillity.

The 1992 amateur Giro d'Italia was held over eleven stages between 16 and 28 May. Marco hid in the peloton for the first four days. Then, on stage five, a thirty-seven-kilometre time trial, he conceded four minutes to the winner, Alexander Gontchenkov, and two and a half minutes to his main rival, Wladimir Belli. But Marco had learned patience. On stage seven, he showed himself, finishing sixth in a small group of the best climbers. Two days later, he sprang the trap. The stage from Verona to Cavalese, way up in the Tyrol, was a 144 kilometre climb into the mountains. For the first fifty-eight kilometres, no one dared attack. Then two lesser riders attempted to build a lead, to be chased down by the Trentino team, helped by the Ukrainians. Then, after eighty kilometres, Marco's team-mates moved to the front of the peloton and raised the tempo to 44 k.p.h. It was the preparation for Marco's first attack of the race. Only Nicola Miceli could stay with him, before he, too, dropped away. Marco finished the stage alone. On the podium, Francesco Moser congratulated him. But it was only a prelude.

Marco lay seventh overall at the start of stage ten, 111 kilometres from Cavalese to the Plan di Pezzé, above the village of Alleghe in the Dolomites. There is a photograph of Marco with Pino Roncucci, taken that morning at Cavalese. 'I'm saying, "What do we want? Do we want to win this blessed Giro?" And he's saying, "But I'm seventh." I said, "Don't you see that Belli is always using a handkerchief? He's ill. If you want to win this Giro, attack immediately – the stage is short."'

Towards the top of the first climb, the Passo Sella, Marco attacked. Two Colombians, Hugo Bolívar and Omar Trompa, went with him. Trompa, perhaps believing the attack was in vain, lost ground, leaving Marco and his breakaway companion with a twenty-two-second lead at the brow of the Sella. Belli, forced into crisis by Marco's aggression, was already two minutes forty-seven behind. At Gardena, Pantani crossed ahead of Bolívar: Belli reached the col five minutes later. On the Campolungo, Bolívar led Marco, helping him extend his lead.

Roncucci, meanwhile, was taking short cuts through the mountains: 'I remember his father and I went to the foot of the final climb, Plan di

Pezzé. By radio they said that he was already second in GC with a deficit of twelve or thirteen seconds. Belli had collapsed: we'd seen it right. He'd lost ten minutes. Marco arrived there at Plan di Pezzé, and I shouted, "If you want to win the Giro, you have to drop him." He shouted back, "I've promised him the stage." And I shouted, "We'll give him a stage next year!" At that point he attacked, and took the jersey, and it was historic.'

One race reporter – again, Roncucci's cuttings are cropped so tight, the publication isn't clear – wrote: 'Marco Pantani realised a masterpiece yesterday, a sporting exploit on the roads of the Sella, Gardena and Campolungo Passes that evoked those of Coppi or Gaul.'

It was a lofty comparison: for Italians, Fausto Coppi has the stature of Ali or Pelé, while Charly Gaul was considered the greatest climber in cycling history. And both men had tragic destinies, Coppi dying young, Gaul falling into alcoholism and near madness.

Marco returned home a champion. He had promised his grandfather this victory. The race finished on 27 June. Three days later Sotero Pantani died. When winning had been new to him, Marco had dedicated a race to Guerrino Ciani, recently deceased. Now, his greatest victory coincided with the death of his beloved grandfather. Sotero's funeral was a peculiarly local, and specifically Communist occasion. The rite is described in a history of the town by a former mayor, Giorgio Calisesi:

> The funeral procession of an old Republican or Communist, preceded by a band playing hymns from the Unification or songs dear to the militants of the International, makes a complete circuit of the monument to Garibaldi – the final affirmation of faith in an ideal that goes beyond death. [*Il canale, il mare, un paese. Per i 700 anni di Cesenatico* (Il Ponte Vecchio, Cesena, 2002), p. 37]

Calisesi's own subsequent funeral followed this ritual. So too did that of Sotero Pantani, whose firstborn, Dino, carried the red flag at the head of the procession. By then, of course, the Berlin Wall was long gone and the Soviet Union was disintegrating. Its denial of the Stalinist terror had always given Italian Communism a self-delusional quality. Now it had lost its bedrock, as well as its credibility. The fall of Communism left Marco, no less than the Eastern bloc athletes of his age, culturally orphaned.

*

I asked the old Vice-President of the Giacobazzi team, Gino Gaioli, about the relationship between Roncucci and Marco. He told me, 'Marco was already a professional in his head. He knew what to eat, how to train. But he was almost unmanageable. If you tried to tell him what to do, he wouldn't listen. If you wanted him to ride at Bologna, say, it was no use saying, "You're riding in Bologna at the weekend." He wouldn't go. Roncucci understood him. He'd say, "Marco, there's a race at Modena, and another at Bologna. What do you think?"' Gaioli recalls a comment by Marco that reveals an unexpected ambivalence in Marco's relationship with cycling: 'He told me, "I hate the bicycle, but I'm certain it'll allow me to live. If it goes well, at thirty, I'll retire."'

Roncucci himself remembers Marco as mysteriously gifted and cursed: 'Marco had a great weight–power advantage. When he was in form, he weighed fifty-five, maximum fifty-six kilos, and he was very strong. He had this ability to wear you down on the climbs: he accelerated suddenly, and again, and again. He destroyed anyone who tried to stay with him.' At a time when heart-rate monitors were becoming an essential piece of training equipment, Marco refused technology. 'We used them for the first two months in 1990, 1991 and 1992. But he said, "Pino, I have ears to hear – the sensations, I *hear* them. I don't need to be told . . ." He had something, you understand? Plus, for me, he had a capacity for suffering, for bearing fatigue, others didn't have. But he lost years to injuries. He was extremely unfortunate. What destiny gave with one hand, it always took away with the other. Without bad luck, he'd have won all three of the amateur Giros he rode. He always had an immense strength that allowed him to get back up again.' Then, wringing his hands, Roncucci skips seven years and adds, 'That strength abandoned him after Madonna di Campiglio . . .'

4
Rite of Passage
(JULY 1992–JUNE 1993)

On 25 July 1992 Marco fell, and spent the week unable to train. It sabotaged his hopes of winning his final amateur race. Interviewed for *Ultimo Kilometro*, Marco explained, 'I'll ride the Florence–San Patrignano [on 2 August], then I'll close as an amateur ... I'd like, perhaps, in my last race to ride a good race. We'll see if the bruises mend and let me close in style.'

The Florence–San Patrignano was actually the third 'Race Towards Life' from the village of Sieci, east of Florence, to Coriano, nine kilometres inland from Rimini. It was restricted to first- and second-category amateurs, although the winner would earn 1.5 million lire (€750). A hundred and forty-two riders representing thirty-two teams, the best in Italian amateur cycling, assembled beside the municipal stadium in Florence for the nineteen-kilometre ride out to Sieci and the starting line. Some chatted serenely; others were tense. Marco's Giacobazzi team-mates were sharing a joke. Marco, of course, lost in concentration, wasn't among them. He was surrounded by future professionals. At least four – Maurizio Nuzzi, Massimo Donati, Andrea Noé and Vincenzo Galati – would compete the following season as professionals, although Galati, a year older than Marco, was the youngest of them, and Nuzzi was already twenty-seven. Others – Alessio Galletti, Luca Scinto, Rosario Fina, Marco Milesi, Gianmatteo Fagnini, Nicola Loda – would be professional by 1995. Other, younger riders would move up in the years to come: Davide Dall'Olio, Leonardo Piepoli, Gabriele Missaglia, Massimo Codol, Elio Aggiano.

But, if Marco felt he was different, he was right. His record in the amateur Giro – third, second and first in consecutive years – had no equal. He alone could dictate terms to a team like Carrera. His mood was also, perhaps, dictated by the conditions: there were 192 kilometres and four categorised climbs ahead, and Tuscany's August heat was beginning to rise. In any case, at these one-day races everyone knew he was out of his element. To win, Marco needed mountains, not these brief ramps.

The peloton was a blot of saturated colour that sped through the Arno valley villages of Pontassieve, Leccio, I Ciliegi. After twenty-nine kilometres, at the foot of the first categorised climb, came the first attack: Luciano Pagli, riding for Monsumanese, on the ascent of the valley wall to the village of Castelfranco di Sopra. He took the mountain prize unchallenged; behind, the peloton, no longer swept along in a single air stream, but fighting gravity, exploded into particles. Then the gradient weakened, the physics of movement found a new balance, and the leading seventeen cohered into a single, separate entity. The incentive of intermediate sprints ten kilometres away at Loro Ciuffenna, and ten kilometres further on at San Giustino Valdarno, powered the leaders over the rolling terrain. Six were future professionals riding for the powerful Domus 87 team: Fagnini, Codol, Loda, Milesi, Galati and Fina. Aggiano and Scinto were there too, with Scinto's team-mate Stefano Santarini, the winner of the first Florence–San Patrignano two years before. Only one of Marco's Giacobazzi team-mates, Davide Dall'Olio, had made the break.

Domus 87 had the manpower to deposit their leader, Nicola Loda, at the foot of the final climb in the best possible position. They had won the first three places during the previous year's race. Such dominance this time would have humiliated Giacobazzi on the day of Marco's final appearance, so Roncucci sent his boys to lead the chase. By Castiglion Fibocchi, after a draining pursuit, Giacobazzi had caught the breakaway, and piloted Marco up to the front of the peloton by the foot of the Válico di Scheggia, the next major climb. Few other teams could have achieved it.

As the two groups merged, something happened of no significance to the race but laden with meaning for the riders: they sped past the last Italian winner of the professional Giro d'Italia, Franco Chioccioli, coming the other way. Then thirty-two, Chioccioli was a native of Castelfranco di Sopra, and these were his training roads. The winner of the 1991 Giro bore a striking resemblance to Fausto Coppi, and was nicknamed Coppino. His was the world Marco would be entering in less than a week. Seconds after the encounter the race crossed another threshold, crossing the N71 north of Arezzo and joining the route over which Miguel Induráin had won stage three of that year's Giro d'Italia, an individual time trial from Arezzo to San Sepolcro held on 27 May.

Marco repaid his team-mates' efforts by joining the attack on the ten-kilometre Válico di Scheggia. As the pitch steepened towards the brow, Marco, Piepoli and Nuzzi found themselves alone. Piepoli took the mountain prize; Marco was second. The acceleration had breached the thread of the peloton and stretched riders out over a kilometre, but these were still early skirmishes. Cycling has something of the frustration fantasy of being chased and being unable to get away. The unwisdom of early, futile energy expenditure had already ruled Pagli, the winner of the first mountain prize, out of ultimate victory.

Fumbling down from the Válico, the peloton reformed. The next climb was a much shorter ramp up to the village of Anghiari. The riders ascended in single file, Marco in seventh position, until the acceleration for the mountain prize. Renato Baldassari crossed first, with Fina second and Marco in third place. It was the halfway point in the race. The climb had split the riders again, but again, tilting vertiginously down the valley wall, they reassembled. Yet the Válico and the climb before Anghiari had weeded out the weak, and of the 142 starters only sixty were still in the hunt.

Before the next climb, the Passo di Viamaggio, Nuzzi launched a solo attack. Thirty seconds back, the chase was led by Marco's team-mates Dall'Olio and Fabio Laghi. The Viamaggio is not steep, but long at eighteen kilometres, and the group thinned as it closed in on Nuzzi. Then the ten leaders cohered into a single group: Fina, of Domus 87, led his team-mate Milesi, followed by Marco and another Domus 87 rider, Vincenzo Galati, glued to Marco's wheel. Then came Nuzzi, Riccardo Faverio, Piepoli, Donati, Nicola Palletti, and finally, slipstreaming and taking on water at every opportunity, the Domus 87 leader, Nicola Loda. The pace was sustained but not frenetic – cycling is a war of attrition; the artillery bursts are sporadic. Kilometre after kilometre the altitude gathered. On the Passo di Viamaggio, at an altitude of 983 metres, with 112 kilometres completed, Palletti preceded Nuzzi, with Marco third. A chasing group crossed the line forty seconds after the ten leaders, followed by ten more, fifteen seconds behind. They were leaving Tuscany now. They would cut across a corner of Le Marche before speeding towards the Romagna hills where Marco trained. To his left was Sársina, the village of his great-grandfather, and the push up to Pieve di Rivóschio, where Sotero had taken his children. Ahead of them, Santarcángelo and Cesenatico: thoughts a racing cyclist, absorbed in competition, can never think.

There were still thirty riders in contention when, somewhere between Badía Tedalda and Pontemessa, Marco missed the break. Six riders, including Donati, Nuzzi and Loda had escaped. Marco's team-mate Dall'Olio had joined them instants before the air had stilled behind them. Marco was one of five riders thirty seconds further back. This chasing group grew slowly, reaching fourteen, before another cell division: at Secchiano, seven of the chasing group broke away. They reached the leaders at Pietracuta; Marco was not among them. As they swung right into the Republic of San Marino and the Acquaviva climb, he had missed another break. Had the thought of his professional debut days later dulled his competitive edge at the decisive moment?

Again, Nuzzi attacked. Only Donati could follow. The acceleration had stretched the group to its elastic limit. For Loda, in third place but riding alone now, there was no way back into contention. On the final climb Donati rode away and won by a minute. Marco ended his amateur career with tenth place. His Carrera contract started the following day.

His final journey as an amateur had taken him past the last Italian winner of a three-week stage race, onto the roads where Miguel Induráin was king, through the hills where Marco's itinerant forebears had trudged from farm to farm, to the heart of the San Patrignano Community, an institution founded in 1978 for the rehabilitation of drug addicts. By the time Marco climbed this last one-kilometre climb towards the finish line, San Patrignano was offering accommodation and education to well over a thousand, mostly young, former drug-users. The race owed its existence to the San Patrignano philosophy. This arduous athletic odyssey across the land, connecting people and places, culminating in infectious scenes of celebration, was not a means to wealth or fame, but a therapeutic instrument for lives devastated by substance abuse. The pages dedicated to 'Sport and Society' in the community prospectus explain:

> Sport above all means respect for yourself and others. It implies the capacity to recognise your own limits and to learn to go beyond

them through work and commitment. It is an encounter with others, a way of relating to them that goes beyond differences or discrimination. It is friendship and solidarity. Sport is the proposal and the practice of principles and values that have an extremely important preventive role regarding the problems of youth and, at the same time, it is an instrument for the recovery of all young people who need activity and paths to re-socialisation and social re-insertion.

Three days later Marco started his first race as a professional athlete, a world with a very different idea of sport. Many years later his parents would call San Patrignano, seeking help for their son. By then it would be too late.

In February 1992, Italy had celebrated the Olympic successes of its downhill skiers. In the space of a few hours at the Albertville Winter Olympics, Alberto Tomba had won the men's giant slalom and Deborah Compagnoni the women's Super-G. Tomba in particular – a dazzling, undisciplined playboy nicknamed La Bomba – became symbolic of Italian sport. Football was certainly Italy's most popular sport, but it was regionalistic and enormously divisive at club level. Skiing, like cycling and motorsport – more motorcycling than Formula 1, in which Italy consistently failed to produce a homegrown champion – galvanised national sentiment in a way only rare moments of international football success could match.

In August that year a series of second-stream races in the seasonal lull allowed Marco a taste of professional road-racing. He responded encouragingly: thirtieth in his first professional race, the Gran Premio Camaiore, a hilly circuit on the Tuscan coast; sixteenth a fortnight later in the Coppa Agostini, at Lissone, within earshot of the Monza autodrome, north of Milan; twentieth the following week in the Giro del Veneto; and third, back in Tuscany, in the Gastone Nencini Memorial time trial to the Passo della Futa. Yet his performances were hampered by painfully misdiagnosed skeletal problems. Due to an asymmetry in Marco's gait, a compensatory, eleven-millimetre spacer had been inserted between one foot and the pedal on the assumption – wrong, as it turned out – that one leg was longer than the other. It was also assumed there was no cure and, as a result, Marco's future at Carrera was uncertain, almost before it had begun. The solution was found when Marco began working with Dr Marcello Lodi. The Carrera riders were treated at the Centre for Biomedical Studies Applied to Sport at the University of Ferrara, run by a medical researcher named Francesco Conconi, famous for having developed a remarkably simple method for measuring an athlete's maximum anaerobic and aerobic threshold, described in the *Journal of Applied Physiology* in a 1982 article entitled 'Determination of the anaerobic threshold by a non-invasive field test in runners', and known simply as the Conconi test. His Centre had become a magnet for top professional cyclists.

Lodi joined the Centre in 1992. A fascinating eclectic, he had a store of biomechanical and homeopathic learning – including dietary means of raising the red-blood-cell count, based, in part, on horsemeat *bresaola*. He diagnosed a misalignment in Marco's cervical vertebrae, probably a whiplash injury sustained in one or other of the serious car accidents (there had been at least three) that Marco had been involved in – at the wheel, not as a passenger – since the age of eighteen. In December 1992 Lodi sent Marco to Este, north of Ferrara, where a physiotherapist, Giorgio Borghesan, confirmed the diagnosis and set to work. Borghesan is a warm, lumbering figure, at least six foot four, and one of many in the cycling community who has lost a close friend or relative (in his case, his son) in a training accident on the road. He told me: 'Marce' – Marcello Lodi – 'called me and said, "I'm bringing you someone who'll win the Giro d'Italia if you can put him right." And in came Marco with his thinning hair and stick-out ears. He had pain in the lower back, shooting down his leg. I was told the problem had tormented him for about a year. He had a misaligned pelvis and first vertebra, and a distortion of the first cervical vertebra at the base of the skull. The two things effectively cancelled each other out. There's a theory that pelvic asymmetries are related to asymmetries of the palate, so Marco had been treated with a dental plate, although the therapy was useless. He came to me for a number of sessions over ten days. Even after the first session he felt much better. We got rid of the platform under his foot and I gave him a programme of exercises.' The therapy may have saved his nascent career; Lodi recalls a conversation with one of the senior Carrera team staff, who wagered him 40 million lire – €20,000 – that Marco would come to nothing. Many years later Marco would remember Lodi's intervention.

Lodi's collaboration with Marco continued on a four-kilometre climb north of Bergamo called the Róncola, where Lodi and a colleague at the Centre for Biomedical Studies, a medical doctor named Giovanni Grazzi, worked with Marco and his senior team-mate Chiappucci, studying the effects of infinitesimal changes in position and technique. Lodi redesigned Marco's frame, repositioned him in the saddle and, for the first time, Marco was comfortable on the bike. Lodi began to transform Marco's pedal style, educating him to use larger muscles, guiding him towards greater fluidity, coaxing the pedal, not forcing it, harnessing the momentum of the muscle mass in motion. He taught him how to add venom to his accelerations by angling his torso. The old stiffness dissolved. In motion, he acquired new grace, a simultaneous fall and tilt united in a rhythmic flow. These lessons would stay with Marco throughout his career.

Soon after Marco joined Carrera, his masseur Roberto Pregnolato followed. Pregnolato had also worked with Chiappucci, the team's great star at the time – the famous tattoo of a comic devil on Chiappucci's arm was Pregnolato's design – and it was Chiappucci who invited him on board. However, from 1993 Pregnolato worked exclusively with Marco. Pregnolato's home town, Modena, forty kilometres west of Bologna, was to become a second home for Marco, and Pregnolato's family a second family. Pregno must have helped Marco adapt to his new environment. The older Carrera riders, starting with the sprinter Guido Bontempi, did not take kindly to Marco's brashness.

In 1993, his first full season as a professional, Marco rode a heavy spring calendar: on 25 February he finished fourth overall in the Settimana Siciliana. Two days later he was ninth in the one-day Giro della Provincia di Reggio Calabria. These were impressive results for a new professional. The following month, he was blooded against stiffer competition. On 28 March he finished forty-sixth overall in the weekend Critérium International in northern France. On 8 April he was ninth in stage four of the Tour of the Basque Country, and the following day he finished nineteenth overall. From Spain, Marco went straight to Belgium for two hilly one-day classics, the Flèche Wallonne and the Liège–Bastogne–Liège. What mattered wasn't that he finished thirtieth and sixty-seventh respectively, but that he finished at all: these were international one-day races at the very highest level. Then, in consecutive weeks, he rode strongly in two smaller, Italian events: twelfth in the

Giro del Friuli in north-east Italy on 25 April; sixth a week later in the Grand Prix at Larciano, near Florence. Marco's physique was able to absorb the work rate, and grow stronger.

Then, in the four-day Giro del Trentino through the mountains around Lake Garda. Marco finished fifth. At a time when his team might have thought of resting him, he was gaining in strength. He made the Giro d'Italia team, and was given the task of riding close to Chiappucci. Not yet swathed in his aura of magic, Marco nonetheless did so admirably, lurching in and out of the altitude to fourteenth place in stage five, ninth in stage twelve, thirteenth in stage fourteen, and fifteenth in stage fifteen. On stage eighteen he abandoned, tendons swollen and aching. It marked the end of his season: it had been a promising start, although nothing suggested Marco would soon displace Alberto Tomba as the symbol of sporting Italy.

5

The First Peak
(1994)

The political parties that had kept a stranglehold over Italian politics since the end of the Second World War – sarcastically dubbed the 'Party-ocracy' – had been going through a profound and dramatic crisis since the 1970s. In a nation where almost every business, newspaper, TV channel, football team, opera house and trade union had a political protector, and where up to a million public-sector positions were said to be in the direct gift of the parties, their crisis was also that of the Republic itself. Yet the potential for reform of the parties, or the State itself, was negligible. Legal investigations revealed a degree of political collusion with organised crime and threats of violence and arson beyond the suspicions of the most hardened pessimist. One estimate put the yearly sums paid in extortion rackets and pay-offs at 30,000 billion lire (€15 billion). At the 1990 local elections four hundred candidates had previously been indicted for racketeering: the criminals were moving into government, and the last bulwark was represented by the judiciary, despite a barrage of legislation between 1987 and 1992 that had imposed restrictions on examining magistrates. However, in mid-1993 something gave, and prosecutors managed to have the parliamentary immunity of 395 deputies and senators – almost a third of the total – lifted. In the analysis of the historian Martin Clark,

> Eighteen per cent of all local councillors were [placed] under investigation; top civil servants and businessmen – including past presidents of both IRI and ENI – disappeared into prison, or killed themselves. By 1994 the net had caught over 3,000 top people. A political and economic class had been brought down. It was a 'legal

revolution', and one quite unique in world history [*Modern Italy 1971–1995* (Longman History of Italy, second edn, 1996), p. 415].

In this evolving context sport played a curious role. On 24 March 1986 Italy's most prominent media boss, Silvio Berlusconi, had been elected chairman of AC Milan, one of the country's most widely followed football teams. After the breakdown of the traditional parties and the flight of his political protector, the Socialist former Prime Minister Bettino Craxi, to Tunisia when his parliamentary immunity had expired, Berlusconi had founded a political party named Forza Italia, run by media and advertising executives using marketing techniques to decide policy and select candidates. As Luigi Crespi, the director of Datamedia and one of Berlusconi's closest advisors, said in a 2001 interview, AC Milan '[is] a symbol of Berlusconi's virtues as an entrepreneur and innovator. He is known more for football than for Mediaset, and AC Milan fans' – there were estimated to be six million of them all over Italy – 'will vote for him more willingly if the team is winning points and playing attractively. His political success may be inseparable from his success in football.' Crespi added that these views were supported by 'objective data'.

The identification of sports fans as a constituency of party-political voters created a disturbing new context for Italian sport. However, that sporting performances are unreliable political allies was proved when Italy's national team conceded victory in the final of the 1994 FIFA World Cup to Brazil when Roberto Baggio missed a penalty after extra time. Baggio's cycling equivalent, with whom the Italian public closely identified, yet who, despite immense talent, never quite realised their vicarious ambitions, was the cyclist Gianni Bugno. At the 1990 Giro d'Italia, Bugno, then 26, had won two time trials and an undulating stage through the Umbrian hills, and held the leader's pink jersey from start to finish. If that wasn't enough, he had won Milan–San Remo and the World Cup overall. It was an achievement of Coppian proportions. World champion in 1991 and 1992, national champion in 1991 and 1995, winner of the Clásica San Sebastián in 1991 and the Tour of Flanders in 1994, Bugno, like Baggio, was a great champion. But Baggio never won the World Cup, and Bugno never won the Tour. If the new Italy was to have its undisputed sporting icon, it would have to look elsewhere.

*

Marco's next target was the 1994 Giro d'Italia, due to start at Bologna on 22 May. After abandoning the Milan–San Remo on 19 March his early-season form burgeoned as the Giro approached: in the Tour of the Basque Country from 4 to 8 April, he was fifty-fifth overall. In Liège–Bastogne–Liège on 17 April, he was sixty-seventh. But on the last day of the month he finished sixth in the GP Industria e Commercio, and the following day he began a string of fourth places: in the GP Larciano, on 1 May, in stage two of the Giro del Trentino on 11 May, in the final classification of the Giro del Trentino on 13 May, and in the Giro di Toscana on 15 May.

Marco went into only his second major stage race with ambition. The former professional rider Davide Cassani, at the time Carrera's press officer, recalls: 'A week or ten days before the start of the Giro, he told me: "If, in this Giro, I don't ride as I say, I'll go back to my mother's kiosk and sell *piadine*."' The Giro started on Sunday 22 May with a minute of silence for the legendary Spanish climber Jesus Luis Ocaña Pernia, the winner of the 1973 Tour de France. Ocaña had been due at Bologna to commentate for a Spanish radio station. Instead, on the Thursday before the race began, he had shot himself in the head at his French home at Caupenne d'Armagnac, near Nogère. Ocaña, the great climber, had been the nemesis of the great Eddy Merckx. Marco would now play Ocaña's part to the Merckx of his day, Miguel Induráin.

In the first week Marco finished consistently high in the leading group, conceding little, attracting still less attention. On stage four, after another hilltop finish at Campitello Matese, he moved into the top ten in the general classification by finishing fifth behind a young Russian, Evgeni Berzin. For the next two days Marco disappeared into the group. Stage eight was a forty-four-kilometre time trial along the Tuscan coast. Amazingly, Berzin won it, beating Induráin by sixty-five seconds. Marco lost five minutes forty-seven seconds, and now lay seven minutes thirty behind Berzin in the general classification. Still, he was fourteenth overall, and the mountains still lay before him. On Friday 3 June, on the stage to Lienz, over the Austrian border, Marco wriggled quietly into the hills and back into the top ten.

Then, the showpiece weekend of great mountain stages. These were the days designed to attract the biggest television audiences, when the hundreds of sponsors who financed the teams and the event hoped to justify the outlay. On Saturday 4 June the riders faced 235 kilometres and six mountain passes from Lienz to the spa town of Merano; Sunday 5 June would take them, for the first time in fourteen years, over the Passo dello Stelvio, at 2,758 metres the highest in Italy, and prone to bad weather: in 1967, 1984 and 1988 the Stelvio stage had been cancelled. After the Stelvio the stage posed the Mortirolo, considered by many the most difficult in cycling. And after that, two climbs of the Válico di Santa Cristina, before the finish in the hilltop town of Aprica.

Marco's team had made Saturday 4 June his day off his *domestique* duties. The cols that formed the backdrop had outlandish names: the Stalle Sattel, the Furkel, the Würzjoch, the Kofeljoch and the Jaufenpass, the last and longest of the stage. Claudio Chiappucci recalled: 'That morning Marco had something big in mind.' Early on, as the peloton lilted though the German-speaking borderlands, there were riders ahead, grouped around Pascal Richard, from Switzerland. On the Eores, Berzin's team, Gewiss-Ballan, began the pursuit. The leading formation fractured, shedding riders. It was raining on the Jaufenpass when Pascal Richard dropped his final companions.

A kilometre before the apex of the pass, Marco flashed out of the chasing group and into the downpour, a blaze of colour against the failing light. With only Richard ahead of him, Marco crossed the col alone, then lowered his backside off the back of the saddle to within millimetres of the tyre. From time to time he took a look ahead, before nodding his head into the tuck, like a downhill skier. It took thirteen kilometres to reach and ride past Richard. That left thirty to the finish line. Behind him, Bugno put his *domestiques* to work, four of them against Marco. But through Merano's streets Marco rose repeatedly out of the saddle, pouring energy into the pedals, then hunched into a teardrop, head hung between hunched shoulders, flying towards the stage finish. His team-car followed close behind, klaxon echoing on the underside of a railway bridge as Marco darted through the arch, shaving the wall, disheartening his pursuers by disappearing from view. Through the town he sped and into the final kilometre.

He looks over his right shoulder – a long look, because the chasers are obscured by the race director's car, now close behind him. He moves to the outside of the bend and, coasting now, pitches himself into the penultimate corner, before accelerating out of the bend. Another long look over his right shoulder. Then, the final bend, and again he heaves his torso into action, wringing more speed from the air. Two gravitational pulls fight for him: the finish line before him, and the mocking voice of the chase. In the final straight he gazes at length over first one shoulder, then the other, and only now, perhaps, does he know he's won. Still he doesn't slow, straightening up, accelerating again, then looking down, hiding his head in his cap. It may be simple shyness, not knowing what to do with his face as the cameras focus on him. Or is he saying something? As he crosses the finish line, he sits up, raises his hands, claps them together, clenches his fists in the sky, then throws down his hands in a sign of completion. It is Marco's first win as a professional.

Forty seconds later Chiappucci, Rebellin, Berzin, Induráin and sixteen others reach the finish line. Marco would have climbed to sixth place overall even without the twelve-second time bonus for the stage win. On the podium, between the Lipton's Ice Tea girls, the celebratory champagne comes in a small bottle. Marco shakes it, pops the cork and holds it to his groin, letting it ejaculate right and left. Not a celebration to please the corporate sponsors. Then he gives the following interview: 'I'd already been launching attacks for some time. They'd all gone awry until now. This time was perhaps the least credible attack because it was from a long way out, but it was the one that came off.' He was now sixth in GC, just five minutes thirty-six seconds behind Berzin, the surprise leader. Yet Marco wasn't content with his win. Davide Cassani recalled: 'That evening, he began to ask about the following day. "But how is the Mortirolo? How is the Stelvio?"' The manner of Marco's victory at Merano had attracted huge public attention in Italy and abroad. It ensured massive television audiences, and a massive pay-day for the race, the sport and its sponsors, the following day.

Italia Uno's coverage started at 12.30 p.m., as the riders reached Prato allo Stelvio, marking the foot of the Stelvio climb. According to the Italian TV audience-research organisation Auditel, within five minutes three million Italian viewers watched as Franco Vona attacked with José Uriarte. Uriarte thought again, leaving Vona alone. Two kilometres from the top Vona had three minutes fifty-four on the group. Behind him, Marco's team-mate Claudio Chiappucci was giving chase. At 1.35 p.m., after seventy-three kilometres, as Vona crossed the highpoint of the Stelvio Pass, the Italia Uno audience had swollen to four million; by 1.55 p.m., at the halfway point in the stage, as Vona entered Bormio after ninety-six kilometres, six minutes forty seconds ahead of Berzin, five million Italians were watching. After a hundred and thirty kilometres, at Mazzo in Valtellina, the slopes of the Mortirolo began. Marco marked time on the lower slopes, then started out of the group. Induráin let him go. Berzin made the mistake of trying to match Marco's accelerations; for a kilometre, perhaps more, it worked, but it was only a matter of time before Marco left him standing. It took ten climbing kilometres for Marco to reach and pass Vona; their trajectories crossed a kilometre before the pass. Marco had laid waste to the peloton: at the summit of the Mortirolo, after 142.4 kilometres, Marco led the Colombian 'Cacaíto' Rodríguez by ten seconds, Gotti and Belli by forty seconds, and Induráin by fifty. He had covered the 12.4 kilometres of the climb in forty-three minutes fifty-three seconds, beating the previous record, forty-six minutes ten seconds, set in 1991 by that year's Giro winner, Franco Chioccioli. Over six million Italians watched him cross the Mortirolo.

Induráin threw himself into the descent in pursuit, with Rodríguez on his wheel. On the advice of Marco's *directeur sportif* Giuseppe Martinelli, Marco relented and allowed them to reach him. They coalesced into a single group, taking the first passage over the finish line at Aprica together, after 174.2 kilometres. But then, on the climb of the Válico di Santa Cristina, from the 181 kilometre point to kilometre 188.5, Marco stood on the pedals and flew away. Induráin remained seated, with little body movement, his once-impenetrable superiority now breached. Behind and to the side, Rodríguez was out of the saddle, oscillating wildly. Marco was incredibly slender, and when he stood on the pedals, there was something unexpected about his movements. As each foot completed its load-bearing cycle and ceased to deliver power to the pedal, the knee bent and moved forward, dragging the foot upward to the start of the cycle. The ankle nearly straightened, and the sole of Marco's rising foot, for a moment, was almost perpendicular to the ground. The illusion was that he was pulling the pedals upwards more than forcing them downwards. It was as if Marco's body was being drawn towards the sky. By the brow of the Válico di Santa Cristina, Marco led Chiappucci by three minutes, and Induráin, Belli and Rodríguez by three minutes twenty-two seconds. The television audience grew from 6.4 to 6.6 million, until, at 5.55, as Marco descended towards Aprica, it peaked at 6,733,000, a market share of 59.02 per cent. The roadside crowds grinned and laughed, craning forwards, pointing, as Marco sped to victory, two minutes fifty-two seconds ahead of his team-mate Chiappucci. He was now second overall, one minute eighteen seconds behind Berzin.

Marco's successive stage wins at Merano and Aprica, and the threat he now posed to Eugeni Berzin, won him eulogies for his style. He was again compared to Gaul and the suicide Luis Ocaña. He was also likened to Gino Bartali, the Florentine who had won the 1948 Tour de France and, so legend had it, saved Italy from civil war. But Bartali had been a champion in the age of radio; Marco had become its greatest television star, and not just in Italy. In Spain, an average of 4,945,000 viewers had tuned in between three o'clock and the stage finish.

For the rest of the Giro the daytime transmissions caused havoc in workplaces all over Europe. Workers downed tools and settled in front of TV sets, or decamped to local bars. Those who could came home early, perhaps interrupting their children's regular viewing to watch the stage. Whether it meant family conflict, as children missed their favourite mid-afternoon programmes, or extra hours of togetherness around the television, Marco entered the everyday lives of millions, to shouts of '*Dai*, Marco!', '*Vai*, Panta!' '*Forza*, Pantani!' or the local equivalent.

Stage eighteen was a thirty-five-kilometre mountain time trial from Chiavari, on the Ligurian coast, to the Passo del Bocco. Berzin won the stage, gaining twenty seconds on Induráin, second, and one minute thirty-seven on Marco. The next day, 10 June 1994, saw a 201 kilometre, border-crossing raid from Cuneo in Piedmont to the ski resort at Les Deux Alpes in the French Alps. That night, before bed, Chiappucci described the mountains to Marco: the 2,748 metre Colle dell'Agnello, the 2,361 metre Col d'Izoard, the 2,058 metre Col du Lauteret and then the stage-finish climb to Les Deux Alpes, at 1,651 metres. Marco must have gone to sleep planning the following day's act of madness.

Soon after the village of Sampeyre, at the foot of the Colle dell'Agnello, not thirty kilometres into the stage, Marco attacked, chasing the remnants of an earlier breakaway. He reached them and passed them, and was joined by two Colombians, Hernán Buenahora and Álvaro Mejía. Mejía then dropped back, unwilling or unable to maintain the pace. The audacity of Marco's attack drove Berzin into crisis, and only the experience of his team-mate Moreno Argentin, twice the world champion, saved him. Marco crossed the Izoard alone, 120 kilometres into the stage, but he had burned massive amounts of energy, and Argentin gained twenty seconds on him during the twenty-kilometre climb. Marco's advantage at the shoulder of the climb was one minute twenty seconds. On the descent from the Izoard, the wind was against him. After seventy-four kilometres in the race lead he recognised that his attack had been in vain and allowed Buenahora to carry on alone. Argentin, leading his team-mate, the race leader for 160 kilometres from the Valle Varaita to the foot of Les Deux Alpes, stood between Marco and overall victory. The stage was won by Marco's Russian team-mate Vladimir Pulnikov, whose contribution to *his* team-mate's bid for victory had been minimal. Marco finished seventh, gaining thirteen seconds on Berzin and Induráin.

One mountain stage remained, but 11 June 1994 was a day of frozen fog in the Alps, and Marco complained he was so cold he could scarcely change gear. Visiblity at the stage finish, Sestriere, was minimal: the town had disappeared into a snowstorm. Marco started the day two points behind the Swiss rider Pascal Richard in the mountain category, but he made no attempt to win it: second places and sub-categories held no interest for him. Richard won the stage and the mountains competition. The following day, the final result was confirmed: Marco was second overall, two minutes fifty-one seconds behind Berzin, thirty-two seconds ahead of Induráin, who was third.

I saw all of this, following the Giro by newspaper, radio and television, first in bars around Umbria and Tuscany, then at a friend's flat in Monfalcone, near Trieste, and finally at the roadside at Sestriere. Franco, my friend, was a shopkeeper who couldn't leave the shop during the day, so recorded the stages on the VCR. I slept on his sofa a few nights, and we acted out together the sports-fan's ritual of video-recording live sports events: the late-night programming, in the knowledge that one false flex of a finger will result in the recording of a 1950s western; the early evening effort to avoid the stage result; and, finally, the 'as-live' tension of the viewing rite, that often extended, given the length of the stages, deep into the night. All of which somehow gave watching on the VCR greater ritual status than watching 'normal' television; and, since the result was known after the first viewing, we could then focus on details, committing Marco's victories to memory in ever-greater detail, intensifying the identification. How many of those magical tapes must still survive, worn but still prized, all over Italy, France and beyond! – precious, magical objects, Marco, the icon, multiplied, consumed, fixed in the imagination, his suffering, portrayed on screen, inversely proportional to the euphoria of the television experience.

On 26 June Marco finished thirteenth in the national championship. Then, he travelled to France for his first Tour de France. He made a downbeat start. On stage nine, an individual time trial from Périgueux to Bergerac, Induráin was breathtaking. Tour de France director Jean-Marie Leblanc described him as 'powerful, supple, magnificent to behold – the aesthetic perfection of the cycling machine.' His closest rival, the Swiss rider Tony Rominger, conceded two minutes. Marco lost no less than ten minutes fifty-nine seconds, which left him fifty-ninth, fourteen minutes forty-seven seconds behind Induráin in the general classification. Two days later, in freezing fog, he attacked eleven kilometres from the stage finish at the ski resort of Hautacam, above Lourdes. Unfortunately for Marco, Induráin's great rival Rominger was suffering lower down on the climb, so the Spaniard seized the moment to attack with such impetus that 2.3 kilometres from the finish line he rode straight past Marco, taking the Frenchman Luc Leblanc with him. Induráin allowed Leblanc to win the stage; Marco finished third, sixteen seconds behind Induráin. He now lay twenty-sixth overall.

Racing resumed after the rest day, when France's Richard Virenque joined a breakaway at the foot of the Tourmalet, fifty kilometres from the finish line at Luz Ardiden. Marco had planned to wait until the last possible moment before attacking, but Virenque's move forced him to change his plan. When Virenque's lead reached eight minutes, Marco drifted out of the yellow-jersey group in pursuit. Three kilometres from the brow of the Tourmalet, Marco had pulled back two and a half minutes, but Virenque defended his lead on the descent of the Tourmalet and paced himself on the final climb to Luz Ardiden. Four minutes thirty-four seconds after Virenque had won the stage, Marco crossed the line in second place. He was now eighth overall.

Three days later, on 18 July, Eros Poli, one of Marco's adversaries as an amateur, attacked early and gained an almost absurd lead of twenty-four and a half minutes by the foot of the imposing Mont Ventoux. It was enough to allow him to win the stage by nearly four minutes. On

Mont Ventoux's lower slopes Marco developed a gear problem. He stopped to change machines, then collided with a team-mate who had waited for him, and fell, taking a blow to his right thigh. Back in the saddle, with eleven kilometres of the climb remaining, he attacked, 'to find out if the fall was serious', as he said after the stage. He quickly gained ninety seconds on the yellow-jersey group, only to be chased down by an alliance of Virenque, Leblanc, Pascal Lino and Induráin. After the stage Marco complained: 'Induráin is still riding after me, even though I'm twelve minutes down, and he's doing it to give his Festina friends Virenque and Leblanc a hand. They're always talking among themselves and their tactics are the same. Leblanc and Virenque have already won a stage each, with Induráin's blessing, and now they're protecting their places. So it's looking increasingly unlikely that I'll win a stage or get on the podium. But Induráin's making a mistake, because he's made room for everyone except me. Now I'm going to do everything I can to blow his plans out of the water.'

On Hautacam and on Mont Ventoux he had accelerated eleven kilometres from the apex of the climb. He did so again on stage sixteen from Valréas to Alpe d'Huez. His fellow Romagnolo Roberto Conti had joined a large breakaway, attacked with sixteen hairpins to go, and crossed the finish line nearly six minutes before Marco. But Marco, who reached the foot of the climb with the yellow-jersey group, attacked with such venom that he set a record time of thirty-eight minutes for the ascent, two minutes seventeen seconds quicker than the stage winner. Marco gained one minute forty seconds on Virenque and two minutes fifteen on Induráin and Leblanc, stepping up to within ten minutes of Induráin, and from sixth to fifth place in GC.

The stage of the 1994 Tour that lingers in the memory is stage seventeen, from Bourg d'Oisans to Val Thorens. On the Col du Glandon, the first climb of the stage, as the TV cameras watched the leading group, Pantani was involved in another fall. Twenty-two kilometres into the stage, riding at high speed, he touched the rear wheel of Alberto Elli. Both men fell, hitting a wall at the roadside. Elli departed immediately; Marco stayed down, losing two minutes as the race doctor, Dr Gérard Porte, examined the wound and ruled out a fracture. The television footage shows Marco wiping his face, looking at his elbow. He had agreed with Roberto Conti to attack on the Col de la Madeleine, but the fall had destroyed their plan. Frustrated, angry, perhaps ready to walk away, Marco watched his knee swell, even as, with three team-mates at hand, he began the chase. It lasted twenty-three kilometres. At the forty-five kilometre mark of the stage, sinking down from the Col du Glandon, Marco and his helpers finally joined the main peloton.

Three times Marco, weeping with pain, dropped back to his team car for permission to abandon. It didn't come, so on the Col de la Madeleine he attacked, partly, as on Mont Ventoux, to test the wounded knee. The move thinned out the group. Far ahead, Ugrumov and the Colombian Cacaíto Rodríguez were already on the thirty-nine-kilometre Val Thorens climb. The pace of the yellow-jersey group was so high, no attack seemed possible. Yet five and a half kilometres from the finish line Marco, still in pain, attacked, sprinting from the back of the group. For thirteen seconds, Luc Leblanc gave chase, before Marco's speed made him think again. At the finish line, Cacaíto dropped Ugrumov to win the stage. Marco finished sixty-eight seconds later, third in the stage but one and a half minutes ahead of Induráin, Virenque and Leblanc. He had leapfrogged into third place overall. But he spent the night in pain and the following day, from Moutiers to Cluses, he couldn't push a big gear. Piotr Ugrumov won the stage, with Induráin and Virenque second and third. Marco was fifth, three and a half minutes down. In the general classification he dropped into fourth place, two seconds behind Ugrumov.

The penultimate stage was a mountain time trial from Cluses to Morzine-Avoriaz. Ugrumov led at every split. Marco lost a minute and thirty-eight seconds to Ugrumov, but gained the same on Induráin. Virenque performed dreadfully and slipped from second place overall to fourth. Marco, in his first Tour de France, had finished third. He stood on the podium in Paris, perched precariously on the top platform of the podium with Induráin and Ugrumov, his sponsor's cap too big for him. He was indisputably Italy's number one cyclist. More than that, at twenty-four he was already one of the most exciting, unpredictable and inspirational performers in sport.

6
Falling
(1995–FEBRUARY 1996)

Marco spent the first four months of 1995 training for the Giro d'Italia. At a training camp he shaved his head. It wasn't his initiative; his teammates convinced him to dispense with the remaining strands. Soon afterwards Paolo shaved his head again, for the first time in years. It was the look he had worn during military service, when he had met Tonina.

As the season progressed, Marco came into form: he was ninety-eighth in Milan–San Remo on 18 March, twenty-fifth in Flèche Wallonne on 12 April, eighteenth four days later in Liège–Bastogne–Liège, and then, on 25 April, he finished fifth in the Giro dell'-Appennino, with a new record for climbing the Boccetta. The Giro was due to start on 13 May in Perugia and Marco, another year stronger, was the favourite. On 1 May he was due to drive to Switzerland to ride in the Tour de Romandie, a stage race through the French-speaking cantons, and to hone his form. That morning, before setting off, he rode alone out of Cesenatico to rehearse on the climbs of the Republic of San Marino. In the village of Santarcángelo, thirty kilometres from Cesenatico, a Fiat Punto approached along the Via Emilia. By the time Marco realised he hadn't been seen, it was too late. The impact flung him onto the asphalt, ripping skin from his face. The driver was from Cesenatico and recognised his victim. He was mortified.

Marco was conscious when the ambulance reached Rimini. Blood tests, X-rays and a CAT scan revealed the extent of the damage: bruising to the right knee and sacrum, a cut and bruising to the right temple, but no concussion, breaks or fractures. All the same, they kept him under observation for two days. Meniscus damage was diagnosed, and Marco started laser treatment and ionophoresis. In a television interview broadcast on 10 May, Marco, his right cheekbone and eyelid covered with cream, was still expecting to start the Giro: 'I needed to spend these two weeks working. Instead, I've been in bed. I'll be rested, but not trained, and I'll pay for it.' On the morning of 11 May he rode sixty kilometres with his team-mate Marcello Siboni, and the knee pain was unbearable. That afternoon he announced he wouldn't be starting the Giro.

Instead, he rode the Tour of Switzerland. On stage seven, the first mountain stage, he was dropped, and during the post-stage massage he succumbed to self-pity, complaining to Roberto Pregnolato that he'd done everything possible to prepare himself, but he couldn't recover. Pregnolato tried to reason with him: 'I told him he never rode well in the first mountain stage. It was the same all through his career.' But Marco decided to abandon. The exchange with Pregnolato became physical, and Pregnolato slapped Marco in the face. They didn't speak again until after the following day's stage, the hardest of the race – which Marco won. With the Tour de France days away, his form was rising.

However, before the Tour Marco switched cranks – the arms into which the pedals are screwed. The change from 172.5 to 175 millimetre cranks was intended to make his pedal stroke more efficient, but Marco began to suffer his old pelvic problems. Over the first eight days and 1,370 kilometres of the Tour de France, the aching became unbearable. After the stage through the Ardennes to Liège he was ready to abandon. A Belgian osteopath was found to manipulate Marco's pelvis. It took him an hour and a half, but he succeeded in truing the alignment of the joint between the ischium and the sacral bone, and restoring elasticity to the cartilage. Two days later Marco, reborn, finished fourth in the stage from Le Grand Bornand to La Plagne, through the northern Alps.

The next day took the race over the Col de la Madeleine and the Col de la Croix de Fer to Alpe d'Huez. Agile and elegant, Marco attacked thirteen kilometres from the finish line. He rode past ten riders and approached the leading group of three: Virenque, Laurent Dufaux and Ivan Gotti. Before he could reach them Gotti attacked. Virenque and Dufaux had no answer, so Marco rode past them both and gained Gotti's wheel. For a moment he sat and waited. Then he stood in the pedals, and darted past. Gotti could only watch. Marco was alone now and the stage, barring disaster, was his. The disaster nearly came two hundred and fifty metres from the finish line when he missed the final curve and rode straight across the road towards the car park. Inches from disaster, he braked and made the turn. The double-take cost him a new record for the climb: he completed it four seconds outside his own time of thirty-eight minutes dead.

Four days after Alpe d'Huez, Marco celebrated Induráin's birthday by rearing into the cloud forty-two kilometres from the finish line at Guzet Neige. Ivan Gotti saw him last, obscured by mist, a faint presence in the whiteness. On the podium, goaded by his fans, he gave the podium girls a shy kiss, wearing his little boy's expression. After the stage, Gianni Mura of *La Repubblica* asked him for the secret of his climbing speed. He told him, 'I love the mountains, but the moment of exertion fills me with deep hatred. So I try to shorten the suffering.' It was not the standard language of the sports interview. In the past interviewers had often found Marco at a loss for words. This new and cryptic lyricism was Marco's solution. It allowed him to be disarmingly candid, but also difficult to decipher. His words revealed contradictions in his relationship with his sport and with himself. The elation of victory, the principal goal of his professional life, had cathartic potential, yet the effort that heralded that elation filled him with loathing.

On the night of 17 July a nightmare woke him. The next day, plunging down the Portet d'Aspet, thirty-four kilometres into the stage, Fabio Casartelli fell on a bend and came to rest in the foetal position, with blood gushing from head wounds. His heart stopped three times in the helicopter and, in hospital at Tarbes, he died. Marco wept on the Tourmalet.

He finished the Tour thirteenth overall, and Best Young Rider for the second year running.

The 1995 World Championships were due to be held at Duitama in Colombia early in October. In preparation, Marco started the Tour of Spain, finishing ninth in stage ten and sixth in stage eleven, before abandoning to refine his form, then taper, in order to peak on 8 October.

Two weeks before the championships, Marco contacted a food-supplements producer named Marco Ceriani, asking for nutritional advice. His speech patterns struck Ceriani: Marco spoke quietly, choosing his words carefully, thinking at length before speaking, never arguing or pretending to know. Ceriani recalls explaining the biochemistry of food supplements, and Marco listening patiently as Pregnolato paced in and out looking at his watch: the lecture was making him and Marco late for a date he had arranged with some girls. Marco told him he followed no special diet; he ate what he liked, which meant pasta, *piadine* and plenty of Nutella. And, before demanding mountain stages, a second breakfast of spaghetti doused in honey and dusted with Parmesan cheese. Ceriani suggests that this was the secret of his success. Marco told Ceriani he didn't trust food supplements: 'You know, I don't want any problems.'

On 4 October, as Miguel Induráin powered to the world time-trial championship, a finish-line tribune collapsed and a number of spectators were taken to hospital as a precaution. Marco's father, Paolo, was initially reported to be among them. This Marco angrily denied: journalists noted his lack of humour, always a sign of good form.

The riders faced fifteen laps of a 17.7 kilometre circuit starting at the village of Duitama, the home town of the Colombian rider Oliverio Rincón, at an altitude of 2,540 metres. After five hundred horizontal metres, the only level stretch on the circuit, they faced an imperceptible gradient of four kilometres, before the road turned skywards on the slopes of El Cogollo, peaking at 2,890 metres. The riders described the gradient as 10 to 13 per cent, despite the official maximum of 8.57 per cent. The circuit was completed by a terrifying descent at gradients of 16 per cent back to Duitama. Claudio Chiappucci described it as the hardest circuit he had ever seen.

The first ascent of El Cogollo saw Gianni Bugno, the putative Italian team-leader, dropped by fifty seconds. He gave chase and rejoined the leading group, only to abandon after lap four. The sixth climb saw Induráin's team-mates raise the pace, reducing the group of favourites to twenty-one. No less than six were Italian: Casagrande, Chiappucci, Lanfranchi, Pellicioli, Piepoli and Marco. Then freezing rain began to fall. Chiappucci crashed on the appalling descent and remounted, despite his wounds. Piepoli went down too, and had to abandon.

With three laps to go Marco launched an exploratory attack. Induráin watched him rise into the thin, cool air, then rode inexorably back up to him. There were abortive attacks from others, but the pace was too high and the race too long to allow them to thrive. On the penultimate lap Induráin punctured. Riding a reserve bike, it took him five minutes to catch the leading group. By then the contenders were down to six: two Spaniards, Induráin and Olano, two Swiss, Richard and Gianetti, and two Italians, Francesco Casagrande and Marco.

Then, the shock of an attack by Induráin. His rivals had no choice but to follow; the effort left them in indescribable oxygen debt. As they gasped for breath, Olano slipped away and into a forty-five-second lead. As Induráin had sacrificed himself for Olano, so Casagrande did for Pantani, burning what remaining energy he had to lead the chase. On the final climb of El Cogollo, Richard dropped out of contention. Marco attacked. Induráin and Gianetti chased him down, and then Marco and Gianetti, working together, gave chase to Olano, whose team-mate Induráin, of course, refused to collaborate. Each time Marco attempted a decisive change of pace, his rear wheel skidded on the soaking asphalt. Olano, despite a puncture that meant he crossed the finish line with a completely flat rear tyre, maintained his lead and crossed the line first after completing 265.5 kilometres in seven hours, nine minutes and fifty-five seconds. Induráin won the silver-medal sprint, and Marco held off Gianetti for bronze. All three crossed the line together, thirty-five seconds after Olano.

On 11 October 1995 Marco reached Italy and sea level with his bronze medal. At Nicola Amaducci's Bar del Corso, Marco carried the champagne bottle around the room in celebration. He was persuaded to take his excellent form to the Settimana Rosa, the series of three one-day races that closed Italy's élite cycling season: the Milan–Turin, the Tour of Piedmont and the Tour of Lombardy. Marco himself had little interest in these end-of-season events; throughout his career his season ended with the Tour de France. But in such form, victory in the prestigious Tour of Lombardy, wistfully known as the 'Race of the Falling Leaves', would have been feasible.

So, on the morning of 18 October, when the riders convened in the pouring rain at Novate Milanese, north of central Milan, for the start of the Milan–Turin, Marco was among them. He was probably there to fine-tune his condition, even if he considered it beneath him. The Milan–Turin was replete with history – first run in 1876, it predated all but the very first events in the history of competitive cycling, and drew a symbolic line from Italy's financial capital to the city of its great industrial workshops – but it was no longer a major date in the cycling calendar.

Because of the cold, he was wearing a woolly hat. His nutritionist Marco Ceriani asked him why he wasn't wearing a helmet. Marco told him, 'Helmets don't keep you warm, and I haven't got any hair. Anyway, helmets annoy me: they imprison my thoughts.'

They rolled the fifteen hundred metres to the race start in Via Di Vittorio and at 10 a.m. they were waved off. The route took them from Novate Milanese to Rho, seven kilometres to the west, then south-west through Vigevano and Casale Monteferrato to Asti, the itinerary's southernmost point, 130 kilometres from Milan. A thirteen-man break-away escaped early in the race. With the nine most powerful teams represented in the group, there was little incentive for a chase, and the gap quickly grew to ten minutes or more. Marco was among the back-markers.

By Asti the rain eased and the riders, on dry roads now, turned north-westwards to Castelnuovo Don Bosco, and then to the one great obstacle: the Superga, the hill that overlooks Turin from the east. At 671 metres, the Superga resembles those abrupt prominences inland from Cesenatico where Marco had learned to ride. But the Superga bears a greater burden in Italian sports history: on 4 May 1949 the aircraft carrying the great Torino football team home from a friendly in Lisbon crashed into the hillside, killing all thirty-one on board. The Torino side, perhaps the greatest club side in the world at the time, had been symbolic of Italy's post-war recovery. Of the eleven Italian internationals who beat Hungary on 11 May 1947, ten had been Torino players. Many who mourned them had little interest in sport.

Marco rode easily up the Superga – with his world-championship form, he can hardly have helped riding away from the bunch – before dropping south to Pino Torinese (485 metres), then turning into Chorso Chieri, a 6.6 kilometre, winding descent to Piazzale Marco Aurelio. The finish-line was 3.6 kilometres from the Piazzale, left along the Corso Casale, parallel to the River Po, passing Piazza Borromini (1.6 kilometres from Piazzale Marco Aurelio), then crossing the river for the sprint finish in the Parco del Valentino. The finish was expected at 3 p.m.

At approximately a quarter to three, Marco lowered himself into his characteristic descending position, with two first-year professionals in single file behind him: Francesco Secchiari, 23, of Navigare, and his former Giacobazzi team-mate Davide Dall'Olio, 25, now with Amore e Vita. The race for victory was miles ahead of them. This was for the pure exhilaration of speeding down deserted roads into the heart of the city. Halfway down Corso Chieri, in the suburb of Reaglie, police were barring the Cresto road to keep the race route secure. Their walkie-talkies always worked poorly here. The transcripts of the police radio communications – translated below, with time codes – provide a vivid commentary to the drama that followed. 'Control' is evidently police headquarters; 'Lima 1' is manning a roadblock some way up Corso Chieri:

After 14:43.44
CONTROL Attention all officers on the race route: before reopening the route, wait for the coach with the 'End of Race' sign.
    [. . .]
14:44.45
LIMA 1 I think the tail-end of the race has passed the Reaglie–Chieri–Corso Chieri junction. There are no more riders. Just be aware that behind the ambulance there's a latecomer. Behind the ambulance there's still one late-coming rider.
VEGA 1 He'll have to follow the Highway Code. After the 'End of Race' sign, the road isn't closed, so he'll have to stop at the junctions, too.
LIMA 1 Lima 1 to Vega 1.
VEGA 1 Go ahead.
14:45.25
LIMA 1 I haven't seen a coach at the end of the race.
VEGA 1 It isn't a coach, it's a minibus, but there's always an 'End of Race' sign. It'll come, or it'll be picking someone up on the way.
LIMA 1 OK, received.
    [. . .]
VEGA 1 Where are you?
14:46.00
LIMA 1 I'm turning into Corso Casale.
VEGA 1 Stop there, and put yourself at the tail-end of the race so your colleagues understand the race has gone past and reopen the road when they see you pass.

14:46.33

LIMA 1 There's already private traffic behind us. We'll try to keep the private traffic behind us.

VEGA 1 Perfect – thanks.

VEGA 90 Vega 1, this is Vega 90. We're at the tail-end of the race.

VEGA 1 Perfect, then inform your colleagues as you pass, so that they reopen the road behind you, thanks.

14:47.00

UNIDENTIFIED Where is the tail-end of the race, please, Control?

CONTROL The tail-end is in Piazza Borromini.

VEGA 21 So here, at the Piazza Pasini bridge, we can open the road?

[. . .]

VEGA 90 Yes. If Corso Gabetti is free, open Piazza Pasini.

[. . .]

14:48.00

VEGA 22 Can we open Piazzale Marco Aurelio?

VEGA 1 Negative: until Corso Casale has been opened by your colleagues, you can't reopen.

14:48.15

CONTROL Vega 22 and Vega 1. Do not reopen Corso Casale – they're still coming down from Pino. Do not reopen.

VEGA 22 Did you receive that, Vega 1?

VEGA 1 Negative because there's noise here. Repeat.

14:48.36

VEGA 22 They're still coming down from Pino. Do not reopen Corso Casale. Keep everything closed; they're still coming down. The tail-end of the race is still in Corso Chieri.

VEGA 21 Who said the end was in Piazza Borromini? Sorry, someone's not giving precise information.

CONTROL Lima 1 from Control, Lima 1.

[. . .]

LIMA 1 I'm reading you.

14:49.43

CONTROL Shouldn't you be at the tail-end of the race?

LIMA 1 There are leftover riders who've been left behind; we're going back along Corso Casale to escort them.

CONTROL Vega 21, keep Corso Casale closed, then.

VEGA 21 We'll close it again because we'd opened it. They'd informed us that the end was in Piazza Borromini.

CONTROL Understood.

14:50.00

VEGA 90 OK, let's have some order. This is Vega 90. I've contacted the last police motorcyclist in the race and he has confirmed that the last riders were where I was. Those who're still behind were private citizens who have joined the back of the race, but aren't part of it.

VEGA 22 Negative: they're all riders, and there are plenty of them.

VEGA 90 Then I've been wrongly informed.

VEGA 1 The moment there's an 'End of Race' sign, even those wearing a race number who are behind the 'End of Race' sign are private citizens.

LIMA 1 Lima 1 to Control.

CONTROL Go ahead, Lima 1.

LIMA 1 There are still riders wearing race numbers proceeding along Corso Chieri and they are turning into Corso Casale as we speak.

CONTROL After the 'End of Race' sign they have to follow the Highway Code. Vega 1 has given these conditions.

LIMA 1 Agreed, but it's not just a few riders, it's twenty or so.

CONTROL If there are still colleagues up there on Corso Casale, let's keep it as closed as possible –

LIMA 1 – to see how the situation is, then I'll pass it on to Vega.

14:52.50

LIMA 1 Lima 1, Lima 1, to everyone who's on the race: keep it closed, there are still about thirty riders at Corso Chieri-Reaglie.

14:54.00

VEGA 90 So there's a good ten minutes between one group and the other.

14:54.20

LIMA 1 The 'End of Race' minibus has just passed. The minibus has just passed Reaglie – location Reaglie.

VEGA 1 Ah, you've found the 'End of Race' minibus?

LIMA 1 The ambulance that should have been at the tail-end of the race – the ambulance is the one that was with the first group.

VEGA 1 Lima 1, from Vega 1: let's stay calm, nothing's going to happen. This lot are used to arriving a quarter of an hour late through city traffic.

14:55.00

VEGA 1 Vega 1. Lima 1's right, the ambulance is with another group. It has abandoned the final group.

CONTROL Control to any Mike in Corso Chieri.

[. . .]

MIKE 10 Mike 10 reading you.

CONTROL Mike 10, can we take a motorbike off and go to check 220, Corso Chieri; the Medical Guard is informing us of a serious road-traffic accident.

MIKE 10 A road accident?

CONTROL Yes, confirmed – 220, Corso Chieri; they're asking us if there's space for a possible helicopter landing.

[. . .]

MIKE 10 What were you saying just now? Now I'm reading you loud and clear.

CONTROL Well, the Medical Guard if possible make a [*static*] 220, Corso Chieri [*static*] a serious road-traffic accident and [*static*] is arriving [*static*] . . .

In the middle of all the confusion, a light-coloured Nissan Patrol 743, a solid, off-road four-wheel drive, had been allowed to turn into Corso Chieri and head out of town, towards the oncoming riders. The weather by now had cleared up: the sky was clear, the temperature pushing twenty degrees, and the road surface dry. Still, the meanders in the road, and the vegetation and walls lining the way, kept visibility down to a few tens of metres. Perhaps sensing something was wrong from the crowds who had not yet dispersed, the car had crawled upwards, scarcely touching 40 k.p.h.

Five hundred metres later, as the Nissan entered a sweeping left-hand curve, Marco, Secchiari and Dall'Olio had appeared. They had veered over to the left-hand side to shorten the bend. The maneouvre placed the Nissan directly in their path. It braked, and came to a stop, but it was too late. Hurtling down and around the corner – the gradient at this point was 8 per cent, or one in twelve and a half – Marco can scarcely have seen it. He and Secchiari flew over the bonnet. Dall'Olio, with a fraction of a second more to react, made the left-front wing. When the dynamic chaos of bodies and machines came to a halt, the car had sustained only minor damage: a broken fog lamp and radiator grill, and a few dents to the bodywork. But the riders' bikes had been virtually destroyed: Marco's Carrera Podium had a twisted frame and a broken pedal; the handlebars were bent at both ends and the gear levers were damaged. The rear wheel was buckled, the front fork sliced clean through, and the front wheel had completely disintegrated. The driver emerged from the car, unsure what to do, wanting to help, but nearby fans turned on him, and he climbed back in, afraid of a lynching. When the paramedics arrived, he moved the car to give them access. Then the first ambulance and police arrived from Pino Torinese.

Marco was loaded into the first ambulance. It took ten minutes for another to arrive for Secchiari and Dall'Olio. Dall'Olio was placed on the only bed. Secchiari sat down, and realised his pelvis was broken. The twisted bikes were loaded on to a car that pulled away behind the ambulances.

By the time the police arrived, the vehicles had been moved to the side of the road, though the impact site was obvious: a puddle of blood two metres long marked the position of the accident. Whose blood it was was unclear: seconds after the ambulances had left, another group of riders had fallen at the same spot. 'As closed as possible', to use Control's expression, had not been closed enough.

By the time Marco reached the Orthopaedic Traumatology Centre (CTO) of the Maria Adelaide Hospital, news of the crash was being broadcast around the world. At the CTO, X-rays revealed the extent of the injuries. Marco had sustained breaks to the shinbone and the smaller bone connecting ankle and knee in his left leg, with a tumour of clotted blood in the thigh, and skinned bruising all over. Secchiari and Dall'Olio scarcely made the bulletins, although Secchiari had suffered three breaks to the right hip bone, and Dall'Olio had a break to the left thigh bone just below the ball-joint, with further bruising and skin loss.

Dall'Olio was informed that the nature of the fracture meant he had to be put into traction, and could neither be transferred nor operated on immediately. He was left on a hard bed in the emergency department and apparently forgotten. As he lay there, he caught a glimpse of Marco being prepared for surgery, and heard a fierce argument between Martinelli and the CTO's chief surgeon, Professor Massimo Cartesegna. Martinelli wanted Marco transferred to another hospital. Cartesegna told him there was no question of a transfer, or of waiting for other doctors to arrive: Marco had to be operated on immediately. Dall'Olio described the atmosphere as tense, but the operation went ahead, on Cartesegna's insistence. The clinical notes describe it as 'Reduction and osteosynthesis employing external axial fixator' – in other words, the stabilisation and joining of fractured bones using an external splint.

A fragment of bone was protruding from a wound to the rear of Marco's left calf. Cartasegna opened the wound by another centimetre and looked inside. The muscle attachments had been stripped from the bones, and in some places the periosteum, the membrane that covers the surface of the bones, essential for growth and repair, had been completely scraped away. He removed four large fragments of de-vitalised bone; then, with the help of 'live' X-ray images on a TV monitor, stabilised the fracture using the external splint, a sprung, telescopic cylinder which compressed the bone fragments into place using five pins screwed through holes in the skin.

After the operation, Marco was moved to ward 8, bed 4. Dall'Olio was in bed 5. When Marco came to, they talked about the accident. Marco's father was with him throughout; he had parked the camper van near the hospital. Martinelli may have been there that evening; he certainly visited the following day, accompanied by a figure with thinning hair whom Dall'Olio believed to be Dr Grazzi. He visited at least twice, perhaps more. Chiappucci made an appearance, too: Secchiari, in the next room, learnt that he and Martinelli had visited, and was annoyed they hadn't stepped into the next room to see him. Roberto Pregnolato and the other *soigneur*, Stefano Chiodini, paid a visit. Alberto Tomba came. So did Marco's Tuscan girlfriend, Sabrina, whom he had kept out of the public eye. Her visit coincided with that of Candido Cannavò and Angelo Zomegnan, director and cycling editor respectively of the *Gazzetta dello Sport*. In their startled presence Marco told Sabrina to leave and not come back, ending their relationship from his hospital bed.

Over the following days, as Dall'Olio understood it, Cartesegna was worried about a haematoma on Marco's leg, and a fall in Marco's blood levels, and considered a second operation to drain the possible haem-orrhage. Marco was given a blood transfusion for his anaemia. Television news footage showed him in his hospital room – white walls, green panels, the fingers of his right hand still covered with tiny cuts, his left eyelid with a superficial wound. 'I'm still in some pain,' he said, 'but over the last two days it has improved; everything has improved. My morale is still a bit low, but, for the rest, everything's going relatively well.' On 25 October Cartasegna told the press: 'The functional recovery of the man is at stake. His competitive activity still represents an unknown.' Marco said something similar to his team-mate Marcello Siboni: 'I don't know if I'll be able to get back on a bike – if I'll ever ride again.'

The accident that had kept him out of the Giro in May had been badly timed, but not serious. This time, his career was under threat, and he had scarcely begun to realise his potential. Even knowing that his left leg would always be seven millimetres shorter than his right, he launched himself into a recovery programme, the rigour of which was almost beyond belief. Photographs depicted him in gruelling physio-therapy sessions, treading water with a huge weight around his neck. Those images inadvertently encapsulated the rest of his existence, for the 18 October 1995 fall never left Marco. The scarring left by the pins would be a constant reminder. For the rest of his life, he would lift his trouser leg to show them to others, and look at them himself. They were his stigmata and they set him apart from other cyclists. However his achievements would measure against those of other riders, his would have been achieved despite this injury.

As soon as he could be moved, Marco left the Turin CTO and was transferred to the San Rocco Ome Hospital in Brescia. An infection made a second operation necessary. The external axial fixator was not removed until 29 February 1996. Marco's protracted rehabilitation was managed, in part, by Fabrizio Borra, a physiotherapist with a studio at Bergamo. Like Pregnolato, Borra was to become one of Marco's closest friends. However, something in Marco inspired jealousy between his confidants, each of whom claimed to have helped him more, or to have been closer to him, than the last. Pregnolato mischievously recalls that Marco visited Borra's centre only rarely. During this period of re-education, Marco grew a moustache and a goatee beard. His father Paolo did the same.

7

A Glimpse Outside

(DECEMBER 1995–DECEMBER 1996)

Marco's passion was karaoke. He went to karaoke bars with friends and owned his own machine. During his convalescence he contacted a music journalist named Gabriele Ansaloni to ask how he could get to sing at the San Remo music festival. Ansaloni invited him to make his public debut as a singer on his television show *Roxy Bar* and, on 30 December 1995, introduced him as 'the greatest cyclist in Italy' at the start of *Roxy Bar*'s hundredth episode. Marco enthused about another guest, the rock star Vasco Rossi, known simply as Vasco. They had met before at a fund-raiser in Modena, and Marco, so shy of public recognition, had remarked to Roberto Pregnolato that Vasco wore sunglasses at night so that people would recognise him. Even so, Marco was a fan: he had followed Vasco's career from the beginning, and described him as 'one of Italy's greats'.

Pregnolato was sitting in the front row, holding Marco's crutches. Marco nervously scanned the audience as Ansaloni quoted his long history of injuries from a newspaper report: 'Ten years ago he fell, breaking his collarbone and right wrist. Since then he has suffered two skull injuries, a fractured toe in his left foot, two cracked ribs and a knee injury that needed eight stitches. In 1990, still amateur, he suffered a dislocated shoulder and two fractured vertebrae in the same fall . . .' Ansaloni broke off: 'Are you sure you're a cyclist, not a motorbike rider?'

Marco smiled: 'It's just as well you stopped there, because there have been lots of others. It's normal . . .'

Ansaloni interrupted: 'It's what? Normal?' And even before Marco could continue, the fascination he was beginning to exert over Italians who had no specific interest in cycling was clear: small, apparently childlike, his vulnerability and misfortune had become a source of national fascination.

'I think everyone encounters problems in his career,' Marco went on. 'Fortunately, I'm still here among friends, enjoying myself, so I consider myself a lucky man.' At this, the studio audience burst into applause.

Marco had chosen to sing '*Io vagabondo*' – 'I'm a Drifter' – by the rock group *I nomadi* ('The Nomads'). But he was suffering the same nerves that had affected his early television interviews, and anyway, the key was too low for him. He garbled the lyrics in verse one. The song should begin: 'One day I'll grow up, and fly into the sky of life.' Instead of '*volerò*' – 'I'll fly' – Marco sang '*Me n'andrò*', meaning 'I'll depart', or even 'I'll disappear into the sky of life.' It is the song of a perpetual child for whom adulthood means death. It was also dreadful, for which Marco excused himself: 'I've sung this song a hundred times with my friends, but singing in front of people . . .'

Vasco completed the sentence through clouds of cigarette smoke: '. . . takes a lot of courage.'

Marco consoled himself with a proverb: '"Sing, and it'll pass," as the old saying goes.'

Vasco agreed: 'It's the best way to face life.'

Ansaloni brought the item to a close: 'Marco, I won't ask you questions like will you be ready for the Giro? Or will you be ready for the Tour? One day, I'm sure, you'll be ready, and you'll win again, that's certain.' His words seemed to mean the opposite of what they said. With reason: his chances of singing at San Remo might have taken a knock, but, more seriously, it was still far from certain that Marco would ride again.

Some sense of Marco's inner life emerges from the people he identified with. Vasco Rossi was one of them. Like Marco, from Emilia-Romagna (Emilia, rather than Romagna), he had founded a local radio station and worked as a DJ for four years before recording two discs, neither successful, and, in 1979, being declared unfit to perform military service on the grounds of drug abuse. After the sudden death of his father the same year, Vasco had thrown himself into his musical career, deliberately rejecting the intellectualism and the political commitment of the popular *cantautori* in favour of provocative, often explicitly sexual heavy rock. Performing the song '*Sensazioni forti*' ('Strong Sensations') on Italian TV, in 1980, he had sung: 'I like you because you're dirty, because you're rude, because you're a woman, because you wear a skirt, because you're a bitch.' When the news magazine *Oggi* ('Today') branded him 'an unsightly, obtuse druggy, infirm on his feet', Vasco was made. His 1983 album *Bollicine* ('Bubbles') sold over a million copies, and the song '*Vita spericolata*' − 'Reckless Life' − became an anthem of Italian youth: 'I want a life of bad manners ... A life that doesn't give a damn about anything, yeah!' In April 1984 − when Marco was fourteen − Vasco was arrested for using and dealing drugs. He spent three weeks in jail.

Another figure whose presence in Marco's imagination reveals something of his inner world was Ambrogio Fogar, a famous adventurer whose escapades had often caused perplexity. In the 1960s he had set off to sail solo round the world. Crowds had gathered for his departure, and gathered, months later, for his return; no one was quite sure where he had been in the meantime. Another venture was Fogar's solo sled expedition to the North Pole. He returned in triumph, but too soon for it to be believable, and it was suggested that he had achieved his goal with air assistance. A volume debunked Fogar's travel writing as plagiarism. Yet Fogar ultimately proved his greatness after an accident during the 1992 Paris–Moscow–Peking rally left him tetraplegic and dependent on artificial respiration. Indomitable, he continued his adventures, strapped to a bed on the high seas. Marco was still on crutches when he visited Fogar's Milan apartment. Years later, as his life unravelled, he addressed Fogar a delirious note.

A third was Charly Gaul. A brilliant climber, often described (as Marco would be) as the greatest in cycling history, Gaul, from Luxembourg, had won the 1958 Tour de France and the 1959 Giro d'Italia. But his life after cycling had been a mess. When he was still riding, Gaul had married above his station, and his wife's family had cut them off. She had then fallen ill with an incurable tumour, and her death had turned Gaul to alcohol. He had opened a bar, drunk most of the stock, sold his trophies and medals to keep drinking and, when everything had gone, he had abandoned society for a house in the Luxembourg forest, not to face the world again for thirty-five years. A second relationship, and a daughter, helped him rebuild his life. Marco, still convalescing, heard Gaul was ill and had Andrea Agostini drive him through the night to Luxembourg to see him. In the event, Gaul outlived

Marco, but by 1996 he was still far from recovered, and Marco's visit helped him turn the corner. Gino Gaioli, the former vice-president of Giacobazzi's amateur team, knew both men well, and told me: 'They fascinated each other. Gaul's frame-size was exactly the same as Marco's, and both men hated publicity and journalists.' Marco's relationship with celebrity, however, had an ambivalence Gaul's lacked. Performing at San Remo would not have been for Charly Gaul.

Unable to train and perhaps still uncertain of his future, Marco met a nineteen-year-old Danish girl, Christine Jonsson, in a Cesenatico nightclub. Christine had been in Italy eight months; on leaving school she had travelled to Italy, where a friend earned a living as a *cubista* – an exotic dancer who performs on platforms or in raised cages (*cubi*) in nightclubs. Christine had joined her at Riccione, south of Rimini, then travelled across Italy, earning cash as a dancer, until she ended up back on the Adriatic coast, in Cesenatico. Marco's parents recall Christine in unflattering colours. Paolo told me: 'She was Nordic; her attitude to the family was different from ours in Romagna. She was cold, and she was with Marco because of self-interest.'

But the cynical woman in Paolo's description was in fact a nineteen-year-old girl who had survived and fled a difficult adolescence: Christine has spoken of an alcoholic mother and a father who adapted himself to constant emotional blackmail. By all accounts, when Christine met Marco, she had no idea who he was. Her Italian can't have been good: she visited Cesenatico library with Marco, looking for material to help her improve it. Tonina first met Christine in the *piadina* kiosk, as she recalls with undisguised repugnance: 'I can remember it as if it were yesterday. This woman got out of the car with him. I was struck by her look. Her hair was shaved at the sides, here at the back' – Tonina gesticulates above her ears, then towards the top of her head – 'and here, she had a crest dyed all different colours.' Even now, Tonina refuses to call it a Mohican. 'She had big yellow trousers, dirty all the way up to here, a jersey tied round here, *black nails*' – and, at this point, Tonina's expression suggests she might be about to throw up. 'He brought her into the kiosk and I gave her something to eat, and then, laughing, I asked Marco, "Where did you hook that? Where's she been with hands like that – scrubbing around in a waste-tip?"'

Three or four months after they met, Christine moved in with Marco and his parents at the flat on Viale dei Mille, and came face to face with the *mamma* complex of single Italian men. A survey conducted in the early nineties had found that a third of all married men saw their mothers every day, and another 27.5 per cent saw them more than once a week. Of unmarried Italian men, seven out of ten over the age of thirty-five still lived with their parents, and so did one in four of those who had divorced. But there was more to Tonina's hostility than maternal protectiveness; she had never trained herself to be parted from Marco and regarded his girlfriend as a threat. After resisting the tidal force of Tonina's claim to her son for six months, Christine moved out. To spend time with Marco, she gave up her nocturnal lifestyle and took a job in an ice-cream parlour.

Marco had already bought a plot of land at Sala, five kilometres inland from Cesenatico, and was having a large villa built with one section for himself and another for his parents. When it was built and there was a wall between her and Tonina, Christine moved in again. Tonina continues, 'I never understood her. When we came to live here,' she says, meaning the villa, 'I suffered because he went to live *that* side' – she gestures towards the wall that divides the villa. 'I can't say I liked the situation, but he was big and he wanted to be independent. I suffered even more when she came to live here, because she didn't do *anything* about *anything*. The sink was always full of dishes. She didn't do any household chores.'

What hurt most, perhaps, was not Christine's failure to become a traditional Romagnolo *mamma*, but her refusal even to aspire to Tonina's standards. Much later – and the chronology leaps four, five, six years in a sentence – came the suspicion that Christine was helping Marco to keep his self-destruction from his parents: 'When I saw the windows always closed, I had to ask her, "Is Marco OK? Where is he?" "Yes, yes, Marco's fine." But Marco wasn't fine. Maybe if I'd realised this before . . .' Suddenly, it isn't clear that we were ever really talking about their first meeting. What came before is now, in memory, contaminated with what came after, and her son's death is too opaque a filter to allow any sort of view beyond and into the past.

The villa at Sala was a curious piece of architecture. An undoored wall separated the area where Marco's parents would live from Marco's much larger space; and, more strikingly, Marco's bedroom was fitted with a security door. Many years later, Marco would lock himself in this secure space to feast on massive quantities of cocaine. At the time it was installed it perhaps suggested no more than Marco's generally paranoid temperament.

During Marco's recovery many teams approached him. The former Rinascita Ravenna rider, Giancarlo Ferretti, who was now the general manager of MG-Technogym, recalled: 'After the Milan–Turin accident, Marco let me know he would like to ride for me. We met three times, without reaching financial agreement. He rightly wanted a sum I couldn't guarantee, bearing in mind the budget I had at my disposal. I remember he asked me because, unlike everyone else who had contacted him, I didn't want to see the X-rays and put him through medical examinations to see if he could still be a champion. I smiled and said I had no doubt that he would be a great rider again.' Marco was looking for a *directeur sportif* prepared to give him blind, enduring faith, and a sponsor with a similar attitude and deep pockets. He was, very soon, to find them both.

Born at Russi, fifteen kilometres west of Ravenna, on 7 February 1921, Luciano Pezzi, known as Stano, served an apprenticeship as a mechanic, but became a professional cyclist. He was one of Fausto Coppi's great *domestiques*, not as a member of his trade team, but as part of the national team that competed in the Tour de France. When he stopped racing in 1959, he became a *directeur sportif* and directed Felice Gimondi to victory in the 1965 Tour de France. But Pezzi was also a businessman, trading in electrical goods with a partner named Romano Cenni. When Pezzi left Salvarani, for whom he had won the Tour with Gimondi, he managed a team sponsored by one of the companies he co-owned with Cenni, Germanvox-Wega. Later he managed a team sponsored by the other company they had founded, Mercatone Uno. Between these two ventures, in the 1970s, Pezzi lent a hand to Rinascita, in Ravenna, and helped make a legendary *directeur sportif* of Giancarlo Ferretti, who had ridden for Rinascita from 1960 to 1964.

In 1994 Pezzi, who was seventy-three, had telephoned Pino Roncucci: 'It was July or August. Pezzi knew Marco's contract finished at the end of the year, so he called me to ask if I'd help convince Marco to sign with him. I said, "I'll see." When Marco and his father asked me my opinion, I said, "With Carrera you've been happy and the team has helped you progress. Look at both offers, then decide, but don't throw money away, because money is money." In the end, Carrera came up with an offer that kept him there.'

Eight months later, after the Santarcángelo accident in May 1995, Pezzi visited Marco at home. Mercatone Uno wanted to return to cycling sponsorship, but only if Marco led the team. Pezzi's patient courting was finally consummated at the start of April 1996, when Marco agreed to ride for Mercatone Uno amid media reports that relations between Pantani, on one side, and Boifava and Chiappucci on the other, had broken down irretrievably.

By then Marco had returned to training. On 23 March 1996 he was filmed for the first time in the saddle since the previous October's collision, wearing Carrera colours. He told the television camera: 'I'd forgotten how beautiful it can be riding a bicycle.' One way or another, a draw as big as Marco had to be incorporated into the television coverage of the Giro: the broadcaster, Mediaset, got him in by having him record the theme tune in the spring. Thanks to his karaoke skills, Marco overshadowed his rivals at the Giro without turning a pedal.

During 1996 Marco's sponsor and nutritionist Marco Ceriani visited Rimini on a number of occasions, to promote his food supplements. At Rimini's Festival of Fitness, in June, Marco made a guest appearance. Ceriani and his staff stayed in a residence on the promenade with spacious rooms where they could discuss their work in comfort: the Hotel Residence Le Rose. Then, or on another occasion, Marco met Ceriani there. If the place lodged in his memory, it must have been with positive associations. He now knew his career had not ended on the Superga, and he was already in training, at the start of summer, among sponsors and admirers, looking to the future – on his way back.

In August, Marco made a first, quasi-competitive comeback at the Nove Colli, the amateur ride over the hardest climbs in the Cesenatico hinterland. Marco appeared on the starting line disguised as a woman, in a black wig and a tight, triathlon-style bodysuit. No one had reason to look too closely, presumably, until the race reached the first climbs and 'she' accelerated easily away from the accomplished amateurs in the leading group. Afterwards Marco joked in dialect with Savini: 'You didn't recognise me?' There were other, semi-formal events, where Marco no doubt received appearance money: a duathlon at Cesenatico, a circuit at Misano Adriatico, a criterium at Arezzo. Late in the season he returned to professional racing in Spain, finishing fifteenth in the Llodio Grand Prix, and riding the first two stages of the Vuelta a Burgos.

Marco's final appearance in Carrera colours took place in November 1996, at a charity event partly organised by Roberto Pregnolato to raise funds for victims of an earthquake that had struck Modena and Reggio-Emilia on 15 October. Each team of three consisted of a professional rider, an amateur and a journalist or other professional. Marco's threesome, completed by Pregnolato and Francesco Conconi, won the three-kilometre time trial.

In Marco's absence suspicions of endemic hormone-based doping in professional cycling had begun to circulate. The substance at the centre of the controversy was a genetically engineered 'copy' of erythro-poietin, the hormone that controls the production of red blood cells. At the Tour de Romandie, a stage race around Switzerland's French-speaking cantons, in May 1996, riders refused to co-operate with Canadian anti-doping researchers who had intended to collect blood for research purposes. Anonymity clauses were drafted, agreements were struck preventing the unauthorised use of the samples, and the project finally got under way at June's Tour of Switzerland, when seventy-seven riders gave blood for testing before stages four and seven. The Giro d'Italia, meanwhile, started in controversy. A confidential source had informed the Nucleo Antisofisticazione (NAS) – the branch of the Carabinieri responsible for investigating irregularities in medi-cines – that recombinant human erythropoietin, or r-EPO, and other, growth-hormone-based drugs were in widespread use at the Giro d'It-alia. The public prosecutor of the district of Arezzo, through which the Giro was due to pass, authorised the searching of the race and its entourage when, after the first three stages in Greece, the Giro crossed the Aegean to Brindisi. The searches never took place: the *Gazzetta dello Sport* got wind of them, published the rumours and forestalled the raids.

Under normal conditions EPO production is triggered in the kidney by mechanisms that detect falls in oxygen levels in the blood. It cir-culates in the blood until it encounters 'progenitor' cells in the bone cavities, equipped with special EPO-receptors. When they bind, each progenitor cell starts to divide, leading to the creation of dozens of 'precursor' cells and, eventually, hundreds of red blood cells. In the final two to three days before the immature red cells enter circulation, their EPO-receptors disappear and new receptors emerge, sensitive to the iron-transporting protein transferrin. Another protein, 'globin', attaches to four 'haem' molecules and forms haemoglobin (Hb). Each haem contains an iron molecule that can attach to an oxygen molecule every time the red blood cell visits the lungs, and then release it when it reaches the tissues. The red blood cells, then, behave like a fleet of heavy goods vehicles transporting fuel from the source in the lungs to the furnaces of the muscles.

The recombinant version of erythropoietin, r-EPO, is taken as a subcutaneous injection, which can be given by a paramedical assistant. In subjects with low levels of physiological EPO due to illness, the recombinant version adds to, or replaces, the real thing. In super-fit athletes, the deluge of r-EPO descends on the progenitor cells, which engender such quantities of red cells that the blood turns to a deep red, hi-tech gel capable of transporting massive quantities of oxygen, one of the ingredients of the muscle fuel ATP (adenosine triphosphate). You don't *need* oxygen to make ATP – it can be manufactured *anaerobically* – but without it, ATP production has an unwanted by-product that soon paralyses the muscle: lactic acid. After an anaerobic effort you're left with oxygen debt – the gasping as your muscles restock with ATP using oxygen taken from the air. Doping with r-EPO makes it possible to work much harder, for much longer, *without* oxygen debt and the lactic acid build-up in the muscles. It is as if entire fleets of extra trucks suddenly started rumbling down the arterial motorways carrying unprecedented loads to the furnaces, that now burn super hot.

Scientists first isolated EPO in 1977. The first patent for r-EPO was granted in 1984 and it entered the European pharmacopoeia in 1988. By 1994 r-EPO use was suspected to be widespread in cycling. Entire teams of riders suddenly seemed vastly superior to others: at the one-day Flèche Wallonne, three Gewiss-Ballan riders – Moreno Argentin, Giorgio Furlan and Marco's rival at the Giro Evgeni Berzin, attacked simultaneously and rode away to victory. Their team doctor, Dr Michele Ferrari, was one of Conconi's ex-pupils. Greg Lemond, the winner of the 1986, 1989 and 1990 Tours de France, believes it was in use as early as the 1991 Tour. He says, 'I remember in particular the stage from St Brieuc to Nantes. The average speed was 31 m.p.h. [50 k.p.h.] – and we stopped twice for trains. Something had changed in the peloton.' Lemond had started the race in top form, intending to win. Trying to maintain speeds even he found extraordinary, he fell ill, and had to abandon.

The great quantities of molecular oxygen r-EPO made available allowed doped athletes to make repeated anaerobic efforts – violent accelerations, for instance. Each time, the oxygen-rich blood-mix replenished the muscle's supplies of ATP. Average speeds improved dramatically. Cycling lost the dead moments when riders were recovering. It was great news for the viewer and, by day, great news for the athlete. The gel-like blood is great for high performance, but totally unsuited to rest, and at night, when the heartbeat slows, its sheer density becomes a liability. It is as if the fleets of heavy traffic rumbling down the motorway with fuel for the furnaces suddenly slowed to a crawl in a potentially catastrophic traffic snarl-up. The athlete has to set his heart-rate monitor to beep whenever his pulse drops below a certain level – say, thirty-five beats per minute. When it sounds, he has to wake up and exercise to coax his straining heart into action. For the cyclist, this means that after riding for a living all day, he rides on rollers at night to stay alive.

Administered correctly to the anaemic, r-EPO has no discernible side-effects or toxicity. In doped athletes, the body's oxygen-sensors respond by cutting the kidneys' EPO production altogether. It can take weeks to restart. There has been no research into the effects of the stress the thickened blood places on the heart, although the deaths of a number of Dutch athletes were attributed to r-EPO abuse in the early 1990s. The breakthrough came when doping doctors learnt to thicken the blood significantly while also keeping their patients alive, using aspirin to lubricate the gel-like blood.

Athletes and their doctors have striven to use medicines to enhance athletic performance since ancient times. Effective means probably date back no further than the advent of amphetamines in the Second World War, and then the development of anabolic steroids – queen among them the steroid Dianabol. However, with genetic engineering and the development of recombinant protein hormones that could not be distinguished from their naturally occurring analogues, the history of doping turned a new page. Yet there was little reputable research into the magnitude of the advantage r-EPO doping afforded until the end of the 1990s. There were basic ethical problems: the quantities taken by athletes far exceeded anything which would be allowable in a controlled experiment. However, papers published from June 2000 in the periodical *Haematologica* by Australian researchers looking for a method of detecting r-EPO hint at its value to trained athletes. In their first major experiment, the researchers divided their athletes – none a member of a national sports team, all signatories of statements of informed consent – into three groups. One group was injected with 50 U/kg of r-EPO three times a week for five weeks, 100 mg of iron once a week, and given sham iron tablets. A second group was given the same r-EPO therapy, sham iron injections, and genuine iron tablets. A third group was given placebo injections and tablets. The experiment was double-blind: neither those administering the therapy, nor those receiving it, were allowed to know which injections and tablets were genuine and which placebos.

By the third week of treatment two values were significantly greater in both r-EPO groups than in the placebo group. The first of these was haematocrit (Hct), a complex word that has become familiar to cyclists and cycling fans. In the nineteenth century a haematocrit was a standard glass tube with a uniform bore in which blood was centrifuged in order to 'pack' the red blood cells at one end. By expressing the height of the pack of red cells as a percentage of the total height of blood in the tube, a value originally known as 'volume of packed red cells', or VPRC, was produced. With time, the word 'haematocrit' has been transferred from the glass tube to the measurement itself. In the classic test, devised by the American physician Maxwell Wintrobe in 1929, platelets and white blood cells form bands just above the red cell column. They are not included in the measurement. As the Australian researchers treated their volunteers with r-EPO, they noted average haematocrit increases of six points; four weeks after the course of injections had been terminated, it remained three points above base levels.

The second parameter was haemoglobin (Hb), measured as g/dl of whole blood. Haematocrit and haemoglobin were still significantly elevated twenty-one days after the five-week therapy period had ended. The effects lasted long after the therapy period had terminated. At the end of treatment the r-EPO groups showed an increase in haemoglobin mass, a key indicator of oxygen delivery, of 7 to 12 per cent, and an improvement in maximum oxygen consumption of 6 to 7 per cent. These enhancements in the ability of the treated athletes to absorb and consume oxygen demonstrated the enormous advantage conferred by r-EPO therapy.

Six to 7 per cent, then, and upwards: it sounds containable, until you consider what a 6 per cent winning margin in the 10,000 metres, or a 7 per cent lead after 200 kilometres of a bike race, would mean. And the testers, it stands to reason, can't risk thickening a volunteer's blood to life-threatening levels, so they use relatively moderate amounts of r-EPO for relatively short periods. There are athletes prepared to pay any price for a shot at victory, so six or seven in the laboratory might become ten or twelve in the field.

In the winter of 1996, a sponsorship consultant named Giovanni Gibosini, who had worked with Marco's teams since the start of his professional career, invited him to San Severino, near Macerata in Le Marche. Gibosini, a booming-voiced, indefatigable coordinator of friends and events, told me: 'I followed Marco's career from the moment he turned professional to the end. He told me he liked hunting, so I invited him down, with some of the other riders, in December and January 1996,1997 and 1998.

'Marco was well dressed in hunting green. He was expert and meticulous with the rifle – a perfectionist. We used to make bets, and Marco would kill six or seven pheasants in an outing. Once, we were climbing, on foot. He was ten metres in front of me. A pheasant turned towards me, Marco spun round, and I remember diving for cover. From that day on, I was very careful. But he was an expert hunter, perhaps better than the hunters who went every day. It made him very happy. We'd walk for miles, then stop at the Trattoria da Marisa at Stigliano and he'd eat *cappellacci al tartufo'* – pasta filled with truffles – 'then we'd go back to hunting, until nightfall.'

Gibosini's memories are of the extrovert, relaxed Marco: 'I don't recall ever seeing him shy. Marco was always ready to laugh and joke. For nearly five years, at Morrovalle, I organised an annual celebration called "Every Year a Champion" and invited a hundred to a hundred and fifty people to eat. Chiappucci came once; Alberto Tomba came. Marco came after the Umbria earthquake' – on 27 September 1997 –

'and took presents to the children at Colfiorito di Foligno. In the evening we had a meal in his honour. Marco used to sleep with friends at the Hotel San Cristino in Morrovalle. He never asked for a lira; not even petrol money. Never.'

8

Climbing Back

(1997)

In 1997 Marco resumed racing with a new nickname – 'the Pirate' – and a new accessory – the bandana. His intimates are still squabbling over their provenance. Roberto Pregnolato says he invented the nickname during an interview, and his sister Oriella, an excellent seamstress, made the first bandana to protect Marco's newly shaven head from the cold. Tonina says Marco couldn't find cycling caps to fit his small head, so she suggested he try a handkerchief, giving birth to the bandana. The artist who designed Marco's 'Pirate' logo, Iuri Scarpellini, says he printed it on a square of cloth, which Marco wrapped around his head. The only certainty is that, by rarely using either a helmet or the 'official' bandanas, Marco managed to upset two different official suppliers.

His relationship with Christine changed, too. He was often away at races, where he needed solitude in order to concentrate. When he came home, he was often so tired he could do nothing but fall into bed. At his suggestion, Christine began to work in Tonina's *piadina* kiosk. Perhaps he was hoping to encourage peace between the two women in his life. Perhaps it was also a form of surveillance: the Pirate could be jealous.

Cycling had also changed. The blood samples taken at the 1996 Tour of Switzerland had an average haematocrit of 46.11 per cent. According to the textbooks, the figure lay within the 'normal' band: Todd and Sanford's monumental *Clinical Diagnosis and Management by Laboratory Methods* gives 40 to 54 per cent as normal; Wintrobe's standard *Clinical Haematology* gives 41 to 51. However, as an average for a population of seventy-seven, the figure was particularly high: data collected by the Scientific/Anti-doping Committee of the Italian Olympic Committee (CSAD) found that the average haematocrit among five hundred elite athletes was 42 per cent. The Tour of Switzerland data only added to suspicions of pervasive r-EPO abuse in professional cycling.

On 24 January 1997, in consultation with the riders, the anti-doping committee of cycling's world governing body, the Union Cycliste Internationale (UCI), reached a decision that would eventually prove decisive for Marco. Unable to detect r-EPO directly, it instituted mandatory blood testing and fixed a 50 per cent haematocrit threshold (47 per cent for women), above which riders would be suspended for fifteen days. After the suspension a second test would be carried out and, if the haematocrit had returned to within the threshold, the rider would be readmitted to racing. Officially, at least, it was called a health measure. No rider has ever spoken candidly of the thinking behind the limit, but there may have been genuine concern about the Russian roulette their doping doctors were forcing them into.

Two years later, at Madonna di Campiglio, Marco would fall foul of this legislation. Shell-shocked by his fall from grace, he would give an account of the meeting at which the riders ratified these decisions in a television interview with an Italian journalist, Gianni Minà:

MARCO I remember that we cyclists – no one else, neither the Federation, nor CONI, nor anyone else – we decided, of our own free will, to submit ourselves . . . I remember there was Bugno, there was Fondriest, there was Chiappucci . . . We decided to undergo these controls, to make ourselves available. And this created the blood tests.

MINÀ Before other sports?

MARCO Yes, and by our readiness we demonstrated the will to defeat doping. And protocols were decided, *perhaps* open to discussion, but, considering that we athletes are not scientists or biologists or people capable of deciding what values were healthy, some doctors decided that a haematocrit value over fifty was harmful, and we accepted this decision, obviously, as non-specialists in the sector.

Like Marco, Bugno, Fondriest and Chiappucci were medically supervised by staff of Francesco Conconi's Centre for Biomedical Studies at the University of Ferrara. Conconi told me the 50 per cent limit was his idea. In fact, Conconi canvassed for a much higher haematocrit threshold. On 24 June 1996 Conconi faxed the president of the UCI, Hein Verbruggen, and informed him:

> I believe that, while awaiting the possibility of identifying commercial EPO in the urine, the UCI could take other actions. The UCI could prearrange for professionals and amateurs selected at random at international races to take blood samples for the determination of haematocrit values. Such determination is quick, inexpensive and reliable. I also propose that subjects with haematocrit values exceeding a certain physiological limit (e.g. 54%) be considered at risk of thromboembolic accidents and, therefore, that they be temporarily excluded from competition. Such exclusion would be considered a health precaution and not a disqualification of the athlete.

Marco's season started in Spain. On 7 March he finished second in stage two of the Vuelta a Murcia. Soon after returning to Italy he drove to Milan to witness the renewal of the team's contract with Marco Ceriani. With him in the car was the Mercatone Uno team marketing manager Davide Cassani, an ex-rider born in Faenza, Romagna. Cassani telephoned Ceriani and told him: 'I'm in the car with Marco. We've passed Bologna – we'll be in Milan in a little over an hour.' As Ceriani tells it, they reached central Milan even more quickly. Milan is 210 kilometres from Bologna. Take off fifty to put them generously past Bologna, and the *average* speed, including a drastic reduction for the traffic in Milan, is 160 k.p.h. No wonder Cassani was, in Ceriani's words, 'Happy, but a little light-headed from the speed of the journey.'

Marco began a dizzying round of races which, it was planned, would steer him towards his best form for the start of the Giro d'Italia. In Belgium on 15 April, Marco took a moment to reflect in public on his hopes for the coming Giro: 'My great worry is that it isn't fully healed. My left leg is still 10 per cent weaker. After extreme exertions, it is more and more lactic. I'll never again be what I was in 1994. I was younger then. No one will every know what I might have achieved without the accident.' Nonetheless, over the following week he achieved his finest ever results in the hilliest of the northern classics: fifth in Flèche Wallonne on 16 April, and eighth in Liège–Bastogne–Liège on the twentieth. Back in Italy, no doubt riding within himself to recover from those performances, he finished thirty-sixth in the five-day Giro del Trentino.

Before the 1997 Giro began, Claudio Chiappucci, Marco's former room-mate and training partner, gave a blood sample for the new haematocrit test. The result was an immediate two-week suspension, which disqualified him from participating in the Giro d'Italia. He announced his intention to sue the *Gazzetta dello Sport* and the FCI. He was the second patient of Conconi's Centre for Biomedical Studies to be suspended that spring for haematocrit over 50 per cent: earlier in the season Mauro Santaromita, riding for MG-Technogym, had been expelled from the Paris–Nice stage race.

The 1997 Giro d'Italia started in Venice. The sprinter Mario Cipollini won stages one and two. Stage three was a short, explosive individual time-trial from Santarcángelo to San Marino, on roads Marco knew well. The winner of the 1996 Giro, a Russian named Pavel Tonkov, won the stage convincingly, completing the course twenty-one seconds faster than Evgeni Berzin. Marco lost time and a team-mate, who fell at speed and was forced to abandon the race. Two days later, Tonkov won again, after a 215 kilometre stage ending on the Terminillo. Marco finished third in the stage, and was given the same time as the Russian. He confided to Giuseppe Martinelli, his *directeur sportif*, that his form would improve before the high mountain stages on the final week.

Then, on 24 May, Marco was among a handful of riders who fell on the descent of the Valico del Chiunzi, about twenty kilometres from the stage finish at Cava de' Tirreni. Roberto Conti remembers: 'We were in a group of about thirty, and I was saying to Marco, "These are dangerous roads. Let's ride either at the front, or at the back, because if there's a fall ..." I'd hardly finished speaking when a cat sprang into Enrico Zaina's wheel, bringing him and the riders behind him down.'

Marcello Siboni adds: 'Marco rarely fell, but when he did, it was serious.' He finished the stage with his team-mates' help, but the fall had caused serious bruising to his left thigh and he abandoned the race. Scans suggested a badly torn muscle: Pregnolato argued that a vein created a shadow in the image, and that the injury was treatable. To his and Marco's frustration, his opinion was brushed off, and Marco returned home to nurse his frustration in an empty house. According to Pregnolato, Marco's degree of dependence on his mother, or a substitute maternal figure, was so great that he would go without breakfast if there was no one to prepare it for him. If Tonina and Christine were at work, Marco would go hungry – despite being an expert chef, when he could be bothered to cook.

Out of action until mid-June, Marco started the Tour of Switzerland on 17 June, only to abandon. Nonetheless, he was strong enough to finish tenth in the GP Larciano on 29 June, which doubled as the Italian national championship. On 5 July Marco started the Tour de France for the first time in two years. The race had two outstanding favourites, and they were team-mates: the winner of the 1996 Tour, Bjarne Riis, a Dane who had once been treated at Conconi's Centre for Biomedical Studies, and Jan Ullrich, Riis's runner-up in 1996, aged just twenty-two. Ullrich was another Induráin: extraordinarily powerful in the time trials, and fast, but with no change of pace, in the mountains. However, Induráin had been a gentle man whose face, when relaxed, loosened into a mild, herbivorous smile. He had matured slowly and, even at his greatest, it was clear that the years would erode him. Ullrich was a product of the East German sports system; he was steely, muscular, and had ten, perhaps fifteen years ahead of him. When Ullrich rode away from Marco on the climb of the Arcalis in the Pyrenees, the succession to Induráin seemed to have been decided. Marco finished second, one minute eight seconds behind his unstoppable rival. On 18 July Ullrich won again, a fifty-five-kilometre individual time trial starting and ending at St Étienne. His margin of victory was remarkable: three minutes five seconds. Not even Induráin himself had achieved such crushing superiority in a Tour de France time trial. Marco, exceeding himself, finished fifth in the stage.

The following day, the riders faced a 203 kilometre stage from St Étienne to Alpe d'Huez. His team-mate Mario Traversoni told me: 'Me, Pellicioli and Siboni set the pace by riding the first 180 kilometres at forty kilometres an hour.' As Marco's *domestiques* dropped away, Ullrich took over in person, forcing the pace on the first hairpins of the climb. Marco followed for five kilometres, then attacked. Ullrich, Virenque and Riis gave chase. With sixteen of the twenty-one hairpins still to ride, Riis surrendered. With twelve to go, Virenque dropped back. Soon afterwards Ullrich too dropped away from Marco's wheel. Seven kilometres from the summit Marco led Ullrich by twenty-two seconds. On the finish line, he clenched his fists and shouted in joy: *this* was the comeback, the return from the fall on 18 October 1995. Marco's time for the climb, thirty-seven minutes thirty-five seconds, a new record, was little short of astonishing at the end of such a long stage. Ullrich crossed the line second, forty-seven seconds after Marco, who now lay third overall.

The following day, from Le Bourg d'Oisans at the foot of Alpe d'Huez to the Courchevel ski station, Ullrich took his revenge. Richard Virenque, second overall but facing a deficit of more than six minutes, attacked early on the stage. Ullrich, relayed by Riis, closed in on him, and the two men finished together at Courchevel. To Virenque, the stage; to Ullrich, even greater security for his overall lead. Marco, suffering from bronchitis, lost three minutes six seconds, despite finishing sixth on the stage.

But the next day Marco attacked on the Col de Joux Plane, dived into the abyss on the other side and finished alone at Morzine after a daring descent. Ullrich and Virenque finished together, one minute seventeen seconds later. There was no changing the general classification now, and on 27 July Marco rode into Paris third in the Tour, for the second time of his career.

9
Pink, At Last!
(END 1997–JULY 1998)

At the end of 1997 the team expanded. Mercatone Uno's *directeurs sportifs* Giuseppe Martinelli and Alessandro Giannelli were joined by Orlando Maini, a former rider who had directed Marco at the 1992 amateur Giro d'Italia. Davide Cassani left the team to pursue his career as a television cycling analyst. A new marketing manager arrived: Alessandro Samek, who had a law degree and market-research experience but was new to cycling. He found Marco an enigma: 'Immediately after races,' he said, 'I can steer him where I want. He becomes completely acquiescent; he'll go to the anti-doping control or the pressroom, and he'll do anything I say without a second glance. But it doesn't last; as soon as he comes around, he recoils from those around him and it becomes difficult even to ask what he wants for dinner. I find it almost impossible to work with him.'

A number of episodes in spring 1998 suggest that Marco's outspokenness was beginning to border on the reckless. In an interview he joked that the only food supplements he used were his mothers *piadine*; this upset Marco Ceriani, the team's food supplement supplier and co-sponsor. At an official reception at Ferrari, he said he preferred Porsches. It was a reaction to the increased commercialism that surrounded him. Ceriani's food supplement firm could no longer use Marco's image alone in advertising: this right had been reserved for major sponsors paying hefty fees. When Ceriani complained, Marco lowered his eyes and nodded, but did nothing to reduce the price.

The enlarged team's first training camp took place at Terracina, south of Rome, in December 1997. Mario Traversoni was there, and recalls the disorienting speed with which Marco could reach unbeatable shape: 'I already had ten thousand kilometres in my legs, because I had to be strong for the first part of the season. I was ready to race. Marco hadn't touched his bike for two, maybe three months. We went on a long training ride, two abreast, but Marco eventually got fed up and, on the next climb, he accelerated. I was the only one who could stay with him, until about three hundred metres from the top, when he accelerated again and I had to let him go.'

The team flew to Valencia, Spain, for their second training camp, and the first races of the season. By the first week of March, Marco was in scintillating form, winning stage four of the Vuelta a Murcia and finishing third in GC. On 10 April he abandoned the Tour of the Basque Country in torrential rain. He didn't want to jeopardise his Giro. Later in the month Ceriani was giving a talk about food supplements at Davide Cassani's cycling school in Cervia, on the Adriatic coast eight and a half kilometres north of Cesenatico, when Marco walked in, to the joy of the students. At the end of April he finished fourth in the Giro del Trentino: perfect form for the start of the Giro d'Italia.

Between Marco and victory in the 1998 Giro d'Italia stood the Swiss rider Alex Zülle. Second in the 1995 Tour de France, he had won the 1996 and 1997 Vueltas a España. He rode like Induráin and Ullrich, defending in the mountains, then gaining time in the time trials. He dominated the Prologue, a six-kilometre time trial through Nice. Pavel Tonkov, the 1996 winner, restricted his losses to twenty-three seconds. Marco lost thirty-nine.

Stages one to five explored the coastline along the Ligurian and the Tyrrhenian Seas – those subsections of the greater Mediterranean – from Nice in France to Frascati, south of Rome. The sprinters' teams combined to ensure mass sprints decided them all. The time gaps separating Zülle, Tonkov and Marco remained stable until stage six, from Maddaloni, in the outskirts of Caserta, south to Lago Laceno. Marco threw down his cap before riding off alone. Zülle's response was decisive: he quickly bridged the gap to Marco, then, incredibly, like Ullrich on the Arcalis the year before, he began to ride away. After a short descent the final kilometres were on the flat. Zülle, the consummate time-trial rider, drove down into the pedals with irresistible strength, adding to his lead. Marco finished fourth and lay sixth overall.

Across the peninsula to Lecce, then up the Adriatic coast to Macerata, the top positions and times in GC remained identical. Stage eleven led to San Marino. Marco, with an acceleration on the final climb, dropped Tonkov and Zülle, took second place in the stage and leapfrogged Tonkov into fourth place overall, fifty-one seconds behind Zülle.

In the final ten kilometres of the stage to Schio, twenty-three kilometres north of Vicenza, Marco attacked in a rainstorm, only to fall twice on the treacherous final descent. Michele Bartoli won the stage, sixteen seconds ahead of Tonkov and Marco, and twenty-four ahead of Zülle. Noè, second on the stage, took the pink jersey. Marco now lay ninth, one second ahead of Tonkov and still forty-three seconds behind Zülle.

Stage fourteen took Marco to his favourite terrain. Low on the final climb to Piancavallo, with thirteen kilometres still to ride, he headed out into space. Tonkov tried to match each change of pace, against the advice of his team director Giuseppe Saronni. Zülle sensibly took the climb at his own pace and recorded the fastest time for the final six kilometres. Marco won the stage, but his margin of victory, thirteen seconds, was narrow considering the energy he had spent, and Zülle won back the pink jersey. It was Marco's first Giro stage win since Aprica, four years earlier, yet his reaction was irritation. 'The game is clear: I attack. The others react, or try to. It takes courage and willpower to ride the way I ride.' He complained the Giro was designed for Zülle. Looking back, Orlando Maini recalls: 'But when he began to complain, to get nervous, it always suggested he was coming into form.' Marco was now second overall, twenty-two seconds behind Zülle. Tonkov was third, eighteen seconds behind Marco.

The following day was the individual time trial. Alfredo Martini, the Italian national coach, reflected: 'The rising mountain roads no longer allow the differences of past days ... A time trial like today's around Trieste can reshape GC more than a mountain stage.' To prove Martini's point, Zülle rode the time trial of his life. The route up the Trieste panhandle was not quite undulating, but nor was it a mirror-flat course for specialists. Yet Zülle covered the forty kilometres at an average speed of 53.771 k.p.h. – faster than the fastest Prologue time ever recorded! Marco, who had started three minutes before Zülle, saw his main rival fly past him and into the distance. Marco lost three minutes twenty-six seconds and finished the stage twenty-fourth. Third on the stage was Tonkov, two minutes faster than Marco. Marco commented: 'It went as I expected. The time trial was too fast; when I saw the route, I was surprised, in the negative sense. I can't develop those speeds. By now, it's Zülle's Giro, unless he has a crisis. I'll attack him – that much is certain; but if he resists, there's not much I can do.'

It wasn't even the last time trial of the race: the penultimate stage held thirty-four more kilometres against the clock. Before then, two transitional stages sandwiched three mountain stages. If it was even conceivable that Marco could claw back the four minutes that separated him from Zülle, and add maybe two more as a cushion against the final time trial, there was still Tonkov – a superlative climber and consistently faster against the clock than Marco, who blamed his seemingly inevitable defeat on the race route: 'A Giro d'Italia with so few climbs can't be a Giro for Pantani. These days, the great stage races are designed for time-trial specialists.' For Marco, cycling was a performance, and failure to provide a show was failure, full stop. 'I'm the only one who tried to create a spectacle on every climb, no matter how small. I don't think Gotti and the others did the same.' Providing a show, of course, meant, not calculated moves with tiny margins of error, but extravagant demonstrations of superiority.

On 2 June stage seventeen took the Giro to Val Gardena. Roberto Conti remembers: 'He should have attacked on the Marmolada, but he'd never ridden it; and it's hard, very hard. I said to him, "When are you going to attack?" He said, "When does the Marmolada start?" I said, "We've already ridden half of it."' Marco accelerated, taking Giuseppe Guerini with him. Working together, they built up a lead of over two minutes on Pavel Tonkov. Zülle, meanwhile, suffered a loss of form and conceded four minutes thirty-seven to Marco and Guerini. Marco allowed Guerini to win the stage. The greater prize – the pink jersey of the overall leader – was his, for the first time of his career. The first ever Giro leader with an earring and a nose stud led Tonkov by thirty seconds, and Zülle by thirty-one.

Barring time trials, stage eighteen, from Selva Val Gardena to Pampeago, was the shortest of the Giro. Pavel Tonkov used it to fight back, winning the stage. Marco's lead at the start of stage nineteen was as frail as tissue paper. The final climb, Montecampione, was nineteen kilometres: close on an hour of relentless climbing. It was very hot that day: as the riders approached it, the asphalt beneath their tyres quivered with nervous, reflected heat.

After something over seven hours in the saddle, Marco throws down his bandana, and darts out of the group with dazing swiftness. For a second you see only speed. Then the bald head and pink jersey. Three lengths behind, catching the slight vacuum created as Marco's body drifts through space, Pavel Tonkov. Both are out of the saddle. Marco's cadence is fast and powerful: he spins the pedals at over eighty-six revs per minute. Tonkov's is scarcely inferior; he turns a heavier gear fives times less per minute. Where Marco's back is straight, Tonkov's is arched in more evident pain. Twenty-five seconds later, on a sharp left-hand bend, they sit. The camera-bike tracks them at 25.7 k.p.h. on a gradient of between 8 and 9 per cent. On the lower slopes they work together, shadow-players taking turns at the front, building up a lead, making sure the Giro will be decided between them.

Then the duel begins. Like a creature equipped by evolution with a single, deadly weapon, Marco begins his series of terse, stinging accelerations. Each time a metre, two metres open between them. Tonkov, more slowly, closes the gap. And each time Marco takes a half-look behind him. Afterwards he told Fabrizio Borra: 'I didn't want to turn around and give him the impression that I couldn't go on. So, after each acceleration, I looked for his shadow to see if he was still there. He always was.'

Climbing at speed makes remarkable demands of both the physique and the imagination. In Marco's case, the imaginative component was formalised into a ritual that started when he threw down his bandana. It was an irrevocable gesture, signalling total commitment to the attack. It was also a challenge, as much to himself as to his rivals. Ivan Gotti once commented: 'Normally riders are afraid of the climbs. Marco wasn't afraid.' Once the attack had started, Marco began to shed everything that was surplus to his very specific requirements. His sensitivity to the force of gravity was heightened to the ultimate degree. On Montecampione this meant not just water bottles and his sunglasses but the diamond stud he wore in his nose, which he jettisoned into the trees. Later he would say he could feel it weighing him down. He would also say he heard his grandfather Sotero speaking to him on the climb; it was he who told him to get rid of the stud. It must be there still, buried in the mulch.

Then, on a left-hand curve 2.8 kilometres from the finish line, Marco delivers another cutting acceleration. Tonkov is immediately out of the saddle. The gap reaches two lengths. Tonkov fights his way back and is on Marco's wheel when Marco, who is still standing on the pedals, accelerates again. Suddenly Tonkov is no longer there. Afterwards Tonkov would say he could no longer feel his hands and feet. 'I had to stop. I lost his slipstream. I couldn't go on.' Marco told Romano Cenni he could taste blood. His performance on Montecampione was close to self-mutilation.

Seven hundred metres from the finish line, the TV camera on the inside of the final right-hand bend, looking down the hill, picks Marco up over two hundred metres from the line and follows him for fifty metres, a fifteen-second close-up, grainy, pallid in the late-afternoon light. A car and motorbike, diffused and ghostlike, pass between the camera and Marco, emerging out of the gloom. The image cuts to another camera, tight on him as he swings round into the finishing straight, a five-second flash before the live, wide shot of the stage finish: Marco, framed between ecstatic fans on either side, and the finish-line scaffolding adorned with race sponsors' logos; largest, and centrally, the *Gazzetta dello Sport*, surrounded by branding for iced tea, shower gel, telephone services.

Then we see it again in the super-slow-motion replay; the five seconds between the moment Marco appeared in the closing straight and the moment he crossed the finish line are extruded to fifteen strung-out seconds. The image frames his head and little else, revealing details invisible in real time and at standard resolution: a drop of sweat that falls from his chin as he makes the bend, the gaping jaw and crumpled forehead and lines beneath the eyes that deepen as Marco wrings still more speed from the mountain. As he rides towards victory in the Giro d'Italia, Marco pushes himself so deeply into the pain of physical exertion that the gaucheness he has always shown before the camera dissolves, and – this must be the instant he crosses the line – he begins to rise out of his agony. The torso lifts to vertical, the arms spread out into a crucifix position, the eyelids descend, and Marco's face, altered by the darkness he has seen in his apnoea, lifts towards the light.

Super slo-mo was just one of the technologies that helped make an icon of Marco. Helicopter images of improving stability and definition had begun to dramatise the difference in scale between the immensity of the landscape and the smallness of the riders. A fantasy of a cycling David taking on the Goliath of the mountains was given stunning visible form. Thanks to these improved aerial pictures, the calm that descends on the peloton as it approaches the foot of the hardest climbs, temporarily neutralising the race, suddenly took on a new tension. Super slo-mo, by contrast, heightened the drama of another, sometimes drameless moment: the instant the stage winner crossed the finish line. Previous slow-motion technology had been limited to playing back standard twenty-five frames per second television tape at eight frames per second. The new super slo-mo cameras filmed at seventy-five, then two hundred, then more frames per second; played back at twenty-five frames per second, the tight image and the illusion of high resolution lodged tenaciously in the memory. Before super slo-mo, finish-line celebrations were generally forgettable. With the crowd dispersed along the roadside and team-mates often far behind them, stage winners had no clear target at which to aim their joy. In any case, the win was followed by an uncertain wait before the meaning and extent of the time gain became clear. In a sprint stage decided by thousandths of a second, the closing metres captured by the super-slo-mo camera are full of sporting meaning. Not so in the mountains, where stages can be won by minutes. In any case, the super-slo-mo image normally frames out the finish line and the clock, and shows nothing of the winner's work rate, muscular toil, or the relative positions of the riders that yield the race result. In the super-slo-mo era, finish-line images combined the iconic traits of still photography with the dreamy quality of slow motion moving pictures, and became unforgettable: Lance Armstrong's celebration at Limoges in 1995, three days after the death of his team-mate Fabio Casartelli, could have been choreographed for super slo-mo, and was immortalised by it.

The super slo-mo sequence of Marco on Montecampione allows us to look intently into his face the way a mother might her baby, or lovers at the moment their affection is first reciprocated, although in this case the intimacy is non-reciprocal. It reveals involuntary micro-expressions normally too fast to recognise, expressions otherwise invisible, that their subject never chose to reveal – a *truth*, we are tempted to imagine, and one not directly related to the outcome of the race. The stretched-out images may mimic, at some level, biological mechanisms that seem to slow time, and are triggered during life-threatening experiences, when we are charged with adrenaline. We may be fooled into connecting the images with a trauma-induced insight into the fragility of our lives. Full of longing and mortality, these pictures explain why Marco's epic duel with Tonkov spoke to a generation. They marked a new phase in his relationship with the Italian public.

At the start of the final time trial, a rolling, thirty-four-kilometre course from Mendrisio to Lugano in Italian-speaking Switzerland, Marco's lead over Tonkov was one minute twenty-eight seconds. There was every reason to believe it would not be enough. Tonkov set off three minutes before Marco. Orlando Maini drove behind Tonkov and relayed split times every three kilometres back to Martinelli. After the first three kilometres Marco had actually gained three seconds on Tonkov. After nine kilometres he had gained six. Twelve kilometres into the race he was ten seconds up on Tonkov. Then, at the halfway point, the picture changed. Tonkov had regained eight seconds. Marco, it seemed, had started too quickly. If he collapsed now, the Giro would fall to Tonkov. With thirteen kilometres to go Tonkov was now three seconds ahead of Marco. There was still time.

Then their times evened out. Somehow, Marco matched Tonkov's rhythm. Ten kilometres from the finish line their times were identical. The realisation must have broken Tonkov's resolve. Over the final ten kilometres Marco pared back five seconds. The dog that ran across the road in front of Marco some four kilometres from the finish line represented the only remaining threat to his Giro victory. Marco managed to avoid it; Martinelli's car was not so nimble. But Marco did not relent and finished the stage with an overall lead of one minute thirty-three seconds over Tonkov. There was no news of the dog, but Marco had won the Giro d'Italia.

That evening, Marco managed to upset the team's official supplier of heart-rate monitors by telling reporters he hadn't used one during the time trial: 'I trusted my feelings.' His team-mates Massimo Podenzana and Marco Velo were second and fourth, respectively, in the stage. However, the dominant performance by Marco's team was marred by the suspension of his team-mate Riccardo Forconi before the time trial could begin, after a mandatory blood test revealed a haematocrit level over the 50 per cent threshold.

The televised post-stage analysis, *Il processo alla tappa* – 'The Trial of the Stage' – far from being forensic, showed an inarticulacy verging on the imbecilic. There was vague talk of elevated levels of red blood cells, but no attempt to connect them with performance enhancement, legal or illegal. Over images of the team hotel of another suspended rider, Nicola Miceli, Nino Farolfi's voice-over observed: 'No one's here. No one wants to speak' – as if both could be true – 'even if it's not doping, but a precautionary measure . . .' Then, over the arrival at the Mercatone Uno team hotel of Roberto Conti and Marcello Siboni – no rebuffed attempt to speak to them made the cut – it continued: 'Forconi is still here. He'll leave perhaps tonight. He's watching the duel which has already started in his room. The joy of Marco's success will cancel out, at least for a moment, his sadness.' No potential connection was conjectured between the dominance of Forconi's team-mates, and his suspension. Giuseppe Martinelli appeared in the studio, but when the *Corriere della Sera* journalist Gianfranco Josti, also guesting, posed a question about the Forconi case, he was interrupted by the compere, Claudio Ferretti: 'No, Josti, I've made an agreement with Martinelli. He's here only for Pantani. For the sake of correctness, I must respect the promise I've made. I understand the demands of journalists, but this is my personal promise to Martinelli.'

Paolo Savoldelli, tenth in GC, was also present. He was asked his feelings about being woken so early. No complaints, he said: 'I wasn't woken up brusquely. I was already awake when they arrived. The doctor called for me at eight fifteen.' Not so Pantani. Another guest, Beppe Conti, leapt to his defence: 'Eight fifteen is an acceptable time. The pink jersey was called at six forty-five.' Claudio Ferretti observed: 'He's first in the classification. They obviously started with him.' What Martinelli and – presumably – no one else present knew was that Marco's blood test that morning had revealed a haematocrit of 49.3 per cent. He had been called at 6.30 a.m. to present himself for testing at or before 7 a.m. He had appeared at 7.17 a.m. No action had been taken.

The *Processo alla tappa* journalists represented not a niche newspaper or magazine, pleading for access to teams and riders, but the principal domestic broadcaster. This gave them considerable power, yet they allowed the opportunity to confront the issue of r-EPO doping to pass them by.

For the final stage everyone in the Mercatone Uno team – riders, mechanics, *soigneurs* – shaved their heads in deference to Marco. After the final procession into Milan, Marco dedicated his win to Luciano Pezzi, now gravely ill. On 26 June Luciano Pezzi died. There had been few figures of authority in Marco's life: Amaducci, of course, and perhaps Savini; Roncucci, certainly and, naturally, his grandfather Sotero and his substitute grandfather Guerrino Ciani. Pezzi had filled the spaces they had vacated. Now, just when Marco was achieving his greatest success, the last of his sobering influences had gone. Years later, Romano Cenni would comment: 'If Luciano hadn't died, if he'd only been able to be near Marco a few more years, things would have turned out differently.' For Roberto Conti, 'Luciano was like a father to Marco.'

Loss had always accompanied victory in Marco's life. His first ever race win had preceded the death of Guerrino Ciani, and his greatest win as an amateur, the 1992 amateur Giro d'Italia, had preceded Sotero's demise. Pezzi's passing was the price Marco had to pay for this, his greatest triumph.

Pezzi had wanted Marco to ride the Tour; to honour his memory Marco decided to go. But if he was to be in France for 5 July, there would be little time to reflect on Pezzi's death and little opportunity for closure. Riding the 1998 Tour de France would be Marco's way of mourning his mentor's passing.

In Italy a craze for bandanas began: official Mercatone Uno bandanas were sold in huge numbers. Then, shortly after the Giro had finished, Candido Cannavò, the director of the *Gazzetta dello Sport*, attended a meeting at the Vatican. Cannavò had come to ask for permission to start the 2000 Giro, the Giro of the Jubilee, at the Vatican. Cannavò feared he might have to preface his appeal by explaining the Giro and its importance; instead, Monsignor Crescenzio Sepe, the general secretary of the Vatican – a man who met daily with Pope John Paul II – was well informed about Marco and the Giro. The Monsignor's father, passionate about the sport, had called him every day during the Giro to update him on Marco's progress. After their meeting Cannavò called Castellano, the director of the Giro d'Italia, with a request: 'If you can get a pink jersey, signed by Pantani, to Monsignor Sepe in two days, the project will be up and running.' The jersey arrived the next day.

10

Double Vision

(JUNE–AUGUST 1998)

On his triumphant return to Cesenatico after the Giro, Marco met Christine at the kiosk. It was late, but they posed for photographers. Then Marco stepped inside to change. But instead of returning to Christine he climbed out of a rear window and disappeared into the nightlife of the Riviera with a bunch of male friends. At ten the next morning he was in Christine's arms again, posing on the Port Canal for more press photographs. It was remarkable their relationship lasted as long as it did.

In 1992 and 1993, when Induráin had completed the Giro–Tour double, there had been just twenty days between the end of the Giro and the start of the Tour. In 1998 the finals of the FIFA World Cup started in France on 10 June. In order not to clash with the final in Paris on 12 July, the start of the Tour de France had been given to Dublin and pushed back to 11 July. This gave Marco thirty-four days in which to party, and then start training for the Tour.

The outstanding favourite to win the 1998 Tour de France, Jan Ullrich, meanwhile, was dieting frantically. After winning the 1997 Tour as a twenty-three-year-old, Ullrich had been garlanded with prizes. According to a survey reported in *Der Spiegel*, many believed Ullrich would develop into the greatest sportsman of all time. Yet the fêting had also exercised his other great talent: for gaining weight. His attempts to reach race fitness in the spring had descended into a vicious circle of self-starvation, illness and more weight gain. In November and December 1997 he had suffered a heavy cold, followed by a painful inflammation of the auditory canal. In January, a high temperature had interrupted his Tour of Mallorca. He had abandoned the Tirreno–Adriatico in March after stage one due to an allergy, and the Tour of the Basque Country after three stages with bronchitis. Yet he turned up at the Tour looking miraculously lean.

At 2.25 p.m. local time on Saturday 11 July a little-known French rider, Denis Leproux, inaugurated the 1998 Tour de France by speeding away from the starting ramp in Dublin, a 5.6 kilometre sprint ahead of him. By then, however, the event was mired in scandal.

Three days earlier, at 6 a.m. on Wednesday 8 July, French customs officers at Neuville-en-Ferrain (North), two hundred metres from the Belgian border, had stopped the first vehicle of the day, a Fiat Marea emblazoned with the logos of Festina, the world number one team with three Tour contenders in Richard Virenque (second in 1997), Alex Zülle and Laurent Dufaux. They soon learned that the driver, a 53-year-old *soigneur* named Willy Voet, had been driving without a licence since a speeding offence in January 1998. The officers decided to search the vehicle; what they found was to transform the relationship between cycling and its public. There were eighty-two vials of Saizen (somatropin, or human growth hormone), sixty capsules of Pantestone (epitestosterone), 248 vials of physiological serum, eight pre-filled syringes containing hepatitis-A vaccine, two boxes of thirty Hyperlipen tablets (to lower the amount of fat in the blood), four further doses of somatropin, four ampoules of Synacthene (to increase the rate at which corticoid hormones are secreted by the adrenal gland) and two vials of amphetamine. There were also 234 doses of recombinant human erythropoietin, made up of ten pre-filled syringes of Eprex 4000, 139 vials of NeoRecormon powder and eighty-five vials of Erantin 2000 powder.

This mobile pharmacy had been due at Calais to sail for Dublin on the 11.45 a.m. ferry. Instead Voet spent the day at Neuville with specialist interrogators and the night in a police cell in Lille with drunks and drug addicts. Only on Friday 10 July, after Voet had been brought before Judge Patrick Keil at Lille's Palace of Justice and charged with importing contraband and the unauthorised circulation of prohibited goods, did news of his arrest reach Dublin. Only on Saturday, Prologue day, through a statement by Tour director Jean-Marie Leblanc, did Voet's arrest become common knowledge. Looking back seven years later, the French rider Philippe Gaumont gave an insight into the riders' perception of the burgeoning storm: after Voet's arrest, the riders were initially nonchalant: 'We almost wanted to say: "Oh, yes? So what?" ... the world of cycling was convinced it was untouchable.' And Gaumont was French: how much less significant Willy Voet's arrest must have seemed to Marco, an Italian on an Italian team, competing, for the moment at least, in Ireland, where his results might even be read as an expression of his remoteness, both from the Tour and from the upheaval to come.

Marco hadn't even bothered to preview the 5.6 kilometre route of the Prologue through Dublin and completed the course forty-eight seconds slower than the winner, Chris Boardman, and forty-three seconds slower than Jan Ullrich – to whom he conceded more than seven seconds a kilometre. Of 189 starters Marco lay 181st.

Stages one and two – through the Dublin countryside, then from Enniscorthy to Cork – were won by sprinters. By the morning of 14 July the Tour was back in France; through Brittany and the Vendée, Marco stayed buried in the peloton, surrounded by team-mates, including Riccardo Forconi, included in the team despite his failed blood test on 6 June. Ullrich always finished towards the front of the peloton; Marco always lagged behind.

Then, at five o'clock in the evening of 15 July, after stage four, Bruno Roussel, the Festina *directeur sportif*, and his team doctor Erik Rijckaert were taken in for questioning, and gendarmes raided the Festina hotel at Cholet. As Marco languished at the bottom of the general classification, gaining and losing nothing on Ullrich, Rijckaert and Roussel faced police interrogation. It took two days to break them down: at 5.30 p.m. on the evening of 16 July Rijckaert began his confession. At 9.20 p.m. Roussel did the same. At 8.30 p.m. the following evening, a statement issued by Roussel's lawyer, M. Thibault de Montbrial, outside the Palace of Justice in Lille, changed cycling for ever: 'Bruno Roussel has explained to investigators, who were in possession of the facts, the conditions under which the supply of doping products to the riders was managed collectively between the Festina team directors, doctors, *soigneurs* and riders. The purpose was to optimise performance under strict medical control, in order to avoid the individual and untrained provision of the riders in conditions likely to endanger their health, as might have been the case in the past.'

De Montbrial then telephoned Roussel's Festina colleague Michel Gros, who was with the riders at the Tour, to inform them of his confession and allow the team to avoid the shame of disqualification by withdrawing voluntarily. Richard Virenque, the team leader and one of France's most cherished sportsmen, refused point-blank. Jean-Marie Leblanc, the Tour de France race director, issued a statement announcing the race organisers' decision to exclude Festina from the race. The following morning Virenque telephoned Leblanc to inform him that the riders didn't accept their exclusion and would start the individual time trial. Leblanc arranged to meet them in Chez Gillou café at Corrèze railway station. The meeting lasted an hour. Virenque came out from the meeting in tears. Philippe Gaumont recalls: 'Finally we understood something serious was taking place.'

On 18 July, in the shadow of Thibault de Montbrial's statement and Virenque's exclusion, the first long time trial of the Tour, fifty-eight kilometres from Meyrignac to Corrèze, began. The Tour had been designed as a time-trial sandwich; on its penultimate day, 1 August, the riders would face another fifty-two-kilometre time trial. By then, of course, the powerful *rouleurs* would have spent days lugging their heavy carcasses over the mountains. All the same, on 1 August Marco was likely to lose a large proportion of whatever he lost now.

Marco's forty-three-second disadvantage to Ullrich had remained unchanged through the first six days of racing. The Corrèze time trial was an important indicator of his form. Marco started at 11.36. One hour, nineteen minutes and forty-six seconds later he crossed the finish line. 'I didn't give it everything,' he said. 'I'd have paid a high price in the days to come, and my form isn't good.'

Three and a half hours later Jan Ullrich started. The lungs bulged in his back accentuated by his body-suit design – pink arms and shoulders, white back, with the three stripes of the brand slicing across the shoulders – which gave him the look of an enormous beetle. He scuttled voraciously into the race lead. Marco's time was the thirty-third fastest, four minutes twenty-one seconds slower than Ullrich's. He now lay forty-third, five minutes four seconds down.

The Festina expulsion had removed Zülle, Virenque and Dufaux, but between Ullrich and Marco there still lay five more potential Tour winners: Laurent Jalabert, the winner of the 1995 Tour of Spain, fourth; in ninth place, Abraham Olano, second in the 1995 Tour of Spain, third in the 1996 Giro d'Italia, and fourth in the 1997 Tour de France; twelfth, Evgeny Berzin, the winner of the 1994 Giro d'Italia; fourteenth, the Frenchman Luc Leblanc, sixth in the 1996 Tour de France; and twentieth, Bjarne Riis, Ullrich's team-mate and the winner of the 1996 Tour. There were also two outsiders of great potential: Bobby Julich, second, and Michael Boogerd, sixteenth. Already there seemed to be nothing but stage wins in it for Marco.

After the time trial he made an appeal to the press: 'The police and the judges will deal with the Festina affair. I hope the journalists will talk about the race.' He wasn't to know that a second scandal had broken earlier in the day. On 4 March customs officers near Reims searching a TVM team vehicle driven by two mechanics had stumbled on a cache similar to that found in Voet's car. The products, including 104 pre-filled syringes of r-EPO, had been seized, the mechanics released and no further action taken. The revelations of the Festina affair had led magistrates to reopen the TVM file, eroding the reputation of the Tour – and cycling – still further.

As the Tour finally approached the Pyrenees, Marco announced: 'Everyone is asking me to save the Tour, to do something. They've finally realised that without Festina the race risks becoming less spectacular. A race with Ullrich in the yellow jersey all the way to Paris would be boring, but try telling the organisers, who repeatedly favour the *rouleurs* and forget the mountains. I don't ask much – just more balance.' Marco remained five minutes twenty-four seconds behind Jan Ullrich until the morning of stage ten. For two nights, Marco complained, he had hardly slept. In the heat of stage nine, he said, he had tried to take on too much liquid. But with the Italian Prime Minister Romano Prodi, an ardent cycling fan, in one of the guest cars, Marco hoped for a stage win.

Marco's heavy head and stomach, and thick fog on the Col d'Aubisque, the Col du Soulor and the towering Col du Tourmalet, led him to ride the first 168 kilometres with caution. On the Col d'Aspin the fog cleared. Then the race reached the final climb of the day, the Col de Peyresourde. At 9.8 kilometres, the Peyresourde was not the most formidable of climbs, although the gradient touched 10 per cent. But it started after 168 kilometres, fifty of them climbing. Besides, Marco had ridden within himself, and Ullrich, his younger rival, was beginning to make mistakes. Halfway up the Peyresourde, the German had taken the front himself, thinning out the group with a sustained display of pace. Then, with one and a half kilometres remaining to the col of the Peyresourde, Marco flew out of the group and was alone. Only Vasseur and

Massi were ahead of him. Vasseur was caught before the col. Marco crossed alone, then lowered himself over his rear wheel for the descent. Forty-two seconds passed. Then Ullrich reached the col, shepherded over by Riis. Fifteen and a half kilometres remained, most of them descending.

Massi was too far ahead to catch. Marco finished the stage alone, but the chase by Ullrich, Robin, Leblanc, Boogerd, Julich and Escartin kept his lead down to twenty-three seconds. Much later, Marco commented: 'If I'd won that stage, I'd have gone home.' But at the time, he complained: 'I want to win the Tour, but I have to be realistic. I've looked at the mountains, and there aren't prohibitive climbs. There are plenty of big-name mountains, but you can ride them on the big chain ring. There's very little terrain for us climbers.' It was either gamesmanship or chronic self-doubt, as his performances soon demonstrated: the following day, early ascents of the Col de Monte, the Col du Portet-d'Aspet, the Col de la Core and the Col de Port stripped away the weak and after 154 kilometres Marco reached the foot of the climb up to Plateau de Beille with Ullrich, Jalabert, Julich, Piepoli, Boogerd, Escartín and Rinero. There were 15.7 kilometres still to ride, and the chase was markedly faster than its quarry, Roland Meier, a Swiss rider on the Cofidis team, who led by two minutes forty seconds. Then, low on the Plateau de Beille, Ullrich punctured. He radioed his team car but had to stop and allow the peloton to pass. By the time the wheel was replaced, Ullrich had begun to panic. He slalomed around riders up to the leading group at high speed, dropping all his team-mates who had stopped to wait for him – including Bjarne Riis. Marco hadn't noticed Ullrich's problem, and was about to attack when his team-mate Roberto Conti told him to wait. Marco allowed Ullrich to settle into the group, then he launched a vicious acceleration. The group was left standing. Suddenly Ullrich was spent; he had regained the group too fast and tender red bulges now formed beneath his eyes, like a man deprived of sleep. Marco's pace was stunning: he rode straight past the lone attacker, Roland Meier, and celebrated on the finish line with a clap of the hands. Meier finished one minute twenty-six seconds later, followed by Julich, Boogerd, Escartín and Rinero. Forced to let them go, Ullrich gave them seven seconds and Marco one minute forty. If this was Ullrich's bad day, he had got away with it and retained the lead in the new GC, with Julich second. Jalabert and Marco were now on equal time, three minutes one second behind Ullrich. The stage win had placed Marco in contention. Ullrich could not afford another off day.

Pantani told the press later: 'My main goal on entering the Tour was to win this stage because it was the most beautiful climb in the race. Now I hope to win the other stage finishing in altitude, next week in Les Deux Alpes. As for overall victory, I think I lost too much energy in winning the Giro.'

Ullrich's team-mates began to grumble. It was far more difficult than in previous years to control the peloton, and Marco's team was making no contribution. Roberto Conti recalls: 'The following morning, one of Ullrich's *domestiques* came up to me and said, "You're sly, you lot! Two minutes today, two minutes tomorrow. Bit by bit, you'll be getting close to the jersey, and you'll have to start helping to control the race." Diplomatically I told him we were only interested in stage wins. "The Tour doesn't interest us."' That was soon to change.

The following day, a rest day at Tarascon-sur-Ariège, was one of great activity involving the police, journalists, and the UCI. Police raided the TVM team hotel in Pamiers, and took in the former Dutch champion Cees Priem and his Russian colleague Dr Andrei Mikhailov, respectively *directeur sportif* and team doctor of TVM, for questioning. Priem and Mikhailov were then taken to Foix, awaiting transfer to Reims. A spokesman for the investigation confirmed doping products had been found at the hotel.

On rest-day evening the teams received a UCI circular informing them that it had decided to bring forward the introduction of a new health monitoring scheme from the start of the 1999 season to the following Saturday. Later still the France 2 news bulletin included an item on doping at the Tour. Reporters were shown rummaging through waste bags left by the Italian team Asics. They found a number of empty medicine boxes.

The following morning a number of riders, Jalabert and Marco among them, led a sit-down strike. After two hours a group of riders was persuaded to start the stage, led by Ullrich's team-mate Bjarne Riis. Telekom was among the first teams to break the strike. Other, smaller groups followed, six and ten minutes behind the leading group. Marco was among the last to resume racing. At the head of the race, Leblanc persuaded the leading group to slow down. With a favourable wind, the stragglers eventually caught them. Into a headwind the 1998 Tour might have ended there and then. As it was, Marco, Jalabert and Luc Leblanc, rebel leaders and dangerous riders, now regarded Ullrich as a strike-breaker. A coalition between them could cost the German the Tour.

The Pyrenees had restored part, at least, of Marco's lost time. Even so, on the morning of stage fifteen – the final uphill finish of the Tour, from the town of Grenoble to the ski station of Les Deux Alpes – Marco needed three more minutes on Ullrich just to draw level. And there was still the second long time trial to come. He'd conceded four minutes twenty-one seconds to Ullrich in the first; he could expect to do the same again. In short, to have any chance of overall victory, Marco had one stage on which to gain seven and a half minutes on the reigning Tour de France champion. Seven and a half minutes! An insane margin: an *unthinkable* one in modern cycling. Marco naturally accepted the challenge.

A bitter morning broke over the Alpine capital of Grenoble that 27 July. The riders huddled in the drizzle and rolled south to the outlying village of Vizille. There they met the gorge of the Romanche river, where nine riders joined an early breakaway. Ullrich had his team-mates raise the pace. This, perhaps, was his first mistake, made even before the race turned north to begin, almost imperceptibly – the incline starts at less than one in a hundred – the thirty-one-kilometre climb to the Col de la Croix de Fer.

As the first skirmishes brewed, hailstones fell and the gradient gathered: 7 per cent, then 8; 9 per cent, then 10. Bobby Julich tested his rivals. His Cofidis team-mate Christophe Rinero followed, then launched his own attack. Much of the peloton was swaddled in ungainly rain capes when a Mapei rider, Daniele Nardello, slipped off the asphalt into the rock and gravel on the inside of the road. Marco fell with him. If time stood still for a moment, the moment quickly passed: Marco remounted and quickly caught the tail of the group.

Rinero sped first across the Croix de Fer. At the village of Saint-Michel-de-Maurienne, after 111 kilometres, the two-phase ascent of the pass up the Col du Galibier's north side began with the 11.5 kilometre step up to the Col du Télégraph. Five chasers made it on to Rinero's wheel. Behind, the first of the riders around Ullrich to attack was Luc Leblanc. Again Ullrich unleashed his team-mates – Aldag, Bolts and Riis – to shadow the offensive. The quickened pace put Laurent Jalabert in trouble. That left one rider less between Marco and the yellow jersey.

Rinero's leading group crossed the brow of Télégraph. After a shallow five-kilometre respite they reached the foot of the great seventeen-kilometre pass up to the Col du Galibier, at 2,646 metres. Three minutes behind them the great Spanish climber José Maria Jiménez darted out of Ullrich's group. Then Leblanc launched a second attack. Escartín and Boogerd followed – and suddenly Ullrich was isolated, leading the chase in person. Aldag, Bolts and Riis, asked to ride too fast too soon, had gone. So powerful was the German's surge that only Bobby Julich went with him. A gap opened behind them. Marco led the rest of the group up to Julich's wheel, and the riders coalesced into a group of six: Leblanc, Escartín, Boogerd, Ullrich, Julich and Marco.

The next attack was Escartín's; he left Leblanc at the head of the group, riding at a hellish speed with Ullrich and Pantani on his wheel. Tell-tale gaps began to open and close; Julich bridged the space behind Marco. The drizzle on the TV camera lens distorted the riders into abstract patterns, illuminated by the dazzle of the motorbike headlights. And Ullrich, perhaps intending to intimidate, was chasing down every attack, squandering energy – playing into Marco's hands.

At this breakneck pace, the hours pass into the twilight of the late afternoon. There is a long right-hand curve. At 3.56 p.m., 4.5 kilometres from the brow of the Galibier, as the knot of riders drifts out towards the centre of the curve, Marco grimaces and flashes away, a brush-stroke of saturated colour in the grey. Ullrich moves instinctively into his slipstream, but there is no attempt to respond. He doesn't even climb out of the saddle. Marco's acceleration lasts ten seconds, then he looks long over his right shoulder to gauge the destruction: it has the flavour of a test, something scripted. But only Leblanc has responded. Marco seems to wait, allowing Leblanc to approach, only to dart away again, leaving the Frenchman with no answer.

Only five riders precede him. Escartín is the first to suffer from Marco's speed. Marco pulls alongside, perhaps slightly behind him, and slows to Escartín's pace. He pauses a second, two seconds, then slips ahead, offering the Spaniard his slipstream. Far behind, Ullrich is being dropped by a number of riders. Two and a half kilometres later Escartín is a distant memory. By the time Ullrich reaches the same spot, one minute thirteen seconds will have passed.

Marco lifts his protective glasses onto his forehead. Ahead of him,

Rinero has attacked, dropping Serrano, Massi and Jimenez. As Marco responds, a fan runs alongside him, eager, reckless in these treacherous conditions. Marco lifts a hand from the handlebars, turns his head, shouts into the fan's face and speeds furiously away. As he approaches Rinero, Marco, sitting, outpaces Rinero, who is standing on the pedals. Marco rises too and lets loose another bruising acceleration. Rinero sprints, matching him for a matter of seconds, but then is forced to relent. Ulllrich passes the sign marking one kilometre to the brow of the Galibier two minutes four seconds after Marco.

With motorbikes ahead and behind, Marco rides between crowds that engulf the road. On the brow of the Galibier, Orlando Maini waits with a rain cape and *bidon*: 'When I saw him appear, I was afraid I wouldn't be able to give him the cape, because I felt more tired than him. He was doing something great, something important, and I felt unable to do it. The moment I passed him the cape I felt liberated. I couldn't make an error.' The Spaniard José Maria Jimenez crosses the col ten seconds after Marco, who calmly pulls up at the side of the road. With frozen fingers Marco needs help to don the cape. Jimenez rides past. Even in the storm of his attack Marco is absolutely sure of every move.

Two minutes forty-nine seconds after Marco, Ullrich passes the col of the Galibier in an eight-man group. He hasn't eaten for ten kilometres – his second mistake – and now, soaked to the skin in gelid drizzle, he decides not to put his rain cape on for the glissade down the south side of the Galibier.

After 164 kilometres, with twenty-five kilometres remaining on the stage, Marco's lead is down to two minutes eleven seconds, owing to the stop to put on his cape. At 4.50 p.m., his advantage equals and surpasses his three-minute-one-second deficit. In the valley, Marco works together with Escartín and Rinero, only to dart away from them at the foot of Les Deux Alpes. Behind him, Ullrich's errors of judgement are compounded by bad luck: on the pinball alley descent from the Galibier, he punctures. He lumbers down the sodden track, plunging towards evening through spaces Marco vacated four minutes ago, and sees Bobby Julich narrowly avoid skidding into the void. On the corridor leading to the start of the final climb, Ullrich powers across to the chasing group, but on the lower slopes of Les Deux Alpes great, dark pouches again form beneath his eyes. The disparity is growing.

Marco enters the final straight of the greatest stage of his life and a great drop of water – rain and sweat – falls from his beard. His eyes are clenched shut in pain, his mouth is an open grimace – and then, the moment of transfiguration as he rises out of his agony, spreads his arms into a crucifix position and, eyes closed, raises his face skywards, an extraordinary image, permeated with longing and mortality.

Five kilometres down the mountainside, Ullrich, climbing listlessly among riders moving at different times and speeds, was disconnected from the commotion of riders swarming upwards. Over the following eight minutes fifty-seven seconds, twenty-two filthy, sodden riders crossed the line. Ullrich was not among them. Then he appeared, shepherded home by his team-mates Bölts and Riis. In his autobiography, *Ganz oder Gar Nichts* – 'All or Nothing' – Ullrich admitted that only the extra week before the Tour had allowed him to get his weight down to seventy-one kilos – less, in fact, than in 1997, but still not the sixty-seven or sixty-eight he was aiming for. Ullrich had started the Tour starving himself in order to lose those extra three or four kilos. His collapse on the Galibier was due to the pressure of Marco's attack, but it was also the logical outcome of too-rapid weight loss.

Marco, meanwhile, in the yellow jersey for the first time of his career, had become a global sporting icon. He led Ullrich by four seconds short of six minutes. Julich and Escartín lay second and third in GC, but they were of no concern to Marco. After the stage he was massaged for an hour, then went for treatment by his physiotherapist, Fabrizio Borra. He ate with the team and with Felice Gimondi. There was a brief toast, but no party or euphoria. Martinelli commented: 'It isn't our style.' In Italy, the television news on Rai3, the Tour broadcaster, opened with Marco's win. Romano Prodi, the President of Italy, was on an important diplomatic mission to Turkey; his visit was relegated to second place in the news schedule. 'Quite right,' he commented. 'His exploit is unique.'

The following day, halfway up the twenty-kilometre Col de la Madeleine, Ullrich attacked from the peloton. Escartín and Piepoli tried to follow, but soon found the oxygen debt unbearable. Only Marco could sustain his rival's pace. During the fifteen kilometres of the descent, Marco offered Ullrich his slipstream no more than twice, pulling alongside and exchanging words with the German. Only then, as the road levelled out for the final flat kilometres into Albertville, did Marco begin to share the load-bearing position into the wind with his rival.

They began to stretch their advantage over Julich and Escartín, cementing Marco's advantage before the final time trial, and making sure of Ullrich's second place overall.

The sprint for the stage victory was a highly ambiguous affair. Marco was ahead. As Ullrich pulled out of his slipstream, Marco glanced to his right, sat up and, incredibly, stopped pedalling. Ullrich drew alongside, gaining a few inches, and Marco stood again on the pedals, turning his feet but coasting. Then he resumed the sprint, looking across twice more at Ullrich, before the German threw his bike at the line – with none of the urgency of a truly contested sprint – and took the stage. By coasting for two full seconds during the sprint, Marco gifted Ullrich the stage.

At 3.35 p.m. on the afternoon of 27 July, twenty minutes before Marco's attack on the Galibier, Ceer Priem and Dr Andrei Mikhailov of TVM had completed the ten-hour journey from their hotel at Foix in south-west France, to the Palace of Justice in Reims, in the Champagne region. At 9 p.m. Priem's interview with the examining magistrate began. At midnight he was charged with transporting toxic substances and storing dangerous goods. At 3 a.m. the following morning Mikhailov was charged with violations of France's 1989 anti-doping legislation.

Meanwhile police raided the TVM hotel in Albertville. At 6.05 p.m. that evening twenty-one police approached the Hotel Million. Some went to the second floor, where the team was roomed; others searched team vehicles outside. The assistant *directeur sportif*, Hendrik Redant, and a mechanic were taken in for questioning and at 9 p.m. the six TVM riders still on the Tour were escorted to the Pierre de Coubertin Hospital for blood and hair tests. They reached their hotel beds close to midnight. The following morning the newspaper *Le Figaro* announced imminent police raids on other Tour de France teams. The riders refused to compete, riding thirty-two kilometres as a group, before grinding to a halt. Laurent Jalabert led the strike, tearing off his *dossard* before the television cameras. Marco, then the rest of the peloton, followed. Jalabert then became the first to abandon the Tour in protest, taking his team, ONCE, with him. As the ONCE riders rode slowly towards their hotel at Aix-les-Bains, the rest of the peloton resumed the stage, still refusing to compete or to ride at racing pace. At the feed zone two more teams, Banesto and Riso Scotti, abandoned en masse. A quarrel broke out between Bjarne Riis, of Ullrich's Telekom team, and Leblanc of Polti.

Riis believed the riders should come to an agreement with the Tour organisers to allow the event to reach Paris; Leblanc was in favour of stopping the race. Leblanc then abandoned.

His namesake, Tour director Jean-Marie Leblanc, assured Riis that he would do everything in his power to prevent further police raids. Soon afterwards, Leblanc informed the teams via race radio that he had obtained a guarantee that riders would in future be questioned in their hotel rooms, and that the high-profile police raids would cease. The stage continued, reaching Aix-les-Bains at 7.30 p.m.: four TVM riders were allowed to cross the finish line ahead of the group.

Leblanc had been bluffing: the evening saw police raids on the hotels housing Casino (the team of Rodolfo Massi, the leader in the mountains competition), La Française des Jeux, and ONCE, whose *directeur sportif*, Manolo Saiz, reportedly asked them why they hadn't done the same to the teams in the recent FIFA World Cup.

The following day's stage from Aix-les-Bains to Neuchâtel in Switzerland started with just 103 riders. Ten metres across the border into Switzerland, Jeroen Blijlevens of TVM abandoned the Tour. His teammate Bart Voskamp said on Dutch radio at the finish: 'I'm relieved to be on neutral territory.' The stage ended in a mass sprint. The positions at the top of GC were unaltered. TVM did not start stage nineteen, apparently fearing arrest at any moment.

Ullrich won the final fifty-two-kilometre time trial. Second was Bobby Julich, sixty-one seconds behind. Then came Marco. 'I'm not a specialist, but I couldn't lose the yellow jersey.' The Tour de France was his. At the team hotel the entire team staff dived fully dressed into the pool. Everyone's left ear was pierced and adorned with a pirate earring. A Paris hairdresser was hired to bleach everyone's hair, then tint it yellow. The blue bleaching foam burned everyone's scalp.

In a post-race live link with Cesenatico, Marco's conversation with Christine was stilted. Christine garbled: 'I haven't much to say. He knows, and we all know: it's time he came home.' Marco added: 'She's shy like me. We'll talk in private.' Once more he dedicated his victory to Luciano Pezzi. Alluding to his aversion to pressure, he thanked his team and those around him, 'because the climate around me helped me keep a clear mind'. After the broadcast someone asked Marco about his immediate plans. 'I'll buy a box of Viagra and lock myself inside with Christine.'

On 5 August he met Giorgio Squinzi, the owner of the adhesives company Mapei and the sponsor of the biggest-budget team in cycling. Press reports said Marco demanded five million euros a year – twice Miguel Induráin's wages at his peak. Three days later it was reported that Marco had decided to stay at Mercatone Uno, 'in Luciano Pezzi's memory'.

With business out of the way Marco celebrated, and on 13 August 1998 Cesenatico became the centre of Italy for a day: 'Pantani Day'. Some say fifty thousand thronged to the town centre to celebrate. Every *piadina* stand in town contributed free *piadine* to the celebration – *almost* every stand; Marco's parents were alone in abstaining. And, shortly before 10 p.m. in Piazza Andrea Costa, the Italian Prime Minister Romano Prodi stood beside Marco and spoke to the crowds: 'In these times when there is so much talk of doping, Marco is liked because he embodies the ideal of the healthy, true sportsman who wins by his exertions on his bike. I'm grateful to him in the name of Italy.' Where Berlusconi had AC Milan, Prodi had Pantani, medically assisted by Prodi's close personal friend Francesco Conconi.

11

Domination

Marco's success gave him almost boundless celebrity. His mobile telephone number rang almost incessantly. This, and a flood of commercial offers, made it essential for Marco to find a manager. He raised the subject with Giovanni Gibosini: 'I said, "Thanks, but I'm not good enough to be your manager. You need a specialist agency."' Marco spoke to Alberto Tomba, whose sister Alessia referred him to Manuela Ronchi, a hard-headed, ambitious young businesswoman and a notoriously tough negotiator. A graduate in languages and literature, Ronchi had gone into sports management and image consultancy because, in her words, 'in the presence of champions, there was an immediate empathy, not an evaluation based on an acquired theory'. She managed the image of the motorcyclist Max Biaggi, the billiards champion Gustavo Zito, the volleyball player Maurizio Cacciatore, the yachtsman Giovanni Soldini, and a number of footballers. She had no interest in cycling; but she could hardly have avoided Marco, who was now as famous as a sportsman could be. 'If he'd gone into politics, Marco would have won the elections,' she told me. 'It was an ambition of mine, after my experience with Max Biaggi, to have another personality of his stature.' Her other clients were leading figures in their sports, 'but if you're not number one in one of the principal sports, you don't have the same visibility'. Then, as if answering her prayers, one of Marco's people called.

Ronchi met Marco for the first time at the Bar dei Marinai along the Port Canal in Cesenatico. They agreed that Ronchi would research the market and estimate the value of Marco's image. At their next meeting Ronchi showed Marco her findings. He thought them over, then contacted her. They met again, and Marco joined the Action Agency over a plate of fish. In October 2004 Ronchi would publish a memoir of her

130

relationship with Marco, which started in August 1998 and ended on Monday 9 February 2004, five days before his death. Ronchi became Marco's rock; when his life began to fall apart, she was always there for him. But Marco lived in many worlds, and if Ronchi's intimate portrayal is an important document, it could also be seen as a self-serving interpretation of those years. No account of the final half-decade of Marco's life can ignore it, even if the truth it purports to relate is far from the whole truth.

Marco's liaison with Ronchi was marked by the usual streak of subversion. Outside education and the social services, women were still under-represented in Italian professional life. Sports management must have been one of the most retrograde sectors, with cycling as steadfast a bastion of male chauvinism as boxing. And Ronchi spoke no Romagnolo: she was an outsider, like most of the women in Marco's life – except for *the* woman of his life, his mother. Ronchi called Romano Cenni at Mercatone Uno and arranged to meet. What remained of the family atmosphere and the regional identity within the team was about to dissolve.

On 3 September Mercatone Uno hosted an end-of-season dinner at the Hotel Monte del Re in Dozza, a few kilometres west of Imola. A Renaissance monastery set proudly on a hilltop, the Monte del Re sits in an ancient cypress grove. Marco, of course, was the centre of attention, but he had always hated official functions. In a corner of the garden he told Marco Ceriani he'd lost his privacy. He complained of being photographed and obstructed, of people hiding behind his car, jumping out of the undergrowth, stalking his family, rummaging through his garbage, ambushing him instead of arranging an appointment. Celebrity was certainly a by-product of his success and Marco undoubtedly found the relative loss of privacy almost impossible to take. Tonina told me, 'He couldn't bear the sensation of being observed.' Ronchi recalls: 'At times, when we were in the car, he would say, "Great: I'm in an anonymous car where I can observe others and they can't observe me."' Yet Marco could also court publicity, and he was wealthy enough to do something about many of these problems, the way other celebrities did – by employing security staff, for example, or restricting access to media outlets who made unauthorised approaches.

He made another guest appearance later that month at the massive cycling trade show in Milan. The team's marketing manager, Alessandro

Samek, had distributed Marco's time in proportion to each sponsor's financial commitment. At each stand, Marco was required to sign great piles of pink and yellow jerseys and bandanas for company directors and suppliers. To Ceriani he described the ordeal as 'torture'. Ceriani had been informed that Marco would arrive at his stand between ten fifteen and ten thirty, and stay five minutes. He was asked not to detain him. In the event Marco stood and chatted and refused to move on at his minders' behest, sabotaging Samek's schedule.

In November, after the route of the following year's Tour de France was announced, Marco was disparaging. By including 118 kilometres of time trials, he protested, 'I'd say they've done everything possible to prevent me winning again.' He refused to commit himself to riding the Tour and started a feud with the organisers that would carry on for years. A week later he attended the presentation of the 1999 Giro d'Italia, whose planners had perhaps gone too far in Marco's favour. He complained about them, too, but this time with humour: 'With five uphill mountain finishes and only two time trials, perhaps they've exaggerated!'

Then he flew to the Seychelles with Christine.

On 4 February Ceriani visited the team training camp at Terracina, and found Marco tense and more closed than in the past. He seemed no longer to trust even those close to him. Marco told him the relentless commotion was unbearable. He said he had thrown away his mobile phone and wasn't planning to replace it. He felt like a hostage, or like a hunted animal – a simile rich in significance for a man who dedicated hours to stalking quarry with a rifle in his hand. Ceriani felt the idea obsessed him.

On 14 February the 1999 Mercatone Uno team was unveiled at the Hotel Monte del Re. Marco and team appeared on the mocked-up bridge of a pirate ship, hammed up with eyepatches, gold chains and earrings. His physiotherapist Fabrizio Borra commented: 'Nineteen ninety-eight was Marco's first year without a fall since 1994. In 1999 you'll see the *real* Pantani.' Marco was then interviewed for the flagship television football programme.

Alessandro Samek was no longer with the team. Instead Marco had brought in his old friend Andrea Agostini as press officer. Yet the team had never been less a band of friends. Ceriani protested that the old

Mercatone family had been converted into a money-making machine. The sponsorship contracts had doubled and, with access to the riders severely restricted, Ceriani was ready to bail out. Only daily calls from Martinelli, he says, convinced him to stay, and even then he had to threaten not to sign the contract to get approval to use a publicity photograph in which Marco was prominent.

Mario Traversoni was no longer part of the team: 'I was out of contract, but I'd won races, and I'd finished the Tour pulling in the hills, even though I'm a sprinter. I went on holiday, confident the contract would be ready when I got back. Instead, by then, I was out of the team. Marco wanted me — he didn't want to change anything — but there were too many people around Marco who were only there because they had an interest in him. Martinelli suddenly thought he was the world's greatest *directeur sportif*. The old group who'd been around Marco began to break up, and mine was the first arse to get the boot.'

Marco's season, this year as every year, started in Spain. He dominated the Vuelta a Murcia with a stage win, fourth place in stage two, the mountains title, and the final classification. On the last day of February he finished eighth in the Clásica de Almeria. Back in Italy, Davide Cassani goaded him over the Milan–San Remo, a race he believed Marco could one day win, and bet him a house he wouldn't win the 1999 edition. On 20 March, on the climb of the Cipressa, Marco flickered away from the peloton before lunging down towards the sea. That he was caught, and finished only sixty-second, didn't concern him. All he wanted was to get Cassani worried.

There was another win on 23 March, in stage two of the Setmana Catalana. Then, despite his enormous strength, it is as if he renounced victory until the Giro. At the Tour of the Basque Country from 5 to 9 April he was fourth in stage two, third in stage three, and eighth overall. At the Giro del Trentino on 26 to 29 April he was fourth in stage two, second in stage three, and third overall. On 2 May he was seventeenth in the Giro di Toscana, around Arezzo.

That second stage of the Giro del Trentino had been won by Marco's team-mate Riccardo Forconi, who had been suspended from the 1998 Giro after failing a UCI blood test. On 17 May an interview given by the *directeur sportif* of Amore e Vita, Ivano Fanini, prompted the Italian Association of Professional Cyclists to issue a statement of censure.

Fanini alleged that Marco had tested high for haematocrit during the 1998 Giro but that the result had been attributed to his team-mate Roberto Forconi, who accepted the suspension. It hardly seemed plausible: in order to switch their results, two, perhaps three medical doctors on the testing team would have had to be corrupted, and probably a UCI official too. On the other hand, Forconi had ridden for Fanini's team for five years before joining Mercatone Uno for the 1998 season, and Fanini knew him extremely well. Mercatone Uno announced that they would sue, although they never did.

This was not the only distraction. With a manager employed to realise his market potential, Marco's face was soon everywhere: news kiosks, sports shops, Mercatone Uno stores, Citroën showrooms, as well as branches of the Romagna Bank, which were handing out yellow jerseys to new clients opening a current account. As the Giro approached, Marco had to take part in television advertisements for Citroën, leering, 'You wanted the bike. Now ride it!' into the camera. After training late into the afternoon, he was required to film into the night. As the Giro route was widely regarded as made to measure for Marco, anything other than total dominance would have been humiliating. He was now losing precious recovery time.

Before the 1999 Giro Marco visited Pregnolato's beauty salon, where a semi-permanent eyeliner was applied to sharpen his gaze. It was rock-star behaviour, and the Italian press ran with the story, writing up Marco as a fashion icon. In the *Corriere della Sera* magazine, Diego Dalla Palma − 'make-up artist to the stars' − illuminated the Italian public with his expert opinion that the measure wasn't functional ('There's no anti-dust make-up'), but intended to 'underline certain aspects of his face'.

While Marco attended to his appearance, the CSAD was preparing to look beneath the surface and into the very veins of the riders at the upcoming Giro. The race organisors had expressed publicly the desire for more thorough testing procedures, and the CSAD had taken them at their word. On 12 May, three days before the race was due to start, the CSAD secretary, Dr Pasquale Bellotti, wrote to the President and Secretary of CONI and the FCI, and to the Giro organising committee at the *Gazzetta dello Sport*, describing a campaign of health tests it proposed to conduct at the Giro d'Italia and appealing for cooperation.

They consisted of combined blood and urine tests which would expose attempts to dilute the blood by detecting low concentrations of creatininuria in the urine. After the Festina affair, none of the institutions wanted to be seen to obstruct the CSAD campaign, despite the fact that it could only target the Italian participants. Already subjected to six-monthly, three-monthly, monthly and unannounced health and anti-doping tests for CONI, the UCI and the FCI, the riders raised a stink.

Marco was at the centre of this, and other controversies. At Agrigento for the start of the Giro, Andrea Agostini had to deal with comments reported in the press that could have placed Marco in contempt of court: Marco, he said, 'has never accused magistrates of abusing their power. He said that he felt a certain irritation at an action by magistrates that led to raids on his home. He described a natural irritation, but he has faith and respect for the mechanisms of justice.'

The race itself started farcically, with theatrical bickering between the principal players and a variety of offstage voices. It would end in tears, if not tragedy. Before stage one, in the oppressive Sicilian heat, Marco was edging his bike towards the starting line when a reporter from a satirical news show pushed a television camera into his face and asked, repeatedly, 'Do you swear you have nothing to do with any doping practices?' After several repetitions of the question Marco stopped, looked into the camera and said, '*Giuro*' – 'I swear.' That evening he was fuming: 'They have no respect for us riders. We have no protection. Suddenly someone like that, with a microphone and a camera, can come up and attack you in front of millions, despite all our hard work. It's not right.' True, the television journalist was chasing a cheap story, and little Marco could have said would have deprived him of it. But cycling's credibility had been seriously damaged by the scandals of July 1998 and, even before the 1999 Giro had begun, two riders had already been excluded with haematocrit values over the 50 per cent threshold. So the question, no matter how rudely posed, was an urgent one. There was self-delusion in Marco's inability to see it.

When the race finally began, the first three stages ended in mass sprints. A searing scirocco blew hard from the south, bringing Marco and others down and sweeping rumours over the race. At the same time, extracts from a book of confessions by the former Festina *soigneur* Willy Voet were appearing in the international press.

At Terme Luigiane on 18 May, Laurent Jalabert, who had moved to

Switzerland and consequently was not taking part in the long-term health monitoring launched by the French Ministry for Youth and Sport on 1 January 1999, took the stage win – victory number 133 in his career. On 20 May, during stage six, the longest of the Giro, Jalabert, in the pink jersey, was held up by a fall. In windy conditions Marco's team piloted the leading group away at top speed, panicking Jalabert into a frantic chase. He closed the gap, but others, notably the climbers Virenque and Heras, lost nearly five minutes. Their challenge to Marco was over before it had begun.

The CSAD had announced on 19 May that the first tests of its campaign, dubbed 'I don't risk my health', would take place between 8 and 10:30 a.m. on the morning of the twenty-first, before the stage start at the Hotel President, Foggia. The tests were a fiasco from the start. At 6 p.m. on the evening of 20 May a meeting was held to brief the team doctors. The race director Carmine Castellano was there, with his race coordinator and representatives from CONI. But the team doctors hadn't been contacted. The Giro organisers claimed they had no idea they were supposed to inform them of the assembly. So, instead of presenting the tests to the team doctors, the meeting moved on to the drawing of lots to select the teams that would be tested the following morning: they were Mobilvetta-Northwave, Ballan-Alessio and Vini Caldirola-Sidermec. The *directeurs sportifs* and team doctors of these teams were contacted and a meeting hastily convened for later that evening. The doctors were shown the rooms to be used for the tests and raised no objections. Yet, later that night, there was talk among the teams of boycotting the following day's stage. The counter-protest came from Mapei, whose *directeur sportif* Serge Parsani commented: 'We hope they'll continue these tests. If someone is complaining about them, it means they have something to hide.' Andrea Tafi, the Italian champion, added: 'They can come every day and test me at home.'

The following morning just sixteen riders adhered to the campaign. The blood collection started at 8.30 a.m. and ran into difficulty immediately. The test tube used for the first collection had a defective lid, so when the tester tried to close it, blood splattered over a table top and on to the floor. The clean-up left the testers with insufficient latex gloves to carry out every collection with gloved hands. When the team doctors and *directeurs sportifs* saw that samples were being collected by doctors with ungloved hands, they seized the moment to goad the testers, who continued despite the tension. By 9.50 a.m. the blood collection was over. The samples were driven the 135 kilometres to Bari, and the results were back in the hands of the testers by 1.30 p.m.

After the stage, the testers met the team doctors of two minor riders whose test results showed anomalies: Filippo Casagrande and Guido Trombetta. Their haematocrit levels were legal – 43 per cent for one, 48 per cent for the other – but their urine showed creatininuria levels far below the normal lower limit of 4 mMol/litre, low enough to suggest either illness or that their blood had been diluted, a standard measure used to lower an artificially high haematocrit. Casagrande and Trombetta were asked to comply with the terms of the campaign to which they had voluntarily adhered by withdrawing from the race and undergoing second level testing.

Trombetta accepted the suspension; Filippo Casagrande resisted, and the following day faxed CONI:

> The undersigned Filippo Casagrande hereby revokes his assent to the declaration of adhesion to the CONI–FSN national campaign 'I don't risk my health' considering that the analyses carried out on 21 May 1999 do not [sic] present the prerequisite guarantees for accurate results to safeguard my rights, therefore I do not accept the suspension from competition.

Four other riders – Mauro Radaelli, Massimo Apollonio, Gianluca Siboni and Mauro Zanetti – faxed similar notes, without the final 'therefore . . .' Threats to boycott the following day's stage in protest were withdrawn, but the tension was high. Marco's was the public face of dissent: 'These tests are no longer being used to monitor our health and prevent problems. They're something else.' In a television interview he got into an argument with the Mapei rider Andrea Tafi. Eugenio Capdacqua, the journalist with *La Repubblica*, later reported that 'more than one interviewee, including riders, expressed strong suspicion of the amazing climbing of some of the contenders'.

At the start of stage eight Andrea Tafi had been subjected to a stream of insults from other riders and, most notably, from Marco. At the back of the group Tafi was reduced to tears. Only support from his teammates and directors stopped him abandoning. Two hundred and fifty kilometres later, on the slopes of Gran Sasso d'Italia, Marco slowly raised the pace. There was no violent acceleration, just a progression between the great snow dunes. In the finishing straight, his face disfigured into a scowl, Marco raised a hand to celebrate the stage win. José Maria Jiménez, second, finished twenty-three seconds later.

After the stage Marco justified his attitude to Tafi with an excess of consistency: 'A year ago, at the end of the Giro, someone at Mapei made very serious declarations about an imaginary exchange of blood samples, and these declarations cast doubt on the credibility of the checks. How can they now say: "Let's do the checks"? Could it be that last year someone wanted Pantani's head at all costs, and didn't get it?'

Stage nine was a thirty-two-kilometre individual time trial starting and finishing at Ancona, a hundred kilometres down the Adriatic coast from Rimini. Trombetta and Filippo Casagrande defied the CSAD testers by starting the stage, though Trombetta ended his protest by abandoning during the stage. Marco was expected to lose time to riders like Jalabert and Honchar, first and second respectively in the 1997 World Time-Trial Championship. He did, but his performance was every bit as good as in his previous Giro time trial, at Lugano in 1998: there, and at Ancona, Marco finished third. Jalabert took the pink jersey by two-hundredths of a second.

But Ancona became another battleground for the CSAD testers. The previous day, Hein Verbruggen, the President of the UCI, had declared their campaign in explicit contravention of UCI regulations, which prohibited all blood testing except its own at international UCI events. Not surprisingly, three of the four teams selected to undergo the CSAD tests before the Ancona time trial – Teams Polti, Saeco and Lampre – refused to take part. The fourth team, Riso Scotti, declared its riders available in principle, but the riders chose individually not to take part. Then Mapei stepped in: in the presence of the President and General Secretary of the FCI, the Mapei team directors, medical staff and riders requested to be tested and adhered enthusiastically to the campaign. Filippo Casagrande, meanwhile, continued to race.

On 25 May the Giro sped into Cesenatico. Marco sent his team to the front for the final three circuits around his home town, which thronged to the roadside to welcome its most famous son. The stage was won by a sprinter, Ivan Quaranta. At 7.35 the following morning Marco was called, via his team, for a UCI blood test. His presentation time, stipulated by the UCI regulations, was ten minutes later: 7.45 a.m. In October

138

1998 the UCI had reduced the time between notification and testing from thirty minutes to ten, to limit the time available for diluting riders' blood to lower their haematocrit. Marco arrived at 8 a.m., a further fifteen minutes outside the time limit. The UCI medical inspector, Antonio Coccioni, was told the delay was because Marco had slept at home that night. The times were recorded on the test certificate and Coccioni issued a warning to Marco and his team management. No further action was taken. In any case, the names of the teams to be tested had been leaked to the press beforehand; the surprise tests were anything but unannounced. For the record, Marco's haematocrit was 47.4 per cent.

Then the indestructible Richard Virenque, who was still maintaining his innocence in the Festina trial despite Willy Voet's revelations, won at Rapallo. As he celebrated his victory, he learned he had been charged in connection with the Festina affair. The pink jersey was still on Laurent Jalabert's shoulders, with Marco breathing down his neck. On 28 May, rest day, Marco reconnoitred the Madonna del Colletto, the final climb of the next day's stage. The roads bifurcated and doubled back on themselves, and he concluded: 'The descent is very demanding and torturous.' Paolo Savoldelli, famous for his breakneck descending, won the stage. Marco finished second, gained one minute forty-one seconds on Jalabert and took the overall race lead.

The following day's stage unfolded like a comic-book plot. At the foot of the final climb, eight kilometres from the finish line at the Sanctuary of Oropa, in northern Piedmont, Marco was near the front of the leading group when his chain came off. By the time the team car reached him, the leading group had sped past and Marco was alone. Five team-mates had been with him in the leading group; they peeled off, waited, and slotted, one by one, into a pace line ahead of him. Together, they sped past the back-markers. Then, as his team-mates ran out of energy, they peeled away one by one, like Olympic sprinters on the track, until Marco was hurtling alone towards the sky. The racing line followed a drystone wall on the left-hand side of the road. There were two and a half kilometres to go when he reached Jalabert. Marco had already overtaken forty-eight riders. The Frenchman surrendered the racing line to Marco in a gesture of respect. Marco darted past. Jalabert took up position on his wheel, but Marco's tiny frame offered little slipstream, and gravity was too strong. Another acceleration shook

Jalabert off. There was no celebration under the cupola of the Sanctuary of Oropa, not even the subdued salute he'd given at Gran Sasso. Marco said it was because he wasn't sure he'd won.

In the interview area after the stage, he reflected: 'It would have been easier to have stopped for breath.' And then, for the first time in the race, he smiled. That evening Marco was asked about the Tour de France. During stage three of the Tour of Germany, Jan Ullrich had touched the wheel of his team-mate Udo Bölts, and fallen, sustaining a knee injury that would keep Ullrich out of the 1999 Tour. 'I'm sorry for him. I hope it's not serious. But I'm not even thinking about the Tour right now. I don't think I'll ride it.' The following day Jalabert out-sprinted Marco to the stage victory at Lumezzane, twenty kilometres north of Brescia.

On 2 June a forty-five-kilometre time trial led through the Treviso flatlands. Marco's lead over Savoldelli and Jalabert, both excellent against the clock, was little over two minutes. The time trial was followed by three severe mountain stages. In particular, the penulti-mate stage took the riders from Madonna di Campiglio, over the Tonale and the Gavia to the horrendous gradients of the Mortirolo, and then across the Valico di Santa Cristina to the stage finish at Aprica. It would provide the most spectacular possible backdrop for whatever epic Marco could invent. Nonetheless, for the Treviso stage against the clock, Marco was insistent: two minutes wouldn't be enough to maintain his lead.

Before the time trial could begin, the CSAD testing team invited the remaining teams to undergo their health checks. That meant Mercatone Uno, Liquigas, Amica Chips, Navigare and Cantina Tollo. The first four refused outright. Cantina Tollo allowed its riders to decide individually whether or not to take part. They unanimously chose not to. That afternoon Marco rode strongly, finishing seventh and conceding just one minute thirty-eight seconds to the stage winner, the Ukrainian Serhiy Honchar. Savoldelli, second in the stage, had clawed back eighty-one of the hundred and twenty-five seconds that separated him from Marco; Jalabert, fifty-seven of the hundred and twenty-six. They now lay second and third in GC, Savoldelli, forty-four seconds back, Jalabert, one minute and nine.

On 3 June his team-mates Zaina and Borgheresi delivered him to the strategic spot, four kilometres from the finish line on Alpe di Pampeago.

Roberto Heras was unable to follow and Marco rode away to his third stage win. That evening he repeated that he had no intention of riding in France in July: 'I'm not going to the Tour to finish third or fourth. There isn't the terrain for my attacks. It's a deliberate stance, a signal to the organisers. We're climbers, who work flat out on the slopes. We're the ones who create a spectacle, but they have no consideration for us. What would I be doing at a Tour where I don't have the terrain to let off steam?' The word Marco used – *sfogarmi* – expresses more than 'to let off steam': it means 'to relieve or give vent to [my] feelings', 'to open [my] heart'. This was his perception of his attacks: an escape valve for something pent up inside.

Whatever he released on Alpe di Pampeago, it allowed him to extend his lead to three minutes forty-two seconds over Paolo Savoldelli. And the following day there were more mountains. Nine kilometres from the finish line at Madonna di Campiglio, as the gradient steepened, five of Marco's team-mates led him and some fifteen other riders, thirty-five seconds behind the remains of the breakaway. Pascal Richard, the Olympic Champion who had been on the attack all day, made one final attack, gaining a fifty-second lead. The Colombian Hernán Buenahora went with him, even guessing that resistence had, by now, become futile. Yet their lead was still intact four kilometres from the finish line – always four, the formula for success – when Marco, chased by Simoni, released a stinging acceleration.

Buenahora had dropped Richard and believed he was heading for a stage win when Marco catapulted past. The Colombian managed to catch Marco's slipstream, but what was, for Buenahora, a fearsome sprint, was a speed Marco could sustain for kilometre after kilometre. Seconds later a second burst of speed from Marco distanced Buenahora, who dropped away. Buenahora's speed was impressive enough, but by the time the Colombian reached the 'Three kilometres to go' marker, Marco led him by thirty-seven seconds. If Marco sat in the saddle at all during that four-kilometre pursuit to the line, the television footage doesn't show it. It was the supreme display of climbing: repeated, unanswerable accelerations followed by sustained speed. Ullrich wasn't here, of course, but the recognised cream of world climbing – French (Virenque), Spanish (Heras and Jiménez), Italian (Simoni and Gotti) and Colombian (González and Buenahora) – was, and no one could rival Marco.

Again, there was no finish-line celebration. Marco's eyes were obscured behind dark, reflective lenses, set in an eccentric yellow frame. His mouth was an open grimace.

12
Madonna di Campiglio
(4–6 JUNE 1999)

Italy was elated. Pier Bergonzi of the *Gazzetta dello Sport*, the organ of the race organisers, caught the mood: 'These are victories that, lined up one after the other, make cycling history.' The editorial of the *Gazzetta dello Sport*'s profoundly Catholic director, Candido Cannavò, was headed, with atypical innuendo: 'In every surge, an act of love.' The race sponsors and television advertisers must also have been celebrating: Marco gave them huge exposure (television viewing figures for the final forty minutes of the stage – mid-afternoon on a Friday – touched five million) and can only have added to the Giro's market value. The superlative sporting performance was also strangely emotionless. He had won every uphill finish except Monte Sirino. He had finished third and seventh in the time trials. Paolo Savoldelli, second overall, was five minutes thirty-eight seconds behind him. There was something unyielding, mechanical – inhuman, even – about Marco's tyranny. It was still theoretically possible to lose the 1999 Giro through a fall, or a catastrophic loss of form, but the real interest of the final mountain stage, from Madonna di Campiglio to Aprica the following day, lay in how Marco would win, and by how much.

Within cycling's small, closed world, however, the acclaim was muted. The last but one of the breakaway riders to see Marco rush past was the reigning Olympic champion Pascal Richard, approaching the end of his career. On the finish line Richard said pointedly that it would have been nice to have been allowed a stage win. Pantani retorted tersely: 'If I hadn't beaten him, someone else would have.' He had a point: Richard had been caught and dropped by two separate clusters of riders giving futile chase, and had finished at the tail end of a third, one minute forty-nine seconds after Marco. Nonetheless, Richard's frustration was widely shared. *Gazzetta* journalist Filippo Grimaldi observed, 'Twenty stages without a single successful breakaway: a record.' During the Giro, the term *fuga da telecamera* – 'the television breakaway' – had been coined to describe doomed attacks made with the peloton's consent to allow minor riders a moment of limelight, and their sponsors a few minutes of airtime. Ronchi told me, 'I was at the finish line with Fabrizio Borra, and when Marco attacked and won, Borra said, "Look, Marco's incredible; he could have saved himself the effort. But you see? He saw all these fans arrive here just for him, and not to win for him would have been to betray his fans." But other voices were saying, "He's over the top; he won't let the others win."' Martinelli told Ronchi that Marco was tense and best left in peace. She didn't see Marco again that evening.

Hints of discontent seeped through even in the *Gazzetta*. 'Insatiable', was Angelo Zomegnan's headline on page three: 'Yesterday morning he'd implied he wouldn't chase breakaway riders, provided they didn't threaten his dominance in GC. But, with less than six kilometres to the finish, put on edge by accelerations from Jalabert and Simoni, the time came when he could no longer bear to ride calmly in his *domestiques'* slipstream.' Elsewhere, Martinelli said his team had wanted the break-away to succeed: 'We did everything we could to let them go. The others brought them back. Vini Caldirola had to protect Gonchar's GC position; Kelme wanted to do the same for Heras. I know how these things work – I've had to chase for a fifth or sixth place in the past. But when Marco sees them accelerating under his nose, he's going to react. It's only logical: he's a champion.' Pier Bergonzi's headline paraphrased Marco at the press conference: 'If you can win, you must.' Marco had continued: 'I hadn't planned to attack today, but Simoni had a go, then Jalabert, and I ended up on Jaja's wheel.' Marco's sense of hierarchy then compelled him to act: 'I'm not a rider who should be on Jalabert's wheel in the mountains, so I left. And when I was on my own, I felt even better. I was in a state of grace.' His explanation continued: 'We didn't light the fuse. It suited me to let the breakaway go. The others brought it back. When Simoni and Jalabert attacked, it seemed to me right to take up the challenge. It's just a shame the climb wasn't steeper.'

At the end of the post-stage press conference Marco was free to return to his hotel for a massage, dinner, and to rest for the following day's rigours. But he displayed no sense of satisfaction. Antonio

Dallagiacoma, the proprietor of the Hotel Touring at Madonna di Campiglio, told me the atmosphere in his hotel that night was far from euphoric: 'Marco came in through the side door, where his father had parked the camper van. Marco had already met my wife in December, when he came to Madonna di Campiglio to train, and he'd stayed at the Hotel Zeledria, which belongs to a friend of my wife. So when my wife saw him come in, she said, "*Bravo*, Marco!" He said, "*Grazie*," but he wasn't all that pleased.' Dallagiacoma also recalls that one of the most senior and respected members of Marco's entourage was sitting on a bench in the hotel foyer when Marco entered. He greeted Marco with something along the lines of, 'What have you gone and done?' 'Marco went straight up to his room,' Dallagiacoma resumed. 'Mercatone Uno had booked the entire second floor, and the cyclists and *soigneurs* distributed the rooms among themselves. They took beds out of some rooms to create more space for massage. Saeco did the same on the first and third floors, though there were also a few private guests on the Saeco floors.'

Dallagiacoma's wife contrasted Marco's mood with that of the other riders in the hotel that night: 'I remember the Saeco riders were generally cheerful, but Marco Pantani had a long face, downcast eyes and no smile. I remember thinking it very strange in a man who had just won the Madonna di Campiglio stage and consolidated his overall lead. It seemed to me he might have been criticised for a victory he should not have achieved.'

By the time Marco reached the Hotel Touring after the post-stage interviews in the evening of 4 June 1999, a number of guests had checked into the nearby Hotel Majestic. They included the UCI medical officer Antonio Coccioni, well known in Italian cycling circles; three medical doctors, Mario Spinelli, Eugenio Sala and the extravagantly named Michelarcángelo Partenope of the Sant'Anna Hospital in Como; the ex-rider Davide Cassani, now working as an onscreen cycling expert for the Italian national broadcaster Rai; and Angelo Francini, the owner of a company that dealt with product marketing at sports events and an Italian Cycling Federation councillor since January 1995. The three doctors asked for a 5.30 a.m. alarm call and were seen no more that evening.

Back at the Hotel Touring, a member of one of the two teams sleeping there asked the owner to unlock the doors the following morning at 6.30 a.m. because the UCI testers would be arriving. Shown photographs of members of the Saeco and Mercatone Uno teams, Dallagiacoma couldn't identify the person who made the request. He could only say it was not Martinelli, Rempi or Corti – probably a mechanic, he said, or a *soigneur* – someone he didn't look at very attentively. Asked why he thought the teams were expecting the testers, Dallagiacoma replied, 'In my opinion it was because several days had passed without receiving them.'

Another of the guests at the Majestic that night recalled: 'Antonio Coccioni, the commissaire responsible for the UCI's surprise controls, was at the Hotel Majestic. It's easy to associate his presence with the controls we're talking about, in that I believe he's responsible for most of them. On that evening, I remember I met Coccioni by chance in the hall of the hotel and he asked me not to make his presence known. But I should point out that in that hotel there were many other guests, including journalists and workers in the publicity caravan of the Giro d'Italia, and it's probable that one of them informed the teams of Coccioni's presence, which implied imminent anti-doping controls that were no longer a surprise. It should be pointed out that in the great stage races it is common practice that surprise controls are held in the last two days of racing on the leading riders in the general classification.'

Another source reported that on the evening of 4 June a telephone call was made to the Majestic to provide the anti-doping officials with the names of the athletes to be tested. The telephone call was received by an official who, being a little 'deaf', repeated in a loud voice the names of the pre-selected athletes, within earshot of their *directeurs sportifs*.

The riders to be tested were chosen by the UCI, or the FCI, in consultation with the race organisers, and communicated to the medical inspector or to the DS of the rider's team. According to UCI protocol, the *directeurs sportifs* of the selected riders should have been notified by the medical inspector no more than ten minutes before the test – although arrival one or two minutes outside the ten-minute cut-off was routinely tolerated. However, it is starkly clear that by late evening on 4 June at Madonna di Campiglio, not only were the following morning's supposedly unannounced blood tests common knowledge; the names of the teams and perhaps of a number of the individual riders to be tested were known to their team directors. It was not the first time: the day before the tests at Cesenatico the names of the teams that would be tested the following morning had been published in a national newspaper. To neutralise the leak, the pre-selected teams were replaced – except for Marco's Mercatone Uno team, which therefore had twenty-four hours' notice.

After three weeks on the road, with blood tests expected at 6.30 a.m. the following morning and a punishing 190 kilometre stage over three great mountain passes starting at 10.50 a.m., Marco might have been expected to take an early night. Yet late that evening he was in the hotel restaurant, eating nothing but four hundred grams of rice, deep in conversation with Candido Cannavò. In an editorial published a year after Marco's death, Cannavò recalled meeting Marco that evening, 'face to face, over an uneaten steak and discussing the future, the wrongs of the world and the suffering of so many children, and planning common initiatives to invest his sporting glory in solidarity.' Events were conspiring to frustrate their charitable ambitions.

Dallagiacoma told me: 'Everyone came here because so few hotels with a kitchen were open. The most important teams were here. Mercatone Uno had sent a menu by fax, so we'd stocked up the ingredients. At 5 p.m. they changed their minds and altered the menu. The roads were closed for traffic, so we had to walk down into town with backpacks to collect the new ingredients and carry them back up the hill. That evening we had more than a hundred and twenty covers, so we had two dinner sessions. People were eating until midnight. We didn't know who they were, or who was paying, so in the end, we put half on Saeco's bill and half on Mercatone Uno's bill, and they paid with their company credit cards.'

Sometime after midnight Fabrizio Borra recollects asking Marco if he was concerned about the following morning's test. Marco's reply was: 'Of course we're ready: do you think I'm stupid? I've already won the Giro. In fact, to make sure we're in the right, let's check.' It was normal for riders to own blood cell counters and to carry out their own checks before the official tests. According to Ronchi, Marco tested his blood in the presence of his father and Fabrizio Borra. The result, she claims, was 48.6 per cent. 'You see?' Marco is said to have commented. 'All within the rules.'

Meanwhile Dallagiacoma saw Marco's team doctor leave the hotel: 'I remember that Dr Rempi went out after midnight. I don't know what time he returned. The last time I saw him he seemed to me to be composed.' Dallagiacoma's wife added: 'I remember perfectly seeing Dr Rempi leave the hotel at about 12 a.m. with a race-organisation hostess with long, black hair and a vaguely oriental look. At the time I remember thinking it was irresponsible, and that if a cyclist was taken ill, he'd be difficult to find. I don't know where he went and I didn't see him come back that night.'

Ronchi told me: 'I'd been invited by the organisers of the Giro d'Italia to a discotheque at Madonna di Campiglio where they'd organised a party, and towards 1 a.m. I met Agostini and Dr Rempi, and I said to myself, "Tomorrow's the Mortirolo stage, and the team doctor is in a disco." It didn't seem very professional to me.'

Rempi hadn't returned by the time the hotel concierge, Santino Battaglia, went to bed, sometime between three and three-thirty. Dallagiacoma opened the door at four, then went to the kitchen to prepare breakfasts – although, he points out, 'The doors were ajar downstairs to allow water hoses and electricity cables to reach the team buses.' Rempi may have returned to the hotel unseen any time after four a.m. 'At seven-thirty, eight, the riders came down and ate eight huge *crostate di marmellata*' – home-made jam tarts – 'and an enormous breakfast buffet. Then, before leaving, they ate pasta and omelettes. There were dozens of journalists and fans milling about the hotel.'

Doctors Sala, Spinelli and Partenope received their alarm call at five-thirty. The pre-stage health tests were governed by strict UCI procedures and using instruments provided by the FCI. These included needles and blood-collection tubes defined in the UCI regulations, and a Coulter Act-8 blood cell counter, calibrated and tested prior to each session, according to UCI rules. A numbered label was attached to each tube after blood collection; the same number was then attached to the documentation against the athlete's name. The doctors were required to avoid the athletes before the controls. They were informed of the athletes' identities by the anti-doping commissaire only at the moment of the blood collection.

Marco's presentation time was noted as 7.35. Coccioni must have informed DS Giuseppe Martinelli that Marco's name was on the list at 7.25. Three hours later Martinelli would reflect: 'If the commissaire had arrived three minutes later, Marco would have been having breakfast

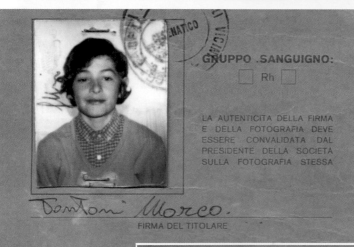

A shy child huddles into the folds of his grandfather's coat. Marco and Sotero, circa 1983.

Full of promise: Marco's 1985 racing licence.

Before.

Winning.

15 September 1985.
The Ilario Vignali Trophy,
at Donnini di Regello, near
Florence. In the portraits,
the unease before the
prying camera is palpable.

Warming down.

Going home.

Marco laughs reluctantly as Eros Poli, the sprint category champion, lifts the tiny overall winner, Cristiano Andreani, after the Giro dell'Emilia-Romagna in May 1990.

Left The podium of the 1994 Tour de France: the imperious Miguel Induráin, with Piotr Ugrumov (left) and Marco, engulfed in an outsize casquette. A decade later, Ugrumov was in his flat in Rimini when Marco's body was found in the Hotel Residence Le Rose next door.

Right Marco with the man who first put him on a bike: Nicola 'Roberto' Amaducci.

Protégé and mentor: Marco and Giuseppe 'Pino' Roncucci, moments before starting stage ten of the 1992 amateur Giro d'Italia. On Roncucci's advice, he would attack early and win the stage and the race.

Bosom friends and mischief-makers: Marco and Roberto Pregnolato.

Marco's final appearance in Carrera colours with two controversial confidantes, Francesco Conconi and Roberto Pregnolato (November 1996).

Marco as rebel leader at the 1998 Tour de France.

Alone in the mountains – but for the broadcast paraphernalia that made him an icon.

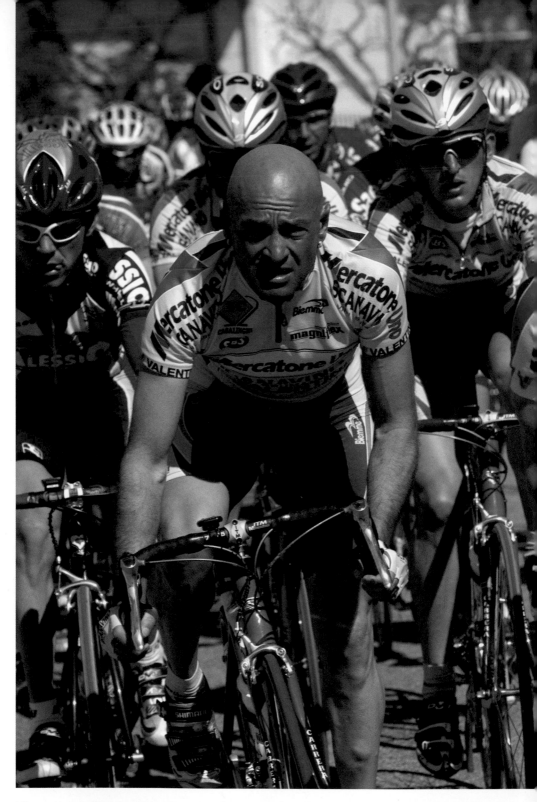

Three years after his last victory – three months after cosmetic surgery on his nose and ears – the aging athlete still has the most recognisable face in his sport (the 2003 Settimana Coppi & Bartali).

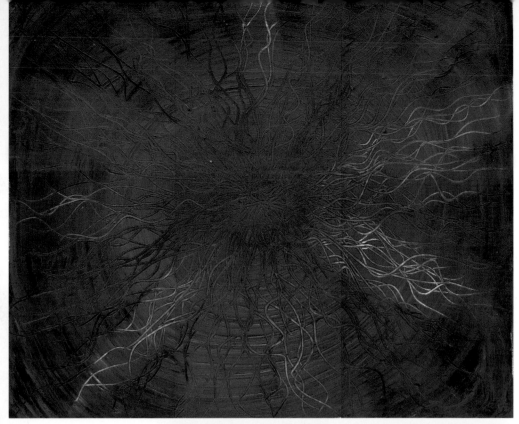

For Lance Armstrong, Marco had something of Salvador Dalí. But his paintings are more expressionist than surreal: an abstract shows a preoccupation with what is hidden beneath (above), while a more disturbing image adorned his bedroom at the time of his death (right).

Two icons of their age meet before the 2000 Giro d'Italia.

3 November 2000. The third accident of the day and umpteenth of the year, speeding the wrong way up Corso Ubaldo Comandini in Cesena. Eight cars were damaged.

Unable to stand, he is half-carried out of the Hotel Touring to face the press. 1.02pm on Saturday 5 June 1999.

Disconsolate at the roadside after a fall on stage eighteen of the 2003 Giro.

and they wouldn't have been able to test him, because the tests have to be carried out on an empty stomach.' As it was, the blood sample was collected from Marco's team-mate Marco Velo, and then Marco was called. Paolo Savoldelli arrived first, and his blood was collected. Only then, 7.46, eleven minutes late, did Marco appear. Marco walked into the tiny room and sat down. Partenope recalled that Martinelli was present, Doctor Sala was behind Partenope, perhaps in the doorway. Spinelli and Coccioni were in the corridor, the room being too small. Coccioni's memory differed slightly: he stated that the blood sample had been taken in his presence, and that Martinelli was either in the doorway or just outside the room.

Marco sat with his arm on the table. The blood-collection tubes specified by UCI examinations were 4.9 millilitre, red-top blood bottles produced industrially by Sasted. They contained the referred anticoagulant for haemochromocytometric examinations, ethylenediaminetetraacetic acid, or EDTA. The tiny droplets, microscopically small, clung to the walls, in suspension. Partenope picked a collection tube at random and attached the blood test-gauge syringe. Marco asked him not to use the torniquet: as the vein was sufficiently large, Partenope agreed. He disinfected then perforated the skin, sank the syringe into the vein and pulled the plunger. Blood flowed in. Partenope then detached the syringe and passed the tube to Sala, who, in the presence of Coccioni and Marco, attached a label bearing the number UCI-IUML 11140. He showed both men that the same code was printed beside Marco's name on the medical inspector's documentation. There was no objection from Marco or Martinelli. Then the tube was stored with the other samples taken that morning. It all took perhaps two minutes. Then Marco and Martinelli left the room. The test tubes were all stored in the same container, inside a bag the testers had brought with them. The medical team never lost sight of it.

They left for another hotel to collect more blood samples, returning with them to their hotel. Approximately an hour after taking Marco's sample, in a room in the Hotel Majestic, the testers calibrated the Coulter Ac*T8 blood cell counter using control blood with known values, provided for the purpose by the manufacturer. Then Dr Spinelli, absent at the blood collection and the allocation of reference numbers, and therefore ignorant of the provenance of each sample, proceeded with the analysis of the blood samples.

Two portions of blood from each numbered sample were tested. According to the testing rules, the higher of the two haematocrit values was discarded, and the sample was said to have passed the test if the remaining value was below 50 per cent. At Madonna di Campiglio, just one sample showed a haematocrit above the 50 per cent threshold. Another portion of blood was taken from tube UCI-IUML 11140 and the test was repeated. Only at that moment, when the over-the-threshold value had been confirmed, did Coccioni cross-reference the number on the tube and learn that the offending blood belonged to Marco.

According to UCI regulations, the medical inspector was required to inform the rider's DS and conduct three further tests in his presence. There was no need to recalibrate the blood cell counter after each examination: it was required neither by the regulations nor by the quality of equipment. However, instead of dispatching Coccioni, the doctors recalibrated the counter anyway, and re-examined Marco's blood sample three more times. Partenope later said: 'We wanted to be sure.' Spinelli added: 'We realised the matter had a certain importance. We'd have done the same for other samples, but in this case, even more so. So we repeated it three more times, making five in all.' Only then did Coccioni inform the team.

Minutes later the test was repeated three more times in the presence of the team doctor, Roberto Rempi, and the team DS Giuseppe Martinelli. Neither made any official observation. That made eight analyses, all of blood taken from the same tube, all of which confirmed the haematocrit of 52 to 53 per cent. The medical bulletin released shortly afterwards by the UCI read: 'Teams tested: Ballan, Navigare, Cantina Tollo, Polti, Amica Chips, Mercatone Uno, Saeco, Once, Lampre. The tests were carried out between 6.40 and 8.05 a.m. The following rider(s) have been declared unfit: Pantani, Marco.'

By then all hell had broken loose. Before nine, rumours that riders had been found positive and banned substances found were flying round the start village. Marco was mentioned. Fabrizio Borra, Pantani's physiotherapist and a man under the Pirate's spell, smelt a plot, Ronchi's book explains. Borra claims the testers were strangely on edge. He says they knocked brusquely on Pantani's door, barking at him to get up at once. When the blood sample had been taken, he adds, they had asked

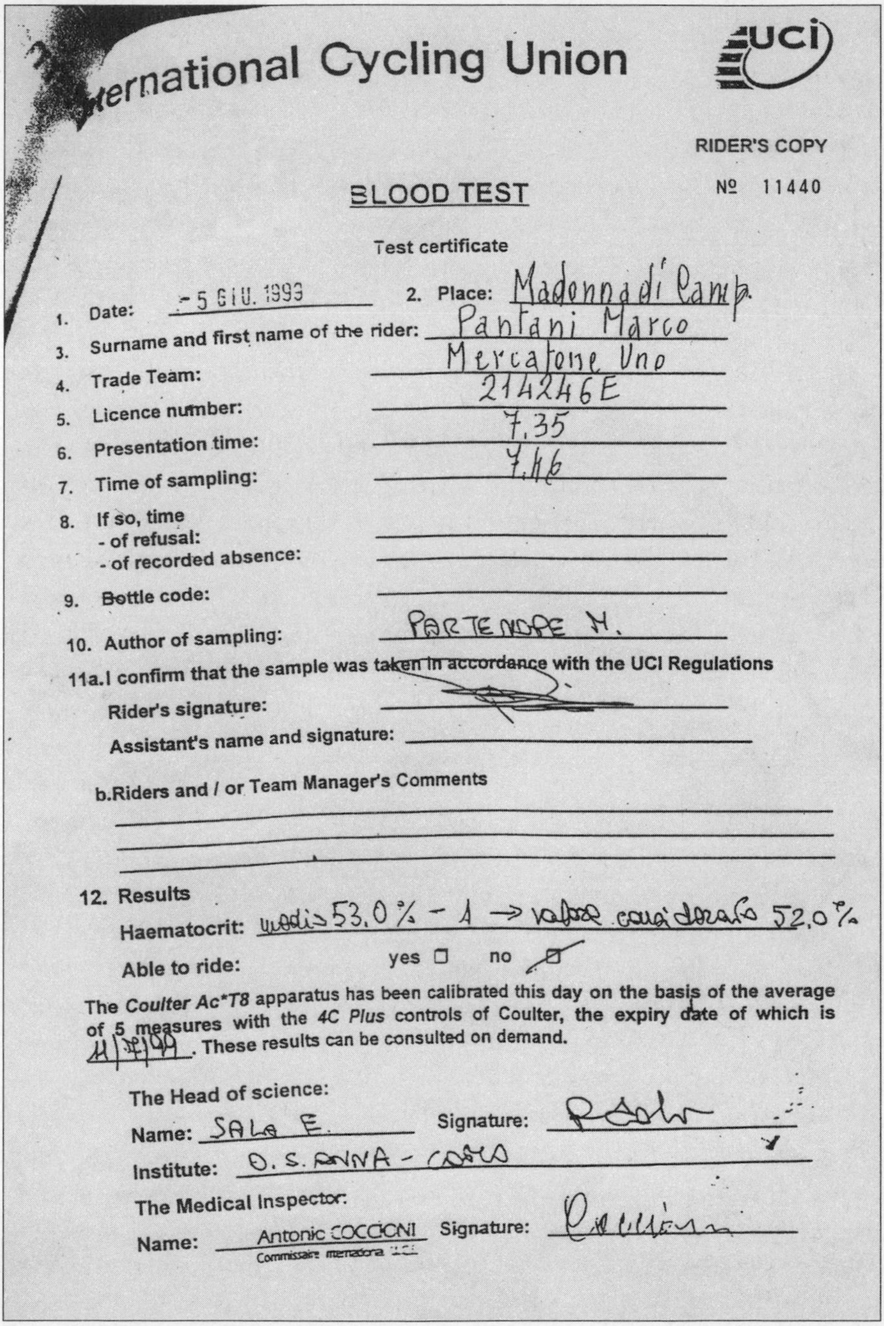

ernational Cycling Union   ⧼UCI⧽

BLOOD TEST   № 11440

Test certificate

1. Date: _-5 GIU. 1999_   2. Place: _Madonna di Camp._

3. Surname and first name of the rider: _Pantani Marco_

4. Trade Team: _Mercatone Uno_

5. Licence number: _214246E_

6. Presentation time: _7.35_

7. Time of sampling: _7.46_

8. If so, time
   - of refusal: _____
   - of recorded absence: _____

9. Bottle code: _____

10. Author of sampling: _PARTENOPE M._

11a. I confirm that the sample was taken in accordance with the UCI Regulations

   Rider's signature: _____

   Assistant's name and signature: _____

   b. Riders and / or Team Manager's Comments
   _____
   _____
   _____

12. Results
   Haematocrit: _uodi> 53.0% - 1 → valore considerato 52.0%_

   Able to ride: yes ☐   no ☒

   The *Coulter Ac*T8* apparatus has been calibrated this day on the basis of the average of 5 measures with the *4C Plus* controls of Coulter, the expiry date of which is _11|07|99_. These results can be consulted on demand.

   The Head of science:
   Name: _SALa E._   Signature: _Rdh_
   Institute: _O. S. ANNA - COMO_

   The Medical Inspector:
   Name: _Antonio COCCIONI_   Signature: _Coccioni_
   Commissaire médecin UCI

Figure 1: UCI blood test certificate, Madonna di Campiglio, 5 June 1999.

him three or four times, in an unpleasant tone, to confirm his name on the test tube. Strange behaviour, says Borra – although Pantani, he goes on, didn't give it any thought at the time, because he was quite at ease. Borra goes on that as he and Pantani sat at the breakfast table, a number of journalists came running towards the hotel: how, he asks, had they come into possession of a piece of news even before the interested party had been officially informed?

Borra's account diverges wildly from that of the testers; the testers didn't knock on doors asking to see athletes. Borra details knocks on doors and tones of voice he didn't witness; he is also naïve to believe the test result could have been kept from the press. 'Why', he asks, 'did they refuse our request to re-test blood from another sample, given that their result didn't coincide with ours?' But the testers could hardly have agreed to give Pantani time to dilute his blood.

For the Mercatone Uno team, the situation was immediately out of control. Manuela Ronchi was wandering around the start village when she began to receive accusing looks and comments. It was a race commentator, Rai's Davide De Zan, who broke the news to her. Ronchi telephoned Martinelli, who swore at her and hung up. According to Ronchi's account, Martinelli was roaming around his hotel room, punching the walls and screaming, 'This should never have happened.' Borra tells us he broke the news to Marco. Pregnolato makes the same claim.

Dallagiacoma recalls: 'When they told him, he shouted. He was in his room. I don't remember what he was shouting, but he was desperate. I wanted to go down and see the start, but two journalists came up in a great hurry, saying "Something terrible has happened. They've excluded Pantani for doping." I closed the fire exits and sent someone to every door. I called the Carabinieri, and told them, "They've stopped Pantani for doping. Send up everyone you have." It was nine, nine ten that morning.'

Ronchi went to look for Marco's father, in his camper van outside the hotel, and found him weeping, his head in his hands. She told him: 'Marco needs you.' They returned to the hotel to see blood dripping from Marco's hand. He had punched out one of the windows. In Ronchi's account, Marco recalled that day some years later, with the following words: 'You know that when I saw Dad come into the room at Madonna di Campiglio, it felt as if I'd become a child again, when I'd been up to something and he came to punish me. I said to myself: "Now he'll give me a slap."'

Meanwhile, a group of NAS officers from Brescia contacted the local contingent from the Riva del Garda section of the Carabinieri, responsible for public order. Five or six officers from Brescia were at Madonna di Campiglio following a tip-off. In September 1998, 'Pietro S.,' an amateur cyclist, had reported to Brescia police that he had been pressured to use doping products. A subsequent investigation had uncovered the use of r-EPO, human growth hormone, ACTH, gonadotropine and anabolic steroids, and had led police to Guido Nigrelli, a coach and pharmacist thought to have supplied Haemaccel, a blood-diluter used to lower haematocrit levels, to Tonkov and the others. The investigators were looking into major races during the period from 1996 to 1999. One of them told me: 'We'd been told by an informant within the cycling milieu that we'd find something interesting for our investigation at Madonna di Campiglio. We were ready to intervene that morning when we heard Pantani had been suspended. We informed the Company Commander, Captain Console, of our presence, and he said something like, "It's just as well you're here!"'

Captain Oronzo Console later gave the following account, in the formal, rather old-fashioned language of the police report: 'We approached the hotel with some marshals and members of the military, and secured the hotel from prying eyes, including journalists, who had an understandable interest in the affair. We contacted Pantani, and his *directeur sportif* who, unless I'm mistaken, was called Martinelli, and other staff and athletes who followed the team. Nerves were frayed and the tension was high, so much so that I remember quite clearly that, in the corridor outside the room of Marco Pantani we heard a commotion and the sound of glass being broken. We entered the room promptly and I remember the windowpane had been broken – we presently understood by the athlete's fist – and the athlete was extremely jumpy, and kept kicking the room furnishings. We invited the persons present to stay calm and asked the athlete to explain his nerves. He repeated, over and again, throughout the period during which we were inside the room, that he'd been found positive, even if the situation was later explained using other terms, and maintained that he'd been cheated, swindled, and both he and *directeur sportif* Martinelli used words whose content could be summed up as: "You are the Carabinieri, your job is to stop these things from happening, etc." In substance, the persons there present – Pantani, Martinelli and other team staff – claimed to be the victims of cheating or swindling.

'I asked if they intended to file a complaint against persons unknown, or anyone in particular, regarding the presumed cheating. At the time, although I was told "Yes" by both the athlete and Martinelli, I had no intention of formalising the complaint.'

The team faced the immediate problem of what to do with Marco. Agostini wanted to smuggle Pantani out of a back door, perhaps accepting a solution offered by Dallagiacoma, who told me: 'We proposed to take Pantani out in our 4x4, across the meadow, and then on to a private road that leads to Carlomagno and the state road. But we'd have had to do it immediately. Soon there was a TV camera at every exit, and it was ruled out.'

At 10.12 a.m. the UCI issued a statement confirming the test result and suspending the race leader from the Giro d'Italia. UCI President Hein Verbruggen was present at Madonna di Campiglio for the stage start: after the defeat of CONI, he suddenly seemed the strongman of the anti-doping movement. Soon afterwards Marco's team-mates announced they would not start the stage. Roberto Rempi, the team doctor, was quoted as saying: 'Perhaps his haematocrit increased because he spent two nights at altitude and he was too dehydrated during yesterday's stage. Last night we carried out tests and his haematocrit was around forty-eight, within the norm.'

At 1.02 p.m., three hours after the UCI statement, Marco walked out of the hotel and into a mass of television cameras. Dallagiacoma told me, 'We wanted to close the doors, but the lady' – Ronchi – 'wanted him to go out and face the press. He was incapable. He had to be held up by three men.' Marco then told journalists: 'I've already been controlled twice; I already had the pink jersey. I had a haematocrit of forty-six. And today I wake up with a surprise. I believe there's definitely something strange here. And I have to say that starting again this time . . . I've started again after serious accidents, but morally this time we've touched the bottom.'

Three minutes later Marco climbed into a grey Citroën. Giuseppe Martinelli was at the wheel. For three hours the two men drove and wept without speaking. When they reached Imola, they went to the Santa Maria della Scaletta Hospital, which issued a certificate showing a haematocrit between 47 and 48 per cent. Mercatone Uno issued a press release later that evening, calling into question the competence of the testers at Madonna di Campiglio. Giorgio Squinzi, the owner of Mapei, was less disposed to discern any mystery in the day's events. 'There is divine, and human, justice at last. This phenomenon had to explode sooner or later. I warned Verbruggen four years ago. We can't go on with this deceit and hypocrisy. The haematocrit of my riders is on average five points lower than when they left Agrigento. Don't let them talk crap: if they have around 50 per cent two days from the end, it means they've been taking top-ups.'

Ronchi met Marco in the team's warehouse at Imola. He held his bald head in his hands, and massaged it, stunned. He repeated words to the effect of: 'Someone owes me an explanation.' Then he returned home. He was in peak condition – perhaps the fittest man on earth, certainly unbeatable by any cyclist on earth – but suddenly he was deprived of anywhere to expend that extraordinary charge of energy, and confined, by shame, to his house. There, besieged by reporters, photographers and television crews, further than ever from his cherished privacy, he locked himself in. He must have been close to madness.

As the doctors drove back to Como and the Sant'Anna Hospital, the gravity of their situation sank in. Given Marco's celebrity, the consequences for the medical team if they had got it wrong would have been catastrophic. Dr Partenope explained: 'I think it's easy to imagine that we wanted to be really sure that there had not been any sort of mistake. So when we arrived at the hospital in Como, where we had an instrument used for the same analysis twenty-four hours a day, we carried out two more analyses – making ten in total.' The tests carried out on the hospital's Abbot Celi Dun 3500 mapped exactly on to the outcomes found at Madonna di Campiglio.

Shortly after those final tests in the Sant'Anna hospital in Como, the Brescia Carabinieri arrived with Captain Console. As Console later told it, 'In accordance with the provisions of the Procedural Code during the period of time before an official complaint is brought, and in view of my assessment of the fact that, if it were a case of fraud – and given the importance of the matter it could be a case of aggravated fraud – I presented the situation to the Public Prosecutor's Office with a covering note of my own, asking him to make arrangements, if he considered it opportune to do so, for the sequestering of the blood samples, both of the athlete Marco Pantani and of the other athletes tested by the doctors, the equipment with which these analyses had been carried out and the material used, reagents, and whatever else had been employed in the operations of collection, analysis and preservation of the blood ... We rapidly received the confiscation warrant ... it happened that the technicians who had carried out the analyses had left, taking all the material with them, and had returned to Como.' The judge noted that the police action was made necessary by the attitude of the Mercatone Uno team staff, who behaved as victims.

Console continued: 'In a somewhat fortunate manner, I recall, we gained Como – profiting from a colleague, a helicopter pilot from Bolzano who was carrying out a wide-range search – where we identified several technicians and the blood samples, presented the confiscation warrant and took charge of all the material, which we took away with us, from which it was directed for analysis to a laboratory identified in the meantime by the Public Prosecutor's Office.'

At shortly after 7 a.m. the following morning the Carabinieri delivered the sequestered materials to Professor Vittorio Rizzoli, director of the Haematology Department of the University of Parma's Bone Marrow Transplant Centre, for counter-examination or, in Professor Rizzoli's words, 'something of the sort ...'

I met Rizzoli at his office in Parma. A gruff, slightly infuriating fellow with a raucous voice, he is unimpressed by fame and seems as comfortable among his blood-cell counters as Marco was with his tools as he stripped down and reassembled his bike. Using the confiscated Coulter Ac*T8 used by the medical team at Madonna di Campiglio, and using the Transplant Centre's own more recent Coulter MAXM, Rizzoli analysed all the blood samples taken at Madonna di Campiglio. 'I carried out the examination on blood samples from a group of athletes, nine or ten of them, whose names I don't recall, but certainly there was a Simoni, a Pantani, then others, foreign athletes too. The portable blood cell counter was brought into our laboratory and we repeated the analyses I'd carried out on my equipment with this Coulter. It was an earlier-generation machine, small, built to be portable. In the end we had three sets of results: one set from our equipment and two from the same instrument, one taken at Campiglio [by the UCI testers], the other at Parma [by me].'

The results were the same for all ten samples analysed. There had been no mistake.

13

Crisis Management

Marco's blood-test result was an enigma. The Giro was already his: why would he dope himself? If he *was* doped, why wasn't his blood diluted to produce a false result? It is clear that Marco was not supposed to win that day, and that doing so caused some discomfort even to members of his own team. It quickly emerged that a number of wealthy team sponsors had been seen expressing anger and frustration at Marco's domination: had they hatched a plot to destroy Marco? What about the bookmakers, for whom Marco's expulsion would surely unleash a windfall? Either way, even Marco's team-mates had heard rumours *the night before the test* that he would be disqualified the following morning. The plot thesis spread like wildfire.

On 8 and 9 June Marco had the opportunity to give his own position, first in a television interview with an eminent Italian journalist, Gianni Minà, and then in a press conference held at Monte del Re. The interview with Minà was tortuous, for Marco could scarcely think, and what he could think he could scarcely express. 'For me it's a rather difficult, rather hard moment in which my thoughts are ... are many, that' – here, a stutter: *'che, c-, c-, c-'* – 'are going through my mind, my head in this ... in this ... in these last two or three days, so I think the house was perhaps the moment ... where I could take refuge and look for explanations.' The turmoil in his psyche can only have been worsened by the director's decision to show the eyebrows-to-chin close-up camera image on a monitor positioned over Minà's left shoulder. It left Marco talking towards a live shot of his own face.

> Anger, frustration, shame are ... are ... are some sensations that, er ... I have inside. The fact that ... that I'd won a Giro d'Italia,

er . . . I believe, in an impeccable manner, after so much work . . . To find yourself before a verdict of this type is certainly a cold shower and . . . Anyone finds themselves before a wall that's falling in on you, something that strikes you in your . . . in your . . . morale . . . in your soul – certainly not an easy moment that . . . It isn't the incident, the incident . . . It's comparable to an accident, but . . . Morale . . . I believe that this time I'm starting from much lower down.

What coherent lines of argument Marco could muster were hollow. The most hurtful thing, he said, was 'that many people who had put me among the stars the night before, threw me in the gutter the next morning'. He was referring, above all, to Candido Cannavò, with whom Marco had been dining the evening before his disgrace. After Marco's blood-test result at the Giro, Cannavò had published a front-page editorial disparaging Marco's team and entourage, who, he wrote, had failed to protect 'Italian sport's greatest patrimony' from 'a foul error'. If cycling's messiah would never be the same again, Cannavò pledged, 'helping Marco reconstruct himself now becomes a mission for us'. However, he added, Marco's would have to be a struggle not against occult powers but against 'hypocrisy, speciousness and the dishonesty of a milieu that led him into an inferno'. Cannavò was as protective towards Marco as he could be, while keeping an eye on reality. Marco would never forgive him for it.

But Marco was committed to finding a conspiracy: he told Minà that two hundred billion lire (€200 million) had been wagered on the 1999 Giro. 'I think I was given very short odds!' he observed, with a faint smile. 'Man', he said, 'is corruptible.' He suggested his blood sample might have been tampered with, or an inappropriate coagulant used.

When Minà raised the involvement of doctors in doping practices, Marco became evasive. And to Minà's question, 'Don't you alert each other? Don't you say to each other, "We have to save each other; there are people who are using us as cannon fodder"?' he replied:

In cycling and in sport doping exists, and I believe it will always exist. [...] [A]s soon as the law is cast, a way around it is found. I'm one of the few athletes who don't train with a heart-rate monitor, who . . . who . . . who . . . who, a little, erm . . . an artisan [*smiles*] among . . . among multinationals [*still smiling – then stops smiling*].

They ought to find a way to find the products in the urine or blood [. . .] because these methods, in my opinion, are scarcely credible.

In another answer, the ambivalence in Marco's relationship with his sport emerges:

Cycling is . . . [*pause, mumbling, looking for the words*] is what has made me great . . . is what has made me suffer, but let's say the thing that's most . . . most important is the pride of a man who has succeeded in winning . . . two great races like the Giro d'Italia and the Tour, and so, the gratification, let's say, as a man, more than as an athlete.

Minà asks him why he doesn't go to the Tour de France and win it:

Because someone will still doubt. What annoys me is that everything is put into doubt, so, already, the fact that there's been this anomaly, eighty per cent of people have put in doubt my career – the Giros I've won, the sacrifices I've made, my injuries, they've put everything in doubt. The man, my family, some say my family has got big-headed, that it no longer allows itself to be as open as it once was.

In her book, Ronchi complains that a recording of the interview was supplied the same evening to the newspaper *La Repubblica*, breaching the terms of the interview and infuriating the other newspapers, which had to wait until the press conference scheduled the following afternoon. I could find no trace of Minà's interview in the 9 June edition of *La Repubblica*, beyond the observation that Marco had spoken to Minà 'yesterday' (Tuesday 8 June) and that the interview would be broadcast 'tomorrow' (Thursday 10 June). On 10 June, beside the account of the press conference, Minà published a short account of his own thoughts about the 8 June interview.

The press conference was broadcast live on Rai radio, and as-live on Rai3 television forty minutes later.

Marco began by taking swipes at the treatment he had received at the hands of the testers: 'I was thrown out of bed and given seven minutes to wash my face, get dressed and appear at something that looked more like an ambush than a health check.' In fact, as we know, Marco had reported for the test twenty-two minutes after he'd been called, and twelve minutes after the official deadline had been and gone.

Action could have been taken on those grounds alone. Indeed, it could have been taken on those grounds at Cesenatico.

Marco denied any use of prohibited substances or practices, and made four points. First, doping would have been out of character. Secondly, only a fool would have taken the risk. Thirdly, the test did not comply with the procedural regulation. And, finally, the UCI regulations were seriously flawed and needed reform. 'It was mathematically certain they'd test me, either at Madonna di Campiglio or the following day. When I heard someone was fifty-two per cent I didn't think it could be me: my conscience was clear ... Three years ago I was one of the riders calling for blood testing. Afterwards they didn't take the statutary second sample to confirm the result: they used blood from the first sample. Two and a half hours later, on my own behalf, at Imola, I gave two more blood samples. My haematocrit reading was about forty-eight, with haemoglobin at 16.5. Someone is bound to say I had had time to dilute my blood. But the haemoglobin content doesn't change. They took the samples from hotel to hotel, there were the anticoagulants, it was hot ... Everything could have changed. The tests should take lots of other parameters into account. They're a mess ...'

Marco's imagination was running riot. The tests were conducted according to the statutes of the UCI, and the Imola blood-test certificate, marked with the time 16.30, eight hours after the Madonna di Campiglio test, would attract the attention of the forensic haematologists when the case eventually came to trial.

Given the opportunity to deny illegal drug use, Marco answered with a fluency and wit that suggested he had been coached since the Minà interview: 'I've never had anything whatsoever to do with doping. You can rule it out completely. I'm clean.' Pantani refused to say when he would race again – if ever. 'My morale is at rock bottom. I need time to think. I don't understand how this happened. And before I get back on my bike, I need to know. To win, it's not drugs I need – it's mountains.'

Asked whether he had received messages of solidarity from other riders, Marco answered revealingly: 'Yes. They've all looked for me. But in this moment solidarity isn't much use.' It was the articulation of Marco's tendency to isolate himself, one he had already acted out when he froze out Pregnolato in 1998. In future this tendency would become acute.

*

The first institution to act was the CSAD. On 14 June the CSAD heard the Mercatone Uno team doctor Dr Roberto Rempi and the *directeur sportif* Giuseppe Martinelli. On 17 June Marco himself sat before the commission in CONI's Bologna offices. Between these two hearings, in another part of Bologna, an investigating magistrate named Giovanni Spinosa sent fifteen members of the cycling community to trial to face doping-related charges. He had brought investigations into Rempi, which concerned a period before he joined Mercatone Uno, to a close, but he had recommended that charges be brought against Dr Michele Ferrari, who had treated friends of Marco's such as Mario Cipollini, and rivals such as Gotti, Tonkov, Olano and Savoldelli; and against Orlando Maini, the *directeur sportif* who had directed Marco to his amateur Giro d'Italia win in 1992 and who had handed Marco his cape on the Galibier during the 1998 Tour. Maini would later be acquitted, but that was far into the future, and, at the time the decision to bring charges against him can hardly have left Marco unmoved.

Nor can the CSAD report, when it was published on 23 June. Marco's contribution consisted of blanket denial and the Madonna di Campiglio conspiracy theory:

> Pantani stated that he had never undergone any doping therapy, that he monitored his haematocrit using the centrifuge mentioned earlier, and that his health was supervised exclusively by Dr Rempi. The athlete could not explain the result of the UCI check at Madonna di Campiglio and intimated, in the absence of proof, that there might have been an alteration of the collected sample, given that in a later test carried out on the same 5 June 1999 the haematocrit level was within the permitted limit.

The CSAD panel was not convinced:

> Serious doubts and confusion surround the legality of the athlete's behaviour and his integrity as a competitive sportsman, in that he has provided no serious explanation of the causes of the sudden haematocrit increase, and has not, therefore, cooperated as he should have in the quest for the truth.

The report qualified Martinelli as 'resolutely uncooperative,' even 'flippant ... insulting the intelligence of those present by stating that in the world of cycling the percentage of cyclists involved in doping is zero.' Nonetheless, 'no elements were found that can attribute to him responsibility for the haematocrit variation that led to Pantani's exclusion from the Giro d'Italia'.

Dr Roberto Rempi, the Mercatone Uno team doctor, got off less lightly. Rempi, said the report, had 'supposedly' been responsible for monitoring Marco's health since Marco's move from Carrera to Mercatone Uno in 1996. As such, Rempi should have had detailed knowledge of Marco's medical history and, specifically, in a resistance sport like cycling, detailed red blood cell data. In any case, the commission observed, haematocrit had been a virtually daily topic of conversation in the media for years.

> However [the report went on], taken at his word, Dr Rempi seems to know virtually nothing about Marco Pantani. He couldn't reply with any precision to questioning about either the athlete's haematocrit and haemoglobin levels during the years during which he has been treating him, or about treatment with iron supplements. [...] [H]e cannot remember, or remembers only vaguely, the values encountered in the period during which he has been Pantani's doctor (the last three years, although, in reality, he cannot even remember the values for the last months: 'I think, between x and y,' he says) and does not appear ever to have looked up Marco Pantani's past values. [...] To the question whether he knew the habitual red blood cell value in Marco Pantani's blood, Dr Rempi said: 'I don't recall.'

Nor could Rempi offer any explanation for the increases in Marco's haematocrit. Rempi provided the commission with documentation of six UCI blood tests conducted between 1997 and 1999 – three of which were at the 1999 Giro d'Italia – as well as the results of the test carried out at Imola on the afternoon of Madonna di Campiglio on 5 June, and the athlete's 1999 medical card, as prescribed by the FCI. Confronted with Marco's minimum and maximum haematocrit values for 1999 – forty-four and fifty-three – Rempi had no explanation. 'He limited himself to observing that this variation could depend on training, without clarifying the meaning of this observation.'

The Imola test, presented as evidence of Marco's innocence, attracted the commission's attention. They pointed out that the haematocrit levels of 47.6 and 48.1 and the haemoglobin of 16.5 and 16.6 were in any case high, compared with what might be expected towards the end of a three-week stage race. On Marco's FCI medical card, Rempi had entered the results of tests carried out at the Sant'Orsola Hospital in Bologna. As well as a very high haematocrit (49 per cent), the commission noted the ferritin level of 1163 ng/ml, vastly higher than the adult male norm, stipulated by the FCI riders' healthcare regulations at 20 ng/ml to 250 ng/ml. To comply with the FCI riders' healthcare regulations, Rempi should have informed the National Health Commission of the FCI in January 1999 when the ferritin abnormality came to light, suspended the athlete as a preventive measure and investigated the cause. Instead, Rempi said he had taken no specific action. 'Clearly', the report concludes, 'he felt unperturbed, knowing the real cause of the value [and] evidently considering the entire picture normal.'

On the subject of iron supplements, Dr Rempi said Marco's ferritin levels were naturally high, and there was no need to give him iron supplements. Yet Marco had told the commission he often took iron throughout the year, on Rempi's prescription.

To the question whether Marco and the other Mercatone Uno athletes took r-EPO and other prohibited substances, Dr Rempi replied: 'Not as far as I know,' 'without', in the report's words, 'being able to express that certainty that should follow from genuine knowledge of the athletes entrusted to his care, and their behaviour, or from the strict monitoring that a doctor can hardly not carry out on athletes, to be certain of working in an environment without doping problems, and therefore "clean".'

Rempi added that Pantani and four other Mercatone Uno athletes regularly checked their haematocrit using a centrifuge. He said he considered it normal that many athletes in the team owned a personal centrifuge.

> When he asks them [says the report], they tell him whether their values are normal or not . . . He doesn't ask the exact value, because he considers it sufficient to hear from the athlete that everything is 'within the norm' . . . He declared that he does not collect the blood sample himself, and does not oversee the successive phases of the blood treatment by the centrifuge. It therefore emerges that Dr Rempi does no more that accept blindly what the athletes tell him, when he remembers to ask.

The commission learnt that Marco checked his haematocrit level on the rest day during the Giro d'Italia. Rempi told them, 'He didn't tell me his value.' As for Marco's own haematocrit check at Madonna di Campiglio, the evening before his ejection from the race, Rempi said, 'I think he told me between forty-eight and forty-nine.' This contrasted with comments Rempi made to the press at Madonna di Campiglio, when he said, 'Last night *we* carried out a test and the value was around forty-eight per cent ...' 'Either way,' concludes the report, 'Dr Rempi has shown that he does not know the significance of a haematocrit level of forty-eight to forty-nine per cent, which is already very high, given that, in the vast majority of cases, elite, non-doped cyclists show haematocrit values around forty-two to forty-three, and even lower.'

On the subject of the use of personal centrifuges, the commission concluded: '[H]ealthy subjects have no reason for constant haematocrit monitoring, given that the haematocrit level, even in conditions of severe dehydration, cannot vary greatly. The self-checking of haematocrit values by the athletes therefore amounts to a completely unacceptable practice ...'

> For Dr Rempi, doping does not appear to be a problem within the Mercatone Uno team [...]. [H]e has clearly never considered the question, considering it a 'non-problem', or one to be sat on – or, if he has raised the question, he must have resolved it in some other way, that is not for public consumption, but which in any case appears to go outside the canons of medical ethics.

In conclusion, the report acknowledged a 'lack of incontrovertible proof that the high haematocrit which led to Pantani's suspension depended on medical treatment carried out by Dr Rempi' and in fact Dr Rempi was never charged. However, it added:

> [T]he doctor's behaviour appears both negligent and in any case in breach of the provisions laid down in [...] the riders' healthcare regulations approved by the Federal Council of the FCI on 15 February 1998. [...] The clinical data relating to the blood collected from Pantani ... would suggest that it is highly likely that the haematocrit increase shown in this case is due to an artificial and exogenous therapy, and one that is in any case prohibited by the existing anti-doping rules.

This deduction is reinforced by the inability of the subject and the other witnesses questioned, to provide any other explanation, supported by objective data.

On 24 October 2005 I spoke to Dr Roberto Rempi to ask him for his version of the events at Madonna di Campiglio and his comments on this damning report. He told me it was time to let Marco rest in peace, and threatened me with legal action if this book gave him grounds.

Soon after the CSAD's damning report was released, far weightier institutions dived in to protect Marco. Late in June, Gianni Petrucci and Raffaele Pagnozzi, the chairman and secretary of CONI itself, granted Marco a private audience. Petrucci denied any persecution of Marco on the part of his organisation. In Ronchi's account, Petrucci described Marco as 'Italian sporting heritage' and invited him to join the Italian team at the 1999 World Championships at Verona – despite the fact that adhesion to the CSAD campaign, which Marco had so signally boycotted, had been deemed a condition for national-squad selection. Days later, Marco was awarded the Collar for Sporting Merit by Italy's Prime Minister, Massimo D'Alema. In July the organisers of the 1999 World Championships invited him to take part in a press conference to publicise the event. There Marco encountered the FCI president Giancarlo Ceruti. Ronchi alleges that Marco and Ceruti arranged to meet in private soon afterwards. In Ronchi's version Ceruti advised Marco that a simple confession that he had gone astray would have ended the matter. Marco, she writes, found the proposal unacceptable.

In the weeks after Madonna di Campiglio, Marco fell into a deep depression. As ever, outside circumstances complicated matters. Soon after his expulsion from the Giro he was the victim of an extortion attempt involving an unborn child. Ronchi has claimed it was a hoax and that no money changed hands; but Paolo and Tonina were more prolix. Paolo told me: 'It was one of these women that . . . he must have had –' (from his gesture I understood 'hundreds of them') – 'you know, like that – spur-of-the-moment adventures, and he was blackmailed by a woman who said she was expecting his child. She asked him for hundreds of millions [hundreds of thousands of euros]. I said, "Where's the problem? If the child is yours, keep him." He said, "She says she can't have him, because she wants to work and she doesn't want kids ..." I said, "Have a DNA test, make sure the child is yours, see how much she wants, then decide." In the end,' Paolo told me, 'the child wasn't Marco's.'

Tonina interjected: 'Perhaps she wasn't even pregnant.'

Paolo resumed: 'In short, they brought a jar with bits of ... "This is ..."'

Tonina took up the narrative: 'They' – meaning Marco and, by extension, Christine – 'kept it in the fridge three months. Think of that!'

I asked, amazed: 'Are we talking about the foetus?'

'Yes, the foetus! I went to open it and inside there was pee.'

Paolo cut in with the coda: 'She was given some money, and the story ended there.'

Marco's parents then learned that Christine had terminated a pregnancy sometime earlier, perhaps in spring 1999. Paolo told me, with some scorn: 'She had wanted to abort because she said she had to go to school in Ravenna.'

Tonina observed, 'The child wasn't Marco's.'

Paolo protested: 'I don't know, but either way, she wanted to abort, and Marco wanted the child. He seemed happy: he wanted a son, a child.'

Tonina objects, 'That's not true. I found one of his notes, which said, "Children? Only people who want them should have them."'

Marco found his public shaming at Madonna di Campiglio unbearable. The humiliation created a background anxiety that accompanied Marco to the grave. In an interview Christine later sold to the Swiss magazine *Hebdo*, she said: 'He returned home and spent days weeping with desperation. We couldn't go out: there were a hundred and fifty or two hundred journalists surrounding the house. They'd put up tents – it didn't seem it would ever end. They'd brought out long-range listening devices and telephoto lenses to search the house. We could see them. Marco spent four days locked in the dark, silent. I couldn't get through to him. I was desperate, but I went back to my job in the *piadina* kiosk ... Then, Marco started going out again at night. It must have been ten days later that he came to see me and told me: "Listen, I've started to take cocaine."'

As she describes it, Marco confessed to taking cocaine fourteen days after returning home from Madonna di Campiglio – four spent locked away in the dark, and ten more after emerging and heading out into the Cesenatico night. This gives the date 19 June 1999. If this chronology is accurate, Marco may have had to choose between cocaine and the 1999 Tour de France. He chose cocaine.

Drug use did not need to mean self-loathing or self-destruction. There were lawyers, dentists and businessmen who sniffed a small amount on a Friday night, with no deleterious effects on their health or professional life. Elsewhere or in the past, instead of cocaine, they might have indulged in an expensive cognac, or a cigar. Despite the fact that the sudden spread of drug usage was the major public-health issue from the late 1970s – the first official death from heroin overdose took place in 1973 – Italy had traditionally taken a rather liberal stance towards drug use. Until 1990 it was not illegal to possess a small quantity of drugs for personal use, although trafficking was a criminal offence. In 1989 there were estimated to be between 100,000 and 250,000 intravenous drug-users in Italy, with far greater numbers using cocaine and cannabis. When, in 1990, partly under US pressure, a new law imposed gaol sentences for possession of more than a 'daily dose', even of soft drugs, the penal system came close to collapse. Within a couple of years, a third of all convicted criminals were drug-users, of whom 14,000 were in prison. Nonetheless, for the young, a night on the town with a cocaine hit was an instant remedy after trouble at work or a broken heart. It was presumably in this spirit that Marco, with a few of his friends, turned to coke. But there is also an asinine mysticism in Ronchi's version: 'After Madonna di Campiglio, someone – I won't name names as a matter of respect – said to him, "Look, if you sniff a bit of coke, the cocaine helps you discover what's behind reality."'

Cocaine works, in part, on dopamine, one of the neuromodulating chemicals (others include acetylcholine, norepinephrine, serotonin) that, among other things, attach emotions to physical and mental functions. The pleasure of a kiss or a warm bath is the product of the release, by nerve cells in the brain, of dopamine messengers into the synapses. Normally, transporters quickly gather up the dopamine messengers and restore them to their nerve cells. Cocaine attaches itself to the transporters and prevents them from flushing out the dopamine. The high lasts forty minutes to an hour. Regular use leads to tolerance, but those early experiences in June 1999 must have been unforgettable. Through cocaine, Marco may have discovered an equivalent to the emotional comfort he longed for.

At least one of his friends believes Marco had used cocaine before 1999. He certainly knew of the drug, notoriously easy to obtain on the Riviera, and he also knew of its destructive effects. At the end of January 1998 an internationally acclaimed artist with a residence in Cesenatico, Mario Schifano, had died after years of cocaine use (a memoire recording his excesses is entitled 'Cocaine for Breakfast'), and Marco had sent condolences and a bouquet to the family. Whether the two men ever met is not documented. But Marco could hardly not have interested Schifano. In the 1990s, among his works depicting rock stars and politicians, landscapes and pornography, a number of canvasses depict sporting scenes. These include sailing, powerboat racing and motorsport, but he dedicated at least three works to cycling. Schifano was also interested in the role advertising and corporate logos played in the visual environment, and Marco, of course, was a walking billboard for dozens of corporate sponsors.

He probably knew Schifano's work. Marco had begun to paint, and some of his own work mimicked Schifano's techniques: Schifano, interested in the relationship between mechanically produced images — photographs, television, cinema – and memory, would take Polaroids of the television screen, print the images on to canvas and paint over them, obliterating sharpness and geometry, exaggerating and distorting colour and tone, defacing the technological image with the elusiveness of sensory memory. Some of Marco's paintings consist of a brightly coloured background covered with a surface layer, which he then scraped away with the point of the brush handle to reveal what was hidden beneath. The relationship between surface and hidden realities preoccupied Marco all his life. So too did the idea that there was a truth that was artistic; he would tell interviewers that his bike was, to him, like a brush to an artist, and that to deny him the opportunity to ride was akin to suppressing an artist's creative urge. The hypothesis begins to emerge that cocaine quickly became, more than mere substance, an *idea* around which Marco began to structure his personality. Schifano's art may have given Marco a template; so too, may the manner of his death.

It was just one of the endless temptations on offer along the Adriatic Riviera. If Marco had been born elsewhere – in the mountains, for example – his life might not have taken the turn it did. The force of this emerges from the picture of the Riviera given in the novel *Rimini*, written between 1983 and 1985 by the author and playwright Pier Vittorio Tondelli, a native of Emilia. Despite its title, Tondelli describes the Riviera as a single entity, extending from Riccione to the south as far north as Lido di Classe, taking in Bellaria, Bellariva, Marebello, Miramare, and Rivazzurra. His novel portrays Beatrix, a German woman who has traced her lost sister to Bellaria, and travels there expecting to find a few hundred metres of sand and a couple of hotels. Instead she finds 150 kilometres of beaches and 'an inferno of motels, residences and apartments, between which millions of people were in simultaneous movement'.

Tondelli's Riviera is one of alcohol, drugs, group sex in hotel rooms and homosexual orgies on the beach. His characters form instant liaisons, often immediately sexual. A local journalist explains that the Riviera's sex industry 'operates day and night: any time you like, there's someone you can enjoy yourself with, who'll fulfil any desire you have – of whatever sort'. Another remarks that, in the major centres, heroin is hard to find in summer, so the addicts flock to the Riviera. Parallel with the sex and drugs industries is a culture of illegal gambling. So dissolute is Tondelli's Riviera that a religious crank identifies Rimini with 'the great whore, enthroned above the ocean' of Revelation, and prophesies the city's destruction on a date foreseen by the Cabbalists. Against this backdrop, a comedy of tender corruption and explicit sensuality is woven. Fiction, of course, but thoroughly researched and not bereft of foundation.

Some years after *Rimini*, Tondelli returned to the Adriatic Riviera for *Sabato italiano* ('Italian Saturday'), a feature film only completed after Tondelli's death in 1992. The 'Italian Saturday' described by Tondelli and his director, Luciano Menuzzi, opens with funereal music over-playing authentic newspaper headlines reading: 'A tragic weekend', 'Fourteen dead and eleven injured', 'From the beginning of the year, seventy-eight deaths', 'War of the discotheques', and so on. These are the records of the 'Saturday night massacre', a phenomenon of the Adriatic coast in the 1980s, where young revellers left the nightclubs, high on ecstasy, and took part in high-speed car races around the city streets. The film traces the evening of three sets of characters as their paths converge, quite literally, in a massive and fatal pile-up at a junction. One character, a garage hand, tells a girl he wants to impress that he is employed to drive through the countryside with reckless speed, to blow out the corrosive air of the *garbino*, the wind that sweeps over the Riviera on summer afternoons, driving everyone insane.

The Madonna di Campiglio scandal did nothing to detract from Marco's commercial appeal. Citroën told Ronchi their Italian sales had increased by twenty-five per cent during Marco's endorsement, which they were keen to extend; and, at the end of July, Albacom wanted Marco to appear at their stand at a trade show in Rimini. Ronchi arranged to meet him that evening, but Marco didn't show. He was at a friend's flat, rummaging around for evidence that he and Christine were having an affair. To try to overcome the crisis in their relationship, Marco and Christine set off in a camper van to drive around Italy. The trip was a disaster.

Eleven days after Madonna di Campiglio, Raffaele Guariniello of the Turin Public Prosecutor's Office began investigations into the medical data Marco had left behind at the Turin CTO after his October 1995 fall. Before the operation to set Marco's broken bones, Marco gave blood for a standard blood test. The results were very far from self-explanatory. They showed blood values that were abnormal, almost bizarre: Marco's haematocrit, or red cell concentration, was 60.1 per cent; his haemoglobin 20.8 grams per 100 millilitres, and his red blood cell count 6,690,000 per cubic millimetre. This extreme haemo-concentration was treated with an infusion of five and a half litres of a balanced electrolyte solution with glucose and Haemaccel, which continued for sixteen hours after surgery. A second blood test, conducted at 7.40 p.m. on 18 October, during the transfusion, gave normal results: haematocrit 42.3 per cent, haemoglobin 14.6 grams per 100 millilitre, erythrocyte count (RBC) 4,730,000 per cubic millimetre. During the days that followed Marco had become anaemic. By 25 October his red blood cell count was so low it was life-threatening. It took a blood transfusion to save his life. Afterwards the surgeon commented: 'I couldn't understand why the haematological rise we normally observe in patients of his age with similar pathologies didn't kick in.'

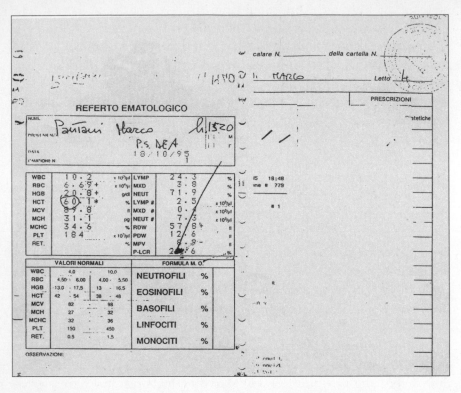

Figure 2: Turin CTO blood test certificate, 18 October 1995.

From the forensic point of view, the episode was suspect, starting with the apparent disappearance of the documents showing the results of the blood test. When the medical files were supplied to Guariniello on 12 June 1999, there was no trace of the test results slip. The anaesthetist swore she had seen the results before surgery; a note she made at the time, showing Marco's haemoglobin value, confirmed her claim. The court finally obtained the results on 22 September 1999 from Marco's insurer, Reale Assicurazione. The results had evidently been kept in Pantani's file at the CTO from 18 October 1995, at least until 8 November, when a photocopy was made and sent to Marco, or someone representing Marco, for dispatch to his insurer. The photocopy shows that the slip was attached to the medical file when it was photocopied. On 19 July 1999 Professor Gian Martino Benzi, one of the forensic haematologists asked by the investigating magistrate to act as an expert witness, had obtained his own copy directly from the CTO. It had arrived with the following note from the doctor responsible for the CTO blood analysis laboratory: 'I hereby produce a copy of the haematochemical tests carried out urgently on 18/10/95 on the patient Marco Pantani, present in the file, and furthermore the print from our computer file – routine exam – in the period 19/10/95 until 27/10/95.' Apparently the slip had been mislaid in November 1995, perhaps during photocopying. Its whereabouts until its reappearance in July 1999 were never established. A clerical oversight, perhaps, but, given Marco's status, the incident took on suspicious overtones. The magistrate described the temporary misplacement as 'worrying'.

If Madonna di Campiglio had been more than Marco could bear, the announcement of an investigation into the Milan–Turin fall was an attack on his identity. He felt that the fall, and his struggle to recover from it, defined him as a cyclist and as a man, and he may have perceived the inquiry as a calculated attempt to humiliate him publicly. In the chronology that emerges from Christine's statements, Marco turned to cocaine three days after the Milan–Turin investigation was launched.

Late in 1999 Marco made an unexpected call to Marcello Lodi, the expert in biomechanics who had worked with Marco in his Carrera days. Lodi recalls: 'It was at night. The telephone was on charge somewhere, and it took a while to find. When I finally answered, I didn't recognise Marco at first. "Marce, it's Marco." "Marco, how are you?" We spoke for a few minutes, and Marco said: "Marce, if I'm going to get out of this, I need you." I asked him where he was: he was in Modena, with Pregnolato. A couple of days later I drove down to Modena to meet him. I thought Marco was referring to Madonna di Campiglio. I had no idea about the cocaine.'

At Modena, Marco asked Lodi to talk to Cenni to discuss a plan to help Marco recover. 'He said, "Marce, when I had problems at the start of my career, you helped me."' Lodi had never met Cenni, so he called Italo Mazzacurati, a former *domestique* of Felice Gimondi under Luciano Pezzi. Mazzacurati brokered the meeting, which was to have been between Marco, Lodi and Cenni. However, the night before the meeting, Marco called Lodi again. 'He asked me if I minded if he didn't come. I said yes, I did mind. He said Manuela wanted to go instead. "Your girlfriend wants to come?" "She's not my girlfriend. She takes care of my image."' The meeting went ahead, with Ronchi instead of Marco.

Lodi described a project that didn't include the Giro. 'I wanted to remove Marco from the Italian cycling milieu, to take him away from the world of doping. To free his mind, I planned to take him fishing in Spain, and then to prepare for the Tour de France.' Lodi had already spoken to Eduardo Castello Vilanova, a former rider – champion of Spain in 1971 – with a property near Castillon de la Plana, south of Valencia.

I spent an afternoon pike-fishing with Marcello Lodi, watching as he whipped the line backhand to a target twenty, twenty-five, then thirty feet away, into the shadows against the bank where the predators had their lairs. 'You don't think anything,' he told me. 'It's a kind of timelessness.' Marco had invited Lodi to fish for pike and black bass in the pools near Cervia and Milano Marittima. Now, fishing was Lodi's proposed therapy to restore Marco to himself, far from the Italian cycling world with its equivocal habits. Lodi wanted Marco to avoid the pressure and innuendo of the Giro, and prepare exclusively for the Tour de France.

At the meeting, Lodi recalls that Ronchi listened in silence. Lodi left believing he had Cenni's agreement. 'When I left, she said, "We'll meet again, you and I." I was rather insulted when she used the intimate form, *tu*, with me. I asked Cenni's permission to leave the meeting – then I never heard anything from them ever again. Many months later, when I heard Marco was riding the Giro, I wrote to Cenni to say I believed it was a mistake for Marco to be there. He never replied.'

On 11 November 1999 Marco was to appear before Guariniello in connection with the Milan–Turin accident. Guariniello had acquired the medical records of each of Marco's serious accidents since Superga. The magistrates threatened to undo everything Marco had achieved in the past half-decade.

Two days before that court appearance, according to Ronchi's chronology, she drove to collect Marco, only to learn of Marco's drug abuse. She told me: 'He said, "No, Manu, we're not going anywhere, because something very serious has happened, and we'll not get out of here." He took me to the apartment of his girlfriend, who'd made herself scarce, probably because, participating with him in a round of cocaine, she'd realised that Marco became uncontrollable, and the reactions of Marco wanting to know the truth had scared her, and she'd left. We went into this apartment and, probably because he was ashamed, he said something like: "Manu, I'm sorry, I've disappointed you, there's nothing to be done, I'm a drug addict, I've started using cocaine, I'm finished, there's nothing to be done."' Ronchi continued: 'From the moment Marco said to me, "Help!" I said, in that moment, "I'll be a friend."'

Then Ronchi made an extraordinary claim:

'From that moment [i.e., November 1999], I never again asked for money from Marco, because the relationship of a manager with an athlete equals a percentage of what you make them earn. But, with Marco, I wasn't only a manager. Because, in the team, I was an administrator, so I was there in the first person. I was the team-manager, I was Marco's manager, and I was the head of communication in the press office. So I had four roles which, in a team budget, corresponds to four salaries. I never took money from any of these. I go four times a week to Cesenatico, what do I do? Ask for a reimbursement of my petrol at the end of the month? How could I have been credible and helped him if I'd made it a question of money? In the end I said, "A friend doesn't do it for money." I had the team, so in theory I should have been remunerated not by Marco Pantani as a person but by the team. But if the company didn't have the money to pay the riders, how could I accept money for myself? In the end, I always thought that, as Marco Pantani's manager, some day or other, there would be some form of recognition. But I considered I'd been paid by Pantani the day he had the world in his hand, and he chose me.'

If, in November 1999 Marco's cocaine abuse was already so serious that it was no longer ethical to accept money from him, why did she not inform his sponsors immediately? Why did she wait, as she says she did, until January 2002? In December 1999, Ronchi claims, Pantani told her he had written to Romano Cenni, the owner of Mercatone Uno, and informed him he was a regular user of cocaine. Ronchi did nothing to confirm this, and only learned that Marco had lied in January 2002. How could Marco's cocaine use not have arisen during sponsorship negotiations in late 1999, 2000 and 2001 for the following season? Cocaine, after all, is on the International Olympic Committee's list of banned substances, and as recently as August 1999 it had been at the centre of a high profile scandal involving the legendary Cuban high-jumper Javier Sotomayor. Marco was habitually and repeatedly in breach of sporting ethics and the anti-doping regulations. If the sponsors who signed wealthy sponsorship contracts knew about his cocaine abuse, then they had behaved unethically by financing his continued sporting activity. On the other hand, if Ronchi had withheld sensitive information, she was open to accusations of misconduct.

If Marco had anything to say to the investigating magistrate Raffaele Guariniello on 11 November, he kept it to himself. Ten minutes after he had entered the court building, he left it. Asked by a waiting journalist if he had exercised his right to remain silent, he blurted a curt 'Yes'. To the follow up 'Why?' he grumbled: 'It's better that way. I've nothing to hide. I've submitted a written statement to explain my position more clearly.' In a press release, the Mercatone Uno team contested the grounds for the investigation and attributed Marco's high haematocrit after the Milan–Turin race to the trauma of the accident. It also revealed that, on 12 July, a claim had been lodged with Stefano Rodotà, the State Guarantor responsible for the use of personal information, to prevent the publication of information relating to Marco's health. The privacy issue related to the press; Marco still risked a prison sentence of up to two years, and a fine of up to fifty million lire.

However, there was worse to come. On 27 and 28 December, following partial disclosures in *GQ* magazine earlier in the month, the journalist Eugenio Capodacqua published a series of damaging scoops in *La Repubblica*, drawing on yet another investigation involving Marco: that of the Ferrara magistrate Pierguido Soprani into three major figures in Italian sport: the scientist Francesco Conconi, Rector of the University of Ferrara and Director of the University's Centre for Biomedical Studies Applied to Sport, Conconi's former assistant, Dr Michele Ferrari, and the former CONI president Mario Pescante, whose organisation had funded the Centre. As early as October 1998 Soprani had informed Conconi, Ferrari and Pescante that they were under investigation for offences related to doping. The investigation was an offshoot of the Giro inquiries triggered prior to the 1996 Giro d'Italia. A Bologna pharmacy, Giardini Margherita, had been identified as a major centre for the supply of doping products. Searches there revealed documents suggesting widespread doping at both the Giro and Tour de France in 1996. The investigation was unusual in that, although self-evident ethical principles were being flouted and public funding misspent – Conconi's Centre had consumed 660 million lire of CONI funding during the period from 1990 to 1996 – it was unclear precisely which ruling in the Italian penal code defined the wrongdoing. Investigators met a wall of silence, although confidential sources and press investigations began to uncover the contours of a covert, state-funded doping system, in some respects comparable to Programme 1425, the notorious East German doping system, the trial of which took place in 1998 and 1999. In East Germany between 1960 and 1990 more than ten thousand uninformed youngsters had been given steroids, under instructions from its highest political office, as part of a quest for dominance in worldwide sport. The Italian programme, if such it was, was modest by comparison, and concerned only top Olympic and professional athletes. Nonetheless, it was still a flagrant breach of sporting ethics.

Until approximately 1979 doping had largely been an individual affair – the athlete advised, at most, by his coach or doctor. The change came with the widespread use of blood transfusions, pioneered in Finland in the 1970s, which required qualified medical support, laboratories and much larger budgets. A long list of witnesses told investigators that Conconi had been administering blood transfusions to Italian athletes since 1979 and specifically at the Moscow Olympics in 1980 and before the 1984 Los Angeles Games. In March 1985 the Italian minister for health had declared blood transfusion for the purposes of performance enhancement in sport illegal. Publicly the Italian sporting authorities had agreed to discontinue the practice; statements from athletes suggested illegal transfusions were still being carried out by staff at Ferrara as late as 1988, despite cases of hepatitis among the athletes treated. The practice of blood transfusion apparently continued until it was outmoded by the advent of r-EPO in the early 1990s, only to return at the end of the decade.

Days after the drama at Madonna di Campiglio, in June 1999, a Swiss television crew had filmed a man throwing a parcel of medical waste from a Lampre team car during the Tour of Switzerland. The waste included empty syringes and cartons which had contained doping products. The footage went to air and prompted Soprani to order NAS raids all over Italy. Towards the end of June the homes of many of Marco's most successful colleagues and rivals were searched, including those of Ivan Gotti, Pavel Tonkov, Paolo Savoldelli and Mario Cipollini. The teams Mapei, Saeco and Mercatone Uno were also targeted; r-EPO was found in the fridge of a former Festina rider, Gianluca Bortolami. Bortolami had had a near miss the previous year, when he had been left out of Festina's Tour de France team at the last minute and avoided involvement in the scandal at that year's Tour.

Then, at the end of December, came Capodacqua's revelations in *La Repubblica*. They were based on incriminating databases copied from hard disks during a police raid on Conconi's Centre on 29 October 1998. In his first article, Capodacqua named the twenty-two athletes treated at the Centre and described as 'EPO-treated' in a file entitled 'epo.wks'. They included many of the most successful Italian cyclists of the previous decade: Gianni Bugno; Claudio Chiappucci; the great Danish Classics rider Rolf Sorensen; the former World Champion cyclist Maurizio Fondriest and his faithful *domestique* Marco Zen. If the allegations were proven, the history of Italian cycling in the 1990s would have to be rewritten.

The following day Capodacqua delivered a blow that would shake Marco for the rest of his life: he revealed that a second file, 'dblab.wdb', contained the results of hundreds of blood tests carried out between 1992 and 1995 on dozens of athletes, some well known, others less so. Among the biggest names included in the file was Marco Pantani. On 16 March 1994, Marco's haematocrit was recorded at 40.7 per cent. Sixty-eight days later, on 23 May – mid-Giro d'Italia – it had jumped to 54.5 per cent. The day after celebrating his second place overall on the podium in Milan, Marco's haematocrit was given in 'dblab.wdb' as an incredible 58 per cent. Six weeks later, after finishing third in his first Tour de France, the level was virtually unchanged: 57.4 per cent. From 23 May to 25 July, then, Marco's blood values were continuously far higher than normal. During this period, he disputed the 1994 Giro d'Italia, Championship of Italy and Tour de France. After 25 July Pantani underwent no more blood tests for the rest of 1994. In March 1995 Marco's haematocrit was given as 45 per cent, but owing to the fall at Santarcangelo on 1 May he missed the Giro d'Italia. On 22 June, as the 1995 Tour de France loomed, the figure had returned to 56 per cent. He would win the stages to Alpe d'Huez and Guzet Neige. This was the last of the entries for Marco in 'dblab.wdb'; with a minimum of 40.7 per cent (16 March 1994) and a maximum of 58 per cent (25 July 1995), the range of variation in Marco's haematocrit shown in the file was 42.5 per cent. The maximum natural variation, Capodacqua notes, is 10 per cent. Marco's altered blood values continued with the haematocrit of 60.1 per cent found after Marco's admission to the Turin CTO on 18 October. Marco was far from unique among the dblab.wdb riders: Claudio Chiappucci's haematocrit went from a low of 35.7 per cent on 8 January 1994 to 60.7 per cent on 17 June: an astonishing variation of *70 per cent*. Guido Bontempi showed haematocrit variation of 54 per cent, Piotr Ugrumov of 40.2 per cent, Nicola Minali of 42.5 per cent, and Ivan Gotti, 40 per cent. None of these degrees of variation could be explained except through critical illness – which none of these athletes appeared to have suffered – or some form of manipulation. Nonetheless, Marco was the star, and he was singled out for extensive description.

No charges had been brought against Marco; there was still room for denial. But the publication presented him with three shattering revelations: the first was that his blood values for the first three years of his professional career had been recorded; the second was that those records, and every other moment of his professional career, were now under scrutiny by the police; the third was that the national press had access to the ongoing investigations. That crippling sensation of being observed was only going to get worse.

On 13 January 2000, Marco celebrated his thirtieth birthday at a training camp in the Canary Islands. Partying with the other riders, Marco produced a bag of cocaine. The evening ended with the cocaine – to which Marco always referred euphemistically as *la roba*, 'the stuff' – flushed down the toilet, and Marco in tears, crying, 'I've let you down' to Ronchi. If her account is to be believed, everyone in the team now knew of his cocaine use – everyone except Marco's doctors and sponsors.

14

The Noose Tightens
(JANUARY–DECEMBER 2000)

Marco's humiliation at Madonna di Campiglio awoke in him a voice, a rant – 'Look what they've done to me. Look what they've reduced me to' – that began to consume him. It would take him over for days and became a hindrance to living. In his cocaine delirium it began to fill books, paper scraps, even bed sheets. These jottings read like cries for help, or suicide notes written years in advance. One he addressed to Ambrogio Fogar, the tetraplegic former explorer he had met in 1996.

He also began to see more of a friend he had known for years. Nevio Rossi had been a schoolfriend of Alfio Vandi, a second-stream professional rider in the 1970s and 1980s. Vandi tells an anecdote about a training ride with Giambattista Baronchelli, who twice finished second in the Giro d'Italia. Followed by a group of teenaged racers, they set off on a long ride to the Tuscan hills. After five or six hours they turned to see who was still with them. Only Marco remained; he chimed in, in dialect, with: 'I've still got plenty left. I'm staying here out of respect.' Vandi and Baronchelli both retired at the end of 1989, so Marco can have been no older than nineteen.

Whether through Vandi, or on Cesenatico's Port Canal – Nevio had a boat, although he wasn't a fisherman – Nevio had met Marco early in the nineties. In 1996 Marco and Christine first visited Nevio's home, in the fields not far from the Rimini North motorway junction. Nevio's other activities at the time were strictly confidential. Only in July 1999 did they emerge from police confessions by two men who had imported large quantities of cocaine, with Rossi's help, during five voyages to the Caribbean, starting in 1993. The allegations were supported by the state of readiness of a boat for another voyage. Rossi and one of his accusers were taken into preventive custody and gaoled at Civitavecchia. Rossi was eventually charged for his role in a massive cocaine-smuggling operation, involving the import of 334 kilograms of liquid cocaine from Venezuela between 1994 and 1997. He had been filmed paying 566 million lire (€283,000) to an undercover agent.

After seven months in the high-security wing of Civitavecchia prison, during which he refused to talk, Rossi was released to serve a further five months under house arrest. It was during this period that Marco was a regular visitor. He loved hearing Rossi's tales of adventure. Through Rossi, as through Mario Schifano, Marco may have built a delusional fantasy of adventure and artistic creativity around his cocaine use.

The DNA test on blood sample UCI–IUML 11140, taken at Madonna di Campiglio, was presented in court on 24 January 2000. It concluded that the genotype occurred in the population with a frequency of 0.000000000041074 per cent. It could belong to Pantani and no one else. The noose was tightening. Tormented by memories of Madonna di Campiglio and the Milan–Turin crash, and under investigation for both, Marco's life was falling apart. His relationship with Christine was in the balance, he was using cocaine regularly, and he was suffering a series of niggling, perhaps non-existent physical problems. His driving had become even more reckless. On 12 September 1999 Marco had lost control of his Mercedes 600 on a bend and destroyed the car. In January 2000 he careened off the Adriatic state road in his Ferrari and on 5 March he crashed his Mercedes 320 into a telegraph pole, close to the villa at Sala. These were just the accidents that made the press. Each time he was unharmed. On 20 March Marco published an open letter: 'At this time, even if I'm physically ready to race, I'm going through a difficult period with too much inner suffering that, despite the enormous efforts of those close to me, only I can overcome.' The letter reads as if written not by Marco but by one of those close to him. And on 20 April 2000 the magistrate investigating Marco's 1995 Milan–Turin fall recommended that charges be brought against him for sporting fraud.

On 4 May 2000 Marco released a statement saying he would not be riding the Giro. Before the Giro could start, Eugeni Berzin, Pantani's old rival, was suspended with high haematocrit. Then, on 13 May, the race began – and Marco was part of it. He was clearly in no condition to ride competitively, unlike his team-mate Stefano Garzelli, who emerged as a contender for overall victory. On the first difficult stage through the Tuscan hills Marco was dropped. He accused the team of doing nothing to support him, talked about abandoning, and then, on the morning of stage nineteen, an arduous mountain stage through the Alps to Briançon in France, he became convinced that someone in the team had sabotaged his bike. He threatened to ride thirty kilometres and then step down. Instead he launched a series of accelerations on the Izoard that weakened Garzelli's main rivals, then dropped back to help his team-mate up the final climb. Finally, he darted away, like the old days, and took second place in the stage behind an early solo breakaway. Marco finished the race a kingmaker, twenty-eighth overall, twenty-one seconds short of an hour behind the winner, his team-mate Stefano Garzelli.

Suddenly Marco became an outside tip for the 2000 Tour de France – until the first mountain stage, when Marco attacked in the rain, and Lance Armstrong rode straight past him. Marco's career as the greatest climber in the sport seemed to be over. Two days later the decline was confirmed when he was unable to stay with the leading group on the lower slopes of Mont Ventoux. Wisely he decided to drop back and ride alone, at a more sustainable pace. When the front-runners went into crisis, he rode back up to them, then attacked. In four kilometres he made five killing accelerations. The Colombian Santiago Botero was the first to give chase, but Marco floated thirty metres ahead of him, and the gap remained. Then, behind them both, as Jan Ullrich led Joseba Beloki, Roberto Heras and Lance Armstrong around the outside of a right-hand curve, Armstrong launched an unanswerable attack. Every three turns of the pedals, he moved a length away from Ullrich and a length closer to Botero. He passed the Colombian at the same rate, fixing him in the eye as he cruised past. Then he bridged the gap to Marco, finally lowering himself into the saddle ten metres before reaching him. On the way past, Armstrong turned to Marco and spoke, before positioning himself in Marco's path, offering up his slipstream. Marco had to stand on the pedals to match Armstrong's speed and even then the American turned in the saddle, looking to make sure Marco was still there, pointing an outstretched finger at the space behind him, to say he wanted to work with, not against Marco, to build up his lead. It was also understated intimidation, as if to say, 'Even at this speed, I'm in complete control.'

In the final kilometre Marco rode alongside the Texan and looked into his face, but there was no response. Each wore his characteristic expression of ultimate effort: the starved, bloodless crescents of Armstrong's cheeks; Marco's creased forehead, contemplative eyes and lips squirming back from his teeth. Both men had pushed themselves to the very limit. Armstrong pulled ahead and looked over his shoulder at Marco. At tremendous cost Marco crossed the line first, taking his first win for thirteen months and eight days. Pregnolato and the other team masseur, Stefano Chiodini, were waiting, beside Manuela Ronchi. The performance stirred Ronchi to tears. Marco shouted at her in embarrassment. Pregnolato recalls: 'He didn't want pathetic people around him. He didn't want to see you cry, or to hear great speeches. All he cared was that you were there. People have often said that Marco never showed any joy when he won a stage. But he preferred to celebrate at the end, when the race was won overall.'

After the stage he told Rai's Alessandra Di Stefano: 'I didn't like Armstrong's company. Armstrong's a great champion, but I'd have liked to have arrived alone.' Armstrong replied: 'I don't know what Pantani's thinking but ... he's just a little shit starter.' A feud began between the two men. Later, Giuseppe Martinelli would say: 'Marco always respected Armstrong. The only thing he couldn't get over was that Armstrong went too fast. He said, "It isn't possible that, on all these climbs, he riders that much faster, given the effort I make."'

On stage fifteen, on the climb to Courcheval, Tonina made a rare appearance at the roadside. As Marco passed her, he accelerated with such ferocity that he was suddenly alone. Leading the stage was the Spanish climber José Maria Jiménez. Marco caught and dropped him, and finished the stage alone. He jumped into sixth place overall, nine minutes three seconds behind Armstrong. A week before, he had been finished. Now, he was a miracle-worker again, and anything seemed possible.

The following day, from Courcheval to Morzine, Marco launched an impossible attack with 130 kilometres to the finish line. It evoked his winning move on the stage to Les Deux Alpes in the 1998 Tour. The move put Armstrong in crisis; bewildered by the madness of Marco's attack, he too suffered a physical breakdown, one of only two in his seven-year domination of the Tour de France. He even called his adviser

Michele Ferrari, Conconi's old associate, for tactical advice. This time, though, Marco's madness ended in failure. Never more than two minutes ahead of the main group, he began to suffer stomach cramps, which ended his attack. But Marco's unpredictability had lost Armstrong one minute thirty-seven seconds to Ullrich, one minute thirty-four to Roberto Heras, and fifty seconds to Joseba Beloki. That evening Armstrong described the stage as 'the most difficult day of my life'. Marco, meanwhile, abandoned. Courcheval had given him what would prove the last win of his career.

Yet Marco remained a magnet for televison audiences. His stage win between Briançon and Courchevel in the 2000 Tour had replaced his win between Merano and Aprica in the 1994 Giro as the most-watched Italian cycling transmission since viewing figures began (in 1985). In eleven of the fifteen most-watched cycling transmissions, he had been the principal attraction. The official figures make no allowance for viewers watching away from their homes; since the Giro and Tour are summer events, the true audiences were probably far higher. And this, for a sometimes complex sport whose long durations are packaged for televison only with difficulty.

Auditel viewing figures for Italian television cycling transmissions (reproduced with permission), in descending order:

Average	Share (%)	Date	Location (Event)	Channel	Main Attraction
6,046,000	54.15	16/7/00	Briançon–Courchevel (Tour)	Rai3	Marco
5,847,000	50.90	5/6/94	Merano–Aprica (Giro)	Italia 1	Marco
5,835,000	58.07	7/6/98	Mendrisio–Lugano (Giro)	Rai3	Marco
5,102,000	49.70	11/6/94	Les Deux Alpes–Sestriere (Giro)	Italia 1	Marco
4,793,000	28.62	28/5/95	Val Senales–Lenzerheide (Giro)	Italia 1	Ivan Gotti
4,617,000	30.13	5/6/94	Merano–Aprica (1st trans.) (Giro)	Italia 1	Marco
4,557,000*	51.03	4/6/94	Cavalese–Montecampione (Giro)	Rai3	Marco
4,465,000	52.22	25/8/91	Stuttgart (World Championships)	Rai2	Gianni Bugno

4,396,000	37.82	10/10/87	(World Hour Record attempt)	Rai1	Francesco Moser
4,369,000	44.70	10/6/94	Cuneo–Les Deux Alpes (Giro)	Italia 1	Marco
4,362,000	50.83	3/6/98	Selva V. Gardena– Pampeago (Giro)	Rai3	Marco
4,356,000	33.59	8/6/96	Cavalese–Aprica (Giro)	Italia 1	Marco
4,292,000	42.97	28/7/98	Vizille–Albertville (Tour)	Rai3	Marco
4,291,000	48.74	4/6/94	Lienz–Merano (Giro)	Italia 1	Marco
4,282,000	40.96	7/6/97	Malè–Edolo (Giro)	Rete 4	Ivan Gotti

*Highest weekday viewing figures since records began.

Before the 2000 Olympic Games at Sydney, a high-ranking official at Rai is said to have commented: 'Pantani is useful to me for viewing figures.' This alone explains Marco's selection: he had never excelled in one-day races, and the Olympic race route didn't suit his characteristics. To make matters worse, Italy's 'Probable Olympians' were obliged to take part in the 'I don't risk my health' campaign Marco had so vociferously boycotted the year before. It meant a series of blood tests that soon embroiled Marco in yet more controversy.

On 1 August 2000 Marco attended his first test:

'I don't risk my health' test 1 August 2000

	Normal range	Marco on 1/8/00
Hct	40–52%	44.5%
Hb	12–16 g/dl	14.5 g/dl
sTfR	0.83–1.76 ng/dL	1.05 ng/dL
EPO	2–16 mU/ml	22 mU/ml
Total reticulocytes	30–80 billion/L	6 billion/L
RDW	11.6–14.8%	15.6%
Ferritin	15–250 ng/ml	636 ng/ml
s-LH	9–22 mUI/ml	8.7 mUI/ml
MCV	82–92 fl	93.6 fl
Platelets	180–400 x 10^9/l	141 x 10^9/l
Serum transferrin	17–52%	70%

Of the eleven parameters measured, only three – haematocrit, haemoglobin and soluble transferrin receptor (a receptor expressed on the surface of human cells that require iron) – were within the normal range. However, the EPO level was high, giving rise to the suspicion that Marco may have been undergoing r-EPO therapy. Yet Marco's reticulocyte count was extremely low. The high value for red cell distribution width (RDW), an index of the variation in red blood cell volume, also rang bells: increases in RDW suggest the presence of an unusually mixed population of cells, suggesting r-EPO abuse. Ferritin concentrations reflect the body's iron stores, so the extremely high ferritin value evoked the iron supplements that have to accompany r-EPO therapy. The tests also examined serum levels of luteinising hormone ('s-LH'). Luteinising hormone is a gonadotropin released by the pituitary gland, and its concentration in the serum is used, for research purposes – the test has no legal validity – as an indirect indicator of growth hormone abuse. With the necessary caveats, Marco's anomalous reading was taken as a hint that, as well as r-EPO therapy, he may have been doped with human growth hormone.

At Salice Terme on 5 September a second battery of tests was carried out on the 'Probable Olympian' cyclists. Once again there were marked anomalies in Marco's results, compared with both 'normal' parameters and the 1 August results:

'I don't risk my health' test 5 September 2000

	Normal range	Marco on 1/8/00	Marco on 5/9/00
Hct	40–52%	44.5%	49%
Hb	12–16 g/dL	14.5 g/dl	16 g/dl
RDW	11.6–14.8%	15.6%	16.1%
Ferritin	15–250 ng/ml	636 ng/ml	1019 ng/ml
Serum transferrin	17–52%	70%	83.5%
Total reticulocytes	30–80 billion/L	6 billion/L	6.5 billion/L
sTfR	0.83–1.76 ng/dl	1.05 ng/dl	0.71 ng/dl
Total iron	65–170 μg/dl	–	238 μg/dl
Reticulocytes	5–20 2×10^3/RBC	–	1.2 2×10^3/RBC

Again, there were many anomalies. Since 1 August Marco's haematocrit had jumped from 44.5 per cent to 49 per cent, while his ferritin levels, already high, were higher still. Both conditions suggested r-EPO therapy. On 13 September a letter from a clinical haematologist privy to the blood-test results was dispatched to the CONI directors, stating his expert opinion that the blood data of athlete MN8916GC – in the event, Marco Pantani – showed 'particularly altered haematological parameters, indicating a condition of erythrocytosis associated with suppression of the erythropoietic activity of the bone marrow and acute iron overload. As a clinical haematologist, my advice would be immediate suspension from athletic activity.'

The CSAD had powers to suspend athletes, but only if it could point to variations from normal 'base' values. Since both tests revealed wild anomalies, the CSAD had no 'base' values with which to compare them, and was powerless. CONI's directors, by contrast, could have intervened, but did nothing. The FCI's chief doctor was informed by telephone of the abnormalities on the evening of the Salice Terme tests and was told that the CSAD had delivered an informal note to CONI's secretary, Pagnozzi, expressing concern over Pantani's test results. But the Secretary General and the anti-doping chief later claimed not to remember the letter recommending his suspension. The case hit the headlines when Pagnozzi, in Sydney, voiced doubts over the blood-test results of a high-profile athlete whose identity he refused to divulge. Marco denied it was him, then Hein Verbruggen, the President of the UCI waded into the controversy with a personal attack on the leading members of the CSAD. On 18 September an ANSA report quoted Verbruggen as saying: 'It isn't my style to launch attacks against just anyone, but I cannot accept that a rider like Pantani, who's a symbol of cycling, is made the object of inferences and manoeuvres that can destabilise him.' He continued, 'I begin to wonder how CONI, which is entirely responsible in my eyes, can tolerate among its staff two figures like [Pasquale] Bellotti' – the Secretary of the Commission – 'and [Sandro] Donati' – the head of scientific research at CONI's School of Sport. It was an attack on the anti-doping movement itself: Donati had been responsible for unveiling Conconi's illegal blood transfusions in the late 1980s and his state-sponsored doping programme in the 1990s. He and his colleagues were not millionaire sportsmen, but committed, knowledgeable and increasingly sidelined campaigners, fighting against entrenched and well-connected interests.

Verbruggen's lack of judgement brought the entire Olympic movement into disrepute.

In fact, Marco's presence at Sydney was surrounded by irregularities. The medical certificate authorising Marco to compete at the Games was dated 28 September 2000 – *after* the Olympic road race had been run. In the subsequent investigation Marco presented a medical certificate dated June 2000, ostensibly to demonstrate that his ferritin levels were naturally high. The certificate proved no such thing: indeed, it showed an EPO level of 72 mU/ml, far outside the 'normal' range of 2–16 mU/ml, and anomalous compared with the 1 August value of 22 mU/ml. It would later emerge that, in July and August 2000, CONI had carried out precisely *no* surprise, out-of-competition anti-doping tests: all anti-doping activities had effectively been suspended for the duration of the crucial pre-Olympic months. Testing conducted under the 'I don't risk my health' campaign ground to a halt in September, when there had been leaks suggesting abnormally high levels of high human growth hormone in Italy's Olympic squad. These leaks were attributed to the CSAD and used as a pretext to dismantle it. On 26 October 2000 the Scientific/Anti-doping Committee of the Italian Olympic Committee – its sole functioning anti-doping organism – ceased to exist.

The issue at the centre of this controversy – Marco's Olympic performance – had been utterly forgettable: he finished sixty-ninth.

Soon after returning home, Marco was involved in yet another bizarre sequence of car accidents. Early on 3 November he drove his metallic grey Mercedes ML 320 four-wheel drive to Cesena police station, where he was involved in minor collisions entering and exiting the car park. Around midday he entered a one-way street the wrong way. Corso Ubaldo Comandini, a narrow, porticoed street in Cesena town centre, was lined with parked cars when Marco sped along it in excess of the 30 k.p.h. speed limit for traffic coming legally in the opposite direction. A witness later recalled: 'I heard a huge bang; I thought it was a bomb and threw myself to the ground. Then I saw the Mercedes on top of the Peugeot.' Marco had touched a small van on one side of the street and driven into a Volkswagon Golf on the opposite side, before mounting, with his front wheels, a Peugeot 405, which then rolled backwards, causing a domino effect involving four other vehicles. The witness added: 'He seemed to be normal.' The police patrol said the same thing.

Marco, then, was apparently not under the influence of cocaine: the cause of the accident was his impulsiveness, now little short of pathological, and indicative, perhaps, of underlying psychological problems.

Meanwhile, the trial at Forlì over Marco's blood-test results after the Milan–Turin accident on 18 October 1995 was drawing to a close with a flurry of legal activity. The nomination of Professor Gian Martino Benzi and Professor Adriana Ceci was highly suggestive of the judge's uncompromising stance: both were members of the CSAD, and Professor Ceci had been the first signatory of a white paper entitled 'Law for the fight against doping and for healthcare in sport' in 1988, and the Senate Health Committee expert consultant during the draught stages of the anti-doping law approved by the Senate on 16 November 2000 but not yet published. In March 1985 Ceci had posed a parliamentary question to the Health Minister, who had declared the practice of blood transfusions for sporting-performance enhancement inadmissible.

Benzi and Ceci were able to compare Marco's blood values with tables of values of elite-level athletes collected by CONI and the UCI in 1998 and 1999, which gave 44.6 per cent as the average haematocrit for professional cyclists, with haemoglobin at approximately 15 and erythrocytes at 4.85 million. By contrast, the expert called by the defence told the judge: 'I'm not a man with any interest in sport.'

Marco's own natural blood values were understood to be approximately 45 per cent, haemoglobin 15.2 and erythrocytes 4.94 million. These values correspond to the test carried out by Grazzi on 6 June 1995 and suspected by the judge at Ferrara to have been falsified – although it was reasoned that the falsification probably consisted of replacing artificially high levels with Marco's real values.

A haematologist who examined Marco on 26 October 1995 told the investigating magistrate: 'A patient who presents haematocrit of 60.1 per cent has to be considered beyond normal limits, even for a sportsman. A haematocrit value of this type is not compatible with a healthy person and is compatible with primary or secondary polycythemia, or with pharmacological treatment.' However, Marco's legal team hadn't even attempted to argue that polycythemia was the explanation of Marco's haematocrit. Instead, they had prepared four lines of defence: each could have raised Marco's haematocrit by a certain number of points. To explain away Marco's haematocrit, they had to total 15 – the difference between the highest estimate of his natural level – 45 per cent – and the 18 October level of 60 per cent. Together, the defence's four arguments would, they contended, explain his anomalous blood chemistry. They were, in order, *dehydration* (responsible for a 5 point haematocrit increase), *altitude* (a 4 point increase, making 9), *plasmorrhagia* (i.e. an abnormal discharge or flow of blood plasma – Hct increase not defined, but the maths shows the defence needed at least 2 points to total 11), and flaws in the *blood collection method* (4 points, making 15).

a) dehydration

The dehydration thesis stemmed, in part, from a note made during the operation by the anaesthetist, suggesting Marco may have been dehydrated. The defence seized on this hypothesis, sustaining it, to use the investigating magistrate's word, apodeictically – that is, as an unquestionable truth – despite the complete absence of any supporting scientific literature. They argued that 5 points of Marco's high haematocrit could be attributed to dehydration. On 28 November 2000 the investigating magistrate cross-examined Dr Daniele Tarsi, a cycling-team doctor for fifteen years, and one, as the investigating magistrate wrote, visibly embarrassed by questions about doping in the world of cycling. Tarsi described haematocrit values measured by the UCI after an intense training ride in Sicily, in torrid heat, which revealed an average increase of 2 to 3 per cent – far lower than that presupposed by Marco's legal team, despite climatic conditions far more conducive to severe dehydration. Benzi and Ceci strengthened the prosecution case by arguing that dehydration would have caused not only an increase in haematocrit but a corresponding increase in salts, including sodium and potassium, and of creatinina. Marco's sodium, potassium and creatinina levels were normal: ergo, no dehydration. The anaesthetist then confirmed that she had suspected dehydration on the basis of the headline blood values, not on the basis of a detailed reading of the clinical or haematochemical data.

Dehydration, in other words, could not have caused or even contributed to Marco's haemoconcentration. The defence had already lost 5 points.

b) altitude

From 23 September to 10 October Marco had been in the Colombian department of Boyacá for the World Championships, at an altitude of approximately 2,500 metres above sea level. Low partial pressure of oxygen at altitude causes renal hypoxia, which stimulates the release of erythropoietin. The defence argued that Marco's Colombian adventure may have added 4 points to his haematocrit. A wide range of scientific research, including a 1994 study by the Institute for Sport Science and Bologna's Sant'Orsola Hospital of athletes who trained at 2,900 metres in Ecuador for between three weeks and a month, showed haematocrit increases during the first four to five days of 3 or 4 percentage points, stabilising at the new level thereafter. However, Benzi and Ceci added that, during the period from 10 to 18 October, when Marco had been back at sea level in Italy, his haematocrit would have been expected to decrease by 1 to 2 points – allowing a net increase of no more than 3 points – and his haemoglobin by 0.4 to 0.7 points. The defence had lost another point.

c) plasmorrhagia

The third, and strongest, of the defence hypotheses was that the injuries Marco had suffered shortly before his arrival at the Turin CTO might have been responsible for his unusual blood chemistry. Plasmorrhagia would have produced a fall in plasma proteins, yet Marco's blood protein values on admission to the CTO were normal.

Benzi explained that there is no loss of blood proteins after the initial trauma; protein levels drop after the second traumatic event – that is, the surgery to reduce the double compound fracture, which carried with it the loss of both plasma (with the resulting oedema) and blood. The 15.20 hrs blood-test results show Marco's protein levels at 7g/d – well within the normal range of 6.5 to 7.8g/d – while a blood test on 19 October showed a fall in protein levels to 4.9, in line with Benzi's prediction.

d) blood collection method

The fourth point of the defence was that the way in which the blood had been collected might have been responsible for Marco's unusual blood chemistry. The defence claimed that the blood collection method could be responsible for a haematocrit increase of up to 4 points. The

191

investigating magistrate established that the nurse who collected Marco's blood had confirmed he had observed the correct protocol. The doctor responsible for the CTO blood analysis laboratory added that analyses were systematically repeated when pathological values were found, and that the calibration of the blood counter was regularly checked. She added: 'The attention given to urgent examinations is probably slightly higher than that given to routine tests . . .'

The court consultants observed that, in the case of an analysis showing an anomalous haematocrit but other perfectly normal haemo-chemical values, there was no reason to suspect that the collection had been incorrectly carried out. Further, the other two riders, Secchiari and Dell'Olio, had reached the CTO at approximately the same time as Marco, and their blood samples were presumably collected by the same staff using the same method. Yet their blood values were absolutely normal.

Marco's defence was in tatters. Their attempts to explain away fifteen unaccountable percentage points had exlained away none. Every other explanation having been explored, the only remaining hypothesis to explain his blood chemistry was the massive abuse of recombinant r-EPO.

The court also examined the life-threatening anaemia that had affected Marco in the days that followed his admission to the Turin CTO. The test on 25 October revealed that Marco's haematocrit had dipped to 15.9 per cent, and his haemoglobin to 5.8 per cent. At 11 a.m. that morning, Marco had given his informed consent to the blood transfusion that would save his life. Without urgent treatment Marco would very likely have died, aged twenty-five, from doping.

Then the anaemia miraculously cleared up. Four hours before the transfusion, Marco's erythropoietin levels had been measured in the hospital laboratory. The results were baffling: 86, far beyond the healthy parameters of 6–16. He should have been piled high with red blood solids; instead, there were virtually none of them. The defence seized on the erythropoietin level as evidence that Marco's erythroid marrow was functioning perfectly. However, according to Professor Ceci, Marco's high erythropoietin level, far from suggesting a healthy ery-throid marrow, was an indicator of r-EPO abuse. Professor Ceci wrote: 'Towards the end of his stay, Marco began to improve, more than might be expected after an infusion of two bags of blood, and with this

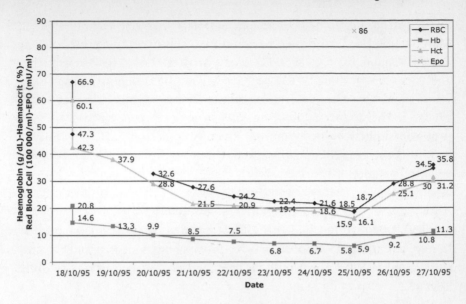

Figure 3: Marco's anaemia after the Milan–Turin crash.

recovery came an increase in reticulytes' – young red blood cells – 'which had been 1.5 per cent, and in the second control were 4.5 per cent ... Either the erythroid marrow had begun to work, late with respect to all that had occurred in the previous days, or ... it can be imagined that [Pantani] had resumed erythropoiesis stimulation which helped him come out of the tunnel.' Independently of the expert witnesses, Massimo Cartasegna, the surgeon who had operated on Marco, had been drawn to the same thought. In court he had described what he considered an inexplicable lack of concern in Marco's doctors and in Marco himself for this acute fall in red blood solids. Their attitude, he said, had left him bewildered. The judge asked: 'Did the various factors you have described lead you to think it possible that, without your knowledge, inside the hospital at Turin, someone – I'm not saying on your staff – may have treated Pantani with erythropoietin?' Cartasegna replied: 'I'm sorry to admit it because it happened without my knowledge, but yes.'

The theory, he said, came to him towards the end of Marco's eight-day stay. It was based on haemotological data alone: there were no witnesses. Davide Dell'Olio, in the next bed to Marco, had told investigators that he had seen no one other than hospital staff administer medicines to Marco. No charges were ever brought. Nonetheless, many months of highly technical debate had led the court to the conclusion that Marco had been treated with r-EPO: he was a doped athlete.

On 6 November Marco's lawyers asked for the judge to be replaced. On 14 November the Court of Appeal in Bologna rejected their request. Then, on 11 December 2000, the day of the judgment, Marco's lawyers presented a declaration, signed by Marco, to the effect that he had never used doping products or practices, as proved by anti-doping control results throughout his career. The declaration had no effect: Marco was found guilty of performing fraudulent acts with the end of attaining, through the artificial improvement of his competitive performance, a result different from that consequent to the loyal and correct conduct of the competition. He was handed a suspended prison sentence of three months, fined 1.2 million lire (€6,000) and banned from attending sporting events or managing sports organisations for a period of six months.

The court passed over an episode of little legal significance but with biographical relevance. Before the operation to reconstruct Marco's leg, doctors needed to establish his family and individual history. Marco's responses to their questions contain important clues to his later decline. After confirming that he was a non-smoker, he gave them information summarised in the curt medical expression *potus saltuario*. *Potus* means 'heavy drinking'; *saltuario*, 'sporadic'. Marco, then, described himself as a sporadic binge drinker. Finally, the clinical notes record Marco's response to the question 'Are you under medical treatment?' His answer is of some importance: it is effectively the first time on record that Marco was asked straight whether or not he was using doping products. We have no direct insight into his thought processes, and we can only imagine that it was without hesitation that he answered: 'No.'

The guilty verdict was based on a highly contested interpretation of the law, and one which Marco's legal team had every expectation of reversing on appeal. There is historical irony in the fact that the passing of an anti-doping law within days of Marco's conviction eventually came to their assistance.

Law 376, dated 14 December 2000 (Law 376/2000), was not without precedent. Its title, 'Discipline for healthcare in sport and the fight against doping', recalled that of Law 1099/1971, 'Healthcare in sport'. Article three of the 1971 law punished 'the use of substances dangerous to athletes' health with the aim of artificially modifying their natural energies'. But, by prescribing no more than derisory fines, it had posed little deterrent, and in 1981, together with all other transgressions punishable only by fines, doping as defined by Law 1099/1971 was depenalised. Then, in 1989, Law 401/1989, known as the 'football betting' act, had been introduced to combat match-fixing. Some legal commentators argued that the expression 'fraudulent acts', used in the text of the law, should be interpreted to include doping, which was clearly intended to falsify the loyal and sporting conduct of the event. The prosecutions against Marco relating to both Madonna di Campiglio and Milan–Turin were based on this interpretation of Law 401/1989.

However, the legislative background to Law 376/2000 gave the lie to this interpretation. In November 1996 Senator Fiorello Cortiana of the Italian Green Party had presented a white paper entitled 'Norms for the fight against doping and for healthcare in sport'. Cortiana's submission made reference to earlier attempts to 'go beyond the pre-existing norms (*vide* Law 26 October 1971, No. 1099)' – thereby spelling out that Parliament did not understand the 1989 law to be anti-doping legislation.

Cortiana's white paper had led to a draft text, approved by the Senate's Permanent Committee on Health and Hygiene on 21 July 1999. This text targeted the supplier of the doping products or the practitioner of the doping method. On 29 March 2000 the First Standing Consultative Committee on Constitutional Affairs gave its support to the law, on condition that the athletes were not to be punished by law. Four months later, on 12 July, the Second Standing Consultative Committee on Justice made its support dependent on the opposite. After long and bitter debate in Parliament, the text drafted by the Justice Committee was incorporated into Article 9 of the new law:

> Unless the action constitutes a more serious crime, whosoever provides to others, dispenses, consumes or facilitates in any way the use of drugs or biologically or pharmaceutically active substances ... not justified by pathologies and which are apt to alter the competitive performance of athletes, or are intended to alter the results of tests to detect the use of such drugs or substances, shall

be punished with a custodial sentence of from three months to three years, and a fine of from five million to 100 million lire.

Law 376/2000 brought Italy into line with the 1989 Strasbourg Convention against Doping, to which it was a signatory. It criminalised doping and introduced sanctions, which included temporary or permanent injunctions prohibiting athletes or those who doped them from taking part in, or even attending, sports events, or working in the medical field.

Marco had played an inadvertent cameo role in the genesis of Law 376/2000, not through any considered contribution to the anti-doping movement, but as a presence in the files confiscated from the Centre in Ferrara. The spectre of a state-sponsored doping system run from the University of Ferrara, and the absence of any specific law against any such system, had ensured that the proposed new law was politically feasible. It filled a void in the Italian penal code; yet, in the short term, it had an unforeseen side effect: by demonstrating Parliament's conviction that doping had *not* been outlawed by previously existing legislation – specifically, by Law 401/1989 – it threw Marco, and the many other athletes accused of doping before Law 376/2000 came into effect, an unexpected lifeline.

15

Blitzed at San Remo

On 10 February the 2001 Mercatone Uno team presentation took place in a new Cesenatico high-rise hotel. Despite the recent setbacks, it was an upbeat display. The word was spread that Marco had been in training since November; climbing the Madonna delle Querce – the 'Madonna of the Oaks' – twenty kilometres from Terracina, only two team-mates had been able to cling to his wheel. Marco's style was quirky, mystical: 'The prerequisites for a good start are in place. I still have a lot to say. I'm my main enemy: if I find myself, I'll be fine, and if I then finish second or third or tenth, it will be of secondary importance. What matters to me is to start the climb back. I'll make the most of every opportunity. After all I've been through, I think everything's in place for a good season.'

In the next breath he spoke of the recent legal developments as 'injustices committed against me': 'I can't pit myself against people who can trap me by virtue of their arguments and education, so it's up to my legal team to show that, without proof, they can't go around accusing and condemning people. My lawyer will fight for me. And, in the meantime, I'll get on with riding and putting myself on the line with the rules and the competition as they are, as I've been doing for the past twenty years.

'I've almost never defended myself, except to journalists and television cameras. I've never felt the need to defend myself because my conscience has always been clear. From my point of view, I've been singled out. Obviously, I've got my position. It's up to others to judge.' Asked if he believed he had made mistakes, Marco responded with words that must have been incomprehensible to those unaware of his cocaine use: 'Everyday I punish myself for the errors I make. I'm far

197

from perfect. I've made many mistakes, although always in good faith and wanting to do the right thing. I've one regret, which is that all these matters have involved people who have nothing to do with them – my family and friends and all those who've wrongly had to bear incredible pressures. Throughout this period, my freedom of thought and expression have been removed, to a degree. I say again, perhaps it's because I've made mistakes, perhaps because I've been singled out or because of judgements made without concrete facts. Whichever it is, I've paid a very high price. I've often been distanced from cycling. Now I want to find myself again. I have to rediscover my enthusiasm.'

One of those present, the *La Repubblica* cycling writer Eugenio Capodacqua, perceptively dissected Marco's words:

> The 'persecution' hypothesis is answered by the numbers that show soaring red blood cell counts on a number of occasions . . . And then we need to clarify what Pantani means by 'clear conscience'. Can your conscience be clear if you've doped, as the Forlì verdict maintains, simply because everyone was doing it? . . . Obviously, it's infuriating to be one of the few in the firing line, especially when it's absolutely plain that Pantani was not the exception in a sport in which many teams were put together on the basis of haematocrit values alone, 'inflated' by r-EPO, that is, by doping.

In television interviews, Marco expressed hopes of riding both the 2001 Giro and Tour as a contender. He had brought his winter training forward and by mid-January he was at a team training camp at Riccione, which would continue at Terracina. However, beneath the public image another legal storm was brewing from which Marco would never recover. During December 2000 Bruno Giardina, the Trento investigator looking into the blood values found at Madonna di Campiglio, had interviewed Marco's team-mates at Riva del Garda. The new law clearly couldn't be backdated to prosecute earlier crimes so, on 24 January, Giardina concluded that Marco should be tried for sporting fraud under Law 401/1989, under which he had already been convicted at Forlì over Milan–Turin. Where all this would lead there was no way of knowing. But one thing was certain: Forlì had ended in conviction and a suspended sentence so, if convicted again, Marco could not be given a second suspended sentence: next time, he would go to prison.

Two days later the Ferrara magistrate Pierguido Soprani recommended that Francesco Conconi and seven colleagues should be
tried for providing r-EPO and other doping products to many athletes.
Among the athletes named in the document summarising the investigation was Marco. If the trial went ahead, it could spell still more
humiliation for Marco.

And the legal headlines kept coming, each one of which must have
sapped Marco's spirit. On 12 February, in Bologna, the magistrate
Massimo Poppi recommended that Dr Michele Ferrari should stand trial
for doping-related offences. The long list of Marco's colleagues and
rivals treated by Ferrari included Lance Armstrong, Claudio Chiappucci, Mario Cipollini, Ivan Gotti, Axel Merckx, Abraham Olano,
Tony Rominger, Paolo Savoldelli and Pavel Tonkov. Poppi found that
the evidence allowed for a prosecution under the laws prohibiting the
illegal practice of the profession of pharmacist, as well as under Law
401/1989. Marco must have reflected that Ferrari's clients were being
treated as witnesses to a potential crime, whereas he was being hunted
like a delinquent. Among those remanded for trial with Ferrari was
Orlando Maini, Marco's DS at the 1992 amateur Giro d'Italia and again
with Mercatone Uno from 1998.

During this period, the team was monitoring Marco's cocaine use
through urine tests. A test dated 17 February 2001 was positive. Four
days later, another past episode resurfaced. On 21 February the Carabinieri visited CONI's Institute of Sport Science in Rome and seized
records of the pre-2000 Olympic health-screening programme. Marco's,
of course, were among them.

The Vuelta Valenciana, his first race since Sydney, started on 27 February. Twenty kilometres from the end of stage one – twenty kilometres
from the finish line – four riders had broken away and were destined
to dispute victory. Marco, comfortably in the main peloton, made a
toilet stop at the foot of the final climb. His team waited for him and he
finished the stage at almost walking pace, more than nine minutes after
the winner, Michael Boogerd. It was a baffling manoeuvre; either Marco
was extraordinarily self-confident, or something was wrong. With six
thousand kilometres of pre-season training in his legs he should have
been comfortable with the pace, despite a bout of bronchitis. After the
stage, he complained, 'I'm tired of having to go from one place to the

next to demonstrate my innocence of doping. Last year was very hard for me. I couldn't concentrate on my work, because, when it wasn't a judge, it was a lawyer demanding my presence. I hope this nightmare will come to an end once and for all, and let me make up the lost time.'

A comment from Capodacqua suggested that Marco's cocaine habit was not totally unrecognised in Italian journalistic circles: 'The Pirate's bitterness and discomfort are understandable, even if, regrettably, Marco has chased himself into the tunnel, and he'll have to find his own way out now, *unless something else lies behind his words.*' The following day, complaining of breathing difficulties, Marco lost eleven minutes thirty-one seconds. On the morning of 1 March, before the start of stage four, Marco abandoned. On 4 March, he abandoned the Clásica de Almeria and, the following week, he pulled out of the Vuelta a Murcia. He returned to Italy, and was immediately summoned to Florence to be interviewed by the Carabinieri about his blood values before the 2000 Olympic Games.

On 30 March the UCI announced new procedures to combat r-EPO abuse. As before, riders with 50 per cent haematocrit would continue to be suspended for fifteen days as a health measure. In future, however, a 47 per cent haematocrit or an unusually high reticulocyte count would trigger the French urine test capable of detecting r-EPO directly. The test was only effective if carried out within three or four days of the last r-EPO injection. However, the red blood cells promoted by r-EPO treatment had a life of 90 to 120 days, which meant that as long as the injections were discontinued four to five days before competitions, r-EPO use could continue with impunity. On 8 April 2001 Pantani's friend and team-mate Fabiano Fontanelli was suspended for two weeks after a blood test at the start of the Tour of Flanders had shown a haematocrit value above the 50 per cent threshold. A positive testosterone test in 1996 made this a second offence. On 13 April Fontanelli's urine test result was published: there was no trace of r-EPO. By then, his fifteen-day suspension on health grounds was over, and he was free to return to competition.

The Forlì conviction and the Trento trial alone would have damaged Mercatone Uno's case for an invitation from the Tour de France. The Fontanelli affair left it in tatters. A French investigation (that would eventually peter out, inconclusively) was already hanging over Lance

Armstrong, the winner of the 1999 and 2000 Tours de France, and with race sponsorship packages awaiting renegotiation, Tour director Jean-Marie Leblanc wanted to avoid any other controversies. Then there were Marco's early season performances:

27 February–3 March	Vuelta Valenciana	abandoned
7–11 March	Vuelta a Murcia	abandoned
24 March	Milano–San Remo	89th
26–30 March	Vuelta Catalana	abandoned
9–13 April	Tour of the Basque Country	did not start
20–24 April	Settimana Lombarda	abandoned

When Jean-Marie Leblanc was asked whether Marco could expect to be invited to take part in the Tour de France, he quipped: 'Pantani? Why, is Pantani still riding?' The only event of note in Marco's spring campaign had been a meeting with Lance Armstrong at the 2001 Vuelta a Murcia, brokered by the Italian journalist Pier Bergonzi to clear the air between the two men. It was a bizarre encounter, as Armstrong later recalled: 'I tried to speak to him in Italian: "*E allora, com'è la forma?*"' – 'So how's your form?' – 'He just laughed: "*Sìì, la forma – la forma di formaggio . . .*"' – 'Yessssss, the form in *formaggio*' ('cheese').

On 2 May, Leblanc announced his decision: Marco would not be invited to the Tour. 'Mercatone Uno', he said, 'is nothing without Pantani . . . And Pantani, for some time now, has done absolutely nothing.' Marco heard the news during the Giro del Trentino. That evening he raged to me and to *L'Équipe* journalist Philippe Brunel against the bosses who were killing cycling and sought to confound his exclusion with that of Mario Cipollini, non grata to the organisers because, however well he had started his many Tours de France, he had never quite got round to finishing one. 'My exclusion, and that of Cipollini, is the death of the Tour. The public want to see a show, not business. I thought Pantani and Cipollini had the right to take part by virtue of what they've given in the past, from 1994 to today. Monsieur Leblanc forgets that, in 1998, he asked me to carry on the Tour, when the race was in difficulty because of the doping affair.' In an official reaction, Mercatone Uno–Stream TV commented: 'Gratitude and recognition belonged to cycling of other times.' They too were living in the past.

Nonetheless, Marco's lyricism was still intact: 'We are all imprisoned by rules,' he told me that night. 'Everyone longs for freedom to behave in the way they see fit. I'm a non-conformist, and some are inspired by the way I express freedom of thought. I've never been meticulous or calculating, either on or off the bike. There's chaos in everyday life, and my riding is instinctive. I respond to the moment. But not everyone sees things that way.' It was an inseparable fusion of inspiration, rancour and insanity. Pure Pantani.

Ronchi saw Marco's exclusion from the Tour as a catastrophe. 'Cycling was the only therapy that could keep him away from drugs,' she insists. 'He needed a powerful motivation, and the stimulus we used to spur him on was to try to beat Armstrong, even in a single stage. The duel with Armstrong had special significance because it meant measuring himself against the best. The only incentive we could give him for him to prepare for was the satisfaction of turning around and seeing he'd dropped him, like in 2000.' But what Ronchi describes as therapy was really little more than gambling with Marco's confidence: there had never been much chance of a Tour invitation. Marco's relationship with the organisers was difficult, his results had been pathetic, and there were French teams who had the organisers' ear. After the usual idle talk of forming a combined team including Cipollini and Pantani, reality sank in. In the following week's edition of *As*, the Spanish sports newspaper, Claudio Chiappucci summed up Marco's career: 'People will be left with the thought that Pantani was a great fighter until he had his haematocrit problems.' Marco must have been incensed.

On the day Leblanc announced Marco's exclusion a Brescia magistrate recommended the prosecution of eighteen suspects on doping-related charges. Many of Marco's oldest rivals were among them. The coming days saw the r-EPO urine test claim its first victims: Bo Hamburger of CSC–World on Line, Roland Meier of Team Coast, both of whom gave positive results in tests taken in Liège, Belgium, on 19 April, the day after Flèche Wallonne. The 2001 Giro d'Italia, from 19 May to 10 June, was the first Grand Tour in which r-EPO tests would be conducted.

However, the war on doping was not an easy one. On 19 May Pierguido Soprani, the magistrate investigating Francesco Conconi, inexplicably abandoned the investigation. In the 21 June 2001 edition of the news weekly *Panorama*, Soprani explained: 'In recent months, the climate had become heavy. Last year the Higher Magistrates' Council started proceedings against me for "incompatibility", probably because I had made accusations about my boss to the same body. I preferred to leave on my own, without too much argument.' Soprani's accusations had been that the inquiry was being hindered; he added that his task had been made difficult by Conconi's political clout – a reference, he explained, not to 'the well-known friendship between Conconi and Prodi, which emerges from the case documentation', but to 'Conconi's visibility and power in his role as Rector of the University of Ferrara'.

Cipollini's exclusion from the Tour de France had had nothing to do with doping, yet Soprani revealed in the interview that the second Italian star excluded from the 2001 Tour, Mario Cipollini, had also shown anomalous blood values. A blood test carried out in January 1996 showed haematocrit and haemoglobin values within the normal range: 43.1 per cent and 14 respectively. On 25 June that year a test undergone at the Policlinico Sant'Orsola-Malpighi in Bologna gave figures of 54.4 per cent haematocrit and 18 haemoglobin. At the 1996 Olympic Games, Cipollini had been either ill or doped.

By the time Marco finished twenty-ninth in the Giro of Trentino from 30 April to 4 May, national elections were looming. In the run-up to the election the leader of the centre-right, Silvio Berlusconi, who was also under investigation, cleverly presented himself and the other Forza Italia candidates as victims of a politicised judicial system which was interfering with ordinary citizens going about their own business. The era of the magistrate heroes was coming to an end. On 13 May Berlusconi won a famous victory. The Giro d'Italia started six days later.

Stage eight was due to depart the Tuscan spa town of Montecatini at 12.10 in the afternoon of 27 May. At approximately 11 a.m. Marco was the last of the Mercatone Uno delegation to leave the Hotel Francia e Quirinale. As he left, a Carabinieri unit from the Florence NAS entered the building with a warrant to search the riders' rooms. That morning NAS units from Florence visited twelve hotels in Florence, Prato and Montecatini, and found a large number of syringes, some containing illicit substances such as corticosteroids.

After stage twelve Marco was lying fifteenth overall, one minute eleven seconds behind race-leader Dario Frigo. The next stage was a 225 kilometre noose-shaped route over four giant peaks. It would have delighted the Pantani of the 1990s; but he could finish no higher than thirty-second, six minutes forty-six seconds behind Gilberto Simoni, who took over the race lead. That evening, police raided a mobile home driven by Ivan Gotti's father-in-law, and discovered so many medicines it took three pages of close typing to list them.

On the morning of 6 June, before the start of stage seventeen, starting and finishing in San Remo, Marco's team-mate Riccardo Forconi was suspended after testing high for haematocrit on 19 May, prologue day. The follow-up test would show him positive for r-EPO. Meanwhile, Marco was suffering yet another inflammation of the upper respiratory tract, the classic endurance-sport illness. On the second of the day's two modest climbs Marco was dropped and ended the day twenty-fourth in the general classification, twenty-nine minutes and nineteen seconds behind Simoni.

Martinelli was livid. In Ronchi's account, he burst into Marco's room after the stage and shouted so long and hard that relations between them would never recover. Marco lay on the bed in tears. Journalists in the hotel foyer watched Pregnolato load Marco's suitcase and bike into his car. Moments later Felice Gimondi appeared and announced that Marco would be sleeping at San Remo. When Marco came down for dinner, he was dejected.

That night in San Remo, over two hundred NAS officers and Guardie di Finanza were involved in surprise raids on every team hotel and vehicle. It became known as the 'San Remo blitz'. The Guardia di Finanza searches were part of a Padua-based investigation into doping among amateur cyclists; the raid on the camper van of Ivan Gotti's father-in-law had been part of this inquiry. The NAS operation continued the investigation that had started the evening after stage seven. It reached the Mercatone Uno team's hotel, the Grand Hotel des Anglais, at 9.05 p.m. Marco, apparently asked to return to his room by a NAS agent, left his meal unfinished. The team stood in the corridor for the room searches. At 11.15 Marco left the hotel with his team-mate Ermanno Brignoli, appealing to reporters: 'Are we allowed to go out for an ice cream?' In fact, they were leaving for a meeting of riders, to be led by Marco and Cipollini. Both men argued to bring the Giro to an end on the spot. After the meeting, however, Cipollini was contacted by the race directors, who persuaded him to change his mind. Marco knew nothing of this change of heart, so the following morning, when he publicised the decision to strike, he found himself alone, arguing with his erstwhile ally.

On 12 June, after a heated four-hour meeting with rider and race organiser representatives, Petrucci, the Chairman of the Italian sports body CONI, called for the FCI to suspend Italian professional cycling for as long as it took to draft a code of ethics which would then be inserted into riders' contracts. The UCI distanced itself from the move: 'Any measures taken by the FCI will be applicable solely to the national calendar.' And the UCI criticised CONI for 'expressing a premature judgement on the development of the judicial investigation'. Mean-while, the commission which would put the new anti-doping law into effect had not yet had its first meeting.

On 14 June the FCI convened to discuss CONI's call for a moratorium. Marco drove to Rome to attend. Just north of Perugia, on the E45, traffic police with a laser gun stopped him for driving at 187 k.p.h. when the limit was 110 k.p.h. Marco's driving licence was confiscated, and he was fined 600,000 lire (€300). A temporary document was issued to allow him to complete his journey to Rome and return home.

The meeting itself culminated in the announcement, by Giancarlo Ceruti, the Chairman, that from Monday 18 June all races in Italy, from junior to professional category, would be cancelled for at least a week. Italian teams were requested to abstain from all races outside the country for the corresponding period. The decision was taken to subject all national squad members to surprise blood tests using the indirect Australian method, based on blood-test parameters, to detect r-EPO abuse. It was a courageous decision, taken in the teeth of hostility from Verbruggen.

Details of the new ethical code were leaked on 20 June. It would outline the rights and responsibilities of riders, team doctors, race organisers and teams. Two days later it emerged that the San Remo blitz had led to formal investigations into eighteen of the twenty teams, and sixty-four riders. Eventually, charges would be brought against fifty-one riders and team staff, including Marco and his *soigneur* Roberto Pregnolato.

205

The 22 June edition of *Sette sere*, a weekly magazine in the town of Faenza, published a highly critical interview with one of Mercatone Uno's longstanding medical staff. Dr Marco Magnani had worked with the team as a medical assistant between 1997 and 2000 before taking over as team doctor in 2001. But he had become increasingly disillusioned and had decided to go public. Marco, he said, was ungovernable. 'I couldn't even get him to agree to a simple operation like weighing him. To get him on the scales, I had to invent a sort of competition with him on who weighed the least. That's how I discovered he was overweight – by six kilos.' On a small frame like Marco's, six kilos was a huge discrepancy and explained his poor performances in the spring. But the interview was of interest above all because of Magnani's allegations that, since early April, he had been under pressure, 'not from the sponsor but from members of the team management', he said, 'to use pharmacological products for ends other than their medical purpose'. He maintained that he had not been taken to the Giro d'Italia because of his refusal to do so.

When I spoke to Magnani in August 2005, the controversy was still fresh in his mind: 'Marco's intractability apparently came from a long way back. He didn't suddenly become difficult in 2000. In the milieu, it was well known that Marco had tremendous mood swings, even as an amateur. There were long periods in which he never spoke, which made life for his room-mates extremely uncomfortable. At root, there were psychological difficulties.' Marco's closest friends said the same. Marcello Siboni recalls: 'He didn't chat much. And you understood immediately, because if you said anything to him, he didn't reply, and you understood he wanted to be in silence.' And Fabiano Fontanelli remembers: 'On the morning of races, Marco was almost unapproachable.'

Magnani was never informed that Marco had a history of cocaine abuse: 'I noticed strange behaviour during the first months of 2001. It was very difficult to speak to him by telephone. He was hard to find, he often didn't answer and, when he did, it was hard to get him to speak. I only learned of the cocaine problem in 2002. This type of information would have been absolutely fundamental for me as team doctor. I didn't know about it at the time, but with hindsight, Marco's behaviour was already off the rails in 2001.' Magnani has vivid memories of being pressured to mis-prescribe medical products within the team in 2001: 'For example, I was asked to treat riders with an anti-inflammatory containing molecules used to treat arthritis or products of other types, antioxidants used in hepatic disease, despite the fact that none of them suffered from the indicated illness. The aim was to reduce the pain induced naturally by muscular effort. We're also speaking of products that are absolutely not for doping.' Not that Magnani denies doping took place: 'It's possible there was doping. I was on the outside. I never noticed any, but it must also be considered that during the most important phase of competition, the Giro, I wasn't there. I don't know about what may have gone on there.' The official team doctors, then, were used as fences by the doping doctors, who were third-party freelancers.

The day of publication brought other, potentially catastrophic news which would hang over Marco until his death. The previous day, Professor Francesco Conconi had been interviewed by Piero Messini D' Agostini, the magistrate whose task it was to assess Soprani's preliminary investigation and decide whether or not to prosecute.

On 29 June Marco was interrogated as a witness, in Florence, by investigators looking into the San Remo raids. In the previous days he had released a television interview stating that the search for ever-better performance led cycling to use illicit products. 'But they're only illegal when they find them on you,' he had claimed. Marco emerged from his hour-long interview declaring himself fed up with being summoned by, he said, 'every court in Italy'.

In August, Marco rode an anonymous Vuelta a Burgos, finishing eighty-first, then abandoned the Vuelta a España on 19 September having achieved nothing. On 23 October 2001 Marco's appeal against the judgment of 11 December 2000 was finally decided. The appeal court found that extended consideration of the meaning of the text of Law 401/1989 and the intentions of Parliament, based on not only the historical context in 1989 but also the parliamentary debate prior to the passing of the new anti-doping law, Law 376/2000, suggested that 'the actions attributed to Marco Pantani, dating to the year 1995, were not considered crimes by the laws applicable at the time'. The 11 December 2000 verdict, then, was overturned on a legal technicality. Yet, after exhaustive re-examination of the evidence, the appeal court could find no fault with the material proof of Marco's r-EPO abuse.

16

The Pirate's New Team

By August 2001 relations between Marco's manager, Manuela Ronchi, and his *directeur sportif*, Giuseppe Martinelli, had broken down irretrievably. Ronchi's solution was to dissolve the team and build a new one. Marco would remain at its centre – ensuring the continued support of Romano Cenni and Mercatone Uno – and he would now be given decision-making powers within what Ronchi proudly announced would be 'an innovative management model'. The formula came straight from Mapei, which boasted ISO certification for its management practices; the old sense of rivalry and inferiority remained vivid. Ronchi and Mercatone Uno held talks with Franco Zappella, the owner of coffee-machine manufacturer Saeco, who expressed an interest in financing a Mercatone Uno–Saeco team, but the project came to nothing. When Marco abandoned the Tour of Spain the negotiations ground to a halt.

When the new Mercatone Uno team finally materialised, Ronchi was unhappy with the budget and terms of the sponsorship agreement, rightly protesting that Marco had won the supermarket chain Mercatone Uno a visibility it could not have achieved through conventional advertising without colossally higher spending. Yet she refused to see that Marco had last won in 2000 and was now in the public eye largely owing to high-profile doping investigations. Marco had become a liability and, in purely business terms, Mercatone Uno's continued identification with Marco was at best a calculated risk, at worst reckless. In any case, by the time the Saeco talks broke down there was no time to seek an alternative second sponsor, and Ronchi was forced to accept terms that made Marco the team's personal financial guarantor and included penalty clauses for race abandons. She told me: 'If I'd told

Pantani what sort of contract I'd been forced to sign, Marco would have lost his last buttress: Cenni.'

Ronchi's much-vaunted 'innovative management' consisted mainly of making inexperience a managerial principle. At Marco's behest, Ronchi took on *directeur sportif* Riccardo Magrini. Magrini had spent thirteen years away from the sport and agreed to return because Marco had asked him. He knew he'd make mistakes, and says he told Ronchi in advance he would need support and patience. His assistant was Massimo Podenzana, who had recently retired from riding and had never worked as a *directeur sportif* before. Ronchi herself had never before managed a cycling team. Fabrizio Borra put together the team medical staff and, incredibly, took on a team doctor who had specialised at Conconi's Centre in Ferrara. His name was Mauro Vezzani and, like many sports doctors, he was a former gynaecologist who had apparently adapted his specialised hormonal knowledge to the field of sports medicine. Magrini told me: 'The internal organisation of the team wasn't up to scratch. We didn't have equipment. Manuela was still looking for a second sponsor as late as the end of January. But the main problem was that Marco was in lamentable condition.'

His substance abuse had taken a new direction. During 2000 and 2001 Ronchi claims Marco had spoken little about his cocaine dependence, despite the February 2001 urine test. In November the new Mercatone Uno team gathered at Montecatini Terme for its first training camp. Marco's mood was buoyant; Ronchi had never seen him so well. In retrospect, it was a warning sign that spoke of the impending crisis. A few days after the end of the camp he stopped answering his mobile phone and became unreachable. His father Paolo told Ronchi that Marco was reasonably well, despite poor spells.

At the start of December a second training camp was due to start at Terracina. This small resort, midway between Rome and Naples, had become a popular destination for cycling teams out of season. Perhaps coincidentally, it was also the location of a major r-EPO manufacturer. Marco failed to show, sending instead a text message to Fabrizio Borra: 'Dear Fabrizio, I authorise you to tell the doctors about my psychological and cocaine problems: help.' Borra immediately drove the 430 kilometres to Cesenatico and brought Marco to Terracina. Christine, it seemed, had left him. Even in Terracina the team staff suspected Marco met cocaine-dealers.

It was a key moment in Marco's existence: his first explicit call for help. But the immediate problem for his doctors was what to do with him. They decided he should sleep in a twin room, accompanied at all times, and be kept at constant training camps to structure his days. Marco refused point-blank. They moved him to a flat in a deserted holiday apartment building at Lérici, just south of La Spezia on the Ligurian coast. The vacant surroundings can only have emphasised the hurt of Christine's absence. Ronchi had moved him and the team into the nearby Hotel Europa when Marco's father called with bad news: the Carabinieri had visited Pantani's villa at Sala with two summonses: one was related to the San Remo blitz on 6 June, when Roberto Pregnolato had been seen disposing of a bag into a bin in the street outside the hotel. Pregnolato insisted that the bag contained innocuous medical waste. The police claimed it contained traces of doping products. The other was in connection with a syringe found in room 401 of the Hotel Francia e Quirinale, Montecatini, on 27 May. For fifteen weeks the syringe had remained unanalysed. Then, on 7 September 2001, lab tests showed it contained traces of the hormone insulin, used alongside anabolic steroids such as testosterone or human growth hormone by bodybuilders to prevent new muscle tissue from being broken down, and taken with glucose by endurance athletes to load their muscles with glycogen fuel before and between events. The hotel's computerised rooms list showed that Marco had been allocated room 418. However, a handwritten list showing team riders and staff and their room numbers was collected from the hotel lobby. It gave Marco room 401. Yet another police investigation was on Marco's tail.

Marco spent Christmas Day in the family home of Massimo Podenzana, and the following week back at the hotel, with team-mates. But he can't have been unaware he was keeping them from their own families, and that, to those who cared for him and depended on him, he was a problem with no solution. On New Year's Eve he cracked, demanding a night off to see the New Year in, and fleeing to Cesenatico. The following morning Christine called Ronchi. She had turned Marco away; now he was at home, in Christine's words, 'harming himself'. Fabrizio Borra and the team's second doctor, Danilo Manari, dropped everything and drove to Cesenatico. They played down the incident: Marco, they said, wasn't in too bad a state. But he had taken cocaine knowing that the renewal of his racing licence depended on a medical examination two days later. The consequences were serious for everyone involved in the team: the precise conditions laid down by the team sponsorship agreement have never been published, but it is possible that the entire team would have folded if Marco had failed to obtain his racing licence. That his self-sabotage may have been deliberate seems never to have been considered.

Marco and six or seven team-mates were due at the cardiology department of Reggio's Santa Maria Nuova hospital on 3 January 2002. Ronchi told me: 'We wanted to do the UCI tests in a public hospital to show people that everything was done with the maximum transparency.' Given the circumstances, this aim could only have been the product of self-delusion. On the evening of 2 January Borra took Marco to the Best Western Hotel in Reggio-Emilia, where he met up with the team. Over dinner Marco was tense, repeatedly leaving the table, never letting his mobile out of his hand. He didn't want to be with the rest of the team. Ronchi took him to one side and he told her his relationship with Christine was beyond repair. More significantly, he said he was ready to give up cycling. Ronchi, accountable for the livelihoods of everyone involved in the team, remembers her immediate reaction: 'I said to myself, "Can he be irresponsible enough to destroy this whole venture?"'

This is the first time Ronchi's book mentions that Marco was ready to turn his back on cycling, although, when we spoke, she told me, 'We took him to ride the Giro d'Italia [in 2000], when he didn't want to ride his bike any more.' Marco had clearly been talking about giving up for two years, although only now did the division between the interests of those who earned their livings from the wealth Marco created, and Marco's own needs as a man with psychic problems and a self-consuming drug dependence, become self-evident.

That night Manari saw a car with Ravenna plates pull up outside the hotel, and Marco get out, carrying a package. When Marco saw Manari, he climbed back into the car, which pulled away. The following morning, Marco didn't answer his door. When his minders finally entered the room, it was to discover that Marco had been smoking crack. There was obviously no question of taking the medical. The other riders were examined and given the all-clear. Marco stayed away. Publicly, Vezzani blamed his absence on night-time diarrhoea and made a second appointment for 30 January.

On the morning of 4 January Ronchi and Magrini dressed Marco and took him with the rest of the team to Bologna airport to fly to Spain. Marco was irate, anxious and full of chatter. Over his mobile telephone, he cried: 'They're taking me away – I'm at the airport!' Ronchi suspected he was talking to a dealer. Ronchi left him at the gate and returned to Milan to meet Marco's lawyer, Cecconi, to be briefed on the Montecatini case. Later, Marco called her from Madrid, demanding to know why he didn't have a first-class ticket. He refused to accept the onward flight had no first-class seats. The lunacy continued in the days to come. He took the keys to a team car, intending to drive to the nearest chemist, only to drive into a coach in the hotel car park. Ronchi convinced Vezzani to go with her to Spain. Her description suggests the confusion Marco engendered in those around him. He was uncontrollable, emotionally in pieces, 'barricaded within himself', desperate. Yet, she writes, he could ride for six hours and drop all his team-mates. 'This was the real Marco,' Ronchi adds. And there was the problem. Marco's body was so strong, he could carry on destroying his mind and identity with cocaine and crack cocaine and still maintain his professional façade. Inevitably, those who earned well from Marco's athletic performances quickly convinced themselves that the key to restoring the man lay in maintaining that façade.

On 30 January Marco duly appeared in the café of Reggio Emilia's Santa Maria Nuova hospital for breakfast. He signed autographs, answered excited questions with monosyllables and left in good time for the examination. In the corridor a member of his team staff stopped him and the medical was postponed for the second time. After Marco's death the hospital's chief cardiologist revealed the truth behind Marco's non-attendance at the medical tests: 'On the basis of information provided by his team staff, we warned them in advance that our public structure would not have given him the go-ahead to resume racing. Probably that's why he missed our tests, and blamed illness.'

Marco was driven back to his hotel room. There he screamed at anyone who came close. Ronchi decided it was time to enlighten Romano Cenni, kept in the dark since 1999. Ronchi claims Cenni's first question was: 'Will he be able to ride the Giro d'Italia?' Danilo Manari argued that publicly recognising Marco's drug-dependence was the necessary first step to recovery. Marco refused. And there was a second problem:

according to the new sponsorship contract, Marco, the cocaine- and crack-user, was also the team's financial guarantor. No one could tell him what to do.

17

Marco's Madness
(DECEMBER 2001–NOVEMBER 2002)

Faced with Marco's inability to obtain medical clearance to compete, Vezzani called the state drug-dependence service (Ser.T., pronounced 'cert') at Reggio-Emilia and was given the telephone number of Dr Mario Pissacroia, a psychoanalyst specialising in the treatment of substance addiction. Pissacroia told me: 'Vezzani came to my study in Modena towards the end of 2001. And there he said to me, "There is a sports champion who is using cocaine." I said, "Who is it?" He said, "Can't you guess?" I said, "There are so many of them!" Then he told me: "It's Pantani."'

Early in the New Year Pissacroia met Vezzani in the hall of the Best Western Hotel in Reggio-Emilia. Pissacroia was led into Marco's room. He recalls: 'Beyond the twin beds Marco was standing with his back to the door, peering out of the corner of his eye at the stranger. He was in a particularly bad state, a state of utter dejection, crouching in a corner of the hotel room. He had the look of an abused child, beaten not once, but many times. He looked at you with suspicion.' Pissacroia knew about problem children: the former president of a centre for specialisation in the treatment of violent and addicted adolescents in Tuscany, he had written a major treatise on the psychopathology of adolescents. Nonetheless, it was made clear to him that his task was primarily to stop Marco's cocaine use and allow him to regain his racing licence. Marco had to be prevented from taking cocaine for two or three months – hardly propitious conditions for psychoanalytical work, but, given the seriousness of the case, Pissacroia could hardly turn the patient away.

Pissacroia's principal concern was Marco's inability to keep his impulses in check. 'It wasn't just depression; it was bipolar disorder –

214

manic depression – and its most important aspect at that moment was the cocaine use. I quickly became convinced that Marco had been using crack over some considerable period.'

Marco, a sexual experimenter who, after that post-1998 Tour interview, had expressed an interest in enhancing the performance of his remarkable physique with Viagra, cannot have been indifferent to crack's reputation. The lungs deliver the drug to the brain in seconds. Users describe the experience as the ultimate pleasure, one with which orgasm, they say, can't compare – at least for the first two minutes. Ten to fifteen minutes of euphoria follow that first hyper-orgasmic high, before the depression kicks in. The quickest way to fight the depression, of course, is to smoke more crack. And as the highs start not to seem so high, and the lows get lower and lower, the user becomes secretive, suspicious and hostile. Marco, with his deep paranoia about plots, food-adulteration and surveillance, was already displaying the classic symptoms of the crack addict.

Pissacroia soon learned that Marco's cocaine habit had been on the agenda every day for some years. There had long been talk of taking Marco to San Patrignano, a strictly disciplinarian community in the Rimini hills. Nowhere in Marco's entourage was there the expertise to manage Marco's problems. Pissacroia had to start from scratch. 'In the past, he had met psychotherapists, said nothing, and afterwards told Vezzani to keep them away. When we next spoke, Vezzani complimented me: he said I was the only one Marco hadn't turned away.'

Perhaps Marco's memories of serious injury and the fear of disability played a part in his decision to allow Pissacroia to stay: Pissacroia, then 49, had tight coils of marble-white hair, dark, penetrating eyes above a Roman nose and walked with a poliomyelitic limp. Marco certainly needed help. 'I spent two to three days there each week. Marco's urine was tested for cocaine two or three times a week. The samples were anonymous and submitted under Vezzani's name to the hospital laboratory along the road. And the compilation of his Multi-Axial Assessment was done with Vezzani, and with clinical psychologists from the Reggio-Emilia Ser.T. We worked in great secrecy.'

The psychiatric diagnosis was reached using standardised criteria laid out in the fourth edition of the *Diagnostic and Statistical Manual of Mental Disorders*, better known as '*DSM-IV*', published by the American Psychiatric Association. *DSM-IV* assesses five 'axes':

Axis I: Clinical disorders and other conditions worthy of clinical
    attention;
Axis II: Developmental and personality disorders, the latter being
    clinical syndromes with long lasting symptoms which
    characterise the patient's way of interacting with the world;
Axis III: General medical conditions affecting the development,
    persistence or exacerbation of Axis I and II disorders;
Axis IV: Psychosocial and environmental problems: events in the
    patient's life that affect the disorders listed in Axis I and II;
Axis V: Using a scale known as 'Global assessment of functioning',
    the mental health professional rates the patient's level of
    functioning at the time of diagnosis, and the highest level within
    the previous year, in order to understand how the previous four
    axes affect the patient and what type of changes may be foreseen.

Axis I of Marco's evaluation contained the somewhat optimistic diagnosis 'Cocaine dependence in initial partial remission', accompanied by
'Cocaine-induced mood disturbances with mixed manifestations'. Axis
II, by contrast, diagnosed his mental illness for the first time. The entry
reads: 'Non-specific personality disorder with narcissistic, antisocial
and obsessive elements, frequent use of denial and manipulation.'
Narcissistic personality disorders consist of a pattern of grandiosity
in fantasy or behaviour and a need for admiration and lack of empathy,
starting in early adulthood – the period when Marco began to use
cycling as an outward persona or mask with which to face the world.
Marco's impulsiveness, reckless disregard for his safety and lack of
remorse were characteristic of the antisocial personality disorders, while
the obsessive-compulsive disorders cover a pervasive pattern of preoccupation with orderliness, perfectionism, and mental and inter-
personal control, at the expense of flexibility, openness and efficiency,
beginning by early adulthood. That many of these behaviour patterns
are inherent in the practice of high-level sport suggests that Marco's
longstanding mental illnesses may have been partially camouflaged
against the backdrop of the sporting world he inhabited.
    Axis III, covering the medical conditions affecting the development,
persistence or exacerbation of Axis I and II disorders, baldly notes:
'Traumatic lesions from sporting accidents'. From the age of fifteen
Marco had suffered a number of blows to the head in training and race

SCHEDA DI VALUTAZIONE MULTIASSIALE

Paziente
Marco Pantani

Reggio Emilia
Dicembre 2001

ASSE I

ICD 10
F. 14.2x

DSM IV

DIPENDENZA DA COCAINA
IN REMISSIONE INIZIALE PARZIALE
304.20

F 14.8
DISTURBO DELL'UMORE INDOTTO DA COCAINA
CON MANIFESTAZIONI MISTE
292.84

ASSE II

F 60.9
DISTURBO DI PERSONALITA' N.A.S.
CON TRATTI NARCISISTICI, ANTISOCIALI E OSSESSIVI
USO FREQUENTE DELLA NEGAZIONE E DELLA MANIPOLAZIONE
301.9

ASSE III

LESIONI TRAUMATICHE DA INCIDENTI SPORTIVI

ASSE IV

CONFLITTI FAMILIARI NELLA FANCIULLEZZA, ABUSO PREGRESSO DI
ANFETAMINE E CANNABIS, CONTATTI CON AMBIENTI ANTISOCIALI,
EREDITARIETA' ANSIOSO-DEPRESSIVA, FORTE STRESS DA COMPETIZIONE,
CONDIZIONE AFFETTIVA INSTABILE E DI DIPENDENZA.

ASSE V

VALUTAZIONE FUNZIONAMENTO RELATIVO AGLI ASPETTI PSICOLOGICI
60/100

INDICAZIONI PER L'APPROFONDIMENTO DIAGNOSTICO E IL TRATTAMENTO

1 PROTOCOLLO FARMACOLOGICO A. P. A. SOSTITUTIVO
2 TRATTAMENTO PSICOPEDAGOGICO DI COUNSELING
(COINVOLGENDO LA FAMIGLIA, LA FIDANZATA
E IL TEAM TECNICO-SPORTIVO)
3 ACCERTAMENTI CLINICO-LABORATORISTICI SPECIFICI
CON FREQUENZA SETTIMANALE
4 DIAGNOSTICHE PER IMMAGINI MIRATE RX, RMN

Figure 4: Multi-axis assessment certificate 2001

incidents, as well as numerous whiplash injuries to the neck in his frequent car crashes. Whether any of these traumas caused lasting brain damage is a question that has never been asked.

The psychosocial and environmental factors listed under Axis IV provide an unprecedented picture of Marco's psychic history: the first element, 'Family conflicts in adolescence', was well known. The second had never been recognised: 'Past abuse of amphetamines and cannabis'. There is no record whether the amphetamines were a performance-enhancing measure in Marco's early sporting life, or used in a recreational context. To these we should add the sporadic binge drinking to which Marco admitted on entry to the Turin CTO in October 1995. Amphetamine, cannabis and alcohol abuse can hardly have been unusual in a young man growing up on the Riviera. Only in the context of Marco's mental illness did they became the precursors of later, harder-drug use.

The list continues with 'Inheritance of anxiety and depression': that Marco's condition had an inherited basis has also been little appreciated. The list ends with two final factors: one is 'Unstable and dependent affective condition', which was clear for all to see. The other must have – *should* have – come as a bombshell to those close to Marco: 'High stress from competition'. Competitive cycling itself had been characterised not as a structure which would hold Marco's fragile self together, but as a complication that aggravated his condition.

The final section provided indications for Marco's treatment. One aspect was substitute pharmacological treatment; this was to be complemented with 'psycho-pedagogical counselling treatment involving family, girlfriend and team technical and sports staff.'

When I interviewed her, Ronchi's précis was this: 'Re-reading the medical records of the whole family, and also of Marco, in the interviews this fact emerged: that Marco was already susceptible as a child to be predisposed to come to the end he came to, from the point of view of the use of drugs, no? Because there was, in his past, probably the fact that when he was born, Tonina had attempted to cut her veins, et cetera, et cetera, involuntarily in the psyche of the child, this trace remained.'

Pissacroia recalls: 'The first phase of treatment required enormous commitment: Marco spoke little, and when he did, he spoke rather like a TV interviewee: there was generally no way into his private life.

We spoke anytime, day and night. I tried to steer Marco into natural conversation with no artificial structure: he had to be guided towards the idea of himself as a person. We spoke for hours and hours. He could be called a difficult patient – very difficult. He had a double diagnosis: as well as the drug addiction, there were personality disorders.

'These counselling sessions, specific for cocaine addiction, were part of a formal therapeutic programme that involved Ronchi, Vezzani, the masseurs and the other cyclists. I was told a former mechanic had been a cocaine-supplier, so I held meetings with the whole team, including the cyclists and the masseurs, and we created a *cordon sanitaire* around him. But you know how a cycling team works: there's a leader, and there are his *domestiques*. The leader takes the sponsor's money and says, "I want this rider, I don't want that one." The *domestiques* are like slaves, and if you don't want to be a slave, you're out of a job. This hierarchical system played into the hands of Marco's drug habit. He corrupted, and knew how to corrupt. He'd bring out a watch, or a Nokia, and say: "Bring me cocaine." All the cyclists knew about Marco's habit.'

Pissacroia's counselling, and the surveillance he organised, had some success, and Marco's addiction improved. In February 2002 Vezzani was able to submit blood and urine samples in Marco's name, and they gave a negative result. Vezzani certified Marco's robust good health, and the Reggio-Emilia health service accepted Marco's racing-licence application, which was issued, days later, by the Italian Cycling Federation. Vezzani and Pissacroia kept the strictest professional secrecy, and there were no leaks. Marco the athlete was back. Pissacroia comments: 'He had been sporadically taking tricyclic antidepressants since 2001. He hated taking them – he felt they altered his identity and numbed his sensations, but without this pharmaceutical help he couldn't survive without cocaine.'

Ronchi records that, on or around 10 February, Romano Cenni took her aside to thank her. Nonetheless, tests on Marco's urine continued to give positive results for the presence of cocaine: police later found positive test markers dated 26 January, 3 February and 16 February. The day after the last of these, Marco started the Ruta del Sol in Andalucia. On 21 February he finished it 102nd. Then came the Trofeo Luis Puig (106th), and the Vuelta a Murcia (57th). Even between races there were lapses. There were also serious organisational problems within the team: first, the riders complained that they had no cycling shoes; then the team was denied an invitation to take part in one of Marco's favourite early-season events, the Vuelta Valenciana. Magrini told me: 'I contacted the organisers, but they were under pressure to invite Spanish, not Italian teams, so they never sent me the forms to enter the race.' Ronchi found fault with Magrini – rather unfairly, as he had said from the start he'd been out of the sport too long.

After the Vuelta a Murcia, Marco returned to Italy, where he and the team moved into Cenni's Monte del Re Hotel. Pissacroia was a regular visitor: 'We coordinated the whole team to keep an eye on Marco at all times, and to watch the entrance of the hotel for suspicious characters. The breakfast room at the back of the hotel was closed off for the team's exclusive use at mealtimes, although Marco was allowed private dinners in the dining room with Christine.' Their on–off relationship was temporarily on again. This special treatment for the team leader, absolutely normal in cycling, could only have exacerbated Marco's unreasonable expectations of especially favourable treatment or automatic compliance with his wishes – a characteristic symptom, in *DSM-IV*, of the narcissistic traits in Marco's personality disorder.

On 23 March he took part in Milan–San Remo, finishing 76th, and then went straight to France for the Criterium International on 30 and 31 March, where he was 65th. However, Marco's cocaine use had re-emerged. It was clear he had no desire to give it up. Pissacroia told him, 'If you take cocaine, you'll never again be a champion.' Marco responded, 'But when I'm not riding, can I take coke?' Pissacroia said, 'But then you'll never be a man.' Marco developed a strange obsession: at night in Reggio, and then at Monte del Re, he was forever pulling back the curtains, looking for NAS officers. It was a paranoid fantasy, no doubt partly induced by prolonged cocaine use.

At Monte del Re, Magrini was replaced by Marino Amadori. Ronchi still had no second sponsor; she argued with Marco and walked out. It took weeks to heal the wounds. Pissacroia (out of competition) and Vezzani (at races) shared the hopeless task of trying to prevent Marco from finding cocaine. Vezzani tested Marco's urine before every race. Pissacroia evolved into the de facto team coordinator, given that no decisions could be taken without his opinion. He liaised with Ronchi, who paid the bills, and the other riders, bearing in mind that those around Marco might also include providers of cocaine. When Marco went abroad, Pissacroia instructed Vezzani, Ronchi and one or two trustworthy riders to accompany Marco and keep Pissacroia in the picture.

But this free-form psychotherapy, the only talking cure Marco would accept, had to contend with other pressures on Marco's mental health. In April, the problem of the syringe found at the Hotel Francia e Quirinale in Montecatini during the 2001 Giro d'Italia resurfaced. On 11 April 2002, the anti-doping Carabinieri in Florence called Marco in for further questioning. He continued to deny ever having used banned substances and claimed that the syringe could not have belonged to the team, which followed 'a rigid procedure for the disposal of medical waste that the team doctor, Andreazzoli, collected in special containers'. The set piece in Marco's evidence was the hotel room distribution. In the interests of privacy, he claimed, the riders swapped the rooms assigned to them by the hotel with those of members of the team staff. This was done through Giacomo Andalò, a *soigneur* who was also the ad hoc head of team security. Marco claimed to have swapped rooms with one of the team mechanics, Dino Falconi, throughout the 2001 Giro.

Andalò confirmed that, each day, armed with the floor plan and the list of rooms reserved for the team, he reallocated the rooms on the grounds of comfort and quiet. He provided the hotel reception with the true list, together with the riders' papers, and fixed a false list beside the lift, to protect the riders' privacy. However, this false list was not used for purely cosmetic purposes: a copy was provided to the hotel, which made corresponding changes to its electronic files, in order to be able to connect incoming phone calls accurately, and so on.

Another *soigneur*, Fabrizio Settembrini, recalled only that the athletes stayed on one floor, and the directors on another. All agreed that the rooms were routinely reallocated, although none could recall where he had slept on the night of 26 May 2001.

However, the day before Marco's interview, the concierge of the Hotel Francia e Quirinale had called the Florence Carabinieri to inform them that a member of the Mercatone Uno team staff calling himself Giacomo had called repeatedly that afternoon, demanding to know whether it was possible to trace the original list of rooms assigned by the hotel on 26 May 2001. He was informed that the relevant papers had been destroyed in March when the bill had been settled – nine months late!

The concierge told them: '"Giacomo" explicitly asked if I would agree to confirm that the room allocation on 26 and 27 May corresponded to our records. I rejected any such agreement, knowing that it was not the case because they had altered our room allocations. I told him: "Absolutely not."'

On 12 April Dino Falconi was heard. Falconi had been a member of the Mercatone Uno team staff for five years. He stated: '[Team members] are normally informed of the rooms allocated to them by consulting a table posted outside the lift which uses a printed organigram of the team.' No one asked him to change rooms. Indeed, the idea of any room change was, he said 'absurd'. Falconi couldn't recall on which floor he had stayed, but he remembered occupying the room allocated to him by the list posted beside the lift, and that there were no riders on his floor. His version agreed with Settembrini's statement that the athletes stayed on one floor and staff on another. The 'false list' story was blown.

Statements from the hotel staff clarified the situation. The hotel concierge, a Signor Terreni, had intended to allocate Pantani one of the largest rooms on the fourth floor – 409 or 421. The hotel proprietor, a Signora Nencini, insisted she had been careful to allocate Marco the VIP suite, room 418. Terreni told police: 'In the event, Pantani chose 401, one of the smallest on the floor.' Nencini expressed similar surprise when Andalò changed the room list and gave Marco room 401, 'one of the smallest and most insignificant' (Nencini). Having said all this, neither Terreni nor Nencini actually saw Marco enter or leave room 401.

In Terreni's words: 'The NAS officers entered the hotel at the moment the final members of the Mercatone Uno team were leaving the hotel. I personally accompanied [the NAS officers] on their search. The inspection started on the fourth floor, which we entered straight away. We stopped the cleaning ladies who had already collected the refuse from rooms 406, 407 and 409, and asked them not to continue their work. We then began the round of the rooms: it is probable that the first rooms searched were 401 and 402.' Three weeks later, Terreni told the Anti-Doping Office of the Italian Olympic Committee, 'Room 401 was inspected at about 11 a.m., at the time the last rider of the Mercatone Uno team, Marco Pantani, was leaving.'

One thing intrigued the Carabinieri: why had Marco's room been falsely attributed to Falconi, clearly not a man prepared to lie to protect him? The likely answer was that Falconi was diabetic and, as a legal consumer of insulin, potentially provided Marco with a last line of defence. If this was the strategy, it was doomed to failure. Falconi made it clear he treated his diabetes with medicine taken orally.

The findings of this investigation were passed to the CSAD, which started its own disciplinary procedure. On 2 May the commission referred the case to the Italian Cycling Federation, recommending the minimum sentence for deliberate doping stipulated in article 130, paragraph 2 of the UCI regulations: a four-year ban.

How did Marco face the threat of a career-ending ban? He rejected the charges out of hand. Pissacroia says, 'He saw it like this: "They should be asking *me* to forgive *them*."' For the moment, the cycling calendar gave Marco's life structure, and team leadership typecast him, although his demands as team-leader far outweighed his performances. Marco can only have been excruciatingly aware of the discrepancy. Days after his interrogation Marco insisted on a private jet to fly the team to Belgium for the two great classics, Flèche Wallonne (17 April) and Liège–Bastogne–Liège. In the end, the team went on a scheduled flight. Once there, Marco's performances were undistinguished. There were no searching attacks on the famous Muurs, and no probing of his opponents' weaknesses. In Flèche Wallonne Marco finished eighty-first. In Liège–Bastogne–Liège, organised by the Tour de France organisers, he rode fifty kilometres, then abandoned. His Belgian performances almost guaranteed there would be no Tour selection: perhaps that was Marco's purpose. It was as if he wanted to punish those who wanted him to ride, and for those who earned their living from Marco's career it must have been deeply worrying.

Back in Italy at the end of the month, Marco was interviewed by members of the CSAD in connection with the Montecatini syringe, emerging from the ordeal an hour later with a personal appeal to the Italian Prime Minister, Silvio Berlusconi, to 'take a look at cycling'. In the Giro of Trentino (25 to 28 April), Marco finished eighty-seventh.

Then the Giro d'Italia approached. Marco prepared by demanding a customised coach to be driven by his friend Nevio Rossi, the former cocaine-smuggler. Mercatone Uno had agreed to supply no more than a team camper van. Ronchi arranged a coach, at a cost of 200 million lire (€100,000). The Giro started on 11 May at the Dutch town of Groningen. Stage three started in Luxembourg, where Marco's friend Charly Gaul, the ageing former Tour and Giro champion, made a guest appearance. Three days later, after a long transfer south, the race reached Italy for a hilltop finish at Limone Piemonte. Marco's performance was poor: twenty-four kilometres from the finish line, on the first steep slopes of the penultimate climb, the Colletto del Moro, he was dropped, and finished the stage flanked by three team-mates, seven minutes after his former protégé Stefano Garzelli had won it. He commented to journalists: 'I'm just not good enough right now.'

Marco was also accompanied by 'security staff': at least one was an off-duty police officer from Forlì, who later faced questions over his presence at the Giro. He claimed he went as a favour to Marco, simply in order to enjoy being part of the Giro. There was also a cook to ensure that Marco's food wasn't poisoned or adulterated with doping products. Rossi says the cook did very little. Some of these individuals were no doubt using Marco, at the very least to earn money. But Marco knew about them, too; he had dirt on them, and could therefore control them. Above all, they were directly within his control – and outside that of Ronchi.

Pissacroia describes a tall, dark-haired character driving a Mitsubishi L200, who would appear at hotels, apparently delivering up to three suitcases, which then circulated among riders. The cases may have contained doping products used by bodybuilders and sold at gyms. At Viareggio, Pissacroia couldn't find the team, which had changed hotels at the last moment. There, too, rumour said the cases were on their way around the hotel. Pissacroia recalls: 'The hotels were heavily monitored by NAS officers, and the rumours of cases being passed around drove Vezzani, his doctor, to distraction. How he put up with it I don't know. He can't have been earning a huge amount.' Marco and his team spent 27 May, rest day at the Giro, at the spa town of Abano Terme, in the hills south of Padua.

There he was visited by the new lawyer he intended to hire: Veniero Accreman, one of Rimini's leading criminal lawyers. Accreman represented both Michael Rocchi, who had made the initial contact on Marco's behalf, and Nevio Rossi, who had followed it up. Accreman, with his son and a colleague, had a four o'clock appointment at the hotel in Abano Terme, but arrived late: the team had changed hotel, not for the first time during the Giro. Accreman described that first meeting to me: 'The impression I had of him when I met him was of an extremely anxious, worried, tense person. I commented to my son: how can an athlete compete like that?' Marco instructed them to contact his former lawyer, Cecconi, for the files relating to the Montecatini case. Ronchi's recollection that she found herself attending a meeting about which she had no advance notice and in which she could say nothing, strengthens the impression that Marco was gradually seeking to loosen her control over him.

The following day, suffering from bronchitis and feeling weak from antibiotics, he climbed off his bike and into the Mercatone Uno team car with Marino Amadori. He was seventy-fifth, fifty-eight minutes forty-three seconds behind race-leader Jens Heppner. As he did so, other legal issues immediately closed in on him. On 29 May the pre-liminary investigation into the blood-test results at Madonna di Cam-piglio ended with the recommendation that Marco be tried for sporting fraud under Law 401/1989. The same day, Carabinieri from Brescia, apparently investigating the arrest of a cyclist with the Panaria team, and the suspension of Marco's team-mate Roberto Sgambelluri, at the start of the Giro, went to the stage finish at Corvara in Badia and searched the hotel room of the Mercatone Uno team doctor, Mauro Vezzani. The following day they visited his rooms at Reggio-Emilia. The *Gazzetta di Reggio-Emilia*, giving details of the investigation, reported that thirty-five phials and twenty pills of morphine – controlled substances – had been found in a kitchen cabinet at Vezzani's home. Vezzani explained that he had taken the morphine from a patient who had died of cancer. Possession of morphine was illegal, even by a doctor, and Vezzani was charged. Furthermore, documents relating to Marco's treatment in January and February – positive urine tests for cocaine in Marco's name and in the name of another Mercatone Uno rider – were seized. Marco's name suddenly appeared in yet another investigation. Soon after the scandal Vezzani departed from the team.

He had been one of the pillars that supported Marco's precarious equilibrium, and his removal can only have jeopardised what stability there was in Marco's mental state. However, the nature of the medical assistance he provided Marco is open to question. In June 2005 the disgraced French rider Philippe Gaumont mentioned Vezzani in his memoir of his own doping experiences. In May 1998, in mid-preparation for the Tour de France, he claims, his team, Cofidis, contracted Vezzani, because what Gaumont calls 'prohibited medicines' could be obtained more easily abroad than in France. Gaumont alleges that Vezzani packed r-EPO and growth hormones in ice to preserve them, and dispatched them in express parcels to the Cofidis riders, with instructions.

After the Giro, Ronchi writes that Pissacroia was so pessimistic about Marco's prospects, he told her to give up on him. Pissacroia's version is rather different, and tells of a burgeoning conflict between those who managed the money and career of Marco the sportsman, and the health professionals hoping to rehabilitate Marco the man. It corresponds with the diagnosis given in the psycho-pathological evaluation: 'My advice was that it was a mistake to insist on keeping Marco in the saddle. The measures taken to give him even the smallest competitive chance were incredibly complex. He was almost impossible to manage: the team was tightly structured around him, yet he constantly reached outside. He maintained his own private cocaine-suppliers, and very probably his own private suppliers of doping products. They may even have been the same people, very likely involved in organised crime. You couldn't take your eyes off him for a moment. At the same time, Marco was no longer sure he wanted to continue as a professional cyclist. If you removed the question of riding – and Marco was extremely wealthy; he didn't need to ride – you were left with the cocaine problem. And the cocaine problem alone might have been manageable.'

Keeping Marco in the saddle was a precarious balancing act. Ronchi writes that the team's main function was to provide Marco with psychological support; strictly sporting criteria had a secondary importance. But using a team of professional cyclists as a vehicle for a symbolic form of communication was an impossibly complex strategy; and Marco's relationship with cycling was complicated enough. At different times and to different interlocutors, he was capable of expressing hatred, indifference and undying passion for his sport. He lived for the moments of exaltation cycling allowed him, yet it was clear that his performances could only deteriorate with age and cocaine use, and that disenchantment became an ever more likely outcome than joy. And Marco only had two strategies for dealing with disenchantment: one was sniffing cocaine; the other was smoking crack.

Doping was merely another form of substance abuse, and the team was embroiled in two doping scandals in the first six months of 2002. On 24 April Roberto Sgambelluri had tested positive for 'Darpoietina' –

in other words, a variety of r-EPO known as NESP. And on 12 June 2002, at the Bank Austria Tour, Valentino Fois tested positive for norandrosterone. On 19 October the Disciplinary Commission of the Italian Cycling Federation examined the Fois case and disqualified him until 11 June 2005. The judgment fined the team, in the form of 'Società Mercatone Uno Sitar SA,' 3,000 Swiss francs for 'objective responsibility'.

I put this to Ronchi, who told me: 'No, you're quite wrong.' But there was no mistake: the case summary is on the website of the Italian Cycling Federation. She started again: 'When a rider is found positive, or something, the rider is always named as liable, and the management company is found to hold "objective liability" because the rider is in any case independent of the management company. But it's a mere procedure.'

In the National Federal Disciplinary Committee archive on the Italian Cycling Federation website, I searched for every case relating to doping in the weeks surrounding the Fois case, to test this contention. The Fois case was number ninety-four in the year 2002. I studied every case involving either a positive anti-doping test or possession of doping substances heard in the period surrounding the Fois case from case 71 to case 128, and found no other instance in which a team management company was fined for objective liability.

At the start of June – a matter of days before the Montecatini case was due before the the CDFN – Accreman received the files. He asked the Commission for a delay, and was given a week. Accreman was informed that Marco's presence would be welcome; he was informally invited to excuse himself before the CDFN. Accreman told me: 'I spoke to Pantani and Ronchi. I found him reluctant; Ronchi was expressly against the proposal. I formed the impression she had great power over him. While I was with Pantani, I had the sensation we'd almost reached an agreement. We were to meet the day before the hearing at Rome. We'd already booked the hotel. Then Ronchi informed us he'd decided not to come.'

In fact, Marco had taken cocaine the night before he was due to travel and was in no condition to attend the hearing. Accreman continues: 'I said, "Big mistake." I related his decision not to come to something he'd said in my rooms: he was talking about the judges who presided over

Italian cycling, then he said, "But I *am* Italian cycling." He had feelings of pride, masking an extremely fragile personality.'

The hearing took place on 17 June 2002. Accreman called for the charges to be dropped owing to the absence of proof that Marco had stayed in the room in which the syringe was found. Professor Giovanna Berti Donini of the University of Ferrara had provided expert opinion that between the moment the syringe was found (27 May 2001) and its analysis (7 September 2001), chemical changes could have taken place. She also sustained that DNA testing could still have been carried out to establish whether or not Marco had used the syringe.

However, the Commission ruled: 'The possession and use of doping substances (insulin) by Marco Pantani is proven.' Marco was handed a 3,000 Swiss franc fine and an eight-month disqualification. The Mercatone Uno team was fined 5,000 Swiss francs. The ban was made public by Manuela Ronchi. Marco issued the following statement on the Mercatone Uno website: 'I'll demonstrate my innocence, but I wonder, when I've done so, who will give back to me everything that has been taken from me.'

Informed of the decision, Mercatone Uno suspended their team sponsorship. Ronchi sustains this was in breach of their contract, but it made no difference. She met Marco at Milano Marittima and gave him the news. He took it badly, throwing his arms down in frustration, before mounting his motorbike and disappearing.

Pissacroia claims Vezzani, no longer an official member of the team, asked him to help fight Marco's ban. The only avenue left open seemed to be that of finding a supportive, and influential, national politician. Marco had been awarded the Collar for Sporting Merit in 1999; Vezzani's idea was to obtain a sort of 'absolution for sporting merit'. He managed to arrange an appointment with Carlo Giovanardi, the Italian Minister for Parliamentary Relations and a prominent resident of Modena, and asked Pissacroia to attend. On the day of their appointment Pissacroia waited in the street outside Giovanardi's office, but Marco never came. To Pissacroia, 'Marco had developed an incapacity to take decisions, and his excessive pride prevented him from asking help from someone from his own region.'

In June 2002 Pissacroia arranged for Marco to enter a private clinic in Rome. Two psychologists from an anti-drug charity gave Marco twenty-four-hour care to detoxify him. His anonymity was kept; the media knew nothing of Marco's presence. He was given thorough medical checks. He was well behaved. Pissacroia visited him twice. On arriving, he tested positive for cocaine, which would have cost him his racing licence had the test result not been falsified by misspelling his name as 'Patani'. A subsequent test was negative. He was tested by the clinic's specialists; not being sports doctors, they had no interest in massaging the results – which may have disturbed Marco. His haematocrit was in the 38–42 per cent band, his blood pressure normal. His resting heart rate was not the expected 50 or 55, but close to 70 beats per minute. He suffered insomnia owing to abstinence from cocaine. Attempting to ride a Giro or a Tour with this physique – a normal adult physique, not that of a world-class athlete – might have proved extremely damaging to his health. The pneumologist found that Marco's great lung capacity was intact, but the first signs of pulmonary fibrosis were evident: precociously aged lungs, with elasticity of the tissue and an irreversible loss of the tissue's ability to transfer oxygen into the bloodstream. Marco greeted the news with a smile and the observation, 'It'll be all the *polvere* I've eaten.' *Polvere* means 'powder' – though Marco was thinking of the dust in the street, not cocaine. Marco left the clinic angry because, he said, they had wasted his time, and his insurers refused to pay.

Pissacroia recalls: 'The first thing he did, like any addict, was go out on a four-day bender. I was livid, and Marco was afraid of me. When we next met, at Cesenatico, he said, "You're not going to slap me, are you?" – the reaction of a child used to being beaten.'

On 12 July 2002 appeals against Marco's suspension were lodged at two courts of appeal: that of the FCI, and the Court of Arbitration for Sport (CAS) in Lausanne. The response of the first of these was instant: in a meeting the next day at the Monti Velodrome in Padua, the FCI Court of Appeal revoked Marco's sentence and cleared him of all accusations. The judgment explains the court's findings that the accusations against Marco were 'founded on pure supposition and on explanations given a posteriori by the officers of the judicial police, never supported by suitable proof demonstrating the case for the prosecution'; 'the witnesses indicated by the prosecution have denied being able to state that they saw with their own eyes Marco Pantani enter or leave room 401'; 'it is not certain, but only supposed that the athlete occupied the said room'; and 'there is no proof that the said syringe can be attributed and/or in any way attached to Marco Pantani'. There was no mention of Falconi's refutation of the 'false list' thesis, or of Andalò's repeated telephone calls to the hotel.

One of the three judges who made up the court was Celestino Salami, now the President of the Emilia Romagna section of the Italian Cycling Federation. Salami, an acquaintance and admirer of Marco since losing the Forlì–Val di Noce to him on 5 August 1984, still speaks of him in glowing terms. 'I rode with him for fourteen years from 1980 to 1993. He was always a phenomenon, and those who say he took doping products forget this.' Another man might have declared his admiration and personal acquaintance as conflicts of interest and stood down before the hearing.

The decision was received with no joy from any quarter. Giacomo Aiello, the chairman of the CDFN, was present at the hearing. When the verdict was pronounced, he stood up, announced his resignation and stormed from the room, slamming the door behind him. Marco's only comment was a paraphrase of his reaction to the guilty verdict of 17 June: 'Even if I obtain justice, who will return what has been taken from me?' Salami told me: 'It wasn't the reaction I was expecting. There was no expression of happiness. It didn't seem to me the reaction of a balanced mind.'

The lawyer representing the CSAD, meanwhile, announced the commission's intention to appeal, while on 26 July the UCI dispatched the following letter to Marco:

> We are astonished to hear of the FCI Court of Appeal decision to acquit you. The UCI does not recognise the competence of the FCI Court of Appeal, whose ruling of 13 July 2002 is therefore not accepted by the UCI. The decision of the court of first instance of the UCI (CDFN) of 17 June 2002 therefore remains in force, to wit:
> - Suspension of 8 months from 18 June 2002 to 17 May 2003.
> - Fine of 3,000 Swiss francs.

While the FCI and UCI quarrelled over their competencies, Marco remained suspended. The appeal at the CAS in Lausanne was pending, but would take months. In the meantime, life went on. Pissacroia told me: 'As Marco was suspended from competition, there were no urine tests. During the months of inactivity Marco began to have doubts. He began to ask, "Can I still be competitive at my age? Even if I give up cocaine?" In my opinion, the answer was more "no" than "yes". A power struggle had emerged between, on the one side, Marco's father, who wanted to convince Marco to continue as a cyclist on the grounds that he had so much more to give, Ronchi, who also entertained the idea of Marco becoming a public figure, with endorsements, guest appearances, and so on, and Marco himself, who entertained the fantasy of marrying Christine and having two children. They would buy a boat and sail together up and down the Adriatic Sea.' Pissacroia interpreted Marco's state of mind as one with huge therapeutic potential, one allowing glimpses of another Marco, dependent on neither doping products nor cocaine.

As Marco's legal team prepared his appeal, Marco faced the problem of how to spend his empty days. He was now based at Cesenatico. He no longer had the identity of a cyclist. In his absence the team no longer existed. Cenni didn't know what to do. Ronchi was deeply stressed. She could no longer find sponsorship. No one would commit themselves for the following season.

Marco's only concern was to rebuild his relationship with Christine. She'd distanced herself, right at the time the suspension had started, blaming Marco's cocaine use and promiscuity. She found a job as a waitress in a bar in central Ravenna. In late July 2002 Pissacroia was on holiday in Corfu. Marco called him five times, and he was compelled to cut his holidays short. On his way to Cesenatico, Pissacroia stopped at Ravenna to talk to Christine. It took another week to convince her to meet Marco, and to drag Marco out from behind his reinforced door, where, alone, he was consuming massive quantities of cocaine, dazed, as if he could bear the outer world only by not existing in it.

'He said he'd rent a flat in Ravenna to be close to Christine. I don't know if he did. But by this stage, I'd talk in terms of psychiatric problems, connected only in part to cocaine.' At the end of the week, Christine appeared on the Port Canal. Pissacroia was there with his companion. They saw kids in the street shouting: 'There's Pantani, there's Pantani!' Pissacroia acted as go-between: 'I made sure they were speaking, then left them to it. Then I went back for what remained of my holiday.'

Pissacroia describes Marco's identity in disarray. 'Marco didn't feel affectionate towards objects or people. He regressed into the infantile emotional mind typical of drug addicts, an extremely primary, archaic sense of affections: "I love Mummy, I argue with Daddy," or, "I understand Mummy, I don't understand Daddy." In this family fantasy, his team-mates were like brothers. This tendency was heavily aggravated by the cocaine. He spread money around, but to those who brought him drugs or women. It was often in the form of a watch or a chain.

'I had to convince Marco's parents to have that enormous house meticulously cleaned, because Marco had hiding holes for cocaine even in the skirting boards. It was as if they were asking for a raid: if Carabinieri had turned up to search the place, Marco would have been destroyed. They agreed to do it only after much persuasion. Then they asked me what to do with what they found. I told them to sniff it!

'Marco was no longer a champion with a doping problem, but an ex-champion with a drug problem and sentimental problems. There were two Marcos: the ageing athlete, repeatedly accused of doping, and the cocaine-user. Neither had much of a future. I wanted to open a space for another Marco – a healthy, human Marco. What this healthy Marco chose to do with his life mattered little: only his mental health mattered.

'He could go without cocaine for up to a week before succumbing to temptation and sating himself on bulimic, almost suicidal quantities, locking himself behind the armoured door of his bedroom. It was the way he was put together. Nonetheless, those week-long periods represented a huge step for him. I asked a volunteer to visit him. Marco didn't want to know: he accused me of wanting to surround him with spies. But the support network was still intact and, to the extent to which it could, it was working.'

Ronchi had stopped paying Pissacroia from the team's accounts in June 2002 on the grounds, she writes, that his advice was always the same and produced no concrete results. What advice Ronchi wanted to hear, and what concrete results she expected, we do not know. The personality disorders described in the psycho-pathological evaluation were long-term conditions that had affected Marco at least since early adulthood. The 'psycho-pedagogical counselling' it recommended had scarcely begun, and had had to contend with the stresses of competition and the additional pressure of summonses, court hearings and unmitigated rumour. Pissacroia continued to see Marco, but their meetings became sporadic. From the end of June Marco's father Paolo paid for his treatment. Pissacroia recalls: 'I remained at the disposal of Marco and his family until November 2002. Late in 2002 Marco called to ask what I was doing for Christmas and the New Year.' Then, it was over, and Marco was in freefall.

18

Stop or Go?

On 26 August, as Manuela Ronchi holidayed in Croatia, she too picked up a telephone message from Marco. She called Tonina, who asked her to come as soon as possible. Marco had crashed the car several more times, possibly under the influence of cocaine. Having dismissed Pissacroia, Ronchi turned, not to qualified psychiatric help, but to another of her clients, a climber, mountaineer and adventurer named Renato Da Pozzo. Seven years older than Marco, Da Pozzo had competed in the rock-climbing World Cup in the 1980s. He had opened new routes up sheer rock faces in Patagonia, reaching the very elite of technical rock-climbing. However, Da Pozzo had grown to dislike the competitive list-ticking of professional climbing and begun to look for alternative approaches. In British Columbia, before attempting a climb on a peak sacred to indigenous peoples in the area, he had approached them for permission, and turned a corner in his career. Rather than visiting, or passing through the landscape, he focused on remaining in it, getting to know its inhabitants and exploring the relationship between the individual and the natural environment. Then, on a 320 kilometre, eleven-day trek in subarctic conditions across Norway, Sweden and Finland, he had experimented with the effects of sleep-deprivation by restricting himself to three forty-five-minute sleep periods a day. Through meditation, the study of indigenous cultures, and readings of Krishnamurti and other mystics, he developed a contemplative, therapeutic programme based on immersion in the landscape. In 2001 he began to welcome healthy individuals seeking a non-competitive relationship with the wilderness to his centre in Norway, 300 kilometres inside the Arctic Circle.

Da Pozzo's transcendental vision of sport seems in harmony with

234

Marco's solo flights through the mountains. In 1997, in his auto-biographical book *Storie di aria, di spazio, di luce* ('Stories about air, space and light'), Da Pozzo expounded his philosophy of sport as a personal exploration of the relationship between the athlete's internal reality – what Da Pozzo calls the man-as-athlete – and the surrounding world, using movement to conduct a dialogue with the world. But look closer, and Da Pozzo's holistic values could hardly be further from Marco's. Marco's first motivation was Da Pozzo's last: winning. And in a professional sport like cycling, by contrast with amateur pursuits like rock-climbing, winning meant money, and lots of it. Money had become Marco's principal means of managing his relationships. He paid more than the street price for cocaine – perhaps a means of ensuring greater purity. And what place could doping have in Da Pozzo's conception of sport as a path to enlightenment? Nonetheless, Ronchi spoke frequently to Da Pozzo about Marco, often calling late at night, seeking coherence and advice. He agreed to meet Marco at his Norway base and design a course that would help him out of the black hole of his existence. But at Cesenatico on the morning of the trip Marco's condition was parlous. He had delusional fantasies that a road accident affecting Christine had been reported on the news, and that Ronchi and her husband were on what he called the guilty list. Ronchi threatened to cancel the journey. Marco's parents could no longer cope and begged her to take him away. Ronchi refused to leave without her husband, who arranged time off work. They drove to Milan, he packed a bag, and they left. On the journey north, Marco slept at every opportunity, waking only to eat and take his prescription drugs. They flew to Oslo, then north to Bodö, then on to Narvik. At every change of plane, Marco had to be physically propped up in order to walk. At Narvik they collected a hire car and drove out to meet Da Pozzo.

He was reassuringly hard-edged: like Pissacroia before him, Da Pozzo's view was that Marco needed to become a man. He was hard with Marco, telling him he was of course free to destroy himself, but that he couldn't involve others. Da Pozzo gave a long, uncompromising talk about his view of Marco's situation and the conditions Marco would have to accept. These also involved medical monitoring by Da Pozzo's own doctor at San Marino. And, like Pissacroia, Da Pozzo insisted that the pressures of continued competition could only jeopardise Marco's prospects. *He had to stop riding.*

Marco, used to being surrounded with luxury, asked Da Pozzo, 'How can you live like this?' and left for his hotel to think about it, with Ronchi and her husband. The following morning he appeared at Ronchi's door in a panic, afraid she had abandoned him. He told her he wanted to leave.

Marco had only ever listened to his grandfather, Sotero, or his grandfather-figures, Guerrino Ciani and Luciano Pezzi. Charly Gaul might have got through to him. Even Pissacroia was silver-haired and walked with a limp. Da Pozzo, broad-shouldered, cleft-chinned, long-haired, didn't have a chance. Marco, who would undergo plastic surgery to pin back his ears within weeks of their encounter, must have recoiled at the sight of him – he could have been a Rimini beach bum.

They flew to Copenhagen, where Marco met Christine's sister, hoping for reconciliation.

In Autumn 2002 Marco went to Greece with his parents. The body of Ronchi's book does not mention that she went too, but a photograph caption explains: 'Above, an image portraying us together during the trip to Greece, in the camper van.' It was there, and in that company, that Marco decided to return to competition. Ronchi's description hints it may not have been entirely Marco's decision: 'It wasn't a choice. The anger I have is that I was the only one to think in a certain way. Keeping him on his bike was the only way of keeping him away from drugs, because the demonstration is that while he was training, his relapses weren't continual, whereas in the summer when he didn't have his bike, for two months Marco didn't stop. He hadn't cultivated other interests parallel to cycling.'

There was talk of Mercatone Uno sponsoring a team directed by the 1996 Tour de France winner Bjarne Riis, including both Marco and Jan Ullrich. But it came to nothing. Then Ronchi believed she had found an alternative sponsor in Holland, and signed a contract which guaranteed 10 million euros a year, only to find the 'sponsor' was a hoaxer. Marco ended up with Davide Boifava, his first *directeur sportif* as a professional, with Carrera. Ronchi says, 'Marco would have preferred never to work with Boifava again. But it was Mercatone Uno's choice. Marco described Boifava as "the least worst option".'

The rest of the year, Marco spent between Copenhagen, Cesenatico, his property at Saturnia in the Tuscan Maremma – and Paris, where, on 24 October 2002, he attended the presentation of the 2003 Tour de

France. It was the last time I saw him. As always, he was in Ronchi's protective presence. He seemed withdrawn. He had facial tics and frequently crumpled his face into the gurning expression of a derelict. Marco apparently spoke to Greg Lemond about depression.

The appeal to the Court of Arbitration for Sport grumbled slowly on through summer and into autumn. Marco was no doubt kept abreast of developments, but the matter was in the hands of his legal team. There was little Marco himself could do.

On 5 November Marco, alone in the house, dialled 118 for the emergency services. An emergency ambulance was soon joined at the villa at Sala by the Carabinieri and the fire service. Marco was taken to hospital, then returned home after several hours. The press reported comments from a family member, describing Marco's security fears. The villa had been targeted by thieves before. At the end of June 2001 a gang of safe-breakers with intimate knowledge of the Pantani villa had tried to gain entry to Marco's safe, first by drilling through the roof, then by entering the house and drilling through an interior wall. The vibrations had set off remote alarms and the thieves had fled empty-handed. Then, four days before the start of the 2002 Giro d'Italia, less focused delinquents had raided the family villa while Marco's parents slept. They had found Marco's wallet, stolen several hundred euros, and escaped in Paolo and Tonina's four-wheel-drive Mercedes.

19

Pursuing Oblivion
(JANUARY 2003–OCTOBER 2003)

In January 2003, his self-perception perhaps altered by drug abuse, Marco underwent plastic surgery to straighten his nose and pin back his ears. It betrayed the depth of the hurt he carried around with him, and the anguish Armstrong's 'Dumbo' jibes had caused him. By making him a poor look-alike of himself, the surgery guaranteed him the very mocking looks he feared.

Soon afterwards his former psychoanalyst was affected by scandal. On 22 February 2003 the Rome-based paper *Il Messaggero* wrote of 'an eminent psychiatrist with dozens of publications behind him, no mere theorist but so expert in the field of drug-dependency that he occupied the post of supervisor in a Ser.T. in a central Italian town'. The Carabinieri of the Rome NAS, the report continued, 'have discovered that the psychiatrist X.Z. (not his real initials), 51, does not even have a medical degree: he is, in short, not a doctor at all. At the top of his academic CV is a high-school diploma, then nothing. Probably, in short, the illustrious scholar was only a liar of genius.' The following day, the *Gazzetta di Reggio* wrote: 'M.P., 51, has been exposed and charged ... He was no more than a brilliant con man.'

Mario Pissacroia was 51, had dozens of works behind him, was a drug-dependency expert and a Ser.T. supervisor in the central Italian town of Reggio-Emilia. He had no degree in medicine – like many Italian psychoanalysts before a change in the law in 1989; in fact, his professional qualifications, gained in France and the United States, translated awkwardly into Italian. But Pissacroia was never 'exposed and charged'; the truth about the scandal resembles a cheap soap-opera plot: a jilted, well-connected lover had planted the story in newspapers of the towns where Pissacroia had studios, and involved the police through a family relation. A brief police investigation established his integrity, the inquiries were closed – he showed me certificates to that effect – and a former colleague at the Reggio-Emilia Ser.T. assured me Pissacroia's psychiatric competence was beyond doubt.

Pissacroia decided the better course of action was silence, despite the damage to his reputation. But Marco was caught in the crossfire: the scandal was brought to his attention and allowed to reinforce his scorn for psychotherapy and psychotherapists.

On 12 March Marco's appeal to the CAS over the insulin syringe was finally decided. The verdict smacked of realpolitik: it allowed Marco to return to competition five days later. Ronchi's book claims that the court cleared Marco on the grounds of lack of proof. Yet paragraph 6 on page 58 of the judgment could hardly be less ambiguous:

> The Court of Arbitration for Sport:
> a)   Condemns Marco Pantani to the payment of a fine of 3,000 Swiss francs.
> b)   Suspends Marco Pantani for a period of six months.
> c)   Specifies that this suspension will end on 17 March 2003.

So, on 26 March 2003, after an absence of three hundred days, Marco started the 'Settimana ciclista Internazionale Coppi & Bartali'. In stage five he was second, and overall he finished tenth. Mario Pissacroia considered his results an irrelevant sideshow to his destruction. In his view, the potentially autonomous Marco, no longer dependent on doping products or cocaine, was destroyed the moment they put him back in the saddle. 'That final year of cycling killed him.'

Marco continued his preparations for the Giro d'Italia with Boifava in Spain. In April he rode the Tour of the Basque Country, then the Tour of Aragon, where he managed fifth place in stage two and fourth in stage three. At the end of April Marco returned to Italy a day earlier than scheduled. He told Boifava he wanted to see Christine. In fact, he spent the night in a nightclub on the Riviera consuming cocaine. Christine had become an excuse he used when he could no longer resist his cocaine cravings. The following day Boifava drove to Cesenatico and found Marco in a lamentable state. The Giro del Trentino was out of the question. Boifava blamed Marco's absence on dental problems.

On 10 May the Giro d'Italia started in Lecce. Marco's Giro was tormented by envy. He saw other riders using lightweight wheels and asked why he didn't have any. He saw his old team-mate Stefano Garzelli, now a star in his own right, with a shaven head and better equipment, provided by Davide Boifava's firm Carrera. Giancarlo Ferretti, Luciano Pezzi's former protégé, recalls an encounter with Marco late in the 2003 Giro. 'I met him, all alone in a hotel, silent and sad, absent. I reminded him that we *romagnoli* are a bit special, with strong characters. And I told him that, thanks to that character, he would come through all his difficulties. He answered with a sad smile and I realised he no longer had any fight in him.'

A fall on stage eighteen cost Marco a high placing in the general classification. The following day Marco attacked the Cascata del Toce, but he was too proud to ask the race-leader, his old rival Gilberto Simoni, to gift him the stage win. On 1 June he finished the Giro fourteenth overall and, within days, his life was in pieces. The Tour de France organisation snubbed his team. Talk of joining another team for the Tour came to nothing. Christine, meanwhile, who had warmed to Marco during the Giro, cooled again, so Marco, in the villa at Sala, sated himself with cocaine.

The following morning he was hallucinating. His old team-mate Roberto Conti contacted his former team doctor, Tino Casetti, who steered them towards Giovanni Greco, a psychiatrist at the Ser.T. in Ravenna. Conti wouldn't give Marco's name, but his refusal to consider taking him to the clinic suggested the patient was a celebrity, and Conti's own profession made Marco the likely identity. There were rumours that Marco was already known to the Ravenna Ser.T. Greco advised Conti to call the emergency number, but this would have made Marco's problems public. So Greco made the visit.

At this stage of his life, Marco owned property worth at least twelve million euros, and received annual rents of hundreds of thousands of euros. In current accounts alone, he kept twenty million euros in cash. He had one of the most recognised faces in global sport – yet he now, inexplicably, turned to the Italian national health service, and a highly professional, but extremely busy doctor, for help.

At the villa, Marco was in a state of acute cocaine poisoning, with psychotic hallucinations. He was given a powerful antipsychotic to bring him to his senses, and an antispasmodic to contain the effects of the antipsychotic. He had been self-medicating with benzodiazepine, on the advice of another cocaine-user; Marco, as always, had looked outside official channels for treatment.

Days later Marco went to Saturnia, where he again slaked himself with cocaine. His father called Greco, who recommended a clinic for drug-related personality disorders, the Parco dei Tigli (Linden Park) in the hills south-west of Padua. Paolo later told Ronchi he'd convinced Marco to go to a clinic. But Marco called her from the clinic and complained, 'My parents told me they were taking me to the thermal baths. Instead they brought me here. I don't want to stay.'

His addiction found no respite, even there. He made friends with a twenty-five-year-old Paduan in a nearby room, known as 'Luca'. Marco asked him if he could obtain cocaine. Luca called a dealer in the town of Bassano del Grappa, fifty miles north of Padua. Marco arranged for one of his Cesenatico friends, 'B.G.', to act as go-between. Marco gave his friend two thousand euros; an hour later, he returned to the clinic with a bag, in Luca's description, 'the size of your fist, weighing fifty to sixty grammes. We consumed some, and I looked after the rest.' The following morning Luca tested positive in a urine test and was moved out. Marco left soon afterwards. Ronchi told me, 'I received a text message, saying: "Manu, I'm on the balcony meditating on my future," and when he sent me messages like that, on the mystical side, something was always wrong. Then he called, and said, "Manu, you have to come and get me because something serious has happened, and I can't stay."' Someone had informed the media that Marco was at the clinic and, that evening, Italia 1 broadcast a live report from outside the gates. Mario Pissacroia, at home, saw it. He had a gut reaction: 'For years Marco had been obsessed with spies and betrayal. When I saw the TV crews outside the clinic, the thought that came to me was this: "We've lost the patient."'

Ronchi collected him, and Marco then published an open letter to his fans:

> After a long and painful reflection, I believe the moment has come to take an honest decision for myself, the sponsors, and all my fans. My world is cycling, but I want to return to it with sincerity and enthusiasm. At the moment, even if I would be physically capable of riding, I am passing through a difficult period, consisting of too much internal suffering that, despite those close to me doing

everything possible, only I can overcome. To do this I need a pause that in my current state I cannot quantify.

It is with this profound recognition that I have come to this conclusion but I hope with my heart that this gesture of humility in recognising a difficult moment can be interpreted as a desire for a new start, this time with the right foot.

See you soon, Marco Pantani.

Meanwhile, Marco's father contacted an old hunting partner of Marco's named Michael – pronounced the French way: 'Michel' – Mengozzi, a nightclub manager, who agreed to spend time with Marco. Marco had first met Mengozzi in 1993, at a team celebration at Mengozzi's nightclub, the 'Controsenso', in Forlì. The son of a wealthy farmer in the hills south of Forlì, Mengozzi had run nightclubs for fifteen years: the Contrasenso was his winter club, holding two thousand; in summer he ran the Fragole amare ('Bitter strawberries', meaning something like 'Tough luck!') at Lido di Classe, on the Riviera, big enough to hold four thousand. Between them, Mengozzi employed seventy staff. He told me: 'I've always worked in discotheques, but I've never had problems with drugs.'

Ronchi recalled, 'It seemed the ideal solution, because you couldn't put a saint around Marco, because he'd never have accepted it. It took someone who could help him enjoy himself in a healthy way, but who knew the milieu and could help keep him away from the wrong people, because if you don't know them, you can't keep them away.'

Mengozzi maintains his bulk pumping iron in his private gym, but throughout our conversation about Marco, he was close to breaking down in tears. 'I weigh ninety-five kilos, so when they introduced Marco as a phenomenon, I didn't believe them. I thought: "How can a kid so small be any good on a bike?" Marco came back and found me a few times, and we slowly became friends. We began to go hunting or fishing together. I've never followed cycling, so he didn't talk about cycling with me, and I never went running after him. If he didn't call for six months, I didn't worry about it. Then, out of the blue, he'd call and say, "What are you doing tonight? Shall we go and eat fish?" We must have gone hunting twenty times. At least eighteen of them, Marco tagged along with me.'

Mengozzi clearly made a deep impression on Marco, whose dream of buying a boat and sailing the Adriatic probably came from him: 'I had a sixteen-metre boat. It was fast, but thirsty. I'd had it five years; it was worth three to four hundred thousand euros. Marco said, "Sell it. I'm not good at sailing, but let's buy a new boat to do trips." I found one, and he said, "Let's buy it together: you buy thirty or forty per cent. I'll pay the rest." But it never happened. It wasn't viable, and I didn't have the money to spend.'

Michael had prior experience with a relation who had a heroin problem. 'I was able to help, but we're talking about someone who didn't have money. Take the telephone and money, and you can control them.' Marco was a more complicated case: 'Marco's problem was that he had money. If you confiscated his money, he'd go straight out and withdraw ten thousand euros from the bank. And with ten thousand euros in your pocket, it isn't hard to find cocaine. The first weeks were hellish. Marco had friends with whom he went to nightclubs. If there was a gram of cocaine around, they'd sniff it, to make a night of it. I tried to tell them they couldn't do that with Marco.'

Initially, Mengozzi went to Cesenatico most days, but they didn't live together. Then, one weekend in July, Marco argued violently with Mengozzi and Tonina, and asked a friend from Rimini to drive him down to Saturnia. Within a couple of hours of arriving, the friend was on the phone to Ronchi. Marco had thrown him out – 'I want to be left alone, I'm free to do what I want' – and locked himself in his room. Mengozzi went to collect Marco from Saturnia, where he'd been smoking crack. He recalls: 'I broke down the door. I showed him I had character, I didn't give a damn that he was Marco Pantani. I wanted to save him. From then, he paid me attention.'

On 21 July he left for Ronchi's Milan home, where Ronchi was heavily pregnant. In Milan he met an old friend, Carlo, and his sister, Cristina. Marco visited the Department of Forensic Medicine of the University of Modena, apparently to determine whether or not he was fit to continue to drive. Greco also put Marco in contact with a doctor at Parma, with whom Marco had an interview lasting several hours. By then, Ronchi recalls, Marco no longer wanted to see Fontanelli or Conti. He wanted to be with people outside the team. Marco had other friends, but, says Mengozzi, few had the discipline to restrain him.

In August, Marco returned to Saturnia. He refused to open the door to his mother or to the doctor. Mengozzi convinced him to move into his farmhouse near Fiumana, in the hills south of Forlì. From September, Mengozzi cared for Marco twenty-four hours a day. He told me, 'I went beyond what friends normally did. That's why he decided to come to my house.' At Fiumana, Marco made friends and discussed a new home with estate agents. He began to train in Mengozzi's gym.

Ronchi told me: 'Dr Greco had, in theory, to have at least one appointment per week, to talk, give advice, prescribe him drugs.' But Greco's work with Marco was fettered by poor information; he was never given more than anecdotal fragments of Marco's clinical history, collected from his family, friends and team-mates. Greco recommended a permanent nurse or counsellor experienced in drug dependence. Marco refused outright, and Mengozzi was left isolated. 'The plan wasn't that Marco would be left with me twenty-four hours a day for months on end, with no support and no advice. I had to call Greco every eight hours. Each time, I had to make an excuse to be able to speak outside Marco's hearing.' And Greco, a busy doctor in a state drug-dependency centre, was often difficult to contact, and his bills for treating Marco were not always promptly paid.

Mengozzi also met Christine: 'I thought she was affectionate. Once she cooked, and it wasn't good, and Marco said, coldly, "This is disgusting."' Mengozzi filled Marco's time with 'simple things', which meant everything from wild-boar-hunting to parties where Marco relaxed in female company, which often meant strippers.

At the start of October, Mengozzi and Marco went to Ronchi's Lake Garda holiday home and met her newborn son. Marco gave him a gold chain with a star on it. He'd bought a similar one for himself.

On 9 October 2003 an old friend of Marco's, Jader Del Vecchio was killed in a road accident at Pisignano, near Ravenna. He was 39. After the funeral Marco wept on his grave. Mengozzi had also known Jader well, and detected something self-pitying in Marco's grief: 'He always had Jader's photo in his hands, but he hadn't been so close to Jader. He probably hadn't seen him in three years.'

Soon after the funeral Marco and Mengozzi went duck-hunting at Posarevac, Serbia ('close to the Danube'). 'Marco and I had an argument, because I was paying for everything. In the summer I'd gone to Saturnia twice a week, and each morning I was the one who got up, went to buy pastries, made the coffee, did the shopping, and paid the petrol and the swimming pool maintenance. Serbia cost me a lot of money, too, and I asked him for fifteen hundred euros as expenses. I was giving him part of my life, my time, and it wasn't for the pleasure. But for Marco, paying a few thousand euros for expenses was something he could use against me the moment it suited him.'

After Serbia, Cuba. One of Mengozzi's hunting party, a restaurateur named Franco Corsini, went hunting in Cuba every year, staying in a holiday village on Playa Girón and hunting with a group leader named Sebastián Urra Delgado. Corsini, Mengozzi and an amateur cyclist named Emilio Faede flew with Marco to Cuba in mid-October. They stayed at Playa Girón and hunted duck and turtle doves.

Mengozzi told me: 'We woke at four thirty, and went out to fire fifteen hundred cartridges a head.' He said there were no parties: 'When you've got up at four thirty you don't want to go after women at night. It was an absolutely normal journey.'

Urra's rather different description leaves plenty of room for other forms of entertainment: 'They spent three weeks at my complex, and I took them out hunting eight times.' Marco met a beautiful young woman named Olguita, and he spent the final few days with her family. Mengozzi recalled, 'Marco spent the evening in front of the television, with her family, embracing. He was probably comfortable with her in a way he hadn't been for a long time.' Corsini added: 'They were marvellous days. Marco was happy.'

Marco located the footballer Diego Maradona at La Pradera clinic in Havana, beside a golf course. He managed to get a message to him that he was a friend of one of Maradona's former team-mates, and coaxed him out. They exchanged no more than a few words over a fence.

There was at least one final night out fuelled by Viagra and perhaps more. Then, they returned to Italy. Mengozzi took Marco to the police station at Forlì to ask how they could bring Olguita to Italy. They learnt it would take at least a month, not because of the Italian formalities, which would have been accelerated given Marco's involvement, but because of the Cuban bureaucracy.

Mengozzi says he kept Marco away from cocaine for sixty-four days, from the start of September to their return from Cuba. His success perhaps lay in his selection of displacement activities. For a man who had described himself as feeling like a hunted animal, as Marco had, stalking wild boar with a gun in his hand was perhaps empowering.

Hunting also represented a route back to Marco's childhood expeditions with his grandfather Sotero; Communist Cuba evoked Sotero's social and political universe. The parties allowed Marco to pursue basic sexual desires. There may have been little growth, then, in all this: Mengozzi's strategy may merely have allowed Marco some weeks of regression into an elementary fantasy world.

20

Campiglio Revisited
(2 OCTOBER 2003)

On 2 October 2003 the Madonna di Campiglio trial came to an unsatisfactory conclusion. As in the Milan–Turin appeal, Marco was acquitted on the grounds that the actions attributed to him were not considered criminal by the laws applicable at the time. But the verdict was a tiny endnote to a detailed forensic exposition by two expert consultants, Professor Vittorio Rizzoli, Director of the Haematology Department at the University of Parma's Bone Marrow Transplant Centre, and Professor Giovanni Melioli, Director of the Cellular Immunotherapy Service of the Centre for Advanced Biotechnologies in Genoa. As we follow their study, if Marco seems to disappear from sight, it is worth remembering that it takes us into his veins and confronts us with the very matter that composed him.

Rizzoli and Melioli began by compiling values for nine parameters: 1. Red blood cells (RBC); 2. Haematocrit (Hct); 3. Haemoglobin (Hb); 4. Mean Corpuscular Volume (MCV), a measurement of the size of red blood cells; 5. Red Cell Distribution Width (RDW), the range of red cell sizes in a blood sample; 6. The platelets produced by bone marrow to help blood clotting; 7. Erythropoietin (EPO) present in the body, whether natural or injected (r-EPO); 8. Soluble transferrin receptor (sTfR), a receptor expressed on the surface of human cells that require iron; and 9. Ferritin, a protein occurring in the liver and spleen, containing iron.

They immediately noticed that the plasma erythropoietin level was below normal in Marco's sample. In other words, every blood parameter – RBC, Hct, Hb, MCV – suggested the massive production of red blood cells, yet the hormone that triggered this production was largely absent. It was an almost exact inversion of Marco's blood

The Death of Marco Pantani

	Normal range	Marco (Sample 11440)
EPO	2–16 mU/ml	0.3 mU/ml
RBC	4.4– 5.4 x 10^{12}/litre	5.44 x 10^{12}/litre
Hct	40–52%	52.5%
Hb	g/dL	17.1 g/dL
MCV	82–92 fL	96.5 fL
RDW	11.6–14.8%	17.4%
Plts	180–400 10^3/l	109 10^3/l
sTfR	0.83–1.76ng/dL	2,349 ng/dL
Ferritin..	15–250 ng/ml	437.7 ng/ml

chemistry after the Milan–Turin crash, when soaring erythropoietin levels had been accompanied by extreme anaemia, prompting suspicions of furtive r-EPO injections by non-hospital staff. Rizzoli and Melioli considered each of the usual theses – dehydration, the action of the test-tube anticoagulant EDTA and the method of blood collection – in turn, and discarded them. They concluded that, barring 'physio-pathological mechanisms totally unknown to the scientific community, which trigger erythropoiesis despite the absence of bodily erythropoietin and affect only élite athletes', the only remaining explanation was r-EPO abuse. The high sTfR and, paradoxically, the extremely low EPO values suggest that the r-EPO injection was recent: the body's inhibition mechanisms, working like a thermostat, had blocked Marco's natural EPO secretion.

They then compared the blood-test results of each of the ten riders tested at Madonna di Campiglio with the nearest thing that existed to an r-EPO test at the time. The three nearest things, in fact: the first was a test devised by the French researcher Dr Gérard Dine. Dine's investigation suggested that if three out of eight parameters were above 'normal' limits, the subject could be considered an abuser of EPO with a probability of 90 per cent. In Marco's case, five out of the eight parameters were above the threshold. The second protocol was the CSAD's 'I don't risk my health' programme, according to which a blood sample was considered suspicious if two out of five parameters were anomalous. Four of Marco's parameters were anomalous. The third was a test developed by the medical committee of the Italian Football

Association (FIGC). Marco's was the only sample of the ten that failed the FIGC test, and therefore the only sample that failed all three.

All his life, Marco sustained that the blood test conducted at Imola some hours after the Madonna di Campiglio debacle should have been sufficient to clear him. The certificate gives a haematocrit value of 47.6 per cent and bears the time '16.30', written in the same hand as Marco's name, in pen.

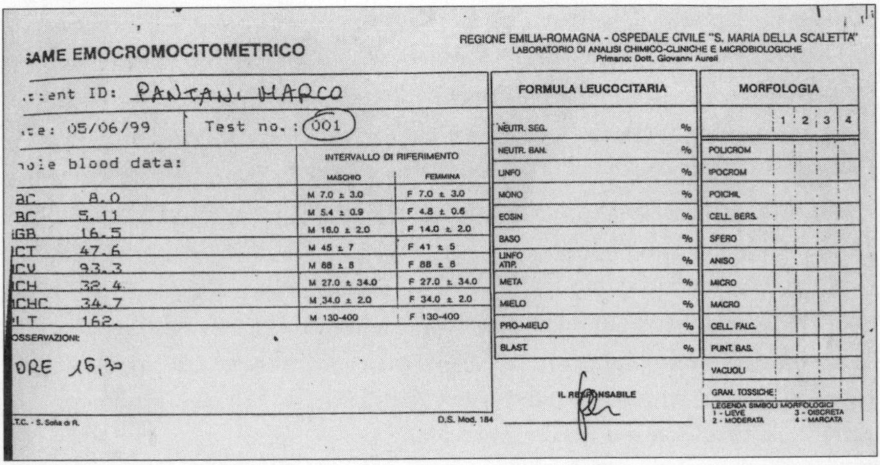

REGIONE EMILIA-ROMAGNA - OSPEDALE CIVILE "S. MARIA DELLA SCALETTA"
LABORATORIO DI ANALISI CHIMICO-CLINICHE E MICROBIOLOGICHE
Primario: Dott. Giovanni Aureli

SAME EMOCROMOCITOMETRICO

tient ID: PANTANI MARCO

te: 05/06/99 | Test no.: 001

ole blood data:		INTERVALLO DI RIFERIMENTO MASCHIO	FEMMINA
BC	8.0	M 7.0 ± 3.0	F 7.0 ± 3.0
BC	5.11	M 5.4 ± 0.9	F 4.8 ± 0.6
GB	16.5	M 16.0 ± 2.0	F 14.0 ± 2.0
CT	47.6	M 45 ± 7	F 41 ± 5
CV	93.3	M 88 ± 8	F 88 ± 8
CH	32.4	M 27.0 ± 34.0	F 27.0 ± 34.0
CHC	34.7	M 34.0 ± 2.0	F 34.0 ± 2.0
LT	162.	M 130-400	F 130-400

OSSERVAZIONI:
ORE 16,30

FORMULA LEUCOCITARIA	
NEUTR. SEG.	%
NEUTR. BAN.	%
LINFO	%
MONO	%
EOSIN	%
BASO	%
LINFO ATIP.	%
META	%
MIELO	%
PRO-MIELO	%
BLAST.	%

MORFOLOGIA	1	2	3	4
POLICROM				
IPOCROM				
POICHIL.				
CELL. BERS.				
SFERO				
ANISO				
MICRO				
MACRO				
CELL. FALC.				
PUNT. BAS.				
VACUOLI				
GRAN. TOSSICHE				

LEGENDA SIMBOLI MORFOLOGICI
1 - LIEVE 3 - DISCRETA
2 - MODERATA 4 - MARCATA

IL RESPONSABILE

T.C. - S. Sofia di R. D.S. Mod. 184

Figure 5: Blood test certificate, Imola, 5 June 1999

Rizzoli and Melioli noted that the certificate bears neither an identifiable doctor's signature nor the official stamp of the hospital. They concluded that a number of parameters, especially the globule volume, raised doubts over whether the instrumentation was suitable, correctly calibrated and operated by qualified technicians, and even whether the tested sample could have been Marco's at all. The Imola certificate was consequently ruled out as evidence in the subsequent investigation, which went on to address, in the first place, whether the Como laboratory technicians had acted properly and competently – they had – and what the reasons were behind Marco's high haematocrit – r-EPO doping. The first case found that, by doping, he had broken the Italian penal code; the appeal found that, yes, he had been doped, but no, there was nothing in the penal code at the time against it. But it left many questions unanswered. Much of the mystery is bogus: why, some asked, would Marco dope himself when he had the Giro won? The answer is that, just as it could take two months to raise a rider's haematocrit using r-EPO therapy, it could take weeks to lower it. The effects of r-EPO cannot simply be switched off.

Others wondered whether rumours circulating the night before the test – that Marco would test high – didn't prove the plot thesis; but since the Festina affair there had always been rumours. That Marco, the world's leading cyclist and the author of remarkable performances, should be at their centre was hardly mystifying. The UCI testers were known in the milieu; so too were the NAS officers from Brescia, who had been investigating doping in amateur cycling for two years. Their presence alone was enough to trigger gossip. Several witnesses reported anger at Marco's domination among a number of high-profile sponsors during the Giro. But there was no way of connecting any plot, real or imagined, with the blood collection. The same was true of the bookmakers.

There were also rumours that the UCI centrifuges had been recalibrated by a point before the tests at Madonna di Campiglio, leading to Marco's downfall. These are to be discounted on three counts: first, any imprecision in so basic a matter as calibration of the equipment would have had professional repercussions for the testers, who were also full-time hospital staff, not to mention the institutional credibility of the UCI and the legal basis of the tests. Indeed, the UCI blood test certificates required the chief tester to complete and sign the following declaration: 'The *Coulter Ac*T8* apparatus has been calibrated this day on the basis of the average of 5 measures with the *4C Plus* controls of Coulter, the expiry date of which is _____. These results can be consulted on demand.' Secondly, the hypothesis has little explanatory force: Marco's haematocrit was not one but two and a half points above the 50 per cent limit. Thirdly, as Professor Melioli told me, 'The Coulter instrument used by the UCI testing team was an automated blood-cell counter that did not require a centrifuge. It calculated the hematocrit by multiplying the red blood cell volume (MCV) for the number of red blood cells. The result is the percentage of cells in a given liquid volume. The "recalibrated centrifuge" hypothesis is technically impossible, in my opinion.'

A final, throwaway comment by Antonio Dallagiacoma, the owner of the Hotel Touring, adds circumstantial evidence to the theory that riders in his hotel that night had oxygen-rich sludge flowing through their arteries: 'The cleaning ladies said they had seen bicycles on rollers in some of the rooms, although I don't know if they belonged to Saeco or Mercatone Uno.' After riding all day, every day (bar one) for three weeks, who would ride at night, unless his life depended on it?

Since, as we have established, the blood test was known about in advance, the only serious question left, then, is this: why wasn't a proven way of circumventing the tests such as blood dilution – an infusion of a blood-diluter like Haemaccel, for instance, or a physio-logical solution (Rizzoli told me, 'If Pantani had simply *drunk* a litre of water two hours before the test, he'd have been three points lower') – used to lower Marco's haematocrit? All of these methods of rehydration were straightforward and, importantly, undetectable by a test that examined haematocrit alone, although not in the 'I don't risk my health' tests, which would explain Marco's boycott. If we knew the answer, we would know what really happened at Madonna di Campiglio.

It is certainly possible that Marco and his helpers assumed they would have plenty of time in which to do so. There is every reason to suspect they had had room for manoeuvre in the past: until October 1998 riders were obliged to present themselves for blood collection within thirty minutes of being called. This half-hour window gave plenty of time for intravenous blood dilution; yet Marco had regularly missed his presentation time in the past and no action had ever been taken. A UCI blood-test certificate dated 8 July 1997, completed at Caen in France, gives a presentation time of 6.56 a.m. and a collection time of 7.07 a.m. – forty-one minutes, in other words, to take remedial action. The certificate for 6 June 1998, the day of the Mendrisio–Lugano time trial, gives a presentation time of 7 a.m. and a collection time of 7.17 – forty-seven minutes to hyper-hydrate. Similarly, at Cesenatico, on the morning of 26 May 1999, his presentation time had been 7.40, but he'd rolled in, with impunity, at eight; given the new ten-minute rule, a total of thirty minutes between notification and testing. Or perhaps, he might have thought, they weren't coming at all: remember Martinelli's comment, 'If the commissaire had arrived three minutes later, Marco would have been having breakfast and they wouldn't have been able to test him'?

I put this theory to a distinguished Italian haematologist, Professor

Giuseppe d'Onofrio, Associate Professor in Clinical Pathology at the Faculty of Medicine and Surgery at the Università Cattolica del Sacro Cuore in Roma, and Director of the Haemotransfusion Service at the A. Gemelli University Polyclinic, also in Rome. He told me: 'It is not clear to me why a phlebotomy of physiological solution wouldn't have been given between seven twenty and seven forty-five: there would have been enough time.' Could there be a simple explanation? We know that the door of the room being used by the blood-testers was open. It is possible that equipment necessary for the infusion could not be moved unseen along the corridor and into Marco's room.

There would, or course, have been no such obstacle *before* the doctors arrived. Indeed, the testers had been expected to arrive as early as 6.30 a.m.: as we have seen, a member of Marco's team had asked the hotel staff to open the doors at that time to let the testers in. Perhaps he was thinking of the morning of the penultimate stage in the 1998 Giro d'Italia, when Marco, as race-leader, had been called first, at 6.30 a.m. Let us assume, then, not that Marco had 'taken a risk', or that there was any botched blood manipulation that morning, but that Marco's blood *had* been diluted and that, if the testers had arrived as expected, he would have been within the allowed parameters. As we know, they didn't arrive at 6.30, or 6.50, or 7.10. Seven fifteen came and went. By then, the effects of any earlier treatment may have been wearing off. The extra liquid would have been filtering through to his bladder.

At Madonna di Campiglio Marco was called at 7.25. He missed the 7.35 deadline, but the testers, this time, were insistent. This time his lateness was not going to be tolerated. The test time is given on the certificate as 7.46: eleven minutes outside the time limit, but nine minutes faster than at Cesenatico, and twenty-one minutes faster than in 1998. Had there been a final, panicked attempt to dilute his blood, foreshortened by the testers' insistence on his immediate attendance? If so, what had his haematocrit been *before* it? Fifty-eight per cent? Sixty? More?

D'Onofrio accepted, in principle, that the haematocrit increase was physiologically possible: 'I think I can say that between six thirty and seven forty-five it is certainly possible that intravenous hydration might have lost part of its effect.' Melioli was sceptical: 'I fear it is unlikely that, after intravenous rehydration, the haematocrit could be modified by several points. I don't believe a haematocrit can be modified by three points in a few minutes. The mechanisms that govern the quantity of liquid in the organism are extremely effective, but probably not so rapid.' Nonetheless, he added, 'The reconstruction could be plausible.' Certainly, it is reinforced by the fact that, in the table of the blood-test values found that morning, the two samples with the highest haematocrit were the later codes – 11440 (Marco) and 11442. Nor is it pure invention: it was passed onto the police investigators by a source who wished to remain anonymous. The same source alleged that the outcome was desired by the directors of some of the other teams, as a result of lost earnings that should have resulted from victories promised by Mercatone Uno and then not conceded. This may be so; but if the fatal delay was conspiratorial, then it was the blandest of conspiracies, in which no impropriety took place. Supposedly unannounced blood tests not having a pre-arranged time, the testers cannot have arrived late. The great conspiracy would have been foiled if only Marco's haematocrit had not been grotesquely, life-threateningly high.

Alternatively, the truth may lie in another hypothesis, which takes into account the characteristics of the stage that was to start later that morning. Stage twenty-one, from Madonna di Campiglio to Aprica, presented blood-dopers with a conundrum. The first serious climb, the Tonale, started within twenty-five kilometres of the stage start; the climb of the towering Gavia, the high point of the race, followed, well before the halfway point of the stage. The athletic advantage of a concentrated stock of red blood cells was going to be required early in the day: no one in contention could afford to start the stage with highly diluted blood. Marco's value for RDW – Red Cell Distribution Width, the range of red cell sizes in a blood sample showing the heterogeneity of the red blood cells – was extremely high: 17.4 per cent, where 'normal' values lie between 11 and 13 per cent; and Gérard Dine's research, mentioned above, gives 15 per cent as the threshold above which r-EPO doping is to be suspected. Today, RDW is one of the parameters used by the World Anti-Doping Agency to test for autologous blood transfusions.

D'Onofrio and Melioli both agree that Marco's RDW level could be explained by the transfusion of a litre of blood. Indeed, the combination of two illegal methods of blood doping, i.e. r-EPO use and autologous blood infusion, can increase their respective efficacy and reduce chances of detection. It is not inconceivable, in fact, that Marco was being treated with r-EPO-enhanced autologous transfusion (EEAT). Transfused blood, of course, has to be kept refrigerated. Any vehicle with a refrigerator would do and there were hundreds of vehicles with refrigerators following the race. Creating a mobile blood bank would hardly present insurmountable difficulties.

A blood transfusion carried out the night before the stage would have given time for excess liquids to drain away, knowing that it would be possible to dilute his blood with physiological solution. However, the following morning, using the team centrifuge, Marco's haematocrit could have been found to be high. If it was necessary to dilute his blood, a doctor would be required – but the team doctor was nowhere to be found. As we know, Ronchi encountered Roberto Rempi at a party at 1 a.m. The hotel staff state categorically that he didn't return to the hotel before 3 a.m., when the night porter went to bed. From 4 a.m. the owner, Dallagiacoma, was on duty. He didn't see Rempi return, although he was flitting between reception and the kitchen and may have missed him. On the other hand, police investigators took the following statement from a witness at the Hotel Majestic, down in the centre of Madonna di Campiglio:

> [B]etween eight and nine that morning, another person appeared in the hotel, [presenting himself] as the doctor of Pantani's team. He went up to Coccioni's room. Then, in a clear state of agitation, this person told me that soon afterwards something serious would happen and he asked me for the telephone number of the Hotel Touring, where the cycling team of Mercatone Uno was lodged.

In the absence of a technician capable of carrying out intravenous blood dilution, we imagine Marco drinking frantically to thin his blood, and delaying the test as long as he could – so long that the Saeco rider Paolo Savoldelli took his test between Marco's team-mate Velo and Marco. Even then there was not enough time, and the UCI doctors found his haematocrit high. In disbelief, perhaps even in fear, they repeated the test, over and over again. Then they informed Marco's team.

Much is known about Madonna di Campiglio, it would seem, and from a wide range of sources. With expert help, a great deal can be gathered from Marco's blood data. Yet once the elements have been identified – the products, the transfusion, the blood dilution, the times necessary for the liquids to drain from his veins – we add and subtract, shorten and lengthen, and draw near, but no nearer the drama that would eventually lead, five years away, to Marco's destruction. The truth is that the mystery in Madonna di Campiglio is not a naturally occurring enigma but a man-made puzzle. One day, when the passion has passed, one of those who know may decide to talk. Unfortunately, as an unburdener of conscience, the truth has a limited half-life; if it is ever, finally, revealed, the opportunity for verification may have passed, and the facts will have become indistinguishable from empty rumour.

A year after her son's death Tonina told me of a link that would have connected a possible plot with Marco's blood-test result at Madonna di Campiglio. One of the testers, she said, had previously worked for Mapei. He had then died a mysterious death in a skiing accident. Paolo added that his body had sunk deep into a mountain lake. The case seemed to have been blown wide open – until I met the testers at Como. All were thankfully very much alive. It was an elementary case of mistaken identity: the former Mapei doctor was Massimiliano Sala (he, too, alive and well); the tester was another Dr Sala – Eugenio – younger, not a sports doctor at all, and unfairly treated, along with his colleagues, by the Madonna di Campiglio affair.

Ronchi continues to defend Marco from charges of doping: 'Marco, unlike all the other riders, was an artisan. He never had a physical trainer, he never had a fixed doctor, and I don't believe he ever abused doping substances. I don't rule out the possibility that he used them, even if I never saw it and I never heard it spoken about, so I can't confirm or deny it. But I use common sense. I presume that, like all the others, he too helped himself, because the effort you make to respond to what the system requires, riding twenty stages of the Giro d'Italia – everyone wants speed and spectacle – a normal human being, I believe, can't do it.'

On the subject of Madonna di Campiglio, Ronchi posed the first question herself, rhetorically: did Marco feel untouchable, and take a risk, even knowing his haematocrit was outside the legal limit? And answered it, too, as best she could: 'I rule this interpretation out a priori, because Marco was too intelligent. He knew the ropes; he'd already won the Giro, and he had no need to overdo it.' Intelligence, however, is no guarantee against human error.

Ronchi continued: 'So, starting there, I ask myself how it was possible that Marco Pantani, with the Mercatone Uno team at those levels [?], knowing that the controls were coming the following day, didn't do anything to make sure he'd be OK.' The very question conceals an admission that Marco was either doped or ill; why otherwise would remedial action be necessary? But Ronchi was unstoppable: 'In the morning they went to find him and they arrived there' – at the Hotel Touring in Madonna di Campiglio – 'and they said, "Take this test tube, look at it carefully" – he wasn't offered five or six test tubes and asked to choose one, as they usually did . . .' But the meticulous police investigations, the trial that tested them and the appeal that re-examined the evidence all established that the testers at Madonna di Campiglio had followed the testing protocols to the letter. '. . . There was a series of circumstances', she continued, 'that aren't proofs, but are circumstances that go back to the start of the Giro d'Italia, when Marco opposed the duplication of the UCI and CONI controls, which lead us to think – and Marco was in the front line – that they wanted to stop Marco Pantani . . . because he had exposed himself by criticising too vigorously the duplication of checks, which didn't mean, "We don't want to be tested," but only that he wanted greater clarity in a system to avoid a situation that continued to be legal, when everyone knew it wasn't right.' No recognition, then, that the 'I don't risk my health' campaign parameters, unlike the UCI test, could detect blood dilution and therefore posed an inestimably greater threat to r-EPO-abusers; or that the CONI leadership warred continuously with the 'I don't risk my health' campaigners and wound up its promoter, the CSAD, as soon as was practical.

'Marco Pantani,' Ronchi told me, 'living in his milieu and his historical era, wanted, with Madonna di Campiglio, to say, "Guys, let's stop a moment, because if we carry on like this, we'll ruin ourselves, and we'll ruin cycling." There, however, he was left alone. The system can't tell people, "You see, we don't stop even before the number one who's winning the Giro d'Italia, in order to clean up our act," when nothing is being done to clean up its act, but it's only trying to sacrifice one individual, and make one individual pay for all the others, when they're still doing what they were doing before. So the real disease of Pantani wasn't EPO; Marco's real problem was that he was the only one who really wanted to put things right, because he was the only one who wouldn't have lost anything, seeing that he was a champion and had been winning since he was eight.'

The argument is rambling, contradictory, incoherent. Hadn't Marco's rivals – Virenque and Zülle, for instance, to name but two massively doped riders – also been winning since they were children? In point of fact, Marco was never a prolific winner, as an amateur or a professional and, on results alone, he belongs to the footnotes of his sport, although, by winning the Giro and the Tour, he had benefited more from doping than they, and perhaps anyone else. And, even in Ronchi's account, he was doped: if not, in what way did he believe he would ruin himself and cycling? Cycling's greatest cheat, then: but also, 'the only one who really wanted to put things right'?

Ronchi is passing Marco for the likes of Christophe Bassons, the Frenchman who rode for Festina in 1998, refused to participate in the team doping programme and was eventually hounded out of sport. Or Charly Mottet, another French rider who rejected doping but finished fourth in the Tour de France. Yet Marco was not even Alex Zülle, or David Millar or Filippo Simeoni, who doped, then repented, and accepted the consequences. Marco, in the end, made no heroic, significant, or even identifiable contribution to the fight against doping except, it might be argued, getting caught.

But Ronchi was still talking: 'I'm convinced, as Marco maintained until the very end, because you don't die if you're not convinced of something, that he had another [blood] value [at Madonna di Campiglio], and that that morning, through how things unfolded – and they need to be reconstructed from the previous evening when rumours were circulating that he'd be stopped ...' And on, and on, and on, desperately, untenably (loyally, even, although loyal to what higher principle isn't immediately clear) defying or ignoring the evidence, out of friendship and a terrible sense of loss, controverting the incontrovertible.

In the end we came back to Marco's mental illness, the anguish he sought to escape through cocaine, the self-destructive, insane bingeing he pursued into the unbeing that lies beyond oblivion. But, here too, Ronchi promised me, 'Mental illness? Absolutely not ... Marco was very, very, very healthy psychologically, I can assure you. Even too much so.' And adds, cryptically, as if we hadn't understood each other at all, and had been at cross-purposes all afternoon, 'Perhaps too intelligent to be a cyclist.'

21
The Ending of Hope
(NOVEMBER 2003–9 FEBRUARY 2004)

The trip to Cuba had awoken a restlessness in Marco, who began to move in circles outside Mengozzi's reach. In the space of four November days the equilibrium Mengozzi had established dissolved. He blamed Nevio for unsettling Marco, and Ronchi for giving him a way out. Perhaps anxious to see Olguita, Marco had contacted Nevio. Mengozzi remembered, 'On the Thursday night, Nevio organised an evening with Siboni and others I didn't know. I wasn't happy, but I said to Marco, "At the end of the evening, come back."' Instead, Marco decided to stay again at Nevio's. Mengozzi called him in the small hours: 'I lost it: I said either he comes back now, or he isn't coming back, although I knew he wasn't ready to stand on his own two feet. I said, "Marco, this isn't a hotel. If you stay Friday, stay on Saturday, too." On the Sunday Marco called and said, "Leave the gate open; I'm coming to collect my things." When he arrived, he said, "I'm going to Manuela's." I said, "We've argued; let's talk, clear it up." Instead Manuela gave him the option of leaving, and he took it. He slammed the door as he left.'

Ronchi had arranged a meeting with another rider, Giovanni Lombardi, in Milan, to explore the possibility of another team. She had told Mengozzi, 'Don't tell him Lombardi's here, otherwise he won't come.'

On Sunday Marco took a few belongings from Mengozzi's house and moved to Ronchi's at Milan. There Lombardi discussed taking Marco to Argentina for a training camp. But Marco, still mourning his friend Jader, and perhaps imagining Olguita was the answer to his grief, fled to Madrid, then flew back to Cuba, alone, to accommodation organised by Pregnolato. Olguita met Marco at the airport; but within a couple of days she'd left him, scared off by his incessant, incoherent chatter. Not even the large sums of cash he was carrying were enough to keep her interested. He also wanted to talk to Maradona again; he had made vague comments about joining him in the clinic. But there was no second meeting: Maradona was no longer on the island.

Marco was now at a dangerous loose end. Olguita's rejection only emphasised his inability to find female affection – an inability that dated to his teenage years and one that had led to a telling comment to Roberto Conti in 1994, after Marco's first major successes as a professional: 'First, women didn't even see me; now they're running after me. Two accelerations at the Giro and I've become *bello*, too!' Now, in a foreign land, where Marco's celebrity counted for little, he was snubbed again. It may have pushed him over the edge. He closed himself into his rented rooms. In the meantime Nevio had arrived from Rimini; he met up with another friend, Enzo, the son of a Riccione hotelier, and moved into another house. With Nevio and Enzo, Marco met other women; Nevio has photographs of Marco with an attractive, dark-skinned Cuban girl taken during the second trip. But the thrill had gone.

One night, Marco escaped Nevio and disappeared. On his return he was hallucinating. His landlady called the doctor at one of Havana's luxury hotels and asked a friend, José, a sometime rickshaw driver, to keep an eye on him; but on another night Marco and José were stopped by police. José spent the night in a cell, and Marco was taken to a clinic to dry out. He gave his bike to José and his watch, a Rolex Daytona, which his friends say was worth sixteen thousand euros, to his landlady's little boy. He took another boy to a clothes shop and dressed him from head to foot. Marco wanted to contact Jader, and was introduced to a blind clairvoyant, but the séance ended in disaster: the medium asked Marco to buy flowers and perfume and cast them into the sea at a specific place. Marco drove, but when the medium told him to stop at a certain point, Marco couldn't understand how a blind man could know where they were. He stormed out of the car and ran off. Soon, he was hopelessly lost in a poor part of Havana. He found a police patrol car, and was driven back to his rooms.

When Mengozzi learned Marco had returned to Cuba, he was livid: 'What made me angry was that Ronchi hadn't even told me. On the Thursday Tonina called me. She said: "Do you know where he is?" I said, "With Ronchi." "No. He went to Spain." I called Ronchi, and she said, "Marco's in Cuba. Didn't you know?" For the previous three months I'd spoken four times a day to Tonina and twice a day to Ronchi. Now, no one had thought to tell me. Ronchi had helped him find the flight. My view of her changed. I understood she played her games to bring Marco back to the bicycle. I realised she'd have ditched me when it became convenient.' Jealousies and possessiveness had begun to unravel the safety net beneath Marco.

Marco began to scrawl disjointed, sometimes heart-rending notes in his passport, then tore out the pages. He made rambling mobile-phone calls to Italy, speaking at length to Pregnolato, who drained two phone batteries trying to work out what was going on. Marco called Greco, and Ronchi, then disappeared. After several days – Mengozzi says ten – with no news, Tonina, on Greco's advice, asked Mengozzi to go and get him. Mengozzi called Nevio in Cuba and threatened him. 'I said to Nevio, "If anything happens to Marco . . ." After fifteen years in night-clubs, I know people.' On Sunday morning Mengozzi tried to find tickets to Cuba. The only seats were in business class, €2,200 each. He called Franco Corsini, and Corsini called Urra, their hunt-leader. Urra asked around and located Marco, who was ill from drugs and had been robbed. Mengozzi called Tonina and said, 'I'm going to need two cars, eight people, and I imagine I'll have to pay people off. I need twenty thousand euros.'

Mengozzi describes his arrival with Corsini, Urra and a group of ex-military men outside Marco's accommodation as 'like the arrival of the Pope. We swept up in two four-by-fours and Marco embraced me. I spent an hour on the telephone with Tonina, two hours with the doctor, who changed the doses, and so on.' Mengozzi reimbursed Marco's landlady for the furnishings Marco had destroyed, he and Corsini reco-vered Marco's bike, and Corsini supposedly drove around for five hours to find the watch. Mengozzi claims they paid five hundred dollars for each; Nevio claims he recovered the Rolex in a matter of minutes. Urra supports Nevio's version : 'Nevio', he told me, 'knew where everything was.'

They took the missing pages of Marco's passport from the bin. As well as making unfathomable references to Santería, the Cuban version of voodoo, his scrawled notes suggested the toll taken by the incessant legal proceedings: 'I've been humiliated for nothing. For four years I've been in every court. Rules, yes, but the same for everyone.' They moved Marco to one of Urra's bungalows on Playa Girón, left a car with the guards and set off around Havana to pay debts. Corsini found the Renault 9 Marco had hired, then abandoned. It had been wrecked.

Marco slept for three days, waking only to eat papaya and potato tortillas and drink water. Urra smoothed Marco's exit with his defaced passport. He told me: 'I've been working with Italian tourists for ten years, so I'm quite well known to the immigration service. A *compañero* there made sure there were no problems.'

Mengozzi took Marco back to Fiumana. 'He'd lost ten kilos. He spent two entire days asleep. I was worried. But when I took him home to his parents, the first thing they said to him was: "Mengozzi wanted €20,000 to come and collect you."' Mengozzi was unrepentant: 'The Cuba trip cost thirteen thousand euros. Marco had cost me a great deal of money at Fiumana: he'd broken things in the house, he'd run up huge phone bills. I'd brought their son back alive, and they accused me of making money out of him.'

Marco was back in Italy by 2 December, when he made large withdrawals from different bank accounts; at 3.37 p.m. 15,000 euros, and at 3.56 p.m. another 10,000. Five days later he withdrew another 10,000 euros. He began to call old friends: on 1 December he called Christine to wish her happy birthday. He spoke to Roncucci; he even called Mario Pissacroia, who recalls their conversation vividly:

MARCO Pronto, sono Marco Pantani.
PISSACROIA Beppe Fanfani [an Italian politician who occasionally rented a house from Pissacroia]?
MARCO No, Marco. It's Marco, don't you recognise me?
PISSACROIA Oh, Marco. How are you?
MARCO I'm well. I've got someone looking after me. What happened about those articles in the paper?
PISSACROIA Soap bubbles made up by jealous colleagues!
MARCO So it's all OK?
PISSACROIA Yes.
MARCO How's your son? [He was ill with non-Hodgkins' lymphoma.]
PISSACROIA So, so. What are you doing for Christmas?
MARCO I don't know. We could do something together?
PISSACROIA Yes. Call me. But tell me where you are.

MARCO Sometimes here, sometimes there. I move about.

PISSACROIA So we'll speak soon?

MARCO Yes, I'll call.

PISSACROIA Merry Christmas and a Happy New Year, if we don't see each
other before.

But Marco never called back.

On 7 December, as Marco slept off his Cuban nightmare, his old
rival the great Spanish climber José Maria Jiménez died in a Madrid
psychiatric clinic, aged thirty-two. He too had been addicted to cocaine.
His death put Marco off clinics.

Through December and January Marco lived partly with Mengozzi and
partly in his own villa at Sala. Greco was called each time Marco
approached self-destruction. Mengozzi arranged for Marco to spend
evenings and nights with women. One night he invited a Polish stripper,
who had performed earlier in the year at a hunting party, to spend the
evening with Marco at the farmhouse. Marco spent three nights with
her. On the fourth, Marco asked her to bring a friend for Mengozzi. The
Polish dancer's friend was another East European dancer; she used the
name 'Barbara' and drove an expensive convertible. Marco quickly
swapped the Polish girl for Barbara, who suggested they needed a little
something to inject some life into the evening. Mengozzi made it clear
that he would have no cocaine in the house. If Barbara was to see Marco,
she would have to promise to keep him cocaine-free. His plea fell on
deaf ears.

Mengozzi and Tonina had begun to identify the telephone numbers
of Marco's dealers from his mobile-telephone accounts. They had
managed to remove them from Cesenatico and Cesena, but serendipity
gave Marco a new supplier. On their second night together, sometime
in late December, Marco and Barbara went to the Pineta, a well-known
nightclub in Milano Marittima. Barbara introduced him to Fabio
Carlino, Marco Cappelli, Rossano Giandomenico and Fabio Miradossa.
Carlino, 26, from Lecce, was the manager of the Le Scuderie nightclub
at Castelfranco Emilia; with Cappelli, also known as Pucci, 38, he also
ran 'Angels Agency.it', a modelling agency for whom Christine Jonsson
had worked. Miradossa, 29, from Naples, lived at Carlino's flat in
Rimini. Investigators described the apartment as 'a formidable logistical

base' for the distribution of cocaine. In the toilet Miradossa provided Marco with a line; they exchanged telephone numbers and, from that evening, Miradossa became Marco's dealer.

Mobile-phone records show that, at 10.46 p.m. on the night of 25 December, Marco, at Fiumana, called Barbara, who was in Riccione. Between then and 0.35 a.m. the following morning he called seven times. She called him back three times. Mengozzi called her once. The call details show her movements: by 23.50 she was in Cesena; fifteen minutes later she had reached Forlì. By 0.22 a.m. Barbara had reached Fiumana. After spending the night together Marco and Barbara agreed to meet the following evening in the Hotel Touring, at Miramare on the Riviera. It was Barbara who suggested the location: she had worked there before. A mobile call at 9.24 p.m. that evening gives Marco's position at the tollgate of the A14 motorway, about to leave Forlì for the hotel.

Miradossa arranged for the delivery of more than seventy grams of cocaine to Pantani at the hotel. Marco knew the deliveryman only as 'Peru'. Other guests saw Marco and Barbara cavorting in a corridor; Barbara was reportedly naked. But the following day, 27 December, under the influence of cocaine, Pantani became moody, and Barbara, frightened, fled the hotel. At 3.59 p.m., and again at 4.27 p.m., Marco sent Mengozzi text messages. At 6 p.m. Mengozzi called Barbara, who was back at Riccione. She told him Marco was still at the hotel. At 6.43 p.m. Barbara called him back. She had returned to the hotel.

Greco arrived at approximately 7.30 p.m. Ronchi had instructed him *not* to apply for a compulsory treatment order. Mengozzi joined him, and they went up to the room. As they entered, Marco took a final, defiant sniff of cocaine in front of them. The temperature was stifling – the central heating was at maximum – and the room was in chaos. They found equipment for smoking crack. There was powder everywhere and a bag of cocaine weighing perhaps fifty grams, which Mengozzi and Greco destroyed. Marco was babbling in Italian and Spanish; he had written on the bed linen. Only after convincing Marco to take several drops of haloperidol, a powerful antipsychotic, could Greco establish verbal contact with him. But Marco struggled free from Mengozzi and managed to swallow five milligrams of an anxiolytic, Alprazolam. After a telephone conversation with Ronchi it was decided Marco should return to Mengozzi's farmhouse. Mengozzi paid for the linen and the other damage, but it took two hours to convince him to leave with them.

The following evening Barbara turned up at Carlino's flat with Cappelli and Carlino himself. The tenant, Rossano Giandomenico, was there. He told police, 'She told us she'd been frightened that night with Pantani at the Touring, because he'd completely lost his head. She said that, after he'd taken the cocaine, he'd become strange and worrying; he'd begun to ramble and had lost consciousness. She left the room as soon as she could. I remember she said something about the cocaine, along the lines of, "But what gear did you give him?"'

On Tuesday 30 December Greco met Marco's parents at Ravenna. He explained the dangers of opposing a compulsory treatment order and advised them to employ a qualified counsellor to support Mengozzi, who had been caring for Marco, with no help beyond sporadic telephone conversations with Greco, for six months. By now, Marco was consuming perhaps a hundred grams of cocaine a week, ingeniously stashed about Mengozzi's property. Mengozzi argued with Marco, and with Marco's parents. When, on Saturday 3 January 2004, Greco met Ronchi and Marco's parents at Fiumana, Mengozzi stayed away. The sole outcome of that meeting was the suggestion, by Marco's parents, that Marco should take another holiday – in Spain, perhaps, or South America.

But Mengozzi was becoming desperate: 'When Marco relapsed, I asked for him to be removed. He didn't obey the rules. They'd left him alone for nine or ten months, unchecked. There was no longer any collective effort. He returned home for a couple of days; Tonina called and said he'd bought more cocaine. I said I didn't want him here. There was no improvement. It had become a game of cat and mouse. He wanted to escape me; I tried to anticipate his moves. In the end I couldn't put up with it any more. I was tired. It was decided that something would happen on Monday [5 January]. Ronchi mentioned a clinic in London. But still Marco didn't leave.'

Nevio Rossi told police that Marco visited him in Rimini sometime early in January 2004 ('a Friday: I suppose it was 2 January'). He told them: 'Marco arrived at my house and showed me the palm of his hand, where he had about fifteen lines of cocaine. More joking than anything else, he asked me if he'd paid too much. He said, "I bought it at Rimini," and I think it was the first time he'd been supplied from here.' Rossi became an easy target for the vindictive after Marco's death. But he protests that, awaiting trial and facing prison, he was the last person who could have provided Marco with cocaine. Blamed and ostracised, he too was about to lose a friend.

Marco saw Barbara twice more in January, at his parents' home. On the first of these visits, Tonina intercepted her with one of Paolo's hunting rifles, as she got out of her car, and, to prevent her from giving Marco cocaine, forced her to strip naked before entering the house. Barbara's less than elegant rejoinder was, 'I bring Marco pussy, not drugs.' The second time she came there was an argument and the Carabinieri were called.

Mengozzi recalled: 'One night, Marco had gone away and I knew he'd taken something. I said I didn't want him here any more. His parents asked me to keep him at least until his birthday because they didn't know what do with him.' On 7 January Marco cashed a cheque for 10,000 euros from a bank in Predappio, close to Fiumana, 'To buy myself a birthday present,' he told Mengozzi. He would be thirty-four on 13 January, and Mengozzi, in a final effort, decided to organise a birthday party to surround Marco with his closest friends, and somehow compel him to understand that help was at hand. But each of Marco's friends suspected the others of giving him cocaine. It took considerable diplomacy to assemble the party and, even then, Marco was ungrateful. He spent the weekend of 10 and 11 January at Verbania, Ronchi's home village, on Lago Maggiore, north of Milan. He left for Mengozzi's shortly after 9 p.m. At 9.07 p.m. he called Miradossa. They met at the Rimini South motorway exit just past midnight. Then Marco called Ronchi and Mengozzi, no doubt to let them know he had nearly arrived.

On 12 January Mengozzi found traces of the drug. He called Greco, who drove down and saw signs of continued cocaine abuse. Marco told Greco he was indifferent at the prospect of his birthday dinner. He said he would have hoped for a different sort of celebration. Greco left. He never saw Marco again.

Tonina was critical of Greco; she said he wasn't available enough. Ronchi told me: 'From the start, Dr Greco told us he worked at the Ser.T. at Ravenna; he wasn't a private doctor who could work solely with Marco. But I think that he tried to keep his distance after several sittings, not because he wasn't a good doctor, but because the case was difficult.'

I put her criticism to Greco. He didn't recognise it: 'I'd like to have seen another doctor who would have gone to the hotel on 27 December, risking his safety and his professional reputation to sort through the drugs and the wreckage. Does repeatedly driving to Predappio in the middle of the night, and taking endless phone calls at 2 a.m., mean unavailability? Probably I'm accused of unavailability because I set limits.'

At the birthday dinner, when one of Marco's oldest Cesenatico friends asked Marco to tell everyone whether or not he had ever provided him with cocaine, Marco laughed: 'Women, yes, but I've never needed your help to get *la roba*!' In Mengozzi's experience, few of Marco's friendships were much more than intermittent contacts. 'You spent a month together, then you heard very little from him for six months.' But Mengozzi remembers the party as a sad affair: 'Marco was in bad shape, and during the dinner he spoke about his problems, telling everyone about the depression, the drugs, his sporting and emotional problems. It was harrowing for everyone.' Often incoherent, Pantani told his closest friends: 'I don't know who to trust any more.'

On the evening of Wednesday 14 January Marco took more cocaine. Mengozzi recalls: 'At 4:30 a.m. I called a friend from Predappio and asked him to help me clean him up. When we went into Marco's room, we had to fight him. I called Greco at 6 a.m. He told me to ask for a compulsory treatment order.' Mengozzi called Marco's parents, who again refused. They reached Mengozzi's at 10 a.m. Mengozzi, Ronchi and Marco's parents all called Greco several times during the day. He told Marco's parents that he was going to recommend a compulsory treatment order. They again opposed him. Mengozzi told them Marco would have to agree to go without money and his mobile phone, and not to leave the house unaccompanied. He'd have to try to do without cocaine. 'I thought we had an agreement,' Mengozzi said, 'but Marco came out of his room and announced, "Ronchi's husband is coming to collect me." She'd given him a way out. Marco's parents began to prepare his things. Ronchi's husband arrived, and Marco took his suitcase and his cocaine and left.' Marco reached Milan on 16 January. He stayed at Ronchi's for two weeks. It was the last time Mengozzi saw him. Ronchi insists there had been scenes of violence between Marco and Michel that justified removing him.

*

Ronchi hoped her home in Milan would give Marco stability: 'His condition when he arrived suggested to me that he had been taking cocaine continuously for months.' But Ronchi told me, exaggerating: 'I spoke to Greco forty times a day,' she says, and adds, 'It wasn't always easy to contact him.' For several days Marco did nothing but eat, sleep and take his prescription drugs. Mengozzi told me, 'He was violent. He talked incessantly, insulting her for her mistakes.' Ronchi contacted Renato Da Pozzo again, but their conversation came to nothing. In her book Da Pozzo is accused of asking 'exorbitant sums', which would have turned Marco against him from the start. She doesn't explain why Marco, deeply ill, and fantastically rich by any reasonable standard, ever needed to know the costs. He spent freely in the cause of self-destruction; it would have taken at least equal and opposite munificence to save him.

Marco continued to smoke large quantities of crack. Greco recalls that he strongly advised them to have Marco hospitalised by force for compulsory treatment. But Ronchi told me, 'It never reached the level where compulsory treatment was necessary.'

Marco phoned Barbara for the last time at 7.03 p.m. on Sunday 25 January. The following morning he asked Ronchi to lend him her car, so that he could drive home to collect clothes. He left the motorway at Cesena at 11.57 a.m. on 26 January and at 12.12 p.m. he withdrew 12,000 euros from his bank in Cesenatico. He drove straight to Rimini; after a fifteen-second phone call to Miradossa, the two men met in Viale Regina Elena – mobile-phone records place Miradossa there at 12.55 p.m. and Marco at 1.13 p.m. – and exchanged money for cocaine. By 5.48 Marco was back in Milan. From then until Friday, Ronchi noticed a marked change in Marco's mood: he hallucinated in front of the television, and babbled.

Greco had fixed an appointment for Marco and Ronchi to see Dr Ravera of the clinic Le Betulle at Appiano Gentile, outside Milan, for 2.30 p.m. on Friday 30 January. Marco's admission to the clinic was arranged for Monday 2 February. Ronchi told me: 'Dr Greco had reserved Le Betulle as a secondary option because, whereas the Parco dei Tigli is a bit more easy-going, the treatment at Le Betulle is much more serious. But Marco's reaction was, "You doctors don't understand anything; who are you to say how I should heal myself? I don't believe in clinics . . ."'

After the meeting Marco burst into tears in Ronchi's car. She took it to be in resignation. It turned out otherwise.

At 6 p.m. on Saturday 31 January Marco's parents arrived at Ronchi's flat. She had invited them to help convince Marco to go to Le Betulle. On the stairs, recalls Ronchi, 'There was a great argument ... and I won't say more out of respect for everyone.' Marco and Paolo quarrelled violently – Marco later complained his father had punched him. He threw down his telephone and stormed out, taking the clothes he had on, his credit card and driving licence, and a considerable sum of money. Ronchi called for an ambulance to treat Tonina, who had fainted. Marco, meanwhile, disappeared.

On 2 February, now in possession of Marco's mobile, Tonina sent text messages to recently dialled numbers. One reached Miradossa (Tonina thought he might be Albanian – 'In any case, he wasn't Romagnolo'), who replied that he didn't know her son, and that, if she continued to accuse him, he would report her to the police. Pantani's parents contacted the drug-rehabilitation centre San Patrignano. Ronchi told me: 'Andrea Muccioli, the community director, told them that Marco would accept treatment only if he was allowed to hit rock bottom. "You don't have a son called Marco Pantani. You have a son who, unfortunately, has a dependence problem and who, like all the others, has to be abandoned."' For the first time, Marco's parents felt able to accept advice coming from an experienced specialist. They prepared the camper and left for Greece.

After a week without a trace Marco called Greco on Friday 6 February. He was at the Hotel Jolly Touring in Milan. Ronchi had searched hotels all over Milan but the Hotel Touring slipped through the net, despite the fact that the Madonna di Campiglio debacle had taken place in a Hotel Touring, as had Marco's Christmas adventure with 'Barbara' at Miramare. He had checked in shortly after 23.30 on the evening of Saturday 31 January, saying, 'I'll be staying a few days.' He had been allocated room 344. He had lowered the blinds and turned the heating up.

After his telephone conversation with Marco, Greco informed Ronchi. She called Marco: he apologised, and asked her to bring him clothes and medicine. She took them round the following morning, leaving them in the hotel foyer together with a letter she had composed, on the envelope of which she wrote the telephone numbers of Greco, Marco's parents and Fabrizio Borra. '"I don't want to see you taken in a strait-jacket," is what I wrote in the letter. "Because I care for you, come with me to the clinic; we'll detox together, and then we'll start again from scratch."' On Sunday the eighth Marco telephoned her to tell her he had decided not to go to the clinic. 'He said, "My parents treat me like a child. They always come to get me. I'm a man, I'm free to take my own decisions." I said, "OK, if you're a man free to make your own decisions, a man is capable of taking the train home; you don't need a manager to reserve you a car or a taxi." It isn't that I didn't want to help him. I wanted to confront him with his responsibilities. He said, "OK, I'll see you on Monday morning."'

On Monday 9 February he phoned Ronchi and asked her to visit him. She told him she wouldn't be able to get there before 2 p.m. By the time she had arrived, he had disappeared again. 'I never saw him again,' she told me.

22

The Last Days of Marco Pantani
(9–14 FEBRUARY 2004)

Marco got out of a black, E-Class Mercedes taxi near Piazzale Gondar, in Rimini, and located Carlino's flat at 23, Viale Regina Elena, where his dealer, Fabio Miradossa, lived. He then walked south along the Viale until he found the hotel Marco Ceriani had used years before: the Hotel Residence Le Rose.

At 2:23 he called Miradossa's mobile from the telephone in room 5D. The call lasted eleven seconds. He called again half a minute later. They spoke for twenty-three seconds – long enough for Miradossa to tell Marco he was in Naples. Silvia De Luigi, on reception at Le Rose, said, 'Signor Pantani left the residence for about twenty minutes after 2.30 p.m. – I knew the time because I was watching television. Then he returned to his room. I remember he made a sign of greeting when he left and when he came back.' Marco walked back along the Viale to the flats at number 23. He range Carlino's bell. Giandomenico later told police: 'When I opened the door, I found Pantani, who asked me if Fabio Miradossa was in. When I said no, he said these exact words: "I've just come from Milan for something; but Fabio isn't in?" I told him again Miradossa wasn't in, that he had gone down south, but that he might be able to find him at the end of the week.'

At 6 p.m., back in his room, Marco called reception. He asked if there was a restaurant nearby, and came down to the lobby, before changing his mind. He asked the new receptionist, Daniele Mangioni, to order a pizza margherita. Mangioni said, 'He added, with humour, on condition it was a good pizza. I replied, jovially, it was edible. At the time, Pantani seemed to me to be composed.'

That evening there was a flurry of mobile-phone calls between Marco, Miradossa, and Miradossa's associates: Carlino, in Rimini, called

Miradossa, in Naples, at 7.03; two minutes later Miradossa called back from his girlfriend's mobile. They talked for six minutes. At 7.29 Miradossa called Marco from a public telephone in Torre del Greco, Naples, close to where he had received Marco's two calls that afternoon. At 7.43 and 7.49 Carlino called Miradossa, using Miradossa's girlfriend's number. Marco called Pucci, Carlino's business partner, at 8.56, and Carlino himself a minute later. At 9.35 Marco received a call in his room from a friend of Miradossa's. Over the next twenty-five minutes the friend made two calls to Miradossa's girlfriend's number, and then, at ten past ten, he called Marco's room from the public telephone at Viale Regina Elena, 83 – opposite the hotel. Moments later the caller called in person. His visit lasted two minutes.

The receptionist, Mangioni, described him as 'young – twenty-eight to thirty; well built, five feet three to five feet five, white-skinned, short, dark hair, dark eyes, unshaven, with no particular accent, dressed in jeans, a dark jersey – brown, I think – under which you could see a light shirt'. Pantani told the receptionist to send him up. Police later compiled a photo album of ten individuals answering the description. The receptionist gave a positive identification of Ciro Veneruso, a thirty-one-year-old factory worker from Naples. At 11.41 p.m. Marco, now in possession of the cocaine – perhaps thirty grams – that would kill him, called Fabio Carlino. They talked for a minute and a half. Then Marco put the phone down. He would never make another call.

For four days Marco was quiet, courteous, more or less invisible. Then, on the evening of 13 February, he emerged from the door of his apartment and spoke to three people living in a neighbouring room. One was Nelson Inglés, a professional basketball-player who played for the Rimini team. Marco emerged while Inglés was waiting for the lift, and stood staring at the door to his room. Inglés asked him if his music was disturbing him. 'He said "No," but he said he'd heard noises and he believed there were people in the flat next to his.' The flat next to his was empty. 'He used the exact words, "I'm mad."' Inglés' team-mate Emanuele Lunedei recalled Marco saying, 'I opened the door because I heard noises. I wanted to see who was making all the noise.' Lunedei continued: 'He seemed confused and there was no logic to his conversation. His mood changed suddenly a number of times.' Gianandrea Pazzini remembered Marco launching into a mad, philosophical discussion with himself – something like, 'Being and not being . . . I don't know if being is the same as not being, so if you're here, you're somewhere else, but they look at you and see what you do all the same . . . There's no way out of the tunnel . . .' This was in Italian. Then, in dialect, he said, *'A ne só sui sará un altr dí per me.'* Pazzini took this to mean, 'I don't know if there'll be another day for me.' He said something similar to Oliver Laghi, the restaurateur who brought Marco his final meal. All four formed the opinion that Marco was mentally disturbed or, at least, suffering depression.

At 10.30 a.m. the following morning Marco called reception. He asked for someone to go up immediately. The receptionist, Lucia, tried to remember Marco's exact words: 'There were people who were disturbing him.' The receptionist and Lorissa, the Ukrainian cleaner, went up. There was silence. They knocked repeatedly on Marco's door, but he didn't respond. They telephoned him from the next-door room; this time he replied, repeating that 'there were people who were disturbing him'. Lucia offered to call for help, but Marco said, 'At this point, it doesn't make any difference.' Soon after 11 a.m. Marco called again: 'He said someone was still disturbing him, it wasn't acceptable, and he wanted me to call the Carabinieri.' Lucia called the hotel-owner, who was away for the weekend. He told her to go up and try to open the door to speak to him. Marco didn't respond to her knocks, so Lucia and Lorissa unlocked the door with the master key and tried to open it. They found it was blocked shut. Marco said something incomprehensible.

Nothing more was heard of Marco until 5.30 p.m., after the change of receptionists, when Pietro Buccellato went up and knocked insistently on the door. There was no reply, and none to Buccellato's repeated telephone calls. The owner called again and, this time insisted. At 8.45 p.m. Buccellato took up two towels. He turned the key and forced back the furniture piled behind the door. He found Marco dead beside the bed in a pool of blood. This time he'd gone too far; from this self-mutilation, this shedding of worldly things, even Marco's indestructible heart couldn't bring him back.

Buccellato called the emergency number for the police and said something like, 'We've a person in a room who shows no sign of life. We think it's the cyclist Marco Pantani.' The operator immediately called Giuseppe Lancini, the commander of the First Section of the

Mobile Squad of the Rimini police, specialising in homicide: 'They called me for an overdose case. I only learned later it was Pantani. I went to the scene, saw it wasn't a typical overdose, and called my assistants.

'Outside the hotel, fans and reporters were beginning to gather. We wanted to inform the family ourselves, so we contacted the Cesenatico Carabinieri and asked them to locate them. They told us the villa was locked up, and the family was in Greece. We called the sister, Manola. She arrived with Mengozzi and another man. Through her we contacted the parents. We spoke to the mother, who then passed the telephone to the father. I asked them when they would be back. The father said Tuesday. I was surprised. I thought they'd return immediately. He said there was nowhere to leave the camper. The man with Manola took the phone and offered to go to Greece and collect the camper, but the father insisted they would be not be back before Tuesday.'

Meanwhile, Paolo Gengarelli, a magistrate from the Rimini courts, was contacted, and took charge of the investigation. 'Every OD has a dealer,' Lancini explained. 'There'd have been a detailed investigation, with or without Pantani. There were clear signs of cocaine in large quantities on the bedside table and on the floor, as well as boxes of psychoactive prescription drugs. From then on, everything was done by my team, not the uniformed police. The scientific police were called, and filmed the scene. When he fell, he hit the ground. There were other injuries to his shoulder. It was hardly surprising: he'd taken the room apart. He'd even pulled out the microwave, which had been screwed in, to put it behind the door. He'd broken the bathroom mirror and removed the mattress covers.

'On the banister of the stairwell leading up to the mezzanine bedroom where Marco's body was found he had tied a sheet and a tube he'd removed from the air-conditioning system. The investigation centred on whether he'd tried to commit suicide before OD-ing. I couldn't exclude the possibility that he'd wanted to hang himself, even if the sheet was too low, and there was no item of furniture below the tube.'

Dr Marisa Nicolini, the emergency doctor, certified Marco dead at 9.20 p.m. Dr Francesco Toni, a forensic doctor, established the time of death at between 2 and 5 p.m. Toni's immediate diagnosis was that death had probably been caused by cardiac arrest with insufficient respiration caused by substance abuse.

At Le Rose, Pantani had unwittingly become a neighbour of an old rival, the last pure climber to beat him at the height of his form. Piotr Ugrumov, a Russian-speaking Latvian, second in the 1994 Tour de France – just behind Induráin, just ahead of Pantani – lived with his wife Anna on the fifth floor of the building facing the hotel.

At 9 p.m. on Saturday 14 February Ugrumov went to collect a pizza from Oliver Laghi, the restaurateur who had taken Pantani his final meal. 'Oliver told me he'd seen Pantani. He said he seemed depressed and vacant. I said, "I'll go and see him tomorrow." At home, the phone went. It was another Russian rider who lived in Rimini. He said, "Piotr, put the television on. Pantani's dead." I went out to the balcony and saw crowds of people in the street. I didn't sleep that night. I knew Marco; we had mutual friends. But no one could get close to him. He felt attacked and isolated. He needed more help than I could have given him.'

Professor Giuseppe Fortuni, a lecturer in Forensic Medicine at the University of Bologna, was contacted to draw up a forensic analysis of the body and the room. I met Fortuni at the University of Bologna's Cesena centre. His warm, brown eyes reminded me of Nicola Amaducci, the youth worker who had first put Marco on a bicycle. But the hair and beard that framed the doctor's young face was white. A veteran of some thirty-five thousand autopsies, Fortuni's had been a life spent among the recently deceased. 'A fine layer of cocaine covered every horizontal surface, even away from the bed. In the final month he had taken it in massive doses. Prolonged cocaine use damages the mucous membranes, so absorbing it through the nose becomes less effective; so, as well as sniffing it, he had eaten it and absorbed it through the gums. He had spent twenty thousand euros on cocaine in the last month alone, and he had consumed it all. There was not even a gram left over. His body contained six times the lethal dose. The little we found was in the mouth, in a little ball of cocaine and bread crumbs that he probably sucked.

'There were traces of mucous and blood everywhere, owing to irritation of the mucous membrane. The internal organs were in good condition, even if the heart showed small infarcts – localised areas of dead tissue – a characteristic sign of cocaine dependence. But he was not physically finished. The cause of death was cocaine poisoning, not physical debilitation, even if there were signs of years of prolonged abuse. It was his mind, not his body, that had gone.

'He had used no other substance. There was, for instance, not a drop of alcohol in the room. There were psychoactive drugs in the room which had been prescribed by Doctor Greco. If he had wanted to kill himself, he had the substances to do so: barbiturates, sleeping pills, anxiolytics. If he'd wanted to, he could have made a lethal cocktail. Instead, he'd taken the prescribed doses. It had probably become an automatic action. I doubt he had the capacity to judge.

'One other thing: everyone said he'd gained a lot of weight. I had heard he was thirty kilograms overweight, but the Pantani I found before me was very similar to Pantani the athlete.' Fortuni described the signs of cocaine delirium: 'He'd destroyed everything in the room: the furniture, the mirrors, the plugs, not in an uncontainable anger, but in a persecutory delirium; in sheer paranoia. Apparently to stop some alien entity from entering, he had piled furniture against the door.' There was no equipment for smoking crack in the room, and nothing was left of the twelve thousand euros.

Marco's heart, refusing to give up, can only have helped him suffer more. Fortuni explained: 'As a means of suicide, cocaine is a poor option. A heroin overdose lets you sleep to death. To kill yourself with coke, you need a lot of money, and even then, you can't be sure it will kill you. Marco probably took some time to die. It was an ugly death.'

Even today, Manuela Ronchi is scathing about Fortuni's autopsy: 'When Marco died, a bone marrow examination was requested. They don't examine the bone marrow in every case. Someone called the magistrate in Rimini to ask for the analysis of the bone marrow, convinced that it would reveal EPO abuse throughout his career. But the examination didn't show this. It showed that Pantani didn't use EPO in the last six months of his life. But it also showed that the organs were intact. If Pantani had used EPO during his career, the examination of the bone marrow would have revealed that the organs were damaged by the abuse. They weren't. So Doctor Fortuni, in his autopsy report, says: "I exclude the hypothesis that Pantani used EPO during the final period of his life because there were no traces. But I do not exclude the hypothesis that he didn't use it in all his existence."' – Ronchi's quotation presumably ends here – 'But he didn't abuse it, because if he'd abused it, traces would have been found in the bone marrow examination.'

I put her views to Fortuni, who told me: 'The bone marrow analysis was requested not by any third party but by the investigating magistrate. It is an analysis that gives useful data regarding cocaine abuse, and revealed in this case that the abuse had been long-standing. The autopsy report itself makes no mention of EPO, which was of no interest to an investigation focusing exclusively on the cause and circumstances of Pantani's death. However, it is true, if fatuous, to say that the bone marrow analysis showed that Marco had not used EPO in the final period of his life, by which we mean, at most, the final one and a half or two months. There were no signs of EPO abuse, but this is not to say that there would have been any signs. It is impossible to say whether, in the course of Pantani's life, he had used no EPO, some, or a great deal.'

Bizarrely, the day after Marco's death Manuela Ronchi mentioned Pissacroia's name in a statement to Rimini police investigators: 'Pissacroia said that it was important to keep Pantani in full competitive activity and that it would not create physical problems; on the contrary, it would stimulate him psychologically.' Pissacroia responded: 'This is false: my view was the opposite. In any case, from 20 June 2002 I was no longer even retained by Ronchi's company.' Pissacroia feels he was removed because he believed Marco's survival depended on the termination of his career as an athlete.

Ciro Veneruso, who had delivered the final, fatal dose, learned of Marco's death that evening. At half past eleven he switched off his mobile phone, removed the SIM card and destroyed it. Rimini police picked him up, with Miradossa and Carlino on Friday 18 May. At first Veneruso told investigators: 'That 9 February 2004 I went to the Residence Le Rose to find Marco Pantani, but I only spoke to him and I never gave him cocaine.' According to the investigating magistrate's report, Miradossa, Carlino and Veneruso, working together, provided Marco with the final thirty grams of cocaine that killed him. Miradossa took the order; Veneruso transported the drug from Naples to Rimini and made the delivery, with Carlino's logistical support. The three were accused of committing crimes in Naples and Rimini on 8 and 9 February 2004.

'Barbara' was also picked up. In reality, she was a thirty-year-old Muscovite named Elena Korovina, who had come to Italy aged twenty-two, married – gaining Italian citizenship – and then left her husband. She had gravitated towards the nightlife of Riccione, where she danced in nightclubs and took money for sex. She told the investigating magistrate after Marco's death, 'He was always talking about that Christine; he said he loved her and she was his love.' Summarising their relationship, Korovina was less than sentimental: 'I met Pantani seven or eight times, but then he turned paranoid and I understood that he was a complicated case.'

Marco reportedly paid Korovina 2,000 euros a night; she normally charged a quarter or a third of that sum. He paid above the street price for his cocaine. In both cases, the money bought silence as well as sex and drugs. Papers found by Pantani's mother, Tonina, when she cleaned her son's room at the family villa, may refer to Korovina. One passage read: 'For some time, some people very close to me who want to ruin me have been making me take drugs, but I'll always be clean. The person I hold most dear is manipulating me.' Another page read: 'Many people over this period of time have made money, even a woman who has been driving me insane.'

'Peru' – in reality Alfonso Gerardo Ramirez Cueva, a thirty-four-year-old Peruvian, who had delivered cocaine to the Hotel Touring Miramare on 26 December 2003, was arrested three days later.

Tonina was unhappy with the investigation into her son's death. For months, extending into years, she raised doubts. In September 2005, in an interview with *La Voce di Cesena*, she observed that Marco's baseball cap had not been found in the room where he had expired. Weeks later she was claiming that two jackets found there didn't belong to him. Someone, she said, had been in the room with Marco.

Her claims had no resonance with those who had combed the tragic scene. Tonina, it was clear, could have no peace. But were there holes in the investigation? Every crime writer knows there is always another door. It might have been possible to enter or leave the Residence via the fire escape, and the receptionist would never have known. And what about the international trafficker Nevio Rossi? Investigators could find no trace of the cocaine Marco had showed him on 2 January. Had Nevio made it up? Was *he* the supplier? Or was there yet another dealer?

But Marco had sniffed massive doses of cocaine any number of times before; he had destroyed rooms at Saturnia, in Cuba, at Mengozzi's, and at the Miramare hotel. In any case, the phone records ruled out third parties: faced with article 586 of the Italian penal code, which covers 'death or injury as a consequence of another offence', Miradossa, Veneruso and Ramirez Cueva had accepted the enticement of reduced sentences, pleaded guilty and told the police what they knew. On 19 October 2005, after plea-bargaining, they were sentenced: Miradossa, the pusher, was given a prison sentence of four years ten months. Veneruso, the courier, was given three years ten months. Ramirez Cueva was given a year and eleven months. The convictions were safe. There was no room for mystery. Only the supporting cast of Korovina, the go-between, and Carlino, accused of providing a logistical base, protested their innocence.

For Marco's former classmate Mario Pugliese, now the chief Cesenatico reporter on the regional daily *La Voce di Cesena*, Pantani's was a death foretold. Pugliese drafted Pantani's obituary a week before he died, and told me, 'It was a surprise to the public, but not to those who knew him. I'd even spoken to my editor about publishing a page entitled "Silence is killing Pantani". But it was too late.'

23

What Little Remains

On 16 February 2004 the judgment of the Conconi trial was deposited at the Ferrara law court. Marco the man had been dead not two days. Now it was possible to approach the truth about Marco the cyclist. The judgment, and many other papers procured during the research for this book, yield a history of Marco's professional career that conflicts in every way with his image as a wholesome heir to cycling's golden age – 'a craftsman among multinationals', to use his own words. Perhaps the most telling document was compiled by Professor Giuseppe Banfi, the Health Director of the Villa Aprica Clinical Institute in Como and a lecturer in Laboratory Medicine for Sport at the University of Milan's School for Specialisation in Clinical Biochemistry, and the Rome-based clinical pathologist we met in chapter 19, Professor Giuseppe D'Onofrio. On 2 October 2001 they were hired to conduct an exhaustive scientific study of evidence gathered by police investigating the activities of the Centre for Biomedical Studies Applied to Sport. That evidence included the files 'dblab.wdb' and 'epo.wks', both of which contained Marco's name beside apparently authentic blood-test data – although this was contested by the defence. On 12 February 2002 their monumental report was complete.

The greater part of it addressed the blood-test data recorded in the database 'dblab.wdb', some of which had reached Eugenio Capodaqua at *La Repubblica* in December 1999. The defence had constructed an elaborate argument to persuade the investigators that the data could not be taken at face value. The researchers at the Centre were obliged to conduct their biochemical and haematological studies using tiny quantities of blood, the argument went. To make matters worse, the blood samples normally arrived semi-centrifuged by the jolts and vibrations suffered during transport. This – the argument went on – raised the danger of rupturing the red blood cells and contaminating the plasma before the blood could be analysed scientifically in the laboratory. So instead of waiting until after the blood test, they systematically removed a small amount of plasma for research purposes *before* blood-testing. It followed that the blood tests returned distorted results – specifically, unusually high levels of haematocrit, haemoglobin and red globules. However, these results remained useful for the study of mean corpuscular haemoglobin – MCH, the relationship between haemoglobin and red globules – a key indicator of overtraining, which was one of the main lines of inquiry at the Centre.

Banfi and D'Onofrio examined the defence arguments in great detail. They carried out laboratory experiments in the presence of the investigating magistrate and experts nominated by the defence and, unusually, cross-examined Conconi to learn more about his unorthodox practices. A rush of arguments emerged to contradict the defence case. Some were highly technical: part of the defence was that the plasma-removal thesis could be demonstrated by studying the relationship between red and white blood-cell populations in the test results recorded in 'dblab.wdb'. Banfi and D'Onofrio devoted twenty-six pages to the question. Nowhere could they find any correlation whatsoever between red and white blood-cell counts that would confirm plasma removal as the cause of the aberrant figures. The two values remained doggedly independent.

Others were elementary: Banfi and D'Onofrio noted that 'dblab.wdb' contained columns for thirty-two different blood parameters; yet, in the two years or more during which it was being compiled, no one had ever thought to add a thirty-third column for MCH, purportedly the entire file's *raison d'être*, despite the fact that the Technicolor-Bayer H*2 instrument used by the blood-test laboratory provided the MCH value automatically. They also observed that the removal of plasma would make it impossible to detect anaemia among the sample donors, and no study of an athlete's health could afford to ignore such a common condition. They pointed out that Conconi and his colleagues were supposedly conducting bona fide research with a view to publication, yet no reputable scientific publication would publish their work without accurate and credible blood test results. Nothing was ever found among the mass of documentation sequestered from the Centre and submitted for consideration by the defence, to support the defence claim that anyone at the Centre was studying MCH at all. The defence thesis lay in tatters.

Intriguingly, among the mass of test results the forensic scientists found perfectly normal blood profiles alongside wildly abnormal ones. To sort the data, they grouped the subjects named in the file according to their disciplines: cross-country skiers (of whom there were thirty-nine), biathletes (eleven), and cyclists (ninety-six). Suddenly patterns began to emerge. In each group a cluster of athletes – generally, the most accomplished – showed haematocrit fluctuations of more than 19 per cent, a far greater variation than could conceivably occur naturally. These fluctuations, moreover, corresponded precisely to the progress of the competitive year: out of season, no data recorded; at the start of each season, the first data and a gradual increase in haematocrit; and during the period of peak competition, peak haematocrit. The cross-country skiers peaked in February each year, the biathletes in December, and the cyclists in May, June and July, the months of the Giro d'Italia and the Tour de France.

The seasonal variations in the twenty-seven cyclists with the greatest haematocrit fluctuation – 20 per cent or more – is shown in Figure 6 (D'Onofrio and Banfi's 'Figure 15'), reproduced below. The graph shows a clear wave pattern, with out-of-season troughs and peaks between March and October. No known pathology could have caused these variations in an individual, let alone twenty-seven individuals, as represented in the chart. The experts concluded: '[A] non-physiological factor intervenes to modify haematocrit in the months from March–April to September, almost always independently of white corpuscles, with greater intensity and homogeneity in one team than in the others [the reference is not to Carrera, with ten riders among the twenty-seven represented in 'Figure 15', but to Gewiss, with eleven] . . . [T]he effects of this external factor cannot have escaped the doctors and researchers at the Ferrara Centre, who often treated the cyclists personally, under various sorts of agreement.'

The riders whose values are represented in the graph included no less than nine of Marco's former or current team-mates – and Marco himself. The analysis leads inexorably to the obvious conclusion: 'It is highly improbable that the cause of these variations can be identified by the

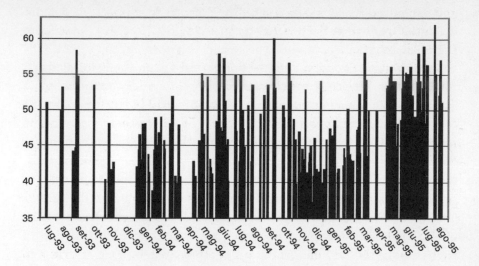

Figure 6: Seasonal haematocrit variations in cyclists with fluctuation >20 per cent, from dblab.wdb (D'Onofrio & Banfi)

systematic removal of plasma from so many samples, in quantities first increasing, then decreasing, more in one team – leaders and *domestiques* included – than in all the others.'

Any subsisting doubts that 'dblab.wdb' contained true values were dispelled when communications from the Centre were seized from Dr Claudio Locatelli, the doctor of the Italian Federation of Winter Sports. The notes informed Locatelli of blood-test results which corresponded to data recorded in 'dblab.wdb'. The meaning of 'Figure 15' in Banfi and D'Onofrio's report, then, is clear: it illustrates massive r-EPO abuse by a large section of the international cycling community to manipulate athletic performance.

The findings confirmed the revelations published in *La Repubblica* in December 1999: it was now clear that everything Marco had achieved between May 1994 and August 1995 had been chemically assisted. The implications for his cocaine treatment were clear: Marco's history of doping had started in May 1994 at the latest; he lived and worked in a milieu where it was normal and accepted. His habitual cocaine use in private life since the summer of 1999, perhaps earlier, meant there was no part of his existence that did not depend on substance abuse. It was entirely possible that he could no longer conceive of himself in-dependently of some chemical prop.

Indeed, Marco's substance abuse may even predate 'dblab.wdb', for his name figures in earlier databases discovered at the Centre at Ferrara. On 18 December 1991, eight months *before* his professional debut (5 August 1992), his name appears in a file entitled 'diana.wdb'. The file contains white-blood-corpuscle data for a number of riders contracted to the Carrera team, perhaps suggesting that the data was used to monitor immune-system responses. But to what? The file name itself may contain the answer: 'diana' may refer to the anabolic steroid Dian-abol, and it is possible that Marco was being equipped with greater muscle mass in view of his professional career. If so, his victory in the 1992 amateur Giro d'Italia was not entirely his own, but gained with chemical assistance.

Yet another file, 'epo.wks', extends this early picture. An entry for Marco dated 13 November 1992 gives absolutely normal values for haemoglobin (15.2 per cent) and for soluble transferrin receptor, the blood-marker Conconi's team was studying at the time as an indirect indicator of r-EPO therapy (1.24 mg/l). A column headed 'Treated: Yes/No', is marked 'No' for this and other entries dated 3 February 1993 and 19 April 1993. However, the soluble transferrin receptor values on those dates are approximately twice the 13 November 1992 value (2.44 mg/l and 2.30 mg/l respectively). The explanation lies in a quite separate section of the file, hidden away forty-eight columns to the right. In this section, the 'Treated: Yes/No' column is marked 'Yes' against Marco's name for the same dates, 3 February and 19 April 1993.

The evidence suggests that Marco underwent his first session of r-EPO therapy during this period. It no doubt helped him through his heavy spring calendar in 1993. The therapy had evidently ended by 10 May 1993, mid-Giro del Trentino, by which time his soluble transferrin receptor value had returned to 1.98 mg/l, and the sole entry in the 'Treated: Yes/No' column is 'No'. The entries for soluble transferrin receptor dated 14 May (the last day of the Giro del Trentino), 27 May and 3 June read 1.65 mg/l, 2.27 mg/l, and 1.93 mg/l. In each case, Marco is described as untreated. These three blood tests, the last of the 1993 season, were conducted under false names: 'Ponti' for the first two, 'Padovani' for the third, perhaps to avoid the same names appearing in quick succession in the test laboratory records. Marco finished the Giro del Trentino fifth overall.

On the whole, however, Marco seems to have been spared extensive blood manipulation in his first year as a professional. Perhaps this was due to the strength of the team, with an accomplished stage-race leader (Claudio Chiappucci), two fine lieutenants (Stephen Roche and Vladimir Pulnikov), an excellent sprint finisher (Guido Bontempi) and a successful classics rider (Rolf Sorensen). Against the names of all these riders, a 'Yes' appears in the 'Certainly Treated' section of 'epo.wks'. Or perhaps it was because, hindered by the back problems for which he received chiropractic treatment, he was not considered a good enough prospect to justify the expense.

For 1994 and 1995, as we have seen, blood values appear for Marco in 'dblab.wdb', considerably larger than 'epo.wks', and quite different in format. In addition to columns giving the name, alias, sport and sex of the athlete, and the date of the blood test, there are thirty-two blood-parameter columns. The first blood test took place on 4 January, during pre-season training. It was apparently conducted under the alias 'Panzani'. The red blood-cell count, and the values for haemoglobin and haematocrit – 4.74×10^{12}/litre, 14.4 g/dl and 43.5 per cent respectively – are absolutely normal. Thirty days later, a test dated 3 February 1994 under the name 'Panti' revealed slightly elevated values, albeit within the bounds of physiological variation: 4.83×10^{12}/litre, 15.0 g/dl and 45.3 per cent. A test conducted on 16 March under Marco's real name showed the lowest blood values on record: red blood-cell count at 4.41 $\times 10^{12}$/litre, haemoglobin 13.7 g/dl and haematocrit 40.7 per cent. Three days later Marco retired from the one-day Milan–San Remo.

The next blood test recorded in 'dblab.wdb' is dated 23 May 1994, day two of the Giro d'Italia in which Marco would win two mountain stages and finish second overall. In the sixty-eight days between 16 March and 23 May, a transformation had taken place. His red blood-cell count had risen from 4.41 to 5.59×10^{12}/litre: a 26.8 per cent increase. His haemoglobin had leapt from 13.7 g/dl to 17.20 g/dl: an increase of 25.5 per cent. His haematocrit had soared from 40.7 per cent to 54.5 per cent – an increase of 33.9 per cent. Over the same period, as his blood levels gradually rose, his racing results improved too.

A test dated 30 June, nine days into the Giro, confirmed these altered

4–8 April	Vuelta al Pais Vasco	55th overall
17 April	Liège–Bastogna–Liège	67th
30 April	GP Industria e Commercio a Prato	6th
1 May	GP Larciano	4th
11 May	Giro del Trentino, stage 2	4th
10–13 May	Giro del Trentino	4th overall
15 May	Giro di Toscana	4th

values: red blood-cell count, 5.56 x 10^{12}/litre; haemoglobin, 16.9 g/dl, haematocrit, 52.6 per cent. Another, conducted on 13 June 1994, the day after the final stage of the Giro d'Italia, showed higher values still: Red blood-cell count, 5.87 x 10^{12}/litre; haemoglobin, 18.6 g/dl, haematocrit, 58 per cent. Compared with the values of the 16 March test, Marco's haematocrit had risen 17.3 points, a percentage increase of 42.5, three to four times the accepted maximum natural variation. With these blood levels Marco had taken the first stage win of his professional career at Merano, and the second the following day at Aprica.

Marco's towering blood values were maintained, no doubt through microdoses of r-EPO, between the end of the Giro and the start of the Tour. On 27 June his red blood-cell count of 6,140,000 was accompanied by haemoglobin at 18.2 g/dl and haematocrit at 57.2 per cent. Then there are four weeks of silence. During this time Marco took two second places in stages of the Tour de France and finished third overall. The Tour ended on 23 July 1994. On 25 July another blood test shows almost unchanged values for red blood-cell count, haemoglobin and haematocrit. His Tour de France performance, like the Giro, had been r-EPO assisted in its entirety. In addition, the 25 July data for Marco include, for the only time in the period documented in 'dblab.wdb', a value for testosterone: 8.5, raising the suspicion that some form of hormonal manipulation in addition to r-EPO therapy was taking place. The 25 July blood test was the last of 1994. Marco's work was done for the year, and the r-EPO therapy no doubt ceased. At the World Championships on 28 August, Marco retired on lap fifteen.

Marco's next appearance in 'dblab.wdb' is dated 4 February 1995. As expected, his red blood-cell parameters are normal: red blood-cell count 4.66 x 10^{12}/litre, haemoglobin 14.6 g/dl, haematocrit 42.8 per cent – almost identical to the 4 January 1994 test. Forty-two days later, on 18 March 1995, he returned slightly elevated values (red blood-cell count 4.89 x 10^{12}/litre, haemoglobin 14.9 g/dl, haematocrit 45 per cent), almost identical to those recorded on 3 February 1994. The expected steep increase took place between 18 March and 1 May 1995, the day Marco was hospitalised after being struck by a car at Santarcángelo during a training ride. The hospital blood test revealed the following elevated values: red blood-cell count 6.00 x 10^{12}/litre, haemoglobin 18.2 g/dl, haematocrit 57.6 per cent. Marco, it would appear, was pharmacologically ready for the Giro d'Italia, due to start on 13 May. Owing to the injuries sustained in the accident, he didn't start. On 22 June 1995, the day Marco won a long mountain stage of the Tour of Switzerland, a major stage race used as preparation for the Tour de France, his name reappears in 'dblab.wdb' beside the values: red blood-cell count 6.09 x 10^{12}/litre, haemoglobin 18 g/dl, haematocrit 56 per cent.

At this date, the databases and other documentation presented at the Ferrara trial turn silent. Their exhaustive, and exhausting, evidence of blood manipulation through r-EPO therapy goes no further than 22 June 1995. The Carabinieri who made the October 1998 seizures were inexperienced in computer searches, and copied the hard disks rather than confiscating them. If files had been deleted, they might have been recoverable from the original drives. Records show that Marco attended the Centre at Ferrara on 13 January and 14 March 1997 for testing on a static bike; the relationship, then, continued. But there are no more blood data.

The picture we have of blood manipulation emerges clearly from Figure 7 (p. 288). As in Banfi and D'Onofrio's 'Figure 15', the out-of-season lows and the peaks timed to coincide with the major events of Marco's career are clear. No known pathology could cause these peaks and troughs in any population, let alone a group of élite athletes in otherwise extraordinarily vigorous health.

For 1997, 1998 and 1999, UCI blood-test certificates show Marco's haematocrit values fluctuating between 45.7 and 47.4, with one exception: the test dated 6 June 1998, on the morning of the penultimate stage of the Giro d'Italia, which has the value 49.3 per cent. These tests looked at haematocrit alone, and were therefore easy to circumvent

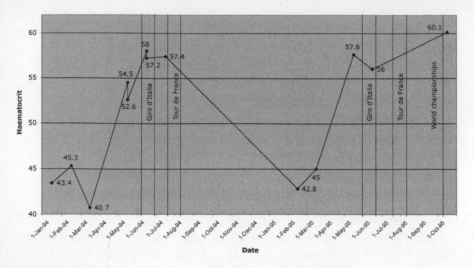

Figure 7: Haematocrit variations 1994–5 from dblab.wdb

through blood dilution. In Figure 8 they are given in cautionary italics. The Madonna di Campiglio figure of 53 per cent, and the pre-Olympic values of 45.5 per cent and 49 per cent complete this survey of a career built on fluctuating haematocrit values, represented here:

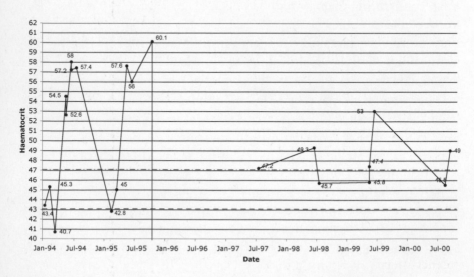

Figure 8: Marco Pantani: a career of haematocrit variations

288

A final consideration emerges from these figures. Since Madonna di Campiglio, mystery had surrounded Marco's natural blood values. In September 2000 only the absence of reliable base values had prevented the CSAD from taking action against him. On 6 June 1995 Dr Giovanni Grazzi had provided the FCI with the following values for Marco: haematocrit 45 per cent, haemoglobin 15.2 g/dl and red blood cells 4.94 x 10^{12}/litre. However, on 1 May and 22 June 1995 – in other words, five weeks before the 6 June test and two weeks after it – 'dblab.wdb' gives far higher values: haematocrit 57.6 and 56 per cent, haemoglobin 18.2 and 18.0 g/dl and red blood cells 6.00 and 6.09 x 10^{12}/litre. These values suggest that the 6 June figures are not to be trusted.

The 'dblab.wdb' figures, however, appear to contain Marco's base values, in the early-season tests. Assuming that the 40.7 per cent figure for 16 March 1994 is abnormally low, perhaps owing to an inhibition response to the initial experimental course of r-EPO we have hypothesised for early that year, the figures of 43.4 per cent (dated 4 January 1994) and 42.8 (for 4 February 1995) are likely to represent natural values. We might adopt the average of these – 43.1 – as Marco's 'base' haematocrit. In the graph in Figure 8, this value is indicated with a dashed line denoting 'Presumed natural Hct.' It allows us to evaluate Marco's haematocrit data with greater precision than the blanket 50 per cent threshold. If we can agree that the greatest natural fluctuation, in the absence of serious illness or some form of blood doping, is 10 per cent, as is widely assumed, any value over 47.1 per cent should be treated as either pathological or manipulated. This goes for every node above the dash-dot line which denotes 'Maximum natural variation'. These suspect values include figures given in three UCI blood-test certificates, one of the 'Probably Olympian' values and, significantly, the figure of 47.6 per cent given in the certificate issued at Imola the afternoon after the Madonna di Campiglio debacle but not accepted as evidence in the trial. Far from proving Marco's innocence, the evidence for the defence seems to support the case for the prosecution.

Marco, of course, was very far from being ill: if anything, he was bursting with the astonishing good health with which his genetic inheritance had blessed him. His haematocrit peaks were invariably timed perfectly to coincide with major sporting occasions. Even the smaller variations are highly suspicious.

*

The Death of Marco Pantani

Years later, rumours still circulated that, during the night before Marco's ejection from the 1999 Giro d'Italia, a member of the Mercatone Uno team staff went into a room housing Saeco riders, looking for some special product to be used the following day. Could this secret substance explain Marco's haematocrit the next day? The answer is surely no: we have no need of additional, mystery substances. There is incontrovertible evidence that Marco's entire career was based on r-EPO abuse, which was both effective and, until 2001, undetectable by tests used in professional cycling. Is it reasonable to suppose that the most successful period of his career, from 1998 until 5 June 1999, depended on anything else?

Epilogue

Marco had been dying a long time. The police investigation into his destruction addressed only the final seven weeks of his life. Much was unknown about him, even to insiders. He had kept his different groups of associates – his team-mates and sponsors; his family and manager; his hunting partners; the various groups of nightclub friends in Cesenatico, Rimini and Modena; those who had doped him; those who had drugged him, and those who had procured him women – in separate orbits, and made sure that none saw more of him than he chose to reveal. Marco's circuitous itinerary towards self-annihilation was his own, but he had many accomplices: abusive pharmacists and counterfeit doctors pre-scribed doping products that alienated him from his achievements; cocaine-pushers provided him with the means of self-destruction; and dealers in fantasies, passionately indifferent to every notion of objective truth, turned him away from reality at every juncture.

On 5 June 1999, seconds after the health test had transmuted a drop of blood into a percentage, Marco and some of those close to him decided to attribute the result to a plot. Their empty fulminations against his unnamed tormentors accompanied the rest of his existence. The fact of Marco's blood-test result was too quickly confounded with the back-ground noise of animosity from the other teams; a simple medical analysis was over-interpreted into an intrigue designed to break him. For years to come, many of those around Marco went into denial, discerning a 'murderous hand' behind his ruin, when the truth was that, if the blood test at Madonna di Campiglio led to Marco's destruction, its murderous efficacy was an invention of its victim.

The idea of sport Marco embodied wasn't one that encouraged ath-letes to face the truth about their existences. It conceived of sport as media content (especially television content), of athletes and events as advertising billboards, and of physical movement as applied science – especially applied *medical* science. To be talented meant not only to have prodigious physical capabilities but also to be responsive to doping products and to be ready to play an almost literally blood-curdling game of Russian roulette using hormones, blood transfusions and steroids. In this high-stakes game the advantage is with the insane. It is an idea of sport that probably doesn't predate the year of Marco's birth – 1970. It didn't die with him.

Dr Giovanni Grazzi, who was Marco's doctor throughout the period covered by the database 'dblab.wdb', refused my request for an interview while I researched this book. He limited himself to the comment: 'The time isn't yet ripe to explain what we were trying to do.' We were speaking sixteen months after the trial of Grazzi, Conconi and their colleague Ilario Casoni had ended in a no-trial on the grounds that the statute of limitations had come into effect. Nonetheless, the judge, Franca Oliva, had written in the final judgment:

> Continuously for a number of years, the accused [i.e. Grazzi, Conconi and Casoni] supported the r-EPO treatment of the athletes named in the list of charges, assisted and encouraged them in the use itself with a reassuring scheme of health checks, examinations, analyses and tests intended to monitor and maximise the success of the treatment in terms of sporting results, and therefore, in reality, cooperated in the therapy and promoted it, as charged, not to mention, as logic dictates, providing all logistical support suitable in order to prolong their r-EPO treatment.

If one day Grazzi feels the time is ripe for his explanation to be heard, what will it be? That the Pandora's box of science cannot be closed, and that doping in sport is as inevitable as nuclear proliferation?

This may be the case. It is probably a mistake to think there are sports that attract 'good' athletes who don't dope, and sports that attract 'bad' athletes who do. There are athletes who are caring, generous, wholly admirable people, except for the fact that they dope, and could not continue to compete if they didn't. The division should be between sports in which doping is highly effective, and sports in which it's less so. Marco's misfortune was to be exceptional in one of the former.

The generalised culture of deception that surrounded him was a background against which Marco's mental illness – from the vaguely insane ambition that characterises most champion athletes, to the clinical genealogy of Marco's most intimate ticks – was camouflaged. The recklessness that drove those extraordinary cocaine binges powered those breakneck descents. The impulsiveness that lay behind his cocaine use, his spending, his reckless driving and attitude to sex made him unreadable as a racer. His reluctance to recognise the feelings and needs of others, masked by the non-reciprocal relationship that is celebrity, gave him his winning coolness. His envy of others, and his belief that they were envious of him, was the very font of his competitive instinct. Cycling's leader–*domestique* system, which allowed him to choose his race schedule, take his sexual partner to hotels, eat in intimacy and drink wine with his meals while his team-mates lived a group existence without these privileges, only confirmed his exaggerated sense of entitlement and expectations of favourable treatment.

He took part in complex doping programmes, yet genuinely feared that his food would be contaminated with a product that would show up in an anti-doping test and destroy him, and convinced himself, after Madonna di Campiglio, that he had been undone by a plot. This terrible, eventually fatal remoteness from reality was cloaked by the fact that he was, for a season and a half, the best cyclist on earth.

Self-importance led him, and those around him, to demand unlimited, unconditional availability from others. In September 2005, in an interview given to *La Voce di Cesena*, Manuela Ronchi claimed she had refused to accept any money from the moment she understood Marco had a cocaine problem (there is no mention of this in her book). To me, she backdated her altruism to November 1999. We have already asked why, if Marco's condition was so serious that it was no longer ethical to take his money in November 1999, Ronchi informed neither his sponsors, nor (and this is astonishing) his doctors, until January 2002. But her claim also raises the suspicion that Marco and those around him came to believe that anyone asking for payment from Marco was breaching his trust.

The sporting values that made this calamity possible were clearly limited neither to Italy nor to cycling. Nor do they belong to the past. A long string of scandals, from Ben Johnson to the BALCO affair, from the old East Germany to the new China, suggests that this idea of sport, in which heavy doping is inherent, is one of the defining open secrets of our age.

Marco's misfortune left a long list of evidence in his wake that made his unmasking inevitable and unleashed a series of legal investigations. He complained – and others have agreed – that he had been singled out. He was: the mechanism that singled him out is called the due process of law. And it would be wrong to think that the law was hostile to Marco, as a major national politician, Walter Veltroni, wrote in the weekly news magazine *L'Espresso* on 11 June 1999. He observed that the doctors who had stopped Marco on 5 June 1999 had 'probably saved his life'. He continued: 'I'm sorry, because legends have been built around him, and sport must also make us dream.' However, he said, 'Today we are discussing the fate of a famous champion, but no one talks about the many adolescent amateurs who are doped, exploited, then thrown away.'

On 15 June 2005 a contemporary of Marco's named Alessio Galletti collapsed and died during a Spanish hill-climb. At the time Galletti was under investigation in connection with doping-related offences; given the evidence to make an arrest, the police might have saved his life. Were *they* not his truest friends? Who *are* the true friends of those who live in a make-believe world – those who conspire to perpetuate it, or those who bring them back to reality?

The strain of pumping thickened blood may have contributed to a spate of fatal heart attacks in the months surrounding Marco's death, involving riders who either lost their minds or died for no discernible reason. They include the following:

10 January 2003 Denis Zanette (ITA), age: 32; team: Fassa Bortolo
Cardiac arrest during dental treatment. Myocarditis (inflammation of the muscular wall of the heart) triggered or aggravated by pulmonary inflammation. No traces of doping products.

5 May 2003 Marco Ceriani (ITA), age: 16
Collapsed with a heart attack after 30 kilometres of a race on 25 April. Died in hospital without regaining consciousness.

3 June 2003 Fabrice Salanson (FRA), age: 23; team: Brioches la Boulangère

Heart attack in his sleep. Forensic analysis of urine, blood and hair revealed no traces of doping products.

14 November 2003 Marco Rusconi (ITA), age: 24; team: Ceramiche Pagnoncelli
Heart attack during a birthday party. Autopsy revealed no doping products and attributed cause of death to a degenerative heart condition.

6 December 2003 Jose Maria Jiménez (SPA), age: 32; team: Banesto/iBanesto.com
Heart attack in a Madrid psychiatric hospital while presenting a slide show of his career. Jiménez, a brilliant climber (champion of Spain in 1995, seven stage wins in the Tour of Spain), died after a long struggle with depression. Served a brief ban for caffeine doping in 1994.

29 December 2003 Michel Zanoli (NED), age: 35; retired
Heart attack. World Junior Champion in 1986, stage winner at the Tour of Spain in 1991. Suffered from mental problems and had apparently served a prison sentence for smuggling marijuana.

12 February 2004 Johan Sermon (BEL), age: 21; team: Daikin
Heart attack in his sleep after an eight-hour training ride. No traces of doping products found. Sermon's decease became public knowledge the day after the death of Marco Pantani.

15 June 2005 Alessio Galletti (ITA), age: 37; team: Naturino–Sapore di Mare
Heart failure during the Subida al Naranco in Spain, when he suffered, collapsed and died.

9 October 2005 Ubaldo Mesa (COL), age: 32; team: Tecos de Mexico
Cardiac arrest while warming up for the Clásico Banfoandes in Venezuela, due to arterial hypertension. No traces of doping products.

Looking back, Marco's successes, like any number of world records, gold medals and winning sequences in recent sporting history, have a phantom quality. They were not what they purported to be at the time, and they would have been struck out had their true nature been known. They weren't events at all, but phantasmagorical experiences with no clearly definable reality, that existed chiefly in the emotions they caused in millions of individual minds. The emotion most associated with Marco is euphoria, yet we now know it was triggered by the poisons that flowed through his veins and made his flamboyant style possible. Those of us who saw him, and were inspired, were doped, at one remove, by those who doped Marco; and, like all drug-induced forms of euphoria, when the drug that induced it was gone, it existed only as memory, and as a terrible temptation to self-deceive.

One of the NAS officers involved in anti-doping investigations told me: 'Every year the names of the same doctors are mentioned. Our activities are absurd – they serve mainly to help them refine their practices.' He was trying to transfer away from anti-doping: it gives him few prospects, and he has kids who'll one day have to be helped through university. Anti-doping is no vote-winner. It has little on its side but worthy causes like public health and sporting transparency. The mass euphoria induced by doped élite sport is far more powerful – although the sponsors who harness it to peddle their products and, even more so, politicians who seek to exploit it for their own causes, should be aware that cocktails of mass euphoria and mass self-delusion can engender all sorts of extremisms.

The current professions of the 'dblab.wdb' riders whose haematocrit variations exceeded 20 per cent suggest that cycling is being run by figures whose idea of sport is Marco's idea: Claudio Chiappucci is a Councillor of the Association of Italian Professional Racing Cyclists (ACCPI); Guido Bontempi, Bruno Cenghialta, Bjarne Rijs, Alberto Volpi and Mario Chiesa are *directeurs sportifs* with major professional teams; Giorgio Furlan is the *directeur sportif* of an important amateur team. Of the riders described as 'EPO-treated' in the file entitled 'epo.wks', Gianni Bugno is a riders' representative, Rolf Sorensen a riders' agent, and Maurizio Fondriest a well-known television cycling pundit. Manuela Di Centa, a skiing champion whose soaring blood values appear in 'dblab.wdb', stood for the European Parliament representing Silvio Berlusconi's Forza Italia party, before gaining the vice-presidency of the Italian Olympic Committee in 2005.

Since Marco's death, the redeeming myth has arisen that, with everyone equally doped or equally clean, Marco would have been equally superior. This, too, is delusion, for this is the certainty doping denies us. A February 2001 paper published in *Haematologica* by the Australian team observes that, although there is a common erythropoietic response to stimulation with r-EPO, 'The type and quantity of globin chain synthesised during the polychromatophilic stage, which occurs after the stem cell has proliferated under the influence of r-EPO, is under genetic control and thus can be expected to show individual variation.'

This individual variation means that, in conditions of widespread r-EPO doping, the best performance is likely to come not from the best athlete but from the athlete with the 'best' response to r-EPO treatment. In other words, there is every likelihood that r-EPO falsified the sporting hierarchy. If sport is narrative, it created a new way of telling, a narrative with a dazzlingly brilliant surface. Within a month of Hein Verbruggen's personal attack on Sandro Donati and Pasquale Bellotti at the 2000 Olympic Games, expert witnesses told the court examining the Milan–Turin case that r-EPO had originally been considered a drug with few applications but was now the world's third-best-selling pharmaceutical; that it had been fifteenth on the Italian health service's list of pharmaceutical purchases in 1998 and had risen to thirteenth in 1999, despite the fact that 50 per cent of r-EPO sold was not registered with local health authorities or hospitals and was therefore not covered by health-service figures. Perhaps this flux of poison has habituated us all to levels of performance that are impossible without it. However, whatever sport is, it is surely not all surface. Sport is also an overcoming, in which the relationship between end and origin matters. When the mask slips, as it did at Madonna di Campiglio, the plunge from the podium to the gutter is no less a construct of contemporary sport than the ascent from youthful hope to triumph.

Many of Marco's fans were so disenchanted with professional sport that they turned their back on it on 5 June 1999. Giorgio Fagioli, the organiser of the first race Marco ever won, was one of them. He told me, 'I haven't watched the Giro d'Italia since that day, even on television.' But there is an alternative to abject disengagement, which may also have a redemptive quality. Watching contemporary sport means acknowledging surface reality as an interim state, prone to re-evaluation, even far in the future. It requires another way of seeing, a double vision or off-centre gaze, like Inuit looking into snow, in which surface appearances are taken not as reality but as gateways to potentially unpredictable truths. We mustn't abandon ourselves to the ecstasy of closure, but must cultivate the more restrained delights in unknowing. There is self-denial in this way of seeing, but only in the conditions it places on the euphoria sport can inspire. The cost of seeing the world through this filter of scepticism may be that we can no longer abandon ourselves to the emotions of the crowd. The past certainties against which the present seems so illusory only seem solid as long as we don't look too closely. Nothing is any longer as it seems. Never write about your heroes, they say. Maybe. But maybe, too, by believing in them a little less, we may credit them with a little more humanity. We may also find we believe in ourselves a little more.

The sheer financial rewards convince many that the duplicity of contemporary sport may be a temptation worth succumbing to. At first sight, everyone benefited from the poisons flowing through Marco's body: his sponsors, the broadcasters and their advertisers, the audiences exalted by his performances and Marco himself. But that temptation came at a price. In the Rai3 studio before Gianni Minà interviewed Marco, Mario Sconcerti of the Italian sports daily *Corriere dello Sport* grumbled: 'I've invested emotion in Pantani over the years, and now this. He owes me, and fans like me, an explanation.' Sconcerti's metaphor suggests depositing something of ourselves in the way we deposit money in a bank. We expect a return on our capital. But the image contains an unacknowledged and opposite element: a claim to own-ership – that idiotic possessiveness that Marco detested and that took its toll on his sanity. When this dimension is spelt out, his debt to his fans is less clear-cut.

Of course, Marco might have taken a stand against what sport has become. But he and those around him, innocent of zeal for any revolution, chose instead to deny reality, even as, after Madonna di Campiglio, teams of investigators scrutinised Marco's achievements and the content of his veins, and denying reality became increasingly implausible.

There is another version, existing largely in rumour, of Marco's down-fall. In the summer of 2002, as Marco gorged himself on cocaine and grieved for his broken relationship, he made forays outside, perhaps in search of affection. There is a rumour, persistent, unsubstantiated, but apparently originating with the police, that in one of his many car accidents in this period a transvestite was in Marco's car alongside him. Could it be that he was homosexual, and destroyed himself out of shame?

It is all too easy to envisage secret homosexual experimentation in Marco's life: there was cross-dressing at the 1996 Nove Colli, and the eyeliner before the 1999 Giro. There was doubtless occasional contact with the transvestites who went to Pregnolato's beauty salon in Modena. There was also, later, the abandoning of a rather attractive, girlish Polish stripper for the taller, more masculine, large-handed Korovina, with a reputation for rough sex. There was talk of a bouquet left at Marco's grave, 'From the man you've never spoken of'. There is a psychological conceit, too: the child grows believing that, if he doesn't become what his mother wants him to be, he'll be rejected; he develops a narcissistic disorder, and a fantasy of a mother–father figure rolled into one, a man who performs the function of a woman.

Around the transit park outside Rimini, beneath great pink lights high above the ground that spell the word 'Gros', the transvestites have replaced women walking the streets, and sell sex to fund their transformation. The turnover is high, but I was told of a pretty blonde on the first corner who might know something. I hired a car – a diesel, which I sometimes stalled, lifting the clutch to pull away but forgetting to disengage the handbrake with my right hand, the 'wrong' hand for a British driver. The starter motor grew hoarser each time, urging the engine into life. I could see myself making embarrassing calls for help later on, and trying to explain my subsequent arrest to my wife. I circled the area many times, but I didn't find the blonde. But suppose she existed, and she'd been prepared to talk: how could I have verified anything she said? In any case, the Riviera – the world – is full of men (women too, why not?) with a secret yearning for a hermaphrodite. They aren't necessarily unhappy. Some must live to be a hundred.

Affection, or the lack of it, no doubt lay close to the root of Marco's predicament. Once sport had solved his material problems, all he needed to do was learn to be happy – no doubt the most arduous skill of all to acquire. Ronchi suggests love was the answer: 'If only he had had a woman who truly loved him, probably he'd still be here.' Perhaps it was that simple: affection, after all, is the building block of every human identity. But Marco had never been able to build any sort of stable relationship. Dependently besotted with Christine, and chronically unfaithful to her, for months he kept a jar supposedly containing the aborted foetus of another lover in the fridge. By the end, he paid for what female companionship he enjoyed. So far gone, Marco lacked not just love, but the structures of the soul that make it possible.

Perhaps the rumour-mongers are the perverts. Certainly they add to the already unsightly struggle surrounding Marco's memory, testimony in itself to the pathos of earthly glory. In death he has many mouth-pieces, many spokespersons at any moment ready to defend his memory or, perhaps, their roles in it. Manuela Ronchi and her Foundation, Roberto Pregnolato's Amici di Marco Pantani, Vittorio Savini's Magic Club, the statue at Cesenatico, the various books ... Everywhere the counters overflow with statuettes of Marco, Marco trademarks, Marco logos, Marco pens, Marco key rings, Marco stickers, medallions, gadgets. The popularity of these items, despite the overwhelming evidence of Marco's doping practices, speaks eloquently of sport's place in our world.

Marco, a standard-bearer for several corporate identities, yet attracted by the freakish and the unspeakable, lived a more than double life. Manuela Ronchi, for instance, never saw him take cocaine for purely recreational purposes. She therefore argues he never did, and that he only took it in enormous quantities in order to harm himself. This view is considered risible by Mengozzi, for instance, or Rossi, or any of the others who knew Marco in a way Ronchi never could.

After winning the 1998 Tour de France Marco remembered his second place in stage ten and revealed: 'If I'd won it, I'd have gone home. I'd have won my stage and I'd have returned home.' Perhaps the shape his life took was that simple: when he had achieved what he felt he was born to, there was no reason to carry on. After years arrested in a state of morning promise by youth and accidents, he had enjoyed a brief, early afternoon moment of realisation. Then hope, with its implicit fear of unfulfilment, gave way to fear, with little hope of overcoming. Looking back, there was always a fatalism in Marco's riding. He won or lost through foolish, inspired deeds with little sense of strategic calculation. The tangible holding-at-bay of the night in those unfor-gettable late-afternoon victories at Montecampione and Les Deux Alpes was always there. For others, stage-racing has always meant weighing up the potential of the stages to come, and riding accordingly – riding, it might be said, in the future tense. Marco had no future tense. His style, in life, like his cocaine use and death, was lyrical, not narrative – a losing himself in time – and, in time (or outside it), the forces that had allowed him to live, consumed him as they consume us all.

MEDICAL TERMS
AND ABBREVIATIONS

BLOOD-TEST PARAMETERS WITH UNITS OF MEASUREMENT USED IN THIS BOOK

EPO	Erythropoietin present in the body, whether physiological (i.e. natural), or injected r-EPO.	Thousand Units per millilitre (mU/ml)
Ferritin	A protein occurring in the liver and spleen, containing iron. Ferritin concentrations reflect the body's iron stores.	Nanograms per millilitre (ng/ml)
Hb	Haemoglobin concentration.	Grams per decilitre (g/dl)
Hct	Haematocrit – the ratio of the volume of the blood occupied by red blood cells, expressed as a percentage. Also known as packed cell volume, or PCV.	Litres per litre *or* %
MCV	Mean Corpuscular Volume – the average volume of red blood cells.	Femtolitres (fl)
Pl	Platelets – tiny cells produced by bone marrow to help blood-clotting.	Number x 10^9 per litre
RBC	Red blood (cells) *or* erythrocyte count.	Number x 10^{12} per litre
RDW	Red Cell Distribution Width – the range of red cell sizes in a blood sample.	%
Reticulocytes	Young, immature red blood cells.	Number x 10^9 per litre

r-EPO	Recombinant human erythropoietin – an injectable, genetically engineered form of the hormone erythropoietin.	
s-LH	Serum level of luteinising hormone, measured as an indicator of possible abuse of growth hormone.	Thousand International Units per litre (mIU/ml)
sTfR	Soluble transferrin receptor – a receptor expressed on the surface of human cells that require iron. Serum levels of sTfR may be used as an indirect marker of supranormal erythropoiesis up to a week after the administration of r-HuEPO, although the effects on performance outlast the sTfR increase.	Nanograms per decilitre (ng/dl)
Transferrin	The main iron-transporting protein in the circulation.	Milligrams per decilitre (mg/dl)
WBC	White blood (cell) count.	Number x 10^9 per litre

ACKNOWLEDGEMENTS

This book started life as a feature in the April 2004 edition of *The Observer Sport Monthly*, commissioned by Jason Cowley. It was Francine Brody's idea that I should write this biography, and she oversaw it from start to finish, under huge time pressures. Mark Rusher was ever present and correct. My agent John Pawsey operated discreetly and effectively in the background, and Nic Cheetham was a cauldron of cycling and literary know-how in the final kilometre.

Conversations with Dr Mario Pissacroia led me to formulate the central thesis of this book: that Marco suffered undiagnosed mental illness for much of his life, which the configurations of modern sport camouflaged. Mario is just one of the psychiatrists whose reputations have been unjustly damaged after having accepted a patient it would have been convenient, if unethical, to refuse. I hope this book goes some way to righting that wrong.

Marco's parents, Paolo and Tonina, were extremely generous to me. The final product will not necessarily please them; I can only ask them to accept that my sole goal has been to compile an accurate, balanced and dispassionate account of their son's life. Marco showed a different part of himself to everyone who knew him. The biographer can do no more than portray as many of these versions of the man as possible.

For the rest, a researcher is only as good as his sources, and I had the fortune to stumble across experts who seemed to have been waiting, theories, solutions and explanations in hand, for someone with the right questions. It was a lopsided transaction, in that many of my sources gave me far more than I could ever return.

Much of Chapter 1 is based on conversations with Mario Pugliese of *La Voce di Cesena*'s Cesenatico bureau, who offered me daring and creative lines of research relating to every period of Marco's life, and was endlessly responsive to my enquiries. Davide Gnola of the Cesenatico library kindly introduced me to the history of his adopted town, and gave me his *Storia di Cesenatico* (Il Ponte vecchio, Cesena, 2001).

In Forlì, the legendary Pino Roncucci spoke to me for hours, provided photographs and press cuttings and went to great lengths to copy videotapes of Marco's amateur performances for me. In Ravenna, Medardo Bartolotti kindly gave me his memories of Marco, and of Rinascita-Ravenna, and sent me a copy of his book *'50 anni rossi e verdi' a cura di Medardo Bartolotti* (Società sportive ciclistica Rinascita-Ravenna–Edizioni Stear, Ravenna, 2000). In Modena, Roberto Pregnolato, who spoke to me at length, lent me DVDs, allowed me to copy photographs and press articles, put me in contact with new informants and allowed me to see the manuscript of his own memoirs about Marco. Pregno also introduced me to Marco's old hunting partner, Giovanni Gibosini, and to Dr Marcello Lodi. Marce generously shared his memories of Marco, and introduced me to the physiotherapist Giorgio Borghesan and Mario Traversoni, who gave me his insights into Marco's motivations, then cooked a delicious pizza for my journey home.

In Nonantola, Bruno Ronchetti shared his reminiscences and kindly presented me with a copy of *La 'Cursa ed Nunántla' e altri sport*. Professor Francesco Conconi kindly agreed to meet me, although I found little of our conversation usable. Daniel Friebe kindly gave me Sandro Donati's email address. With a few wise words, Sandro directed me towards the truth that underlay Marco's career.

For the Mercatone Uno years, Romano Cenni provided me with an interview, a collection of videos and a guided tour of his museum in the Mercatone Uno building at Imola. For the period from 1998 until Marco's death, his agent Manuela Ronchi gave me a long interview and accepted difficult questions unflinchingly. At Madonna di Campiglio, Antonio Dallagiacoma and Santino Battaglia of the Hotel Touring (highly recommended!) kindly answered my questions. UCI 'vampires' Drs Michelarcángelo Partenope and Eugenio Sala kindly met me at the Sant'Anna Hospital, Como, and answered further queries by telephone. Professor Vittorio Rizzoli gave me expert haematological opinions. Professors Giuseppe d'Onofrio and Giovanni Melioli were of inestimable help, very kindly looking over the chapter 'Campiglio Revisited' and

The Death of Marco Pantani

helping me refine my hypotheses. Professor Gian Martino Benzi made himself available for further assistance. The Colombian rider Hernán Buenahora gave me his memories of that fateful stage.

The Rimini lawyer Veniero Accreman spoke with me at length, and kindly presented me with his autobiographical book *Le pietre di Rimini* (Pietronen Capitani Editore, Rimini, 2003). His colleague Massimo Cerburi was also generous with his time.

Marco's former doctors Danilo Manari and Marco Magnani, and his 2002 *directeur sportif* Riccardo Magrini, kindly agreed to speak to me.

For the final period of Marco's life, first among my informants was Andrea Rossini of the *Corriere di Romagna*, whose book *L'Ultimo chilometro*, written in a weekend, is the authoritative account of Marco's final weeks, and has been plagiarised by a number of Pantani biographers. Andrea gave me access to material I would never even have known about without him. His *L'Ultimo chilometro* deserves to be brought up to date and republished. Nicola Strazzacapa of *La Voce di Cesena*'s Rimini bureau supplemented Andrea Rossini's assistance. Without their local knowledge I could never have found Michael Mengozzi and Nevio Rossi, both of whom have lost a friend and have been accused of the sins of others.

Franco Corsini agreed to a telephone interview, and put me in touch with Sebastián Urra Delgado in Cuba. Dr Giovanni Greco spoke to me briefly. Renato da Pozzo was extremely helpful; unfortunately, lack of time made deeper collaboration impossible.

Thanks also to: Giuseppe Lancini, the commander of the First Section of the Mobile Squad of the Rimini police, specialising in homicide, and his colleagues Dario Zammarchi and Giuseppe Malazzoni. Investigating magistrate Paolo Gengarelli. Lawyers Massimo Cecconi and Giuseppe Napoleoni. Former investigating magistrate Pierguido Soprani. NAS officers in Florence and Brescia.

Pier Luigi Salinari of the *Gazzetta di Modena* gave me a precious line of enquiry. Michel Beurat kindly sent me the 22 April 2004 *L'Hebdo* magazine containing his interview of Christina Jonsson; the publisher Editore Christian Maretti of Cesena kindly presented me with two books relating to the artist Mario Schifano: *Cocaina a colazione* by Marina Ripa di Meana and Costanzo Costantini (Maretti Editore, 2003) and *Mario Schifano* by Vittorio Sgarbi (Maretti Editore, 2005).

Acknowledgements

Steve Docherty helped me with a number of TV-related themes and put me on to Paul Ryan of the television production company Sunset and Vine, who provided technical details about super slo-mo. I enjoyed a stimulating exchange of emails with David Eagleman of the Department of Neurobiology and Anatomy, University of Texas over the neuroscience of super slo-mo. Jeff Quenet directed me towards Philippe Gaumont's testimony about the 1998 Tour de France.

I acknowledge the assistance of the librarians of the British Library, Essex University Library, the Essex County Library in Harwich, Essex, the Biblioteca Gambalunghiana, in Rimini; of the Biblioteca Malatestiana in Cesena and the Biblioteca Estense in Modena. Thanks also to the archive department of RCS/*La Gazzetta dello Sport*.

Max Devitor sent me books and helped me with transport, logistics, and with obtaining books in Italy. Mick Tarrant sent me a pile of magazine and newspaper cuttings, as well as valued friendship. Prof. Riccardo Steiner provided me with psychoanalytical texts. An old friend, Franco Fabris, first interested me in cycling, and, with his partner Marina, let me sleep on the sofa after watching those incredible stages of the 1994 Giro.

In Modena, my landlord was Maurizio Muzzarelli; in London, Gary Imlach provided a roof, a table to work on, and his flawless judgement. The finishing touches were added at Bucaramanga, Colombia, at the home of Victor Hugo Peña, and in Medellín, at the home of Marlen Toro. Keith Egerton copy-edited the manuscript with his remarkable eye.

My translations and adaptations of the complexities of Italian legal discourse, medical and haematological usage and police vernacular benefited from the generosity of Dr Isabella Schiavon, who helped me with medical Italian, Drs Gerald Rix and Chris Strachan, Celia Strachan and Helen Rendell, who corrected and commented on medical issues, translations and adaptations, and Micaela and Elliot Kemp, who helped me with police radio communications lingo. I would also like to thank Jeremy Verrinder and the University of Westminster staff who taught me technical translation some years ago. All infelicities are, of course, my own.

My mother, Anna Rendell-Knights, was incredibly generous throughout. My father, John Rendell, was always ready to read draft chapters with a sceptical and attentive eye. My wife Vivi agreed to interrupt her career, uproot her life to Italy, read and re-read drafts, and give support of every imaginable kind. This book is as much hers as mine.

INDEX